Please return or renew by
latest date below

LOANS MAY BE RENEWED BY PHONE

DEC 23 1976 LW

AN INTRODUCTION TO POLITICAL ECONOMY

AN INTRODUCTION
TO POLITICAL ECONOMY

By
V. W. BLADEN

Revised Edition

UNIVERSITY OF TORONTO PRESS

First printed September 1941
Reprinted April 1943
Reprinted and appendix added September 1943
Reprinted August 1945
Reprinted March 1946
Reprinted August 1948

Second edition September 1951
Reprinted July 1953
Reprinted March 1955

Third edition October 1956
Reprinted January 1958
Reprinted September 1959
Reprinted September 1961

PREFACE

This introduction to political economy was written primarily for students in my introductory classes in the University of Toronto. I had in mind the different needs of those members of the classes who would study the subject intensively for three more years in the honour course in political science and economics, and of those who might take no further courses in economics at the University. It was intended to be read along with other books, for it made no pretence to completeness either in its scope or in the treatment of individual subjects. It was hoped that it might prove useful in other universities to supplement the regular text-books, or other books, in use therein, and that it would be found useful by general readers who wanted to know what economics is and how economists think. Its ideal was that expressed by Mr. J. M. Keynes in his introductions to the Cambridge Economic Handbooks: "Economics does not furnish a body of settled conclusions immediately applicable to policy. It is a method rather than a doctrine, an apparatus of the mind, a technique of thinking, which helps its possessor to draw correct conclusions. . . . [this volume] is not directed towards making original contributions to economic science. Its object is to expound its elements . . . so that the number of those who can begin to think for themselves may be increased." I wanted, too, to introduce the student to the literature of the subject, in order that he might see the economist at work with this technique and that he might realize that the science is continually developing, that it is dynamic not static. For this reason I gave a number of foot-note references, but I tried to restrict the references to materials which can be read with interest and understanding by students at the beginning of their study of economics. The theory of money and the theory of employment have developed with great rapidity in the last twenty-five years. The literature is difficult and controversial. For this reason I have not attempted in dealing with these topics to indicate my indebtedness to particular writers, nor have I given references to the literature. To scholars the debt will be obvious; to the students, for whom this is written, the references would be useless.

Some advice given by Professor Pigou to students of economics in his *Apologia* in *Economics in Practice* deserves to be repeated here for the benefit of those who are foolish enough not to read the whole essay.

v

There is a third characteristic of the economist's work. His subject matter in the last resort is economic life in its full concreteness, a moving, breathing process among actual men and women in their factories and their homes. But the great majority of economists are, from the very nature of their occupation, more or less cloistered persons. Their contact with the thing they study is, in the main, not direct, but through the printed page. They therefore lack that intimacy of touch, that feel of reality, which is vital to full understanding. . . . Therefore it is up to the economist, when he is young and his mind is plastic, to take whatever opportunities he can find for direct acquaintance with the life of men and women in factory and field; to understand machinery; to see for himself at first hand how businesses are organised and run. Marshall in his youth had what he called his Wanderjahr. He told me once that, had he been planted in a desert island, he thought he could have re-designed the great majority of important machines currently in use—other than electrical machines. He used to go round factories and study the work that was being done until he could guess within a few shillings the rate of wages that the men he saw were earning. That way,— and if you will reread, as I have lately done, the earlier chapters of *The Wealth of Nations*, you will see that it is pre-eminently the way of Adam Smith—that way, and not by sitting in our studies, as some of us have done, is how the really great economist prepares himself for his work.

This book was written at the end of the thirties and its character was conditioned by the experiences of that decade. When, in 1951, Miss Kemp revised the book for me, some sections were added to "bring it up to date"; but the bulk of it was unchanged and has become "dated." Since then I have returned to my first year class and have become aware of the need for more drastic revision; the times have changed and so have I. Perhaps the book should be revised still more. Perhaps it is still too much a product of the thirties; but so is my economics largely a product of that period of trouble. I hope that my students will realize that problems and conditions change, that it is futile to apply the "conclusions" and policies of the thirties to the world of the fifties, or those of the fifties to the world of the sixties. I hope that they will also realize that the "technique of thinking" which helped "its possessor to draw correct conclusions" in the thirties will still help him in the changed conditions of the fifties and in other conditions, as yet unforeseen, in the sixties.

I am most grateful to Mrs. Ward for typing large parts of this manuscript, for editing the whole and for remaking the index.

V. W. BLADEN

May, 1956

CONTENTS

AN INTRODUCTION TO POLITICAL ECONOMY

CHAPTER I

THE BASIC CONDITIONS OF SOCIAL WEALTH

"THE really fundamental questions of economics," it has been said, "are why all of us, taken together, are as well off—or as ill off, if that way of putting it be preferred—as we are, and why some of us are much better off and others much worse off than the average."[1] In this chapter a preliminary answer to the first question is outlined: in a sense the whole book, indeed the greater part of economics, is an attempt to provide a more complete answer. In developing this answer it is convenient to examine first a smaller and simpler society than the nation, or the society of nations, which is the ultimate object of our study. In particular we want, for simplicity, to consider first an "isolated" community, and since no examples are available in real life we find it necessary to imagine one. If we were concerned with a group of communities trading with each other the same fundamental conditions would determine the aggregate wealth of the group, i.e. explain why all of them "taken together are as well off as they are," but we could not answer this question for any one of them without considering why some of them are "much better off and others much worse off than the average." We begin, then, with an account of the conditions of wealth in an imaginary isolated community. This community is supposed to be completely self-sufficient: its members work to produce things for their own consumption alone, and consume nothing that they have not themselves produced. We could think of a Robinson Crusoe, or better still of a Swiss Family Robinson, but we prefer to imagine a somewhat bigger group, though one equally isolated.

Conditions of wealth in an isolated community. How plentifully the isolated community of our parable will be supplied with the "necessaries and conveniences of life" will depend on: (1) the natural qualities of the members of the community; (2) the original quality of the physical environment; (3) the heritage of accumulated improvement; and (4) the good judgment with which the efforts of the group are regulated.[2] Each of these conditions is elaborated below. The

[1]Edwin Cannan, *Wealth* (London, 1930), p. v.
[2]Compare chap. i, "The Fundamental Conditions of Wealth for Isolated Man and for Society," in Cannan's *Wealth*.

importance of plenty, or the dependence of happiness upon an adequate provision of "necessaries and conveniences," will be taken for granted for the time being. At the end of the chapter some of the problems of the relation of wealth and welfare will be discussed.

The natural quality of the people. Health and strength, intelligence and character are too obvious conditions of wealth to require discussion. One has only to contemplate the time wasted in sickness (health it should be noted is a major part of well-being as well as a condition of increased production of wealth), the jobs left undone because the man's strength is unequal to them, the jobs done slowly because clumsily, the jobs done improperly because carelessly. Less obvious conditions are the age and sex composition and the size of the community. Each new mouth is accompanied by another pair of hands; but the mouth requires food for several years before the hands can help to produce it, and may continue to want food long after the hands have lost their strength and their cunning. The larger the proportion of the community at the productive ages, say between 16 and 65, the more favourable the condition for the production of wealth. One might go further and say the larger the proportion of *men* between these ages the more favourable the condition; but the productive disabilities of women are in part conventional. The poorer the community, and the larger the proportion of its members employed in agriculture, the less important will the sex composition be. More difficult problems arise in connection with the size of the community. These will only be suggested here: more mouths mean more hands, but needs and productive power do not necessarily increase in the same proportion. The bigger the community the more fully specialized may its members be; each member may be put to the task for which he has a natural aptitude, and may develop his skill by constant practice. Thus a community of one thousand may be able to produce more than ten times the wealth which a community of one hundred could produce.[3] But increased size has disadvantages too, arising from the greater difficulty of co-ordination, and the limitation of resources. Increasing intensity of cultivation will yield increasing supplies of food, but beyond a certain point the additional effort required to produce additional quantities of food will increase. It may be more than twice as hard

[3]For the classical account of the advantages of specialization, or "division of labour" see Adam Smith, *Wealth of Nations* (1776), chap. I. That "the division of labour is limited to the extent of the market," or the size of the community, is demonstrated in *ibid.*, chap. III: "There are some sorts of industry, even of the lowest kind, which can be carried on nowhere but in a great town. A porter, for example, can find employment and subsistence in no other place. A village is by much too narrow a sphere for him; even an ordinary market town is scarce large enough to afford him constant occupation." Cf. Cannan, *Wealth,* chaps. II and III.

to produce the food for a community of two thousand as for a community of a thousand located on the same land and possessing the same knowledge of the technique of agriculture.[4]

The original quality of the environment. The importance of the physical environment is also obvious, the importance, that is, of a fertile soil, a convenient topography, availability of such natural resources as wood, minerals, fur and fish, and the presence of sources of water power. The climate is also of great importance, affecting needs as well as productivity: a long cold winter makes necessary better houses and fuel to heat them, better stabling for the cattle and more work to care for them; it means a shorter growing season for annual vegetation and winter killing of perennials; and it precludes the performance of many kinds of work, for example outside construction, for several months in the year. Adequate rainfall in the growing season and sufficient sunshine for ripening are clearly important. The detailed study of resources, or the physical basis of the wealth of particular communities, is the task of economic geography. It is important to emphasize the "subjective" or "relative" nature of the concept, "resource." Things are considered resources only as they are "capable of serving man's needs. In other words, the word 'resource' is an expression of appraisal and, hence, a purely *subjective* concept. . . . Coal, simply because of its physical structure or chemical composition, would not be a resource; but it becomes one because man possesses wants which can be satisfied by releasing its stored-up energy and turning it into heat or work or some other usable form, and because man possesses the power to utilize coal in that manner."[5] Resources are "relative" to wants and knowledge. The land of the Canadian prairie was a very minor resource till the world wanted more wheat, and till the development of early maturing varieties of wheat and of dry farming techniques made its production in the Canadian Northwest feasible.[6] It is also proper to emphasize the strategic importance of those resources which provide sources of mechanical power, and of the minerals which permit the construction of machines to develop, and to be driven by, such power.[7] Finally, we should not ignore the amenities of the locality, beauty of scene and opportunity for recreation, contributing directly

---

[4]See Cannan, *Wealth*, chap. III. The relation between the size of the population and the wealth of the greater societies of the real world is discussed below, pp. 110–17.

[5]E. W. Zimmerman, *World Resources and Industries* (New York, 1933), p. 3: the first three chapters are concerned with "resource appraisal."

[6]See below, chap. VI.

[7]See Zimmerman, *World Resources and Industries*, chaps. IV and V. "Generally speaking, therefore, before the mechanical revolution agriculture was a fairly hopeless undertaking. . . . People raised food and feed today to generate the energy required to raise food and feed tomorrow" (p. 63).

to the welfare of the community and so, perhaps, indirectly to its productivity.

The heritage of accumulated improvement. It would be difficult to distinguish in fact the original qualities of the people or of the environment from the improvements made in the past, but the theoretical distinction is valuable because it draws attention to the possibility of further improvement. Consider first the improvement of the members of the family; the improvement of physique by sound diet, of character by good training, the development of skill by education and practice, and the accumulation of knowledge leading to improvement in technique. Consider next the improvement of the environment; clearing of land, fencing, possibly draining, and careful cultivation such as improves the fertility of the soil. Consider, too, the improvement of the livestock, vegetables, cereals, and grasses, by selective breeding. Finally, consider the accumulation of equipment; durable goods which yield an income of services *directly* like houses, or furniture, increasing the health and comfort of the family, or *indirectly* like barns, increasing the health and comfort of the cattle and so increasing their contribution of beef and milk. The accumulation of suitable tools and implements will further increase the effectiveness of the community's work. Again we must emphasize the strategic importance of that part of the accumulated equipment which provides, and uses, mechanical power.

The judgment with which the efforts of the community are regulated. Given the quality of the people and the environment, and the accumulation of equipment, the wealth, or well-being, of the community will depend on the judgment with which its efforts are regulated. This phrase covers judgments on a variety of problems, and incidentally brings us very near to the heart of our subject. Let us consider first the importance of deciding what things to produce. Notice that there is not enough labour to produce everything that is wanted; labour is scarce and must be economized. Not only is labour scarce, but so are horses, ploughs, cleared land, etc. The relative importance of things to be produced must be correctly judged; the more important things must be chosen ahead of the less important things, the community must be sure of bread before making cake. But the problem of economical choice is more difficult than that: it is always a matter of estimating the importance of a little more of this and less of that. It is a question not of absolute acceptance or rejection; but rather one of degree. One can have too much bread and too little cake. When you have a lot of bread a little more cake may be more important than a little more bread. A little more of the important things of which you have large supplies is less important than a little of one of the less important things of which you have none. It is not enough to produce large quantities of things, they must be the "right" things, in the "right" proportions, to provide the greatest well-being. (We assume, for the time being, that the people are the best judges of what is "right" and that there exists a satisfactory mechanism for directing productive effort into the "right" channels.) The choice of the "right" amounts of the "right" things is complicated by the preference of members of the community for one kind of work rather than another; a little more vegetables and less meat may be preferred, but not enough to outweigh the dislike of a little more hoeing. Another complication arises from the relation of wants to particular kinds of activity: "the longer a man stokes a furnace," says Professor Pigou, "the more keenly will he desire the hot bath which it provides him; while access to a hot bath will render him at once more willing to resume the task of stoking and more efficient in performing it."

Judgment is also involved in the choice between provision for present needs and provision for future needs. We have already noticed that the capacity to produce now is greater, the greater has been the accumulated improvement of the past. In the present it is possible to increase consumption for a short time by using up accumulated stocks and failing to make repairs or to replace worn-out equipment; but this means reduced capacity to produce in the future. Only in emergencies, such as illness or war, is it likely that such action would be justified. In ordinary circumstances good judgment requires at least maintenance of the accumulated heritage, and generally some further accumulation, especially if the population is increasing. How much accumulation is reasonable involves nice judgment. The greater the labour devoted to provision for the future, the less is available for provision for the present; the greater the labour devoted to accumulation the less important is each new improvement likely to be; the less the labour devoted to present consumption the more important is each new sacrifice. Judgment is involved not only in choosing how much accumulation but also, of course, in choosing which of possible improvements are the most important: is it to be improved fencing or a new roof on the barn? Our self-sufficient community is not likely to be able to devote much of its energies to accumulation. It will, by reason of its smallness and its isolation, be hard put to it to raise the food and feed required now to generate the energy to raise the food and feed for tomorrow.

The amount of labour to be distributed between different uses is not fixed; it is limited by the physical capacity of the human beings and by the necessity of a certain exertion to produce enough to live. Under some circumstances the margin between these limits may be small: where there is any margin between them the choice must be made between more goods, the result of more labour, or more leisure, that is more time to enjoy the goods one has. Here again the element of judgment is involved if the greatest well-being is to be achieved. Judgment is required in allocating the work between members of the community, so as to utilize to the full natural and acquired skills, to develop new skills by practice, and to reduce the burden of toil by consideration of the individual preferences for, and aversions from, particular kinds or work. Nor should one forget that "the rational thing to do is to be irrational, where deliberation and estimation cost more than they are worth."

There is judgment, too, in the choice of technique. This is in part a matter of scientific knowledge of how to produce a given result, but it involves problems of economical choice in view of the fundamental scarcity of resources. Of two ways of doing a job the better cannot be chosen on purely technical grounds.[8] If one way requires more man-power but less horse-power than the other, the wise choice between them will depend on the relative scarcity of man- and horse-power. Judgment is also necessary in dividing the product among the members of the community: the rule might be "to each according to his need," to each an equal share, or to each that which induces the maximum productive effort from the group as a whole.

Finally, one must draw attention to the element of uncertainty: uncertainty as to the result of one's efforts to produce owing to natural hazards, e.g. drought or disease, and uncertainty as to one's future needs and desires. Uncertainty enormously increases the difficulty of exercising good judgment. The difficulty of forecasting becomes par-

[8]"There is a common misconception that it is possible to measure or discuss efficiency in purely physical terms. The first principles of physics or engineering science teach that this is not true, that the term efficiency involves the idea of value, and some measure of value as well. It is perhaps the most important principle of physical science that neither matter nor energy can be created or destroyed, that whatever goes into any process must come out in some form, and hence as a mere matter of physical quantity, the efficiency of all operations would equal one hundred per cent. The correct definition of efficiency is the ratio, not between 'output' and 'input' but between *useful* output and total output or input. Hence efficiency, even in the simplest energy transformation, is meaningless without a measure of usefulness or value. In any attempt to understand economic efficiency, the notion of value is more obviously crucial since most economic problems are concerned with a number of kinds both of outlay and of return, and there is no conceivable way of making comparisons without first reducing all the factors to terms of a common measure." F. H. Knight, *Economic Organization* (New York, 1951), pp. 9–10.

ticularly important in relation to the production of long-lived durable goods.

The individualistic order. So far we have assumed that there exists in our imaginary community some satisfactory mechanism for directing productive efforts into the right channels. Choices have to be made and the welfare of the community depends on right choices. Who then is to make the choices? We might have assumed a paternalistic dictator choosing for the community, or a democratic council in which communal choices were arrived at by discussion and agreement. It would be natural to imagine some such planning authority in a small community, and the establishment of a similar planning authority to make these decisions for whole nations has long been urged by socialists. The absence of a planning authority might be expected to spell chaos: yet in the real world such planning is conspicuous by its absence. For most countries there is no central authority prescribing a plan, deciding what is to be produced, in what quantities, by whom, and for whom. There has grown up, with no one devising it, and few understanding it, a system which we may refer to as the "individualistic order." The individualism is sufficiently obvious. The typical member of a modern community has carried specialization to the limit. He probably makes nothing that he consumes, he does not even make anything for sale. He sells his services, and the services of his property if he has any, to business men, or corporations, who buy them with a view to producing goods for sale at a profit. He relies on being able to buy with his salary or wages (and property income, if any) the things he wants to consume. He renders himself progressively more helpless and more dependent on others by specializing for continually narrower occupations, relying on other people being prepared to buy his services and on being able to buy what he needs with the proceeds. If the individualism is obvious, the order is less obvious. Yet the fact that most of us go to work day by day doing our specialized jobs for money, which is only useful if we can exchange it for the things we want, is evidence that there is some order. We shall find that this order is regulated by prices, or changes of relative prices. It will therefore be the purpose of the next two chapters to provide a preliminary explanation of the function of prices in the economic system. We shall see later that even in the most individualistic orders there is a considerable measure of social control, especially under the stress of war; it can also be shown that even the planned economies continue to utilize much of the mechanism of the price system of the individualistic order.

If we suppose our imaginary community to be individualistic and regulated by the price system, we must notice the possibility, or probability, of the existence of involuntary unemployment, people who want to work but who can find no opportunity to work for pay. We shall then have to add a new condition of wealth, viz., full employment of men and other resources. The failure of the individualistic order to guarantee such full employment constitutes one of the most serious criticisms of that order; and the explanation of why it fails to guarantee full employment, and the appraisal of plans intended to promote fuller employment, constitute two of the most difficult tasks of the economist. To the individual unemployment is even more serious than to society. The unemployed have no title to a share in the produce (except so far as public relief and unemployment insurance benefits are available, in which case there is a title to a much reduced share); and, further, unemployment may, through non-use, result in deterioration of the quality of the services which the unemployed worker has for sale in the future. Unemployment, then, reduces the total income of society and increases the inequality of its distribution.

In the individualistic order the share of the social product that one can claim depends on the price one can command for one's services or the services of one's property. The obvious characteristic of the distribution of income which results is its inequality. This constitutes another of the serious criticisms of the individualistic order, and in most countries some steps are taken to redress, even if only in small part, this inequality. One consequence of this inequality of income is that an increase of the income of the community cannot be assumed to mean an increase in the supply of the "necessaries and conveniences" to each member of it. Thus an increase in the income of the Canadian economy will mean very different things according to its distribution between individuals, classes, and regions. An increase in the income of Canada resulting from the rise in the price of gold would affect different people from those who would be affected by a similar increase arising from a rise in the price of wheat, and would probably affect favourably more of those who are already better off than the average. If we are interested in well-being we shall not be content to know that the national income has increased, we shall want to know how the increase has been shared.

Conditions of wealth in a new country. In marked contrast with our imaginary isolated community are the "new" or "pioneer" countries of reality.[9] Such countries, e.g. Canada, Australia, Argentina, are closely dependent on other, and particularly on older, countries. They

[9]See W. A. Mackintosh, "Some Aspects of a Pioneer Economy" (*Canadian Journal of Economics and Political Science*, Nov., 1936), and A. F. W. Plumptre, "The Nature of Political and Economic Development in the British Dominions" (*ibid.*, Nov., 1937).

produce large quantities of relatively few staple products for export; with the revenue derived from the sale of these exports they buy from other countries large quantities of a variety of things for their own use, goods for present consumption and equipment to aid in future production. Their resources, therefore, have to be appraised not only with reference to their suitability for producing the things they want themselves, but largely with reference to their suitability for producing the things they can export to greatest advantage. New elements of judgment are involved: judgment in deciding how much of the resources of the community should be devoted to producing goods for its own use and how much in producing goods for export; judgment in deciding what combination of the possible products for export will realize the greatest income of foreign funds, especially sterling and U.S. dollars; and judgment in deciding what to buy with these funds. The relative prices of the things exported and the things imported become a fundamental condition of wealth, and skill in forecasting changes in export prices and in adjusting production to such changes becomes an essential part of the good judgment required.

Foreign trade offers the prospect of greater wealth, and a higher standard of living, to all countries as a result of each specializing in the production of those things for which its people with their total resources are most fitted to produce, and of each being able to purchase the things its people want, but are not particularly qualified to produce, from other countries whose people are so qualified. The readiness of some of the old countries to abandon the advantages of this "international division of labour" in favour of "autarky" (the newfangled word for self-sufficiency) is in part dictated by military necessity (defence, as Adam Smith said, "is of much more importance than opulence"); is made more tolerable than it would have been in the past by the enormous productivity of modern machine industry; and has some justification, perhaps short-sighted, as a means of insulating a country from shocks generated in an unstable, almost chaotic, world. For the "new" countries autarky has no attractions. For them the emergence of a staple export has been, and remains, the condition of growth. The pioneer country has to build up quickly a vast equipment, roads and railways, power plants and factories, houses, hospitals and schools. Isolated and unable to export staple products, the pioneer country would produce barely enough of the necessaries of life, and would be able to devote but little effort to "improvement." With a market for its staples the pioneer country can maintain a high standard of living and provide for "improvement." The prospect of rapid growth emerges with loans from the old to the new countries. The new country is not restricted to that rate of improvement which its own surplus energies would permit. It may tap the surplus energies of the older countries, by borrowing money in those countries and buying from them the materials necessary for constructing new equipment. With additional equipment the new country can produce more, more for its own use and more for export. Out of its increased revenue from export it must pay interest on its loans; but, if it has borrowed wisely, and spent the borrowed funds wisely, it will be better off in spite of, or rather because of, the debt. We must notice, however, that the debt charges will be payable in the currency of the lending country. As long as the pioneer country had no debt it would be interested only in the *relative* prices of its imports and exports, but once it has any substantial foreign debt it will be interested in the *absolute* price of its exports. If the price of its exports falls the real burden of its fixed foreign money obligations would rise; it would take more bushels of wheat to pay its interest.

The pioneer country is subject to all the uncertainties of our imaginary isolated community and to new uncertainties. It is subject to uncertain variations in the prices of its exports and imports. The prices of the staple products which it sells will be found generally to be subject to wide fluctuations, the prices of the things it buys, largely manufactured goods, will be found to be much steadier. Relative prices will, therefore, generally be more favourable to it when the prices of its exports rise, and, since rising export prices also relieve the burden of its foreign debt charge, its prosperity will wax and wane more or less directly with the price of its staple products. The pioneer country is also subject to great uncertainties because its growth is so rapid. It has no long record of steady growth to provide a basis for estimate of the possibilities of continued steady growth along the same line. The physical resources are only partially known, and the rate of growth is so rapid as to be cataclysmic and unpredictable in its effects in the markets of the world.

Wealth and welfare. So far we have pictured the community with certain recurring wants, to satisfy which there must be made available a flow of goods and of services rendered by persons or durable goods. We have been concerned with the conditions under which these wants will be most fully satisfied, and have suggested that well-being, or welfare, is a matter of an adequate supply of the means of satisfying these wants. But though the economist directs his attention to the behaviour of individuals as they attempt to provide for the maximum satisfaction of their wants, he must not be supposed to have adopted the view that happiness is a function of the supply of material goods, or that wealth and welfare are directly correlated. He may have strong sympathy for the view expressed by Colonel de Stancy in Hardy's *Laodicean* that "the world has not yet learned the riches of frugality," or that expressed by Prosper Profond in the *Forsyte Saga* that "life's awfully like a lot of monkeys scrambling for empty nuts." It is for the sociologist to explain how we have come to want the foolish things we do want, and for the moral philosopher to judge the wisdom of our choice. The economist accepts the individual as he is, and studies his attempts to satisfy his wants as they are; when he talks of the individual choosing the "right" things in the "right" proportions he means "right" relative to that individual's wants, right or wrong as those wants may appear according to some particular standard of moral or aesthetic judgment. The choice of rum by the drunkard is in this sense a "right" choice from the point of view of the economist, however much economists in general may disapprove of drunkenness, or even of the moderate consumption of rum.

Wealth and illth. "Living intelligently," says Professor F. H. Knight, "includes more than the intelligent use of means in realizing ends: it is fully as important to select the ends intelligently, for intelligent action directed toward wrong ends only makes evil greater and more certain." In similar vein Cliffe Leslie emphasized the supreme importance of studying the kind of wealth that people want. While Cliffe Leslie[10] felt that the nineteenth century had seen almost as remarkable an improvement in the kind of things people wanted as in the provision for satisfying these wants, Ruskin[11] felt that his generation were producing as much "illth" as "wealth." Amongst the "illth" may be included armaments. Peace, and the prospect of enduring peace, would enable us to devote our energies to producing more desirable things than munitions. Our wealth (in the economist's sense) would be no greater—it might even be less, for under the stress of war and preparation for war we may work harder, work longer hours, and more of us may work—but our well-being would be incalculably greater. Writing in 1917, Professor Cannan said: "If the [international] system which prevailed before the war is to continue, the cost of preparedness will then be not on the old scale, but on the new and immensely higher scale suggested by the experience of modern war which society now enjoys. There is, indeed, no reason

[10]T. E. Cliffe Leslie, "The Love of Money," in *Essays in Political Economy* (London, 1888). "New desires for health, decency, knowledge, refinement, and intellectual pleasures, have, in fact, revolutionised production. The antithesis to modern wealth is not so much poverty as a different kind of wealth. The change is more remarkable in the quality than in the quantity" (pp. 7-8).

[11]See John Ruskin, *Unto This Last* (1862).

why, in that case, international competition in preparedness should not absorb every particle of human energy that is left after providing the barest necessaries of efficiency . . . for able-bodied adults and children."[12] In the light of World War II and the cold war which has succeeded it, Professor Cannan's statement has new relevance.

While classifying without hesitation armaments as "illth" rather than wealth, one must remember that there are those who would not do so. Hermann Goering asserted that the Germans preferred guns to butter and would not have acquiesced in their description as "illth." If one asks why they preferred guns one might find a cleavage of opinion: to some, guns now seemed to promise more butter in the future, to others, national power and prestige seemed to promise a satisfaction greater than could be obtained from any quantity of butter. As long as the Germans preferred guns, other countries found a preference for guns forced on them. Again the reasons were mixed: to some, the guns promised a maintenance of the supply of butter, to others, national integrity and maintenance of the liberal democratic tradition overrode questions of wealth. In these countries armaments might be considered "illth"; but they were "necessary illth," or wealth relative to the unhappy circumstances which made such provision for defence necessary.

It is clear that if *wealth* depends on producing what people want most, i.e. what they consider the more important or right things in what they consider the right proportions, *welfare* depends on the soundness of their judgment of the relative importance of things. The deliberate choice of guns rather than butter seems to us a glaring example of deterioration of judgment in this matter; but, though there may be agreement that some things are bad, it is not easy to find any two persons who agree as to the best way for any particular individual to spend his income. In face of this disagreement as to what constitutes a right choice, economists have deliberately narrowed their field of inquiry to the organization by which people satisfy their wants as they are. For many economists that is simply a convenient separation of fields of inquiry, implying no judgment as to the wisdom of the choice; but many of the great economists from Adam Smith to the present day went further than this. To them it appeared that individuals ought to be free to choose what they want however foolish their choice. These "liberal" economists might admit that a benevolent, omniscient despot could choose more sensibly for his people than they could for themselves; but they knew that governments were never

[12]See note, dated Feb., 1917, on page 1 of some of the earlier editions of *Wealth*, e.g. that of 1923.

omniscient and were often stupid and inefficient, and that despots were rarely benevolent. To Adam Smith, writing in 1776, these things were particularly clear; for the government he knew was very interfering, extremely inept, and certainly not concerned mainly with the good of the people as a whole. But even granted a benevolent and intelligent despot who could choose more sensibly than his people, the liberal would still prefer to leave the individual free to choose. For he believes freedom to be an end in itself, and an essential constituent of welfare. He prefers freedom to make mistakes to faultless regimentation.

In no country is the free choice of the individual entirely superseded, in none is that choice entirely free. The totalitarian state interferes more with that choice, the liberal democratic state less; but both interfere. The interference assumes many forms: prohibition of the consumption of some things, compulsion to consume other things; deterrence by taxation from the consumption of some things in as great quantities as would be chosen apart from such taxation, and stimulation of the consumption of other things by subsidizing their production and providing them at less than cost; and education or propaganda to mould the free choice of the individuals into the pattern approved by the state. There can be no doubt that such interference can contribute to greater welfare, though there is no guarantee that it will. The method of moulding wants has the advantage of maintaining freedom while possibly improving the choice. But moulding wants is a technique better known to modern manufacturers than to modern governments; through advertising manufacturers seek to make people want what they can most profitably supply, rather than what is best for the citizen or best for the state. In so far as advertising provides information as to what is available it contributes to improved choice; in so far as it moulds the wants of the people it has potentialities for good and evil which are dangerous in the hands of the profit-seeking manufacturer, and, perhaps one should add, in the hands of the ambitious, war-like statesman. In the education of the consumer lies a way to increased welfare, a defence against improper advertising, a defence against unwise propaganda. But who will control this education?

Competitive consumption. In assessing the importance for welfare of an adequate provision of goods and services one must take into account the "competitive" nature of consumption, i.e. the desire to "keep up with the Joneses." One may be content with little as long as one's associates have little, discontented with much if one's associates have more. One may have little use for a radio, yet be unhappy without one, if the possession of a radio has become a mark of distinction.

Nicholas Barbon drew attention to the problem as early as 1690: "Man being naturally ambitious, the living together, occasion emulation, which is seen by outvying one another in apparel, equipage, and furniture of the house: whereas, if a man lived solitary alone, his chiefest expence would be food."[13] But it was Thorstein Veblen in his *Theory of the Leisure Class*[14] who elaborated this idea and showed its serious implication. "The end of acquisition and accumulation is conventionally held to be the consumption of the goods accumulated." If this were the case one could conceive of satiation, and one would certainly suppose that, till the point of satiety were reached, welfare would be increased as more goods were acquired. But, says Veblen, "the motive that lies at the root of ownership is emulation. . . . The possession of wealth confers honour; it is an invidious distinction." In earlier times trophies of the chase and of war constituted the basis for such emulation and invidious comparison, but "as industrial activity displaces predatory activity in the community's everyday life and in men's habits of thought, accumulated property more and more replaces trophies of predatory exploit as the conventional exponent of prepotence and success." The possession of property becomes then a basis of popular esteem "and therefore it becomes also a requisite to that complacency which we call self-respect." The significance of all this Veblen sums up as follows:

In the nature of the case, the desire for wealth can scarcely be satiated in any individual instance, and evidently a satiation of the average or general desire for wealth is out of the question. However widely, or equally, or "fairly," it may be distributed, no general increase of the community's wealth can make any approach to satiating this need, the ground of which is the desire of everyone to excel everyone else in the accumulation of goods. If, as is sometimes assumed, the incentive to accumulation were the want of subsistence or of physical comfort, then the aggregate economic wants of a community might conceivably be satisfied at some point in the advance of industrial efficiency; but since the struggle is substantially a race for reputability on the basis of an invidious comparison, no approach to a definitive attainment is possible.

It is the same problem as that involved in the competition of armaments: as each country increases the weight and efficiency of its armaments its relative strength remains unchanged. There is no end for any unless all call a halt.

Importance of activity. A misconception may arise from the economist's emphasis on wants and their satisfaction. One may feel that

---

[13]Nicholas Barbon, *A Discourse of Trade* (London, 1690, reprinted by Johns Hopkins University Press, 1903), p. 34.
[14]New York, 1919. See especially chaps. II and IV.

activity is important only because of the results achieved thereby. In fact it is a human characteristic to enjoy activity itself. Nor should one ignore the social element in this enjoyment, the satisfaction of working as a member of a social group, the satisfaction of sensing the social approval of that activity, and the element of emulation. For discussion of this subject we turn to Professor Knight's *The Ethics of Competition*.[15] "When we consider that productive activity takes up the larger part of the working lives of the great mass of mankind, it is surely not to be assumed without investigation or inquiry that production is a means only, a necessary evil, a sacrifice made for the sake of some good entirely outside the production process. We are compelled to look for ends in the economic process itself, other than the mere consumption of the produce, and to give thoughtful consideration to the possibilities of participation in economic activity as a sphere of self-expression and creative activity." Or again: "Economists and publicists are coming to realize how largely the efficiency of business and industry is the result of this appeal to intrinsic interest in action; how feeble, in spite of the old economics, is the motivation of mere appetite or cupidity; and how much the driving power of our economic life depends on making and keeping the game interesting. A rapidly growing literature on 'incentive' is a witness to this awakening."[16]

Finally, we should consider the economy not only as supplying goods for people, but also as moulding people. Does it mould people into a desirable pattern? To Ruskin it appeared that there was a premium on the less desirable characteristics, for success in the business world seemed to depend on them. "In a community regulated by law of demand and supply, but protected from open violence," Ruskin said, "the persons who become rich are, generally speaking, industrious, resolute, proud, covetous, prompt, methodical, sensible, unimaginative, insensitive, and ignorant. The persons who remain poor are the entirely foolish, the entirely wise, the idle, the reckless, the humble, the thoughtful, the dull, the imaginative, the sensitive, the well-informed, the improvident, the irregularly and impulsively wicked, the clumsy knave, the open thief, the entirely merciful, just and godly person." This view can scarcely be waived aside as valueless, and stands as a challenge which must be considered in any evaluation of our welfare.

[15]London, 1935. See his suggestive discussion of business as a game and his evaluation of the quality of the game, pp. 63-6.

[16]See V. W. Bladen, "Economics and Human Relations" (*Canadian Journal of Economics and Political Science*, Aug., 1948), especially pp. 303-4. Cf. E. H. Phelps Brown, "Prospects of Labour" (*Economica*, Feb., 1949, pp. 6–9); and O. H. Taylor, *Economics and Liberalism* (Cambridge, Mass., 1955), pp. 310–11.

CHAPTER II

THE PRICE SYSTEM

THE fact of *scarcity*, that is the fact that the things which men want are not available in such quantities that they can *all* satisfy *all* their wants, makes imperative some form of "rationing," i.e. some method of restricting consumption to that amount, or rate, which is consistent with the existing stocks, or rates of supply. At any one time there exists a given *stock* of each commodity available for consumption; somehow this stock must be divided among the people. There is not enough to go round, so some method of sharing must be adopted. We are generally concerned, however, not with stocks but with *rates of flow*. Wants are recurrent, and stocks are replenished as they are used; we are concerned, therefore, with adjusting the rate of consumption of various goods (i.e., the quantity of them consumed per unit of time, day, week, or year, as the case may be) to the rate of production (i.e., the quantity produced in the same unit of time). Again, the stream of production is insufficient to meet the drain which people would make on it if unrestrained, so that some method of restraint, some form of rationing, is necessary. Within the family, restriction of consumption by each of its members to a rate consistent with the rate of supply available is achieved by mutual consent or by parental authority. In the American, or the Canadian, economy as a whole this rationing is, in the main, performed automatically by the prices asked by the owners of the goods.[1] This social function of rationing is not performed as a public duty, nor is it performed consciously. It is incidental to the pursuit of maximum profit by the owners of the goods in question. Each owner wants to sell, and wants to sell at the highest price possible. To sell all he wants to sell he must offer his goods at prices low enough to tempt people to buy, and to consume, the available supply. To sell at the highest price he must offer his goods at prices only just low enough so to tempt people.

Rationing of consumers' goods. The simplest case of price rationing is seen at an auction sale where a single unit of some commodity is being offered, say an oil painting. The owner wants to sell it at the

[1]See Barbara Wootton, *Plan or No Plan* (London, 1934), especially chap. I; also G. Cassel, *Theory of Social Economy* (London, 1923), pp. 64-81.

highest possible price. There are many who would like to own the picture; of these some would pay only a low price, others higher prices. As the bidding rises the less anxious buyers are eliminated and the one prepared to bid the highest price secures the picture. The rationing price must in this case restrict the demand to one. The owner has secured the highest price offered, and the picture has gone to the man ready to pay most for it. The rationing is efficient, it works; but it is important to consider whether the result of the rationing is consonant with our feelings of justice. For this purpose imagine the owner to be a philanthropist who, wanting to get rid of the picture, announces that it will be given away at a certain time. One hundred people come to receive it, and the philanthropist has to decide to which of them to give it. In the absence of certain restraints of civilization the strongest man (or the cleverest strategist) might get it. It might be left to chance to decide, possibly by drawing lots. The philanthropist would like the picture to go to the individual most able to enjoy it; but it is not easy to determine who this is. The first arrival might be assumed to be the most anxious, but chance and the unequal distribution of leisure would influence the times of arrival. Somebody might then suggest that the owner put it up to auction and find who would pay most for it, taking readiness to pay as an index of intensity of desire. This would be a comparatively satisfactory method on one condition, a condition, be it noted, not fulfilled in most auctions, and not fulfilled in the economy which we study. That condition is equality of money incomes. Where money incomes are unequal the same price offer represents entirely different intensities of desire. If one individual bids more for one picture than for another picture, one may suppose he wants the one more than the other. If of two persons having the same income and similar obligations, one bids substantially more than the other for a picture, it may be supposed that he wants it more than does the other. But the fact that the wealthy man bids ten times as much as the poor man tells nothing about their relative intensities of desire for the picture.

If not wisely or justly, at least efficiently, price does ration. In a fundamentally individualistic order the difficulty of rationing in the absence of price adjustment, and the tendency of price rationing to re-assert itself, may be illustrated by reference to the problem of "scalping" in connection with the tickets for a hockey match. If the price of tickets is such that all those who want tickets at that price cannot get them, the result is twofold; first the inconvenience of a queue since those who come first will get tickets; second, resale of tickets at an advanced price, i.e. scalping, which is illegal in many jurisdictions.

Thus the price system reasserts itself, for the same reason that it established itself, viz., the self-interest of individuals who see a chance of reselling at an advanced price and thus securing a profit.

Supply and price. If the rates of supply of all goods were fixed, the only problem would be that of rationing; rates of consumption would have to be adjusted to the rates of supply, and this might be achieved, as in the case of the auction, by the mechanism of prices. But the rates of supply are not fixed; they change and change in large measure in response to changing prices. If the rate of supply of some commodity, say bacon, is so small in relation to the wants of the people that a very high price is necessary to ration that supply, the producers of bacon will be encouraged by the high price, and the consequent high profits, to produce more bacon. As the rate of supply increases the price will fall. It must fall if the increased supply is to be sold, for the restriction on consumption must be relaxed. If the supply increased very greatly the price might have to fall so low, in order to induce people to increase their consumption of bacon enough to eat up the increased supplies, that it would be no longer profitable for the less efficient bacon producers to continue to produce. They would turn to some other line of production, the supply would decrease, and the price rise to curtail consumption to the new rate of supply. A stable adjustment would be reached only if the rate of supply were such that the "rationing" price for that quantity would be high enough to persuade producers to maintain that rate of supply and not high enough to persuade them to increase it. Such a stable adjustment is not easily, or perhaps often, achieved. Rates of supply are influenced by other factors beside price, e.g. the supply of bacon might be reduced by a failure in the corn harvest or by an outbreak of hog cholera. Consumption habits change especially as incomes change, e.g. an increase in employment and in the incomes of wage-earners would increase the amount of bacon that would be bought, if available, at any given price, i.e. would increase the rationing price for any given rate of supply. Finally, the response of supply to price may be too great, so that one may find an oscillation between scarcity, high prices, and good profits, and plenty, low prices, and losses, rather than the stable adjustment that one would prefer.[2] But if this stable adjustment is not

---

[2]E.g., the "hog cycle." "Adaptation to any super-normally or subnormally favorable situation is possible only with a technological lag, corresponding to the time it takes to rear an animal to the requisite age, substantially fixed and the same for all producers who, being faced by the same situation, have to make their decisions about the same time" (J. Schumpeter, *Business Cycles*, New York, 1939). This lag is from fifteen to eighteen months. The response of the farmers is found to be generally greater than would be justified by the increased demand, and the lag is long enough for considerable further changes in the demand to take place before the response to the original change is complete.

achieved, there is a strong tendency towards it; and relative rates of supply of various goods are adjusted, more or less, to the preferred patterns of consumption of the people as expressed in their price offers. That which was relatively scarce, in view of their anxiety to buy, becomes more plentiful as producers are tempted by the high price; that which was relatively plentiful, becomes more scarce, as producers turn from it to more remunerative lines of production.

Rationing of producers' goods. Though the rate of supply of any one commodity can be increased, and is likely to increase in response to a high price, the fundamental fact of scarcity remains. The things necessary for the production of goods for consumption are scarce, i.e. are not available in such quantities that *all* the things people want can be produced. For instance there is a limited labour force and there is a limit to the amount of work which any man can do. It is necessary, therefore, to distribute the labour force between the various possible lines of production: to increase the supply of any one commodity more labour must be available for its production, and so less labour will be available for the production of some other goods, and their supply must decline. This distribution of labour between alternate uses is achieved by a process of price rationing. Business men, and business corporations, anxious to produce goods for sale at a profit try to hire labour. There is not enough labour to satisfy all their requirements so that the drain they would like to make on the labour force must be curtailed. A price, or rather wage, is established which excludes the less anxious buyers. Those producers who will pay the highest wages obtain supplies of labour, but those who expect to sell their products most profitably will be prepared to pay most. Thus supplies of labour are attracted to the production of those consumers' goods which are relatively scarce and the prices of which are therefore relatively high. Land, machinery, raw materials, etc., are "rationed" in this same way.[3] They must be "rationed" because they are scarce. In the absence of any other system of rationing, they are rationed by price. This is not done deliberately in the public interest, but is the result of individual self-seeking. Each worker, or owner of something useful in production, wants to sell his services, or the use of his property, at the highest price possible; each producer with a prospect of high profits wants to secure a supply of the necessary means of production and is willing to offer a price high

[3]Cf. H. D. Henderson, *Supply and Demand* (Cambridge, 1922), chap. vi. § 5, "The Necessity of Rent." "The way in which the land of the country is used, the way in which it is apportioned between the countless alternative employments that are possible is a most important matter. . . . How is this apportionment effected as things are now? The answer is clear: mainly by the agency of rent or price. The business which finds it worth while to offer the highest rent or the highest price of land will, as a rule, be able to command its use."

enough to exclude from the market producers of other goods whose prospects of profit being smaller are less keen to buy.

In this preliminary picture of the operation of the price system in rationing scarce means of production, we have considered only the effect of the price in permitting the production of more of certain goods and less of some others. But changing prices of these things determine not only what will, and will not, be produced, but also determine *how* these things will be produced. For the production of most commodities does not involve the use of various ingredients, various kinds of labour, raw materials, machinery, etc., in invariable proportions. One can usually use a little more of this and less of that, and yet produce substantially the same article. One can economize raw materials if one is extravagant with labour, and one can economize labour if one is extravagant in the use of mechanical power.[4] A rise in the price of some one thing will lead, therefore, to economy in its use in producing the things which are made and to a reduction in the output of those goods. We should notice that the supplies of many of the things which we have referred to as necessary for producing other things are not fixed. The means of production are themselves produced by the use of other means of production. At one time a particular machine may be scarce, its use must be restricted, and will be restricted, by the high price which its owners will ask. But more machines of this sort can, as high prices make their production profitable, be produced and will be; more steel, more skilled labour, etc., will be bought by the producers of these machines, less will be available for producers of other things. Again we find that these means of production can be increased; more labour can be trained to a particular skill, more steel can be produced. But it takes time to train labour; and it takes time, and steel, to build additional plants for the production of steel. If we go back far enough we come to certain fundamental scarcities, an ultimate scarcity of human energy and human ability, an ultimate scarcity of land and natural resources, and, in a less absolute sense, a limit to the aggregate amount of human energy and natural resources which the people are prepared to devote to increasing equipment rather than producing things for current consumption.

[4]Cf. J. M. Clark, *Economics of Overhead Costs* (Chicago, 1923), pp. 73-6. "Part of the efficiency of a garment cutter consists in planning his cuts so as to economize his material, but it would not pay him to spend all day to save a few inches. . . . By giving the cutter more cloth per garment he can do his cutting with less perfect planning and therefore more rapidly, and can turn out more garments in a day's work." How careful the cutter should be must depend on the relation of the price of cloth to the wages of cutters.

Scarcity. This emphasis on the fact of scarcity may seem strange in view of the unemployment of the thirties. Although our experience in World War II was a reminder of the reality of scarcity, nevertheless the popular view is that the economics of scarcity is outmoded, and that the economics of plenty should supersede it. But even when, in periods of unemployment, we must concern ourselves with the need for creating plenty we cannot ignore the problems of scarcity. For the resources that *are* employed are rationed to the highest bidders, the goods that *are* produced are rationed by the prices asked. The system is at work, even when it is working badly. And it still has to work in periods of full employment, for the greater plenty then possible is less than enough to satisfy all our wants. And if the prospects of greater plenty through full employment were very much greater than they are, satisfaction of our wants would still be far off, for the more others had, the more each would want. To eliminate scarcity one would have both to increase the supply of goods enormously and to change human nature to eliminate the competitive element in consumption.

Money incomes. So far in this discussion of the rationing of scarce goods amongst consumers, and of the adjustment of the rates of supply of various goods to the rates of supply preferred by consumers, we have taken the incomes of the consumers as given. Given these incomes one can say that the prices of various commodities determine the share of the available supply that each consumer secures, and the size of the supply that will be available. But these incomes themselves are determined in the process of price rationing. The money income of the individual (gifts, charity, public assistance, apart) is the result of selling goods, personal services, or the services of property. Those who are lucky enough to own supplies of the more scarce goods, or who can supply the more scarce services, are able to command high prices and to enjoy large incomes. They thereby command a large share of the goods being produced, and their preferences exercise a great influence on the direction of production in the future. The result is not necessarily just: in fact, one may say that great inequality, which is the inevitable result, is in most systems of ethics always on the defensive. However our primary task is explanation, not justification or condemnation. We shall find that this automatic determination of incomes in the market is subject to considerable modification through political action, e.g. considerable transfers of income from the rich to the poor are made by the mechanism of taxation and the provision of social services.

Interdependence of prices. Finally one must notice the interdependence of all these prices. The price which will ration any one commodity cannot be determined apart from the prices of a host of other goods, nor apart from the incomes of the consumers who are to be rationed but whose incomes are determined by the prices of a host of other goods. For instance, the price which would ration the supply of coffee will be higher, the higher is the price of tea; and lower, the higher is the price of coffee pots; it will be higher too, the bigger the incomes of the coffee-drinking public. The effect of the price of any commodity on its supply, similarly, cannot be determined apart from the prices of the many alternative products which might be produced. Thus a given rise in the price of whole milk will produce a greater increase in the supply of whole milk the lower the prices of butter, cheese, and pork. Because the complication of the price system as a whole is bewildering it has been the practice of economists to construct (in the sense of set up in imagination) simplified model systems in order to study the elementary relationships which exist, but which are so overlaid as to be difficult to detect in the real world. Chapter III is devoted to the construction and examination of one such simplified model, an imaginary handicraft system. Study of this model should give a more adequate appreciation of the unity of the system of prices; in the remainder of this chapter the piecemeal study of the function of particular prices is continued. The general discussion of the function of particular prices in controlling consumption, production, and incomes is supplemented by a study of the system under war strain.

The political economy of war.[5] The organization of an economy for war changes drastically the nature of economic judgments to be made, and the methods by which the activities of the country are regulated. In peace, the production and distribution of goods are largely determined by the free choice of individuals. By offering more or less money for goods, the individuals in the economy can encourage or discourage their production. In war, individual choice of what is to be produced becomes more and more curtailed in favour of the social choice of war goods, and the government, acting as the agent of the country in conducting hostilities, becomes the chief arbiter of the allocation of labour and resources. If unemployed labour and resources exist at the outset, it may be possible to meet war demands without interfering with civilian requirements, but as the slack in employment is taken up, it becomes more difficult to meet both demands. Increases in war production draw on labour and resources used in civilian industries, while increases in imports for war compete with civilian imports for a limited supply of foreign exchange. The fundamental scarcity of labour and resources becomes increasingly apparent.

[5]A. C. Pigou, *The Political Economy of War*, revised ed. (London, 1940).

If war were a leisurely and normal occupation of an economy, involving only a small proportion of labour and resources, it would be possible to carry on war activities within the framework of the price system. The government would be a consumer of a range of products peculiar to war and would obtain them in the same way as any individual purchaser. The problem of obtaining personnel for the armed forces and war production would be no different from the problems of maintaining a civil service and building roads, schools etc. But the impact of war on the economy is tremendous. Insatiable war demands soon force the economy to a maximum employment of labour and resources. Each change in war requirements necessitates a shift in the productive structure. At one time, more tanks are required; at another time, more ships and planes. The war cannot wait for the business man to debate whether it would be more profitable to produce tanks or planes. The reactions of the price system to changes in demand are too slow to make it an efficient medium for the proper allocation of the productive machinery of the nation in time of war.

Civilian demand also increases rapidly in wartime. Incomes rise sharply as the unemployed return to work, as the employed work longer, and as the young, the retired, and the housewives enter employment. Although the supplies of some essential consumers' goods can be increased, they must be shared with allied countries which find themselves cut off from foreign sources. Supplies of luxuries must not be allowed to increase, since their production would draw on the same scarce labour and resources used in war production. Therefore civilian goods are never in sufficient supply to satisfy demand. If prices were allowed to rise to ration the scarce supplies, many unfortunate groups whose incomes did not keep pace with the rise in prices would not be able to buy the necessaries of life.

The price system, thus, cannot fulfil efficiently in wartime the two functions it has in peacetime: the rationing of products and the allocation of labour and resources. It would be likely to involve a clash between individual choice in consumption, and the social objective of winning the war: between civilian demands and war demands. Such a clash would lead to a cumulative rise in prices. War demands, by creating employment, give the individual more purchasing power to back up his demands for civilian goods. The government would be forced to bid even higher prices for labour and resources for war production, thus creating still higher money incomes, and still more urgent demands for civilian goods. Rising prices of civilian goods would hamper the war effort by delaying the necessary shifts of labour and resources. Rising money incomes would also increase the demand of individuals for non-essential imports, and thus compete with war demands for scarce foreign exchange. Rising prices would also create discontent among the groups whose incomes did not rise as rapidly as prices; they would find their standard of living falling in favour of the groups who owned the scarce supplies. The resultant disruption of production because of strikes, or a fall in productivity, would have serious results for the economy. The uneven rise in prices would cause a redistribution of income in such a way as to place the burden of the war upon the groups with the weakest bargaining power.

A government faces two major economic problems in wartime. The first is concerned with the proper allocation of labour and resources to meet the requirements of war. This allocation must have regard not only for the needs of the country itself, but also for those of its allies. The second problem is that of the equitable distribution of civilian production. The price system alone cannot be relied on to solve either of these problems; there develop therefore various types of control: price control, rationing schemes, subsidization and government production. Some of these controls will be discussed with reference to the experience of Great Britain in World War I and of Canada in World War II. The purpose of this discussion is to throw light on the operation of the price system rather than to study war controls for their own sake. That the controls were as limited as they were in Canada in World War II and that so much was left to the price system can be explained by the success of the government in persuading its citizens to spend less, to save and buy bonds, and in forcing them to spend less by the severity of its taxation. The task was lighter, however, because of the amazing productivity of the economy and the consequent fewness of serious shortages.

Rationing of consumers' goods in World War I, Great Britain. As long as essential foods, such as meat, butter, tea, and sugar, were comparatively plentiful, as they were in peace time, rationing of supply through price changes was accepted in Great Britain without much question or understanding. But with shipping losses from submarine warfare mounting, the drain on shipping for transporting troops and munitions increasing, and the need to conserve foreign assets for the purchase of war supplies growing, these essential foods, largely imported, became very scarce. They became so scarce that the rationing price, the price that would have restricted consumption to the appropriate rate, would have been very high. The scarcity was made more severe by hoarding in response to the fear that supplies would become unobtainable, reinforced by a desire to provide for future requirements before the price rose. The moral sense of the community revolted: there would have been whole sections of the community who would have suffered real privation, while other, wealthier, sections would have got almost all they wanted. Nor was it altogether a matter of morals: maintenance of munition production at a high level was dependent on maintenance of an adequate diet for the worker, and on maintenance of his morale by eliminating new sources of irritation and discontent. Discontent would be aroused not only by the unsatisfactory nature of the rationing, but also by "profiteering." The high rationing prices would mean high profits, big incomes for certain lucky groups of people who owned the scarce goods or the scarce means of making the scarce goods. Indeed it was often to prevent such profiteering that prices were first controlled, and only later that steps were taken to provide an alternative method of rationing supplies and maintaining output. Various methods of solving the problem of rationing in the absence of price changes were adopted in succession. First there were attempts to persuade people voluntarily to restrict their purchases; then there were attempts to ration the retailers, leaving them to ration the consumers; and finally there was introduced a general system of direct rationing of consumers, the amount of certain essential foodstuffs which each person might buy being fixed, as was the place where he might buy them.[6]

Let us consider the case of sugar. The outbreak of war in 1914 cut off the normal supply of sugar from Central Europe. The British government established a commission to buy elsewhere the necessary supplies; private importation was forbidden, the commission being given a monopoly. Adequate supplies were available in the first two years of the war to satisfy all demands at comparatively low prices. In 1916, however, the demand began to outrun the supply. Since the government owned the sugar the problem was purely one of reasonable rationing, and no profiteering problem was involved. The commission restricted sales to wholesalers to a percentage of the amount handled by each in 1915, and met increasing stringency of supply by reduction in this percentage. The wholesalers were instructed to treat the retailers in the same way, and retailers were relied on to restrict sales to customers in a similar manner. This left the essential rationing to the retailers. The method proved unsatisfactory; the retailer had no record of the amount taken by each customer in 1915, and no way of knowing

[6]See W. H. Beveridge, *British Food Control* (London, 1928), especially chap. x; also A. C. Pigou, *The Political Economy of War* (London, 1921), chap. xII, "Rationing of Consumers."

how much sugar his customers bought from other retailers. Many retailers adopted the plan of allowing customers to buy sugar in proportion to their purchases of other groceries: a plan which caused much resentment as penalizing the poor. Leaving the rationing to the retailers opened the way to favouritism, and suspicion of favouritism. "It is probable," as Professor Pigou has pointed out, "that rich people will, in practice have an advantage over poor people, because, since they are more valuable customers, shopkeepers may be more anxious to oblige them. Realization of this fact is naturally very irritating to poor people—more irritating than a knowledge that the rich are getting the stuff while they are not, under a regime of uncontrolled high prices—and the desire to obviate this source of irritation may play a part in deciding politicians to adopt a policy of rationing in war time." It should be noted, too, that an equal percentage decrease in consumption would be unfair: a 50 per cent reduction for a family previously using 24 ounces a week would cause less privation than an equal percentage reduction for a family previously using only 12 ounces. The scheme of control was supplemented by propaganda to persuade people voluntarily to restrict their purchases to three-quarters of a pound per week per person; but though enough sugar was released to permit this rate of consumption many people found they were unable to buy so much.

A really serious shortage of foods developed at the end of 1917, and with it, in the absence of any rationing by prices or by authority, came the "queue," to deal with which emerged, at last, a complete system of ration cards. The story is told by Sir William Beveridge, then in the Ministry of Food and himself playing an important role in the drama:

Retailers found themselves unable to buy enough margarine, butter, bacon, or tea to meet their customers' demands; the public rushed from shop to shop, and realizing that supplies were limited, began to wait outside the shops even before they opened. The "food queue" made its first appearance in October at Woolwich, owing to special circumstances; by the end of November queues were prevalent in all the larger towns, and in December they grew worse.

Letters from wives complaining of food shortages and the strain of queues were said to be causing unrest in the trenches. For about a year plans—conflicting plans—had been under consideration for authoritative food rationing. As a result of the "queue" danger one of the plans was hurriedly adopted.[7]

[7]The history of the introduction of food rationing provides a useful lesson in politics as well as economics. Sir William Beveridge's comment thereon is important for the political economist. "The history of rationing gives much

The beginning [says Sir William Beveridge] was fixed for Monday, 25th February. The interval before that date was one of great anxiety. The London queues had attained gigantic proportions, and ran through a regular weekly cycle. Small on Monday, they rose on Tuesday, usually fell a little on Wednesday and Thursday, and rose rapidly through Friday to a peak on Saturday, when in each of the four weeks preceding rationing about 500,000 persons were counted standing in food queues in the Metropolitan Police District. The suffering involved led to discontent which was daily voiced more and more loudly in the press and in Parliament, by deputations and by threats of strikes among munition workers. . . .

It had an immediate and almost unqualified success. In the first four days of rationing—from Monday 25th to Thursday 28th February—there were practically no food queues in London at all. With the end of the week came a revival of anxiety; on Friday and Saturday queues were seen again in many parts of London. They were, however, as the figures showed, far less than in the week before; they were not due to the same causes as before, namely uncertainty as to where food was to be obtained and the desire of each individual to be first in the field; they represented the inevitable delay in shopping due to the unfamiliarity of the public and the shopkeepers with the system and to the time taken in presenting cards and detaching coupons. The following week saw the success of the scheme assured; the queues to all intents and purposes vanished from London for ever.

Supply and price in World War I.   When prices were not allowed to increase to perform the rationing function, this involved an interference with the "scarcity indicator" and might have been expected to reduce production and make the scarcity more intense. The story of English housing after World War I is a flagrant example of the muddle which can develop. The government passed legislation restricting the

---

food for thought as to the nature of political action. From the outside the solution of the problem of everywhere coordinating supply and demand and the dramatic destruction of the queues appeared a triumph of concerted intelligence in foreseeing difficulties and planning how to meet them. Intelligence and planning there certainly were. But at bottom the success of rationing is a supreme case of muddling through by brilliant improvisations, made necessary by shifting policy and division of counsels. It is a sober statement of fact that the Ministry of Food made its own and much of Lord Rhondda's reputation by putting accidentally into practice one system of rationing while it was formally engaged in devising a different system. It was little more than a further accident that saved Lord Rhondda from being driven by the Prime Minister to supersede at the last moment the officials who were organizing his imminent victory over the queues, and to instal in February 1918 a brand new Director-General of Rationing who at worst would have postponed or confused the scheme and at best would have let it run and gained its laurels. Another reflection of like nature relates, not to the form of rationing, but to the policy of rationing. In this matter the Government of 1917 appears almost incredibly hesitant and slow, obviously far behind public opinion, led by events and not leading, afraid where no fear was. Rationing was in effect demanded by the public long before the Government could be got to decide that it was necessary and that the public would stand it; when it did come it was accepted without question by acclamation" (p. 229).

extent to which rents of small houses might be raised. Houses were very scarce and the rationing rent would have been very high. With rents kept low, profiteering might be eliminated but chance or favouritism would determine who would secure a house to live in. The price system, however, was liable to reassert itself with the emergence of "key-money," a high price paid for the key to the house which was leased at the compulsorily low rent. But, so far as the control was effective, or expected to be effective, low rents deterred new construction, thus preventing the only remedy for scarcity from operating. One control made necessary another, rent restriction made subsidizing of the building industry necessary; but the government was half-hearted in adopting this policy. Happier stories of price control can be told for food; the solution of the rationing problem has been described above; some of the supply problems are discussed below.

The control of food prices involved less difficulty in relation to supply, though problems did arise. A large proportion of the food supply was imported. For these supplies the Food Controller had to pay the competitive world price. The price was comparatively high and provided an adequate stimulus to production. In the case of most of these foods the price to the consumer in England was high enough to cover the cost of the imports; but in the case of wheat, flour, and bread, the price to the English consumer was kept very low and the loss was borne by the Treasury. More difficult problems of the relation of supply to the price offered, or expected, arose in connection with domestic production. First let us notice the experience of the Food Controller with potatoes in the spring of 1917. The crop of 1916 had been poor, and the shortage of labour had combined with bad weather to make harvesting difficult. The price of potatoes rose and complaints were rife. The Controller therefore issued an order fixing a maximum price to growers, and a maximum retail price. The price was considered too low, and potatoes disappeared from the market. "The War Cabinet," says Sir William Beveridge, "turning aside from the prosecution of the war, after anxious deliberation, on 17th February raised the price of potatoes by £1 per ton and telegraphed their achievement to the Lord Mayors."[8] But Liverpool and Manchester, in spite of the War Cabinet, still sought in vain for potatoes. Either one has to rely on a tempting price to bring forward the supply voluntarily, or one has to resort to compulsory requisition. Fixing prices leads to trouble if one does not control supplies. We may next cite an example where a price was deliberately fixed so low as to discourage production of the food in question, the price of butter being brought down to encourage

[8]Beveridge, *British Food Control*, p. 42.

English farmers to produce whole milk rather than butter. It takes from 2½ to 3 gallons of milk to make a pound of butter, yet for various reasons, at a time when milk was selling at, or above, 2s. a gallon, the price of butter was fixed at 2s. 6d. per pound. The result was the almost complete disappearance of home-made butter. This has been cited as an instance of the neglect of sound principle in price regulation. But, says Sir William Beveridge, "the Ministry of Food knew perfectly well what it was about, and was deliberately following the advice of the Food (War) Committee of the Royal Society in discouraging the conversion into butter of milk that might be consumed in a different form."[9] If milk prices are fixed, those of butter and cheese must be fixed too; for if there is any shortage of milk (the only reason for price control) "the shortage will be turned into a famine, as much milk as possible being diverted for sale in the uncontrolled forms."

Rationing of producers' goods in World War I. Fundamentally, this control of supply through price is, as we have said earlier, a matter of rationing, by prices, of the means of production. In war time this system of automatic rationing broke down in industrial production even earlier than in food consumption. In many cases the supplies were left in private hands; but buyers were given priority certificates and sellers were forbidden to sell to buyers with certificates of lower urgency until those with certificates of higher urgency were satisfied. In other cases the government requisitioned the whole supply, sold the appropriate quantities to the firms engaged on war contracts, and distributed the surplus, if any, according to some system of priority to other firms. The reason for control always lay in the fixing of the price below the level which would have adjusted purchases to the degree of scarcity existing. The British Ministry of Munitions, for instance, fixed at an early date a price for shell steel, whereupon the price of commercial steel rose higher and manufacturers concentrated on making it. This was, of course, at the expense of shell steel, and prices then had to be fixed for all steel. The Ministry was next obliged to arrange for the distribution of the available steel between the many uses for which it was required and amongst the many factories involved. For once price was fixed, nothing but deliberate allotment could decide who was to get the steel. An elaborate priority organization was built up, arrangements were made to co-operate with the Allies, and similar controls were extended over all the raw materials required for munitions.[10]

[9]*Ibid.*, p. 165.
[10]Pigou, *Political Economy of War*, chap. xiii, "Priorities and the Rationing of Firms."

For further illustration of this problem one may turn to the contrast between the automatic allocation of tonnage in peace time through the operation of the freight market and the authoritative allocation under the "allied shipping control" in World War I as described by Sir Arthur Salter[11] Director of Ship Requisitioning and Secretary of the Allied Maritime Transport Council.

The allocation of the world's tonnage to the world's needs is normally effected by the intricate but automatic process of the freight market. . . . All over the world the merchants estimating the demands of their own particular markets in wheat, in wool, in coal, in cotton, make their purchases and then look round for the freight to carry them. Some are able to wait, others must ship at once. Knowing the elasticity and the nature of the consumers' demands for their own commodity and the nature of their contracts, some are prepared if necessary to pay an increased rate for transport, others prefer to cancel or postpone. Each gives orders to his agent on the freight exchanges of the world, such as the Baltic in London, to bid for tonnage within specified quantities, dates, and rates. Similarly the owners of disposable tonnage give instructions to their brokers on the same exchanges to accept within specified conditions the best offers available. So the haggle of the market excludes the marginal need and allots the available tonnage in exact accordance with the relative strength of the economic demand. Exactly what the world most wants (as measured by the price it is prepared to pay) is transported up to the limit of the total carrying capacity. What is left behind is exactly what the world least wants (as measured by the price it refuses to pay). . . . All that the system needed in order to allot the transport exactly to the supplies for which there was the strongest effective demand was that the offers of merchants with goods and of owners with ships should be brought together in the big freight markets such as the Baltic in London or the Collier exchange in Cardiff. The brokers in these exchanges would know the current freights offering in their own line of business, and something about the seasonal changes likely to raise or lower them in the near future. A good broker would perhaps have a flair for any new or exceptional circumstances, even outside his own special market, which might be likely to influence rates. Neither broker nor merchants, however, except in the most superficial sense, determined the rates or the allocation of the ships. They were only the instrument through which the economic demand of the world effected its own adjustments. They did not know—they did not need to know—no one needed to know—what were the total demands of the world or of any particular country, how these compared with the total transporting capacity of the available tonnage, still less what was the intrinsic importance of the different supplies competing for tonnage measured in terms not of money but of the public interest. We shall see therefore that when the freight system was broken by the pressure of the war, and it became necessary to allot transport on a deliberate judgment of the relative importance of different supplies, the problem could not be simply solved by turning it over to experts—for such work there were no experts.

[11]*Allied Shipping Control* (London, 1921), especially part i.

When the war broke out the normal freight system was modified by the government's use of the power of requisitioning. It took the tonnage it required for military purposes and paid for it at prescribed rates without regard to the market. Apart from this the price system continued; the tonnage available was less by the amount requisitioned, what remained was rationed via the freight market. Rates soon soared. The effect of high rates on the cost of living caused discontent, high profits in shipping even when heavily taxed were unpopular, and essential supplies for the many were excluded by the readiness of the few to pay high prices for less essential goods. "It became impossible," says Sir Arthur Salter, "to assume, because there was a stronger economic demand for barley for brewing than for wheat for bread, that the importation of barley was more necessary to the country than the wheat; but under this system it was the barley that came in." To meet these problems a system of licensing of imports was adopted: this excluded non-essentials, thus freeing tonnage for essentials, and relieved the pressure in the market, thus easing freight rates. By the middle of 1915 the freight market, even assisted by prohibition of imports, was clearly inadequate:

Now the wheat imports would be endangered. Now some essential raw material would be missing. No central survey of any of these vital supplies was made during peace or the earlier period of the war. Large numbers of individual merchants considered the probable demands and profits of their own particular markets and made their own arrangements without any comprehensive plan or programme. With freights jumping as they did in 1915, the risks became too great for this merchant or that; he failed to buy or charter; and at the last moment the Government (which had accepted no general responsibility for the supply in question) would be faced with a grave emergency. These emergencies were for a long period met, in the British manner, by improvised solutions, each meeting the need of the moment, but failing to prevent the recurrence of similar difficulties; each continuing while it was useful and being terminated or supplemented when it proved useless or inadequate; but each leaving some permanent contribution towards the complete system ultimately evolved.

The use of requisitioning was extended; e.g., tonnage was requisitioned in 1915 to transport wheat. Control of free tonnage through a system of licences was attempted. But the complete centralization of shipping control by the Allies was not achieved till the allied governments acting as one had become practically the sole importer. They then had to determine for themselves, how much wheat, how much sugar, how much steel they would import when they could not transport all they wanted to buy of them all. The problem became one of allocating tonnage to the preferred uses by the one buyer rather than rationing tonnage between the many intending buyers.

Canadian price control in World War II.[12] At the beginning of the second world war, the belligerent countries were emerging from the depression of the thirties. Canada had considerable unemployed resources, substantial supplies of some essential foods such as wheat, and relatively free access to supplies in the United States. The war, therefore, in its early stages, did not impose a critical strain on the economy as a whole. Certain commodities, however, especially wool and sugar, were in very short supply. In order to meet this situation, and to provide safeguards against any undue enhancement in the prices of food, fuel and other necessaries of life, and to ensure adequate supply and equitable distribution of such commodities, the government established the Wartime Prices and Trade Board, by Order-in-Council (P.C. 2516) on September 3, 1939. The Board was given very wide powers: power to investigate, to call for books, to enter upon premises; power to license, to buy and sell, to take possession of and allocate supplies; power to control imports and exports. In August, 1941, the Authority of the Board was extended to cover all goods and services which did not fall within the special jurisdiction of a Controller in the Department of Munitions and Supply. In November, 1941, the Board was assigned the task of administering the "price ceiling" (P.C. 8527 and P.C. 8528). This "ceiling" came into effect on December 1, 1941. From that date the highest price at which any person might sell any goods, or those services listed in the Regulations, was the highest lawful price at which he sold those goods or services during the "basic period," September 15 to October 11, 1941, unless the Board ordered otherwise. Not until July, 1942, did the Board undertake the onerous task of "coupon" rationing of consumers. Sugar first became subject to such rationing; tea and coffee followed in August, and butter in December; meat was not rationed until May, 1943. (Rationing of gasoline had been introduced in April, 1942, but was administered by the oil Controller in the Department of Munitions and Supply. Rationing of "liquor" was a responsibility of the provinces; in Ontario such rationing came into effect in October, 1942.)

[12]See A. F. W. Plumptre, *Mobilizing Canada's Resources for War* (Toronto, 1941); the *Reports* of the Wartime Prices and Trade Board, especially for the period Sept., 1939 to March, 1943; two essays by Kenneth W. Taylor, "Wartime Control of Prices," in *Canadian War Economics*, ed. J. F. Parkinson (Toronto, 1941), and "Canadian Wartime Price Controls, 1941 to 1946" (*Canadian Journal of Economics and Political Science*, Feb., 1947). Other valuable articles in the *Canadian Journal of Economics and Political Science* include S. Bates, "The Price System and the War Economy" (Aug., 1941), and Monteath Douglas, "Limitation of the Financial Factor in a War Economy" (Aug., 1942). See also *Report of the Royal Commission on Prices* (1949), vol. II.

Selective price control, 1939–41. In these early years the Wartime Prices and Trade Board concerned itself with organizing an adequate supply, rather than with the fixing of maximum prices of scarce necessaries. Maximum price orders were used only as a last resort. The problems involved can be illustrated by reference to wool and sugar.

The outbreak of war faced Canada and the United States with an immediate shortage of wool and great uncertainty as to the future supply of imported wool. The price in the United States rose rapidly and Canadian stocks began to move across the border. The Board appointed a Wool Administrator with the power to organize supply and allocate wool in Canada. The export of wool from Canada, except under special permit, was prohibited. Provision was made to allocate the available wool so as to permit the fulfilment of any contracts, and generally to establish priorities.

The problem of sugar was in the beginning a psychological one. Panic consumer buying of sugar caused an artificial shortage. Over 40 million pounds above normal consumption disappeared quickly into consumer hoards. To remedy the situation manufacturers were asked to turn over their excess stocks to the government to be directed into retail channels. The sight of adequately stocked shelves, coupled with an intensive publicity campaign reassured consumers and the panic subsided.

The price ceiling. By the end of 1941 the situation had changed, and new problems had arisen. War demands increased enormously following the fall of France, and civilian demands were rising with consumers' incomes. At the same time supplies from the United States tightened after Pearl Harbor, while labour and material shortages began to impede the growth of domestic supplies. During 1941 there was a steady rise in prices, and in December "selective" control was replaced by complete "price ceiling" control over all commodities, rents and wages. This "police" control was reinforced by publicity and propaganda encouraging consumers to "hold the price line," and by taxation and bond drives to relieve the consumer of his purchasing power.[13] Confidence that the fiscal policy of the government would make the task of the Wartime Prices and Trade Board in policing prices a possible one made the propaganda more effective, for it eliminated the speculative inclination to buy now before prices rose still more.

Price freezing meant a drastic interference with the process of rationing by the price system. The government was reluctant to

[13]Cf. K. W. Taylor, "Canadian Wartime Price Controls 1941-1946" (*Canadian Journal of Economics and Political Science*, Feb., 1947, p. 81 ff.).

institute an extensive rationing programme of its own, because of the tremendous administrative machinery involved. However, the absence of price rationing meant that chance and favouritism determined the distribution of scarce supplies in the legal market, while "black markets" developed as eager consumers reverted illegally to the price system. In this situation public discontent grew, and appeals for authoritative rationing forced the government to ration certain essential foods, such as butter, sugar, meat, tea, and coffee, and other necessary goods, such as fuel oil and gasoline. Some goods were rationed by asking producers to allocate available supplies to their customers in proportion to the total amount supplied by them to each retailer in the year 1941. This method ensured a roughly equitable regional supply as long as the distribution of population remained the same, but it meant that any shift in population would distort the system by making goods plentiful in those centres which lost consumers, and scarce in those centres which gained them.

Methods of rationing.[14] Conditions of supply and demand varied so widely from one commodity to another that different forms of rationing had to be used to meet each new situation. Since acute shortages developed before the necessary elaborate compulsory rationing systems were set up, an "honour system" was introduced in Canada, based on the co-operation of consumers. In January, 1942, for example, it was declared illegal for any person to purchase more than three-quarters of a pound of sugar in a week. Tea, coffee, meat, and gasoline were also rationed in this way for a time, but the fact that co-operation was not complete caused much bitterness, while the system focused public attention on shortages and intensified them to some extent by encouraging panic buying for hoarding purposes.

The "honour system" was replaced by coupon rationing of certain essential commodities, such as sugar, butter, and meat. Upon the surrender of certain coupons issued to him by the government, each individual was entitled to purchase a fixed quantity of these goods each period. Flexibility in the ration, according to changed conditions of supply, was achieved by varying the dates on which coupons became valid. In some cases, where large sections of the community used some substitute instead of the scarce product, the substitute had to be rationed too.

Difficulties would have been encountered, for example, if attempts had been made to ration tea in Canada without rationing coffee at the same time. Some families may use a pound of tea a week, while other families do not use a pound of tea in a year. If the weekly ration were fixed on the basis of

[14]See J. H. Richardson, "Consumer Rationing in Great Britain" (*Canadian Journal of Economics and Political Science*, Feb., 1942); International Labour Office, *Food Control in Great Britain* (Montreal, 1942).

the average per capita consumption, the amount would have come well below the reasonable minimum requirements of the regular tea drinker, but if the ration were fixed to give the regular tea drinker a reasonable minimum, then many people would have coupons far in excess of their needs. Fortunately, in this case, the trouble could be overcome by rationing tea and coffee together, but it is not always possible to find a complementary commodity, or group of commodities, which can be rationed together with the first one to provide some freedom of consumer choice.[15]

One method of restricting consumption of a group of commodities, while allowing consumers some freedom of choice in purchasing individual items within the group is "point" rationing by which certain coupons are valid for the purchase of a variety of related goods, each item requiring a specified number of coupons. The more a purchaser wants of one item, the more he is limited in his choice of other items, so that in effect a "coupon price" system is superimposed on the normal price system. As supplies of a given commodity change, the number of coupons or "points" required for its purchase may be altered so that demand is adjusted. "Point rationing" was worked out in detail in Great Britain[16] and the United States, but the Canadian government used it only in modified form; for example in meat rationing, where various quantities of the different kinds of meat could be obtained for one coupon. Some English economists proposed to control the amount of purchases by limiting the total amount of money that could be spent by one individual in one year on all commodities. The scheme was ingenious but impracticable not only on administrative grounds but also because any specific amount that could be chosen would be beyond the purchasing power of low income groups and disastrously inadequate at higher levels.[17]

[15]Wartime Prices and Trade Board, *Report, Sept. 3, 1939 to March 31, 1943* (Ottawa), p. 60.

[16]The British experience with American brands of canned pork meats offered an interesting example of the operation of the points rationing system. When the scheme came into operation on December 1st, 1941, canned salmon and American canned meats were rationed on an equal basis of 16 points a pound. Canned salmon was well known, and very popular with the British public, but the American brand names of "Spam" and "Mor" were unknown to the housewife, who was under the impression that the cans contained dog meat. Canned salmon disappeared quickly from the shelves in the first period, while canned meats moved very slowly. In the second period, the points value of the salmon was increased to 24 points a pound, and the canned meats were decreased from 16 to 8 points a pound. This drastic revision of points value was accompanied by articles in the press explaining the contents of "Spam" and "Mor." Despite the publicity, the British housewife did not change her buying habits immediately. The next revision of point values in March, 1942, increased American canned meats to only 12 points a pound, while at the same time, salmon was increased to 32 points a pound.

[17]See M. Kalecki, "General Rationing" (*Bulletin of the Oxford Institute of Statistics*, Jan., 1941); also J. T. Polak, "Rationing of Purchasing Power" (*Economica*, Aug., 1941).

Where supplies were quite inadequate to meet basic needs, or where differences in individual needs made equal rationing impracticable, other methods were devised. In rationing oil for heating purposes it became necessary to recognize the fact that homes were of different sizes. In this case rationing was based on a percentage of the previous year's requirements. Where the commodity was in general use but in widely varying quantities, a basic ration was issued plus additional amounts in accordance with "need" as determined by the administration. Gasoline rationing in Canada followed this method.[18]

The rationing of durable consumers' goods, such as stoves, plumbing supplies and tires, presented a slightly different problem. Since these goods were purchased infrequently, a system of permits was used to allocate the scarce supplies to particular classes of buyers and if supplies were not enough to satisfy the demands of everyone in the selected group the permits were granted on a priority basis.

In view of the diversion of a large part of Canada's resources to war, and the wide interference with the operation of the price system, it is surprising that the Canadian economy functioned with so little in the way of compulsory rationing. One explanation is the tremendous increase in productive capacity which took place during the war. Drastic scarcities of consumers' goods developed in only a few instances. In the case of durable goods the problem was not an important one because the public could postpone purchases for several years. In other cases scarcities gave rise to queues and shopping difficulties which helped to discourage buying, but did not create serious discontent. The success of fiscal measures also eased the supply problem by discouraging demand. "Psychological" controls such as "make it do" campaigns gained the support of large groups which deliberately abstained from buying goods in short supply. As a result of these various factors, authoritative controls were largely confined to producers and retailers where they could be easily administered, and there was little direct interference with consumers.

Rationing of producers' goods in World War II. The allocation of raw materials to war needs and civilian requirements demanded careful control. In the case of some strategic materials, control was relatively easy because production was concentrated in a few hands;

---

[18]Gasoline rationing illustrates the difficulty of psychological controls where the commodity is considered a basic necessity. The possession of a privileged ration gave the owner some prestige, and many methods were attempted to get a "privilege" ration. Also, recourse to the "black market" was probably more frequent in the case of gasoline than in other commodities. The existence of a differential ration lent a competitive flavour to the procurement of supplies.

informal negotiations could be carried on, and allocations made without much fear of evasion. The existence of governmental agencies in other countries simplified the control of imports. At first, the government operated within the price system, establishing agencies to secure needed supplies at reasonable prices. Later the diversion of raw materials into war industries became more urgent, and the government resorted to measures of compulsory control such as price fixing and priority systems.

The control of steel in Canada illustrates the elaborate system used to allocate strategic raw materials. In conjunction with the other allied countries, it was decided from time to time what goods were necessary to carry out the plan of war. On the basis of these decisions the steel controller in Canada indicated the type of steel most urgently required by grading in a priority system. To ensure that the raw materials were at the right plant at the right time, steps had to be taken to procure needed supplies and to get priorities in transportation. Scrap steel, an important element in steel production, was allocated to the various mills on the basis of their needs. Scrap dealers were licensed, and special checks made to ensure that no dealer or plant stocked scrap in excess of requirements. Finally, the steel not used in war production had to be rationed on a priority basis, and the whole programme had to be co-ordinated with the needs of other government agencies for labour and raw materials.

Rationing of producers' goods under price control was much simpler than rationing of consumers' goods because of the relatively small number of producers and their active co-operation through trade associations.[19] The "prestige values" of active co-operation on the part of large producers far outweighed any short-run advantages that could be obtained from attempting to evade the regulations. Moreover, the regulations were strengthened by using administrators drawn from industry, who were familiar with the problems involved and able to design efficient controls.

Supply and price in World War II. To maintain the stability of the economy by legal control of prices, the government "froze" to a large extent the existing structure of prices. Low prices prevented large-scale profiteering, but they also discouraged increased production of some essential goods, while in some cases the ceiling price was high enough to encourage too great a supply of non-essential commodities.

[19]For a discussion of the problems of strengthened monopolies arising from the active use of trade associations by wartime agencies, see Report of the Commissioner, Combines Investigation Act, *Canada and International Cartels* (Ottawa, 1945), p. 57.

The upward rise of prices before controls were imposed had been uneven, some rising much faster than others, so that the problems necessarily arising from "freezing" the price structure were made more serious because it was a distorted price structure which was frozen.

Since price no longer determined the increase or decrease of supply in response to demand, a whole battery of controls had to be used to gain the necessary flexibility. Appeals to patriotism encouraged increases long after the stimulus of price had gone. Specific taxation discouraged production of some products; subsidies encouraged production of others. Production directives, simplification and conservation programmes, and priority systems were used to enforce compulsory increases and decreases in supply. Finally, where the goods required were of a novel and strictly wartime nature, the government itself set up Crown corporations to produce them.

In the case of those commodities where the number of producers was large, innumerable difficulties arose in the attempt to increase supplies without price incentives, especially where higher prices existed outside the country. These problems were particularly acute in agriculture. Patriotic appeals had resulted in enormous increases in agricultural production, but the failure of agricultural prices to rise in pace with industrial prices before price control was enforced created much discontent. The muddle of meat illustrates clearly the type of problem which developed. For a time a controlled and uncontrolled market in meat existed side by side, because civilian purchases of meat were subject to price control but governmental purchases were not. Moreover, until 1943, meat prices in the United States were not under price control, although the Canadian market had been controlled since the end of 1941. Rising meat prices in the United States during 1942 and vigorous bidding by government agencies for cattle for military purposes made it profitable for the producer to withhold cattle from the civilian market in order to sell for export under the export quota system or to sell directly to the government. Beef supplies disappeared from the controlled civilian market and were available only at black market prices. To redirect supplies to the civilian market the government raised the price of beef. Export to the United States was more stringently controlled and military purchases were made subject to price control. Subsequently, dissatisfaction over prices again led producers to withhold supplies from the market, and in October, 1942, a further upward revision of price was allowed. Even this increase failed to bring forth an adequate supply for domestic consumption and overseas commitments, and in

1943 meat rationing was introduced. It remained difficult to maintain a supply sufficient to provide the ration considered desirable. Under the price ceiling, control over the supply of beef was inadequate, and it became necessary to resort once more to the price system for a solution.

Subsidies formed the main method of stimulating increased supply under the price ceiling. Payment of a certain amount per unit of production increased the income of the producer and therefore his incentive to produce, without directly increasing the price of the commodity. However, subsidies sometimes upset the delicate price balances of related goods, and made further controls necessary. These problems were particularly acute where all the products were made from the same raw materials. In order to meet the cheese requirements of Great Britain, the Canadian government encouraged production by paying a bonus to the cheese producers. The supply of cheese increased enormously, but only at the expense of butter and milk, as producers shifted to the more profitable business of making cheese. Matching subsidies then had to be granted to the butter and milk producers.

Imports presented another problem which could only be solved by subsidy payments. Prices in other countries were not subject to the same control and in most cases they rose drastically. As shortages developed, it became difficult or impossible to import needed goods to be sold at controlled prices, and to maintain imports of essential goods such as petroleum, vegetable fibres, wool, raw cotton, tea, oranges, and rice, subsidies were paid.

Specific taxation was applied to luxuries in order to discourage their consumption. Early in the war, taxes on items such as tobacco, jewellery, liquor, and motor cars were increased, but these controls were largely offset by rapidly rising incomes. Better results were obtained by direct prohibition of production or by priority controls to prevent the diversion of materials into luxury industries.

Control over prices sometimes made it necessary for the government to enter production.[20] A good example is the case of housing. The mushroom development of war industries in certain districts caused a concentration of population which would have forced rentals up rapidly. Excessive rents would have made it impossible to maintain

[20]Other motives also inspired the government; the urgency of speed, great need for secrecy, and insurmountable financial risks made it necessary to use Crown corporations rather than to try to encourage private producers to enter the field in the production of war goods such as ships, explosives, precision instruments. See Colonel W. E. Philips, "Some Experiences in the Administration of a Crown Company" (*Commerce Journal*, April, 1946).

labour in the war industries, unless the government was willing to jeopardize its wage stabilization programme by offering very high wages. The shortage of building materials and labour would have created difficulties in expanding housing accommodation even if rents had been allowed to rise. Rental control kept rents at a reasonable level but did nothing to increase accommodation. The government therefore embarked on a programme of housing construction in areas where it was essential that labour be retained to keep war industries at full capacity.

CHAPTER III

THE PRICE SYSTEM IN A HYPOTHETICAL HANDICRAFT ECONOMY

In Chapter II we examined the price system piecemeal, or bit by bit. We saw how the supply of a particular commodity was rationed by price, and how this rationing price influenced the future supply of that commodity and the present income of those equipped to assist in its production. We noted, however, the difficulty of treating each price separately. What price will ration the supply of any one commodity depends on what prices are established for a host of other goods, some of which are competing substitutes for the one, others of which are complementary goods which are consumed along with it. Similarly we noted that the supply of any commodity which may be expected in response to any given price of that commodity will depend on the prices of many other goods the producers of which compete for the same types of labour or instruments of production. So completely interrelated, or interdependent, are all these prices that it becomes necessary to get some understanding of the system of prices as a whole. But this system is so complicated and bewildering that we approach an understanding of the price system in the real world by studying the price system which might rule in a simple model economy constructed in imagination.

In the first part of this chapter we describe in some detail one such hypothetical model economy. The specifications for this model are selected with a view to the greatest simplicity consistent with its usefulness in demonstrating more clearly the essentials of the price system in the complicated real world. The simplicity of the model is extreme, indeed the conditions described are fantastic; but an understanding of its working should enable the student to look at the complications of the real world with a new eye for the pattern. In the second part of the chapter we proceed to complicate the model by adding new characteristics intended to draw attention to some other fundamental tendencies discoverable in the real world. But before the complication proceeds far, the difficulty of explaining or understanding the working of the model increases beyond the limits set for this introductory volume. In this second part we shall not attempt, therefore, the same rigorous exposition, but shall content ourselves with a general indication of the character of the problem and of the broad lines of its solution.

The method here used for purposes of introductory exposition is also one of the techniques used by economists in extending the boundaries of knowledge. It is the method of the economic theorist; it is only *one* of the many techniques available, but it has proved, and is likely still further to prove, valuable as long as it is used in close conjunction with the other techniques. The economic theorist, the economic historian, the statistician, to cite only three types of skilled workers in the economic workshop, must work side by side. As in physics, the theorist suggests hypotheses which the experimentalist tests, and the results of experiments suggest hypotheses which the theorist pursues, so in economics the hypotheses of the theorist fertilize the work of those who study directly the real world, and the study of the real world suggests new models for study by the theorist, new models which in turn provide more fertile hypotheses. Further discussion of the theoretical method, however, is out of place and likely to be of little use. The proof of the pudding is in the eating; conviction of the value of a scientific method comes from its use.[1]

Specifications of the model. In our handicraft model we suppose that each family makes one complete article for sale with a negligible equipment of tools. The income of each family will then be derived directly from the price of its output, and all the problems of dividing the proceeds from the sale of a product jointly produced by two co-operating families, or between families that work and families that own equipment, can be avoided. We further assume that the amount of any commodity that each family can and will produce in a given period, say a week, is fixed, and is equal to the amount of that commodity which any other family could produce. The weekly income of each family is, then, the product of the number of units of the commodity it produces and the price per unit of that commodity; and the rate of supply of each commodity is the product of the number of families engaged in making it and the number of units of that commodity that can be made in any selected unit of time by each such family.

The model is characterized by *"free enterprise"*: that is, each family is free to make anything it wishes, and for which it has the necessary skill. Two corollaries follow from this condition of free enterprise, viz. *mobility of labour* and *free competition*. Each family

[1]See E. H. Phelps Brown, *The Framework of the Pricing System* (London, 1936), introduction and chap. I, sections 1 and 3.

is free to move, and does freely move, in and out of trades as attracted, or repelled, by the expectation of higher, or lower, earnings. Each family is free to enter any trade to compete with the existing producers in that trade, and is, of course, liable to have others enter and compete with it in whatever trade it has selected.

It must be noticed that the conditions in this model are not only unlike those of the real world today, but are also unlike those of the real world of the past when a handicraft system of production prevailed. In the historical handicraft system free enterprise was restricted by the regulations of the guilds. To practise a trade one had to become a member of the guild; entry to the guild was sometimes restricted to sons of members, sometimes involved a heavy entrance fee, and in either case required a seven years' apprenticeship. If the trade was crowded the guild often regulated the amount of work which its members might do, multiplied holidays, prohibited night work, etc., in order to restrict total output and to divide the business equitably between its members. Prices were highly customary, and often regulated by the authority of the guild or the town; they were not flexible.

We endow the families of our model with a considerable measure of *economic rationality*; the heads of the families are "economic men." Each family is supposed to be intent on maximizing its income of goods and services for consumption, its provision of the "necessaries and conveniences of life." This means that each wants to sell dear and buy cheap. Each will try to maximize its money income by moving from the trades where earnings are relatively low into the trades where they are relatively high. (The high mobility we have assumed depends on this assumption of economic rationality.) Each in spending its income will behave with such regularity that one can state precisely how much of any commodity can be sold, i.e. will be bought, at any price. Each will be tempted to increase its consumption of any article by a fall in its price, and to increase its consumption by a predictable amount in response to any given fall in price: each, similarly, will be persuaded to restrict consumption by a rise in price, and to restrict by a predictable amount in response to any given rise in price. We suppose that if a purchaser is in doubt whether to purchase one unit of A or one unit of B, each of which costs one dollar, he can be said to want them with equal intensity. If then the price of A falls to 90 cents, he can have one unit of A and 10 cents worth of something else, or he can have one unit of B with nothing else. If he were previously undecided between one unit of A or of B at one dollar each, he will surely now choose one unit of A at 90 cents rather than one of B at one dollar. We eliminate the random element of impulsive purchases, erratic behaviour in the market, and assume that purchasers' habits remain stable over long periods of time. We do not suppose the inhabitants of our model to be "as gods knowing good from evil": they may want silly, even harmful things, but they know what they want and seek to acquire it.

We next lay down two conditions in order to eliminate the difficulties arising from *speculation*. First, we assume that each family spends all its income in the week in which it is earned, and spends no more in that week. We endow each family with a small stock of money, but we suppose, for the time being, that each is content to hold just that much unspent. No family spends more than its income, thus reducing its stock of money; no family spends less, thus increasing its stock of money. Secondly, we assume that each family consumes what it purchases. Again we must endow each family with some stock of goods on the shelves, but we suppose that consumption and purchase just keep pace. No family consumes more than it buys, thus reducing its stocks of goods; no family consumes less than it buys, thus increasing its stocks. Present rates of consumption and purchase are adjusted by present prices to the present rate of production: no family, anticipating a fall in the price of some commodity uses up its present stock and accumulates money while the price is high, and then replenishes the stock by spending the accumulated money when the price falls. We shall have to note some such possibilities later, but to handle these complications at this stage would confuse the picture. We must also rule out speculation by the producers: each producer will sell all he produces for whatever price he can get now. If this price is unsatisfactory he will move to another trade. He will not produce speculatively for stock in the hope that the price may later be higher. Nor will he restrict his output in the hope of raising the price. Such action by an individual would be useless because each individual is producing so small a part of the total requirement; and any attempt at restriction of output by the whole group of producers of some commodity would be wrecked by the influx of new competitors coming to take advantage of the relatively high prices. In the absence of speculation and under the condition of competition what is produced weekly will be sold weekly at whatever price can be secured. The prices will therefore be extremely flexible.

Prices and incomes. Each family by specializing in the production of some one commodity will have rendered itself completely dependent on the unconscious co-operation of the other families for the provision of the necessaries of life. Each family must be able to sell its product, and hopes to sell it dear; but each must be able to buy what it needs and hopes to buy these things cheap. There is, however, a limit to the power of each to sell dear: if some can sell dear, that occupation becomes relatively attractive and others move into the trade, the supply of its product increases, and the price falls. The price must fall in order to induce further consumption to take up the increased supply. As the price falls the influx of new producers is checked. This same process happening in the trades producing the things the family wants to buy constitutes a limit to the risk of having to buy dear, or of not being able to buy the things it wants. If the price of some goods it wants to buy is relatively high, there is likely to be an influx of workers, an increase in supply, and a fall in price.

Under these conditions there will be a rough equality of income, the more complete, the more uniform the skill of the families. If some family, or small group of families, possesses some rare skill or some secret process, for the production of some much wanted commodity, the supply of that commodity may remain so restricted that its price may remain high. The earnings of such favoured producers will continue higher than those of producers generally. There could be no influx of new competitors to increase the supply and bring prices down so that earnings are again in line with the rest of the economy. There could be no such influx because there would be no others possessing the skill, or sharing the secret. If the group is relatively small so that concerted action is possible there may be a further restriction of output by deliberate agreement. It may be discovered that a smaller aggregate output could be sold for a greater aggregate revenue, that a 10 per cent reduction in output would increase the price by, say, 12 or 15 per cent. Such monopolistic restriction is ruled out, however, in our model for there is no scarcity of skill and mobility of labour is effective: any temporary success at deliberate restriction would be the signal for an influx of new producers to share the higher earnings.

In the study of this price system the analogy from mechanics of a system of equilibrium of forces is of great assistance. We shall try to show the conditions under which our model would be in equilibrium, so that each and every individual with perfect freedom to change his rate of consumption of each of the products has no incentive to change, and that each and every individual with perfect freedom to move from his present occupation to another has no incentive to move. Freedom to change yet no change, perfect mobility yet no movement, such are the characteristics of the economic equilibrium.

These characteristics may be better understood if we study this equilibrium in two steps; we consider first a temporary, or "short-run" equilibrium, and then a more permanent, "long-run" equilibrium. Before proceeding, however, we must emphasize the fact that we are discussing what would happen under the simple conditions of our model, if there were no change in the basic conditions during the period necessary for the establishment of equilibrium. Any change in consumption habits, any change in methods of production, would change the equilibrium position. We may later perform some simple exercises on our model by introducing some simple changes in these basic conditions and tracing the changes as a new equilibrium is established.

Middlemen. Even in this simple model we need to introduce a group of middlemen, or traders. If the number of workers in each occupation is considerable, and if the distances involved are great, buyers may waste a great deal of time finding producers with stocks for sale, or producers may waste a great deal of time finding buyers for their wares. This waste can be reduced by establishing a market place where buyers and sellers congregate at stated times. A greater economy may be achieved by some men specializing as traders; they will buy from the producers at their places of work, and make the goods conveniently available to the buyers. It will pay the producer to sell cheaper wholesale to the few traders than retail to the many consumers, because in the time saved from selling he can produce more goods. It will pay the consumer to pay more in the nearby store where a variety of goods is available for inspection and comparison, because in the time saved in buying he can produce more goods. The middleman buying cheaper and selling dearer is able to make an income for himself. Unless this income is roughly equal to the incomes of the producers, no men will specialize as middlemen; if this income is bigger than that of the producers more will enter trade and the competition of new traders will reduce the spread between the retail and wholesale prices till the incomes of the traders are reduced to the general level. We may conclude that our model society might produce more goods in the aggregate as a result of withdrawing some men from production to act as middlemen or traders. The service performed might be useful. We also conclude that the price charged for the service will be reasonable as long as there is free competition. The traders in our model, however, are different in many respects from those of the real world. They do not speculate, but replenish their shelves as they sell thus maintaining their stocks without change. They compete; they are not able to build up monopoly positions as sole sellers in a particular locality or to a particular class of buyer. They sell, yet do not indulge in the arts of salesmanship; they sell what people want rather than persuade people to want what they have for sale. In the real world we may find too few middlemen in some trades, and too large a proportion of the energies of the people devoted to salesmanship rather than to production in others.

Equilibrium. While we assume perfect mobility we shall not suppose it to be instantaneous. At any one time the numbers in each occupation may be taken as given, and this may be supposed to imply that the rates of supply of the various goods are given (we neglect the possible variation in the amount of work done and the amount of goods produced by the workers). Short-run equilibrium requires then a system of prices such that the consumption of each commodity is restricted sufficiently and only just sufficiently, so that the whole current supply is purchased. With any set of prices which does not achieve this exact rationing there will be unsatisfied buyers trying to locate supplies and offering advanced prices, or there will be unsatisfied sellers trying to locate buyers and offering at reduced prices. The system will not be in equilibrium. But the changes in prices which result will be tending to establish equilibrium. Again we must emphasize the interdependence of these prices: the problem is not one of finding a price that rations sugar, a price that rations tea, a price that rations cake, and so on; the problem is one of finding a set of prices for sugar, tea, cake, etc., which if ruling simultaneously will adjust consumption of each of these goods to the supply of each of them. The interrelations are the result partly of the relations of the goods in a pattern of consumption; the more tea is bought the more sugar and the less beer will be wanted. These interrelations also result from the fact that they are all purchased out of the same limited money income; if the price of tea falls, more tea will be bought and unless the purchases of tea are in exact inverse proportion to the price there will be either more or less money spent on tea. If more money is spent on tea, less must be spent on some other thing, or things; if less is spent on tea, there is more to be spent on other things. So a change in the price of one good will have repercussions on the prices and rates of consumption of others, and the changes in the prices and rates of consumption of these others will have further repercussions, and so on. The metaphor of the ever-widening circles when a stone is thrown into a still pond naturally comes to mind. These interrelations can be more complicated if the patterns of consumption of different groups of producers are widely different: if, for instance, the brewers are teetotallers, and the butchers vegetarians. Such complications call for mathematical symbols for precise explanation, but there is no need to go deeper into the problem.

If the short-run equilibrium discussed above results in unequal earnings in different occupations, the condition is one of long-run disequilibrium. There is perfect mobility and consequently there will be movement. Workers will leave the less remunerative to enter the more remunerative occupations. The supply of some goods will increase and their prices fall, the supply of other goods will decrease and their prices rise. The patterns of consumption will change to adjust to the new rates of supply; this change will be in response to the changes in prices and the changes in the incomes of the different groups of consumer-workers. (It is worth pointing out at this point that the consumer and the producer are one and the same person viewed from the different sides.) Change will continue till a system of prices, a pattern of consumption and a pattern of production is established such that workers are so distributed between occupations that, though free to change, no individual sees the possibility of improving his own position by changing. Equilibrium is established.

Adjustment to changing wants. With our model in long-run equilibrium let us suppose that there occurs a sudden change in consumption habits, such as would result from a widespread adoption of vegetarianism. A large group of people try to buy more vegetables, and are less inclined to buy meat. In the short-run the rates of supply of vegetables and meat are fixed, and the rates of consumption must be adjusted to the given rates of supply. The price of vegetables rises sharply, that of meat falls sharply. The more convinced vegetarians secure their vegetables at a price, the less convinced vegetarians are deterred from their new dietary practice by the high price of vegetables, and the temptation to eat meat is made more severe as meat becomes temptingly cheap. Those who do not adopt the change in dietary habit, are affected by the change in relative prices: they buy less vegetables, releasing supplies for the ardent vegetarians, and they buy more meat, consuming the supplies released by the vegetarians. In time the high price of vegetables will induce an influx into market gardening and the low price of meat, a withdrawal from meat production, till prices of vegetables fall and prices of meat rise so as again to give roughly equal earnings in the two lines of production. There will, of course, be secondary complicating effects which we intend only briefly to indicate. The temporary prosperity of the vegetable growers is likely to lead to an increased demand for luxuries, while the depressed condition of the meat producers will force them to abandon for the time being the consumption of things that had become almost necessaries. This means that many other prices besides meat and vegetables will be affected. Then, too, those who now buy more vegetables at higher prices will have less to buy other things with even though they are buying no meat; and those who now buy more cheap meat and less dear vegetables are not likely to be spending exactly the same amount as before on meat and vegetables combined, so that they too will have more, or less, money to spend on other things. Finally, when the new rates of supply have been established, more vegetables may mean more butter is needed; less meat means less mustard is called for.

Equilibrium and order. This discussion of equilibrium in our model suggests that there will be "order," but it is natural to ask whether it will be a sensible order. In the simple conditions of this model it can be shown to be a very sensible order. This can, to some extent, be deduced from what has been said about the impact of vegetarianism. Sensible adjustment to such a change in consumption habits would involve, in a planned economy where the planning authority tried to meet the wishes of the people, a change of plan, a change immediately in the rationing of supplies and a change in the production plan for the future. The changes which would thus be made by authority in a planned economy of this type would in our individualistic model be made without consultation, automatically, through price changes. But the changes would be substantially the same. However, the authority in the planned world might disapprove of the vegetarian craze and refuse to promote the adjustment; it might itself be composed of fanatical converts and make it difficult for those who did not conform to the new practice; or it might be little concerned to meet the wishes of the people and unwilling to make any adjustment. It is not enough, however, to consider whether the automatic *changes* expected in the model are similar to those that would be made by a planning authority which tried to give the people what it wanted. Would the pattern of production and consumption established in the model in equilibrium be similar to that which such a democratic "plan" would establish? In answering this for the case of our model it is necessary, first, to emphasize the fact that under the conditions of our model incomes would be equal. With incomes equal it is reasonable to suggest that readiness to pay is a reasonable, if rough, measure of how much a thing is wanted. Now in equilibrium, with earnings equal, if men were moved from their trade to any other, their product could only be sold by tempting people to increase their consumption of this product by lower prices, i.e. they would be making less wanted things. The position of equilibrium is one which corresponds pretty well with the wants of the people. There are some who would say that the consumer does not know what he wants, does not want what he needs, and often does not get what he thinks he is getting. True, some consumers will make mistakes, and a dictator would, perhaps, toy with the possibility of deciding what was best for the people instead of letting them decide for themselves. But freedom of choice is, or has become through use, desirable in itself; freedom to make mistakes and possibly to learn from experience seems to many preferable to an externally ordered life, however well ordered. Freedom of choice becomes then for the liberal, one might almost say for the truly adult, not merely a means to maximum satisfaction, but a desirable end in itself.

Lest this favourable judgment on the reasonableness of the individualistic order in our model be taken to suggest an equally favourable judgment on the reasonableness of the individualistic order in the real world, certain qualifications should here be mentioned. In the real world incomes are very unequal, and readiness to pay is no measure of intensity of want. The price system produces the things which sell. Luxuries are produced when the supply of necessaries is still inadequate. The pattern of production achieved through price adjustment is very different, then, from that which would be aimed at by a benevolent planning authority whether it tried to give the people what they wanted, or what was best for them. But planning authorities are not necessarily benevolent, or intelligent. They may prefer guns to butter; they may prefer might to comfort; they may be concerned to give the mass of the people enough to allay discontent rather than to create positive contentment. We must be careful not to compare an ideal price system with the most objectionable kind of planning by the worst possible dictator, nor to compare the worst features of the real price system with an ideal kind of planning by an ideal dictator.

The state and free enterprise. In spite of the contrast we have drawn between an economy regulated by some political planning body and one regulated automatically by the free functioning of a price system, it must not be supposed that no political organization is necessary in the latter case, or that no planning can be undertaken if the price system remains. The functioning of free enterprise in our model, as in the real world, is dependent on the existence of some authority to guarantee personal freedom, property rights, and the performance of contracts, and to establish standards of weight, measure, money, and possibly of quality (e.g. the British Pharmacopoeia). There is also required an authority to arrange for the provision of certain services which must, or can best, be provided communally rather than individually, e.g. the provision of roads, sanitary services, fire protection, education. The authority which provides these services of police protection, courts for the enforcement of rights, sanitary services, etc., is the state. To provide these services it must raise funds by taxing its citizens. To the extent of their tax contribution the individuals give up the direct decision as to how their income shall be spent; by spending its tax revenue the state directs resources to the ends it chooses. There is some planning, but the planner operates through the price system. The planning may go further, but still stay within the price system. The state may encourage the production of some commodities by a subsidy (or tariff protection if we admit foreign trade) and may discourage by discriminatory taxation the production of other goods, or may even prohibit the manufacture and sale of others. The planning authority works through the price system, influencing the profitability of various trades with a view to stimulating increased production in some and decreased production in others.

If some sort of a state is necessary for the functioning of even a free economy—and how necessary it is has been only roughly indicated above—it must not be assumed that the state is only a means to an economic end. However dangerous and distasteful may be the glorification of the state in the totalitarian philosophy, and however much one may insist on the liberal doctrine that the good of the individual citizen is paramount, one must not forget that there is a value for the individual in feeling himself a member of a greater society, of a state. Individual happiness depends on belonging to groups, churches, trade unions, lodges, cities, nations, empires. Some of the groups have economic objectives, e.g. the trade union or the wheat pool, yet they are wrongly appraised simply by reference to their efficiency in achieving these objectives. Their value is, in part, in providing some satisfactory group life. What is true of the smaller groups is also true of the greater political societies, nations, and groups of nations.

In the remainder of this chapter we complicate our model by introducing problems of growth, growth of population and growth of wealth, and some incidental problems arising therefrom. The object is to prepare the way for the discussion of similar problems in the real world, to provide something in the nature of a map of the forest lest we get lost in examining the trees. We shall not attempt a completely satisfactory, or rigorous, solution of the problems of our growing model; we shall be content to indicate the nature of the problems and the broad lines of their solution, and we shall end the chapter with an excursion into the real world with the help of a "sketch map."

Growth of population. Consider first the problems of population growth. The people in our first model constituted a stagnant pool, the

people of our new model, as of the real world, constitute a pool fed by
the stream of births (and of immigration) and drained by the stream
of deaths (and of emigration). The level of the pool rises when the
stream feeding it flows faster than the stream draining it. But the
analogy of the pool breaks down, for it ignores the process of aging;
the drops of water entering the pool of population are not just like the
other drops in the pool, nor like the drops draining out. The new
arrivals are mostly babies with very different needs from those of
adults, and constituting no present addition to the labour force: the
immigrant stream brings adults, usually young adults constituting
about equivalent additions to consumer demand and productive
capacity, but also constituting a significant addition to the ranks of
parents and therefore promising shortly an increased stream of births.
Even when we suppose there to be no changes in habits of consumption, the growing economy, because of its changing age distribution, involves adjusting a growing labour supply to meet a regularly
changing set of wants; now more cradles, now more schools, now more
coffins. But the changes are largely predictable, and adjustment is to
that extent easier.

This adjustment to changing demands calls for mobility of labour
between occupations. We endowed our model with this characteristic,
but in the real world such mobility is very limited. The high-school
teacher cannot quickly change to be a tobacco farmer and later an
undertaker as the changing wants of an aging population make themselves felt. But again we have to take account of this process of growing up and dying. The workers in any one trade constitute neither
a stagnant pool, nor a cistern perfectly connected with the other
cisterns (other trades) so as to maintain an equal level of wages in all.
Each trade constitutes a pool fed by a stream of young learners and
drained by a stream of deaths and retirements. Adjustment to change
comes, mainly, from a change in the relative volume of the streams of
learners entering the trades. There may be, almost certainly will be,
some movement of adults from trade to trade if the differences of
earnings become considerable; but smaller differences in earnings will
promote the slower, yet sure, adjustment that comes from a change
in the rate of entry. Now it is clear that adjustment to change will be
more rapid in a growing economy where all the pools are rising;
cessation of expansion in a trade then constitutes relative shrinkage.
With no adults moving, the change in the proportionate distribution of
labour is quickly made. And if adjustment is easier with a growing
population, to some changes adjustment is less necessary.[2] Consider,

[2]See below, pp. 114–15.

for instance, the vegetarian movement in our model as changed to allow for growth. A smaller percentage of the population will buy meat which suggests the need for an immediate fall in price to stimulate those who still want it to buy more, and to ensure an ultimate reduction in the number of people growing beef. But it is a smaller percentage of a growing number of people who will buy meat. Apart from the vegetarian movement the number growing beef would have been steadily growing to provide for the steadily growing population: after the vegetarian success, the immediate fall in the price of beef deters new people from entering the trade, completely or partially, and the supply of beef without becoming absolutely less becomes relatively smaller. Growing population takes up the slack, renders unnecessary the actual movement of adults, and makes short the period of depression for the particular trade.

Growth of wealth. We next provide for growth of wealth, i.e. for accumulation, in our model. In the first, simplest, model we supposed that the income of goods and services produced in a given period was sold, and consumed, in that period. We explicitly ruled out accumulation of stocks of consumable goods, i.e. goods which are destroyed as they are used; and, implicitly, we ruled out the production of "durable" goods, i.e. of goods which last through several periods and yield in each some services which constitute part of the income of that period. We will still ignore the accumulation of stocks of consumable goods, but we shall now introduce the accumulation of durable goods. We were concerned exclusively with income, we shall now be concerned with income and wealth, wealth as the source of income (perhaps also as an end in itself). Two kinds of durable goods may be distinguished; those which give direct satisfaction to their owner by providing useful services, e.g. a house providing a regular income of shelter, comfort, and, perhaps, prestige, and those which enable the owner to produce more and better articles for current consumption, or for further accumulation, e.g. a lathe, a plough, or a workshop. We shall continue to assume, fantastic as it may seem, that each durable good can be completely made by a single family, and that in each case at least one can be made in the income period selected. This eliminates any difficulty about the income of the *producers* of durable goods, in each period (week or whatever period we choose) each family realizes its money income by selling the product of that period, and is therefore in exactly the same position as the producer of consumable goods. We do allow, however, difficulty to develop so far as the *buyer* is concerned, for we introduce, in small degree, the problem of "lumpy" expenditure. To buy out of current income one of the instruments which took a whole period to make would take, since incomes in our model are roughly equal, roughly the whole of the buyer's income for that period. To this we shall return.

The right amount of accumulation. We must now refer back to our earlier discussion of the conditions of well-being for any economy. One of these conditions was the prior accumulation of wealth; another was the good judgment with which existing resources are directed to the many alternative lines of production, and here good judgment in deciding how much to produce for current use and how much of one's energies to devote to further accumulation of wealth was seen to be of very great importance. One may add that our present well-being depends not only on the amount of the prior accumulation but also on how sensible was the character of that accumulation, i.e. on whether we have accumulated the more useful things rather than the less useful. Similarly good judgment in present accumulation involves good judgment not only as to the amount of further accumulation, but also as to the kind of wealth to be accumulated. In the planned economy these decisions, like the decisions as to the detailed composition of the stream of goods for current consumption, would be determined authoritatively by the central planning authority. In our individualistic model durable goods will be produced when buyers offer prices for such goods which promise incomes for their producers roughly equal to those generally available in the economy. The decision to accumulate is made by individuals, and the decision what to accumulate is similarly made by individuals. The price system is again in evidence, providing an automatic solution of the problem. But we do not intend to suggest that the "automatic" solution is the "right" solution. Some doubt as to its "rightness" is expressed by H. D. Henderson in *Supply and Demand.*[3]

We in the twentieth century owe much of the material wealth that we enjoy to the fact that over the last century men saved as largely as they did. But our natural gratitude should not restrain us from doubting whether they were really well advised to do so. If we ask the question *how* they managed to do so, our doubts are deepened. For first place among the explanations must be assigned to the inequality in the then distribution of wealth. It was because many men in England were rich enough to save that our railways were built, and the resources of new Continents were opened up. But England, a century or even half a century ago, was not really a rich community. And if the national income in those days had been distributed more evenly among the people, can we doubt that they would have spent a far larger proportion of it on immediate needs; can we doubt that they would have been right to do so? We may rather doubt, in view of the reactions of poverty on physical and mental efficiency, on social harmony,

[3]Cambridge, 1922. See pp. 131-2.

even possibly on population, whether we today would have been really injured as much as might appear. How, then, can we suppose that the sum of the amounts which it suits individuals to save will bear any close relation to the resources which the community can properly devote to future ends? Are we to regard an unjust distribution of wealth as a mysterious dispensation of Providence for securing perfect harmony between the future and the present? The point need not be laboured further. There are no grounds for assuming that we save, as a community, even roughly what we ought to save. If we wish to believe we do, we must turn for support from economics to theology.

But if we doubt whether the automatic solution was "right," we find it hard to lay down any principles to guide a benevolent planning authority, or to judge the wisdom of any plan. It is interesting to note that the Five Year Plans in Russia involved very rapid accumulation of productive equipment, so rapid as to involve, in view of the real poverty of the Russian community, a severe "tightening of the belt." Were these plans "right"?

Saving in the model. We must now consider the problems arising from the inevitable lumpiness of expenditure on durable goods to add to the store of wealth. Take an implement which is the product of one week's work of the families that produce it. How is the buyer to spend a whole week's income on one article, which will give an income of satisfaction, or increase his earning power, for years, but which will be of but little use in the current week, when his weekly money income is barely enough to buy the necessaries of life during that week? No pulling in of the belt will suffice. How then is the problem to be met? The first obvious possibility is for the buyer to accumulate week by week what little money he can spare from the purchase of necessaries till he has enough to buy it. This involves relaxing the monetary condition of our simplest model, viz. that no family spend in any week less, or more, than is earned in each week. The result of this prior accumulation, if we permit it, would not be serious in our model because of certain other assumed conditions; but the nature of the problem becomes apparent and it is possible to point out some characteristics of the real world that make the problem in fact extremely serious. First, consider the absurd extreme; suppose everyone wants to accumulate more money and therefore decides to spend nothing out of this week's income, then no one has any income, for no one has been able to sell anything that he produced. Secondly, suppose *some* families want to accumulate more money for some lumpy expenditure in the future, and therefore decide to save, i.e. not to spend, a *part* of the incomes they receive in each of the following few weeks. At the old prices all that is produced, and was sold before this saving habit developed, cannot be sold; but under the conditions of our model prices are flexible, and at lower prices the whole output is again sold. If the saving is done at the particular expense of a few luxuries, their prices will fall particularly low, and if the saving keeps up there will be some movement of workers out of those luxury trades into others. Prices as a whole being lower, money incomes will be lower, but real incomes (i.e. the amount of goods and services which a man can buy with his money income) will be more or less unchanged. Those who were trying to save a given sum of money to buy a given implement will find it harder to save that amount of money out of their reduced incomes, but will not now need to save that amount since the price of the implement will also fall. Those who do not save will be able to buy more than they expected each week as each week's income, though smaller, is spent with prices again reduced to maintain sales in face of the continued saving.[4] *Qua* consumers the spenders gain in each period from the low prices, *qua* producers they lose as they sell at lower prices; but when they spend their lower incomes they find prices still lower. The reverse takes place when after some weeks the savers spend their accumulations of money: prices and money incomes rise. Thirdly, let us notice two conditions in which there would be none even of these minor difficulties. First, if each week a few more begin to save, but each week a few reach their objective and buy their implement, the two groups may counteract each other. Some spend less than their income, others spend just that much more than their income; the process of buying and selling goes on with prices and incomes unchanged just as when everyone spent exactly as much as he earned. Secondly, if each week those who save lend the money they save to a group of borrowers, who spend it immediately on the purchase of some implement, again the two groups, savers and borrowers, counteract one another. The savers spend less than their income, the borrowers spend just that much more than their income. The total amount spent creates incomes in each week as large as those of the previous week. This gives us a clue to the solution of the difficulty of capital formation in the real world, but we must first introduce one further complication into our model, viz. price rigidity.

We shall not attempt fully to explain why the perfect price flexibility of our model is not realized in the real world; a partial explanation lies in the absence of perfect competition in large sectors of the

---

[4]This fall in money-incomes and in prices would induce the non-savers to hold *less* money unspent and so would enable the savers to accumulate *more* money. The complications which would arise if the non-savers would not part with any of their customary stock of money, or if more money were made available by the state, cannot be discussed here. See below pp. 69–74.

economy. The Royal Commission on Price Spreads (1934-5) drew attention to the different behaviour of prices and production in the agricultural implements industry and in agriculture: in the former prices fell from 1929 to 1932 by 3 per cent, production declined 91 per cent; in the latter prices fell in the same period 52 per cent and production *increased* 13 per cent. Mr. Lloyd Reynolds in his *Control of Competition in Canada*[5] presents the results of a study of prices in four groups of industry; a monopoly group, a group where the number of producers is relatively small and where price agreements are known, or believed, to exist, a group called competitive, though probably not so perfectly competitive as agriculture because of the development of special markets in which individual producers have a sort of monopoly, and a group of agricultural producers where competition is nearly perfect. "Between 1929 and 1933," says Mr. Reynolds, "the prices of the monopolized goods fell about 10 per cent, while under price agreement the decline was about 13 per cent. . . . Competitive prices, on the other hand, fell by 36 per cent and prices of farm products were cut in half." Mr. Reynolds properly points out that through secret discounts prices in the first two cases may have fallen somewhat more than appears, but allowance for this would not materially change the picture.

Saving in the model when prices are rigid. In our model, so far, we have assumed complete flexibility of prices, in the real world we find only limited flexibility, and flexibility of varying degree in different industries. We do not intend to suggest that inflexible prices are the sole source of difficulty in the real world, but they are *one* source of difficulty and study of this difficulty does enable us to develop some useful principles. We therefore revise our model to investigate the problems arising from saving when prices are imperfectly flexible, and the simplest alternative assumption, though somewhat fantastic, is that of perfect inflexibility, or rigidity, of prices. We shall not attempt to lay down conditions for the model which would make this assumption follow from them, as flexibility followed from the conditions of the earlier model; we simply make an arbitrary assumption of rigidity. We suppose that the families have been spending in each week the income of that week, no more, no less. We then suppose that some families want to accumulate more money to purchase in the future some expensive implement, and therefore decide to save, i.e. not to spend, part of their incomes in each of the following weeks. At the old prices all that was produced would only be sold if everyone spent all he earned. With this outbreak of thrift in some families all that is pro-

[5]Cambridge, Mass., 1940, pp. 71-8.

duced cannot be sold at the old prices, and prices, we assume, cannot fall. Goods are unsold, and money incomes are reduced. Since prices do not change the lower money incomes mean lower real incomes. The community could still produce just as much of the "necessaries and conveniences of life," but the producers would not be able to sell what they produced, and therefore would not be able to consume what the other producers could easily produce for them. Unable to sell they will each reduce their production. The full resources of the community will not be utilized, one of our conditions of wealth will not be fulfilled. The difficulty can be solved, however, exactly as before. If those who save, i.e. spend less than their income, lend to borrowers who spend that much more than their income, the whole output can again be sold at the rigid prices, and production again flows freely. There will, of course, be difficulties since the borrowers are not likely to buy the same things that the savers refrain from buying.

The borrowers who spend more than their income will mainly be buying new durable goods. Some indeed will be spendthrifts careless of the future, some will be unfortunates in temporary difficulty, others will be paying for education in the expectation of higher earnings in the future as a result. But if the amount of borrowing is to be adequate there must be much buying of durable goods, and of productive equipment. If the incentive to borrow to spend for such purposes (or to invest, as economists now call it) is not adequate to take care of the thrift of the people the difficulty which develops is cumulative. For if in the first week goods are unsold and incomes consequently reduced, the prospects of selling goods in succeeding weeks become less, and the incentive to build new equipment to produce more goods becomes weaker. So borrowing and spending in excess of income by one group to offset the saving of the other group becomes still more deficient. But saving, too, will shrink. For, though the underlying force of thrift remains unchanged, the savings of the people will fall as their incomes fall. With lower incomes those families which had decided to save more may reverse their decision, and some who had hoped to save something may save nothing. The aggregate savings of the community will be reduced. Income will shrink to the size which leads people to save just that amount which borrowers are prepared to spend.

How big an income the community can enjoy, or how completely it may utilize its capacity to produce, depends, then, on the relation between the amount the people want to save out of any given income and the amount that borrowers are ready to borrow and spend, or the amount of investment. The enjoyment of the large income which would result from full employment of its resources is dependent on "investment" on a scale adequate to offset the savings that would be made out of an income of this size. If with full employment and the 1939 level of prices the money income of the United States had been 100 billion dollars, and if out of their big incomes the people only spent 80 billion dollars on consumption and tried to save 20 billion dollars, this high income level could have been maintained only if investment amounted to 20 billion dollars. For incomes arise from spending; only if 100 billion dollars is spent can there be 100 billion dollars of income. If only 10 billion dollars is spent in investment, the income of the community will shrink to that level at which only 10 billion dollars is saved. This might be about 75 billion dollars; 65 billion dollars might then be spent on consumption which, together with the 10 billion dollars spent in investment, would maintain the 75 billion dollar income.

Saving and investment in the real world. In the real world, to which we turn for a time, the desire to save is strong, widespread, and constant in operation. The motives for such saving are many and varied. Intelligent provision for the future, provision against death, sickness, disability, unemployment, is important. But, as Professor Knight puts it, "It is mostly a matter of social standards, of what is 'good form,' 'the thing' or not the thing to do. The fact of possessing an accumulation of goods confers social prestige and in addition vast power over one's fellows. . . . The rich man will be in a position to make his favor solicited, his ill-will feared, and may, of course, turn his situation to material profit." That saving is more a matter of "social standard" than intelligent individual planning is, perhaps, an important reason for that constancy, or regularity, of the desire to save which we want to emphasize. The amount of saving does vary in the real world, but this is mainly the result of variation in money incomes, rather than any variation in the underlying "thriftiness" of the people.[6] Contrasted with this constancy of thrift is the irregularity, in the real world, of the desire to buy, generally to borrow to buy, durable goods. We cannot here attempt to explain this irregularity, but we must state

[6]For preliminary investigation, or our rough "sketch map," it is useful to treat the amount of saving as determined mainly, indeed solely, by the size of income. Serious error may result if at a later stage we neglect the elements of instability in consumer behaviour. We must not take the sketch map as adequate in finding our way in the intricate real world. See A. F. Burns, *The Instability of Consumer Spending,* Thirty-second Annual Report of the National Bureau of Economic Research (New York, 1952).

it as a fact. We may quote Professor Hansen's testimony[7] before the Temporary National Economic Committee (a select committee of the United States Congress).

I should like to call attention to what seems to me to be a fact, namely, that economic progress even in the nineteenth century, came by spurts and not at a uniform rate. Such notable students of economic development as Spiethoff, Wicksell, Cassel, Schumpeter, and Robertson stress the discontinuity, the jerkiness and lumpiness of economic progress. . . . It is my view that the deep and prolonged depressions of the nineties relate to a cessation of growth of the railroad industry. There was a temporary lull before the electrical and automobile industries emerged, and similarly in the decade of the twenties . . . we are having a similar experience. The great automobile industry has risen to maturity and no comparable new industry has appeared to fill the gap.

Professor Hansen here stresses the jerkiness of the progress of invention, of the emergence of new industries; the jerkiness in the business decision to exploit existing inventions is equally striking as waves of optimism and pessimism succeed each other.

The variability of "investment," or of "income producing expenditures that offset saving," in the real world is shown in Table I which is adapted from one presented in the evidence of Dr. Currie[8] before

TABLE I
NATIONAL INCOME AND INVESTMENT 1921–38, UNITED STATES
(billion dollars)

	Aggregate national income	Aggregate investment
1921	64	10
1922	64	12
1923	75	17
1924	75	13
1925	80	17
1926	85	17
1927	83	16
1928	86	16
1929	90	18
1930	80	12
1931	64	8
1932	47	2
1933	46	3
1934	56	6
1935	62	10
1936	71	14
1937	79	14
1938	71	9

[7]*Investigation of Concentration of Economic Power: Hearings before the Temporary National Economic Committee, Congress of the United States* (Washington, 1940), part IX, "Savings and Investment," pp. 3496–3518.
[8]*Ibid.*, pp. 3521–38.

the Temporary National Economic Committee. Not only does it show the variability of investment, but it also demonstrates a relation between aggregate income and investment similar to that which our theoretical analysis suggested. It seems clear that the people of the United States could have enjoyed a money income of something like 90 to 100 billion dollars if there were sufficiently obvious and tempting opportunities for "investment" on a scale of from 19 to 20 billion dollars annually. If "investment" fell to 2 billion dollars, as in 1932, income might be expected to shrink below 50 billion dollars, at which level only 2 billion dollars would be saved. This decline in investment between 1929 and 1933 cannot be analysed in detail, but one may note a decline in expenditure on industrial plant and equipment from 10 billion dollars in 1929 to less than one billion dollars in 1933, on private housing, from 2.8 to 0.3 billion dollars, and a decline in consumer credits from 0.9 to 0.1 billion dollars.

This fluctuation in the income of the United States, and the general doctrine of the importance of investment, was very clearly stated by Professor Hansen before the Temporary National Economic Committee. We quote a part of his testimony:

This income stream is large or small according to the volume of purchases currently made. These purchases are of two kinds; one type consists of the purchase of consumption goods and services; another type consists of the purchase of capital equipment, industrial plant and machinery, public utility and railroad equipment, commercial and residential building, and the like. There are, therefore, two streams of expenditures continually going on; one stream consists of expenditures for consumption and the other consists of expenditures on capital outlays on plant and equipment. How large the income stream will be, whether 60 billions or 80 billions, depends upon the volume of these two expenditure streams. Now the expenditure stream which is mainly responsible for the rise and fall of the total income is the outlay made on equipment and plant expansion. When large expenditures are made on industrial, commercial, residential, and public construction; when office buildings, hotels, apartments, houses, school buildings, and public works of all kinds are being erected in large volume, when investment is made on a large scale in railroad, utility, manufacturing and mining, and agricultural equipment, the income is lifted to a high level and it can be maintained on a high level so long and only so long as large capital outlays of this sort are being made.

Thus in the good years from 1923 to 1929, inclusive, the total volume of capital outlays amounted to the vast sum of $128,000,000,000. I am taking the figures from Dr. Kuznets in his monumental study on National Income and Capital Formation, made in the offices of the National Bureau of Economic Research. Of this total, one-half was expended on replacements and renewals, and one-half for plant expansion and new construction. This includes business capital outlays as well as residential capital outlays and outlays for public construction. Average annual expenditure on capital outlays for this seven-year period amounted to 18.3 billions of dollars. It required this volume of capital outlay to lift the national income to 77 billions, the average income figure for this period of high prosperity.

These figures suggest that reasonably full employment and a fairly satisfactory income level, such as we had in 1923 to 1929, require a quite extraordinarily large volume of expenditures on capital goods. It is the margin of income which is created by the capital-goods industries that fills the gap between prosperity and depression. No high level of employment and income has ever been achieved without a large outlay on plant equipment and new construction.

The right amount of accumulation when unemployment exists. Before leaving the subject of accumulation we must notice a paradox. In our earlier discussions of the conditions of well-being we have pictured a community choosing more of this and therefore less of that. More equipment meant less cake now though it might promise more and better cake in years to come. In a planned economy where all resources were utilized the accumulation of durable goods would involve a sacrifice of present consumption. The Russian Five Year Plan did mean less cake, almost less bread. In our model with perfect competition and flexible prices it seems reasonably clear that all resources would be utilized, and so more lathes would mean less cake. But in the real world of the thirties we seem to have been able to have more lathes and more cake, to have more cake only if we made more lathes. For unless we bought more lathes many unemployed workers would have no income wherewith to buy cake, and so cake makers would be idle. We could have more goods for present enjoyment by refraining from adding to our stocks of wealth if our inclination to save declined *pari passu* with our inclination to buy such additions to our accumulated weath, or if we could find some way of maintaining production in the face of declining sales and, or, declining prices. As it was we could, paradoxically, have our cake and eat it.[9] This leads to one more comment. We have said that it is hard to determine what is the "right" amount of accumulation. Now we can suggest one criterion: the right amount of accumulation (from one point of view) is an amount sufficient to take care of the saving that people want to perform when the income of the community is at the high level at which resources are fully utilized. This is the "right" amount in the sense that it is the amount which guarantees full employment. It is better even to accumulate the wrong things and maintain a high level of income and productivity, than not to accumulate enough, and so slow down the production of consumable goods. We can have more pyramids and more cake, we can have more

[9] Cf. A. C. Pigou, *Economics in Practice* (London, 1935), chap. II, "Economy and Waste."

armaments and more cake. All this is true only if people stubbornly save, whether other people want to accumulate or not. One must add, of course, that this holds only up to a point. If we want to spend on armaments on a scale bigger than would just offset our savings with the people fully employed, somehow the people have to be made to consume less.

Canadian national income, 1928–55. So far we have discussed the problem of saving and investment and the level of income by reference to the experience of the United States in the depressed thirties. When we turn to consider Canadian experience in the same period we find it necessary to introduce a new item, exports. When we go beyond the thirties (whether we are concerned with Canada or the United States) a third item becomes important, government expenditure, and we begin to be concerned with the problems of too much, rather than too little, expenditure, i.e., with the problems of inflation. In Table II figures for the period 1928 to 1955 are given, showing the size of the national income (or gross national product) and the amount of investment, exports and government expenditures. We shall discuss briefly the experience of three periods, the thirties, the war, and the post-war inflation.

The thirties. The collapse of investment in Canada from around 1.4 billion dollars to 200 million dollars parallels the fall from 12 to 2 billion dollars in the United States, so that it may seem unnecessary to look for other factors contributing to the decline in income and employment. However the fall in exports, and the consequent reduction in the income and therefore in the spending of all export producers, must have had a further depressing effect; and that same decline in exports contributed, no doubt, to the decline in investment. Imports fell off too, indeed fell by a greater amount, from 1.9 billion dollars in 1929 to 800 million dollars in 1933. The importance of this decline in mitigating the "employment effect" of the decline in exports requires brief explanation. Spending (whether it be consumer spending, investment, or purchase for export) puts income in someone's hands available to be spent. To the extent that some of that income is saved (not spent) income at the next remove must decline unless there is an offset, say investment of an equivalent amount, spending by business making up for the saving by consumers. Out of the 6.2 billion dollar income of the high employment year of 1929 saving would run to perhaps 1.0 billion dollars; if investment were less than this income would fall. But out of this income Canadians would also spend nearly two billion dollars on imports, which is "not spending" in Canada; it does not put income in the hands of

TABLE II

CANADIAN NATIONAL INCOME AND SOME OF ITS COMPONENTS, 1928-55

	Gross national product	Gross domestic investment	Exports of goods and services	Government expenditures
	(all figures in billions of dollars)			
1928	6.1	1.3	1.8	0.6
1929	6.2	1.4	1.6	0.7
1930	5.5	0.9	1.3	0.8
1931	4.6	0.4	1.0	0.7
1932	3.8	0.2	0.8	0.6
1933	3.6	0.2	0.8	0.5
1934	4.0	0.4	1.0	0.6
1935	4.3	0.4	1.1	0.6
1936	4.7	0.5	1.4	0.6
1937	5.4	0.7	1.6	0.7
1938	5.2	0.6	1.4	0.7
1939	5.7	0.9	1.5	0.7
1940	6.9	1.2	1.8	1.2
1941	8.5	1.3	2.5	1.7
1942	10.5	1.4	2.4	3.7
1943	11.2	0.7	3.4	4.2
1944	12.0	0.8	3.6	5.0
1945	11.9	0.7	3.6	3.7
1946	12.0	1.9	3.2	1.8
1947	13.8	3.0	3.6	1.6
1948	15.6	3.2	4.1	1.8
1949	16.5	3.2	4.0	2.1
1950	18.2	4.2	4.2	2.3
1951	21.5	5.4	5.1	3.2
1952	23.3	4.6	5.6	4.2
1953	24.4	5.4	5.4	4.4
1954	24.1	4.4	5.1	4.4
1955	26.6	5.7	5.7	4.6

Data from *National Accounts and Income and Expenditure 1926–1950* and later annual volumes (Ottawa, Dominion Bureau of Statistics).

Canadians, and from the employment point of view it is like "saving." However, this "not spending" in Canada, this saving and importing, was offset by 1.4 billion dollars of investment and about an equal amount of exports. Income and employment were high. Then exports fell 800 million dollars and investment fell by 1,200 million dollars. Income (and employment) shrank till at the lower level of 3.5 billion dollars saving fell to 200 and imports to 800 million dollars at which point the reduced investment and exports were just adequate to offset this "not spending" and income ceased to decline. If imports and saving are so important it may be asked why we emphasize the change in exports and investment. The reason is that it is usually changes in exports and investment that set the process in motion; imports like saving are expected to vary mainly as a *result* of changes in income. Finally one should notice that in a relatively "new" country investment involves a large imported content; so that the decline in investment associated with the decline in income makes for a rather larger decline in imports than might otherwise be expected.

World War II. Throughout the thirties variation in the amount of government expenditure was small and, for the purpose of this elementary exposition, negligible (in a fuller and more rigorous study of the period government finance could not be neglected). After 1940 government expenditure changed from year to year by bigger amounts than either investment or exports. From a pre-war level of 700 million dollars government expenditure rose to a peak of 5 billion dollars in 1944. With this high level of government expenditure the problem was posed of what happens when consumers, business, exporters, and government want to buy more than the total product available when full employment has been achieved.

In 1944 with a national income of 12 billion dollars and with the habits and conditions (including tax rates) of the thirties, expenditure on consumers' goods would have run at about 8 billion dollars. But if the governments were to have their 5 billion dollars worth of goods, and if private investment was to amount to 800 million dollars, there would only be some 6 billion dollars worth of goods (at existing prices) to be bought by consumers. By this time employment had already increased beyond what was previously thought of as "full" and little further increase was possible. Under these conditions either prices would go up, or consumers would have some two billion dollars "burning a hole in their pockets" and threatening a conflagration that would have endangered the "price ceiling."[10] That the "ceiling" was maintained was the result of the increase in taxation which made it harder for many people to spend, and of the success of the government's propaganda in persuading people to save. Taxation enters the picture as an offset to government spending rather as imports are to exports and saving to investment. One must remember however that taxes are not all paid by reducing expenditure; they may reduce saving and thus fail to have their full effect in offsetting government expenditure.

[10] Compare the estimates of national income, desired expenditure on consumption from such income, and amount of civilian goods available for the three years 1951–3 given in "Thinking Ahead" (*Harvard Business Review*, Jan., 1951).

Post-war inflation. After the war the national income rose from its war-peak of 12 billion dollars in 1944 to 18.2 billion dollars by 1950 and to 26.6 billion dollars by 1955. A glance at Table II will show the main factors at work: investment rising to 4.2 billion dollars by 1950, and 5.7 billion dollars by 1955; exports rising from 3.6 billion dollars in 1944 to 4.2 billion dollars in 1950 and 5.7 billion dollars in 1955; government expenditure falling at first but with Korea and "cold war" rising again to 4.6 billion dollars in 1955. Some other factors need to be added, particularly to explain the rise in income in the first half of this period. Pent-up consumer demand was released, consumer expenditures rose from 6.2 billion dollars in 1944 to 6.8 in 1945, 8.0 in 1946, and 9.1 in 1947. In 1945 and 1946 imports fell. Finally price controls were relaxed, and prices rose. Indeed the figures of gross national product for the period reflect changing prices as well as increased production. If the product is priced at 1939 prices (or the gross national product measured in 1939 dollars) it appears that the increase from 1939 to 1944 was 63 per cent (in actual dollars it increased 108 per cent); the increase from 1939 to 1950 was 80 per cent (in actual dollars 219 per cent); the increase from 1939 to 1955 was 125 per cent (in actual dollars 366 per cent). That the increase in "real income" was as great as it was is to be explained by increasing population, improving technology, accumulating productive equipment, and high employment.

CHAPTER IV

MONEY AND THE PRICE SYSTEM

Why people hold stocks of money. It must first be emphasized that while people want money, while most people want as much money as they can get, they want it to spend, or to lend. They want to buy goods and services for present enjoyment; they want to buy durable goods which will give them an income of useful service in the future; or they want to use their money to secure more money as a source of such things in the future or as a symbol of success and a source of power. To use money as the source of further money income they may lend at interest, buy durable goods to lease for a rent, buy a share of the profits of an enterprise, or buy instruments which will increase their own productive power and consequently their earnings. They may, however, buy things without thought of the money income to be derived from them in the expectation that they will later be able to sell these things at a higher price, and thus realize capital gains.

Money is, then, a source of pleasure or gain if you do not hold it: money held in the pocket (or in the bank) gives no pleasure (except to those psychopathological cases known as misers) and no return. "It locks up in a barren form resources that might yield an income of gratification if invested, say in extra furniture; or a money income if invested in extra machinery or cattle."[1] It is not, however, quite barren; a stock of money on hand is a convenience. "A large command of resources in the form of currency renders their business easy and smooth, and puts them at an advantage in bargaining."[2] The convenience and advantage of a stock of "barren" money must next be investigated.

Convenience. Consider first a hypothetical model in which each man receives income and spends it all in the same period. Each is paid monthly, for instance; and each spends his month's income in that month. If we impute to them a miraculous degree of intelligence, foresight, and capacity for quick decision, we should not need to endow them with any money to hold. They would know immediately

[1]Alfred Marshall, *Money, Credit and Commerce* (London, 1923), p. 45.
[2]*Ibid.*

69

what they wanted to buy and might buy immediately. Money would always be on the wing and never come to rest. But consider by contrast the man of the real world in receipt of a monthly salary. Even if he is going to spend in the month his whole salary he is not likely to know on his monthly pay-day exactly what he is going to want to buy with it during the next month. On any day in the month he will be holding some money unspent to meet the expenses which he has roughly budgeted for but cannot exactly foresee. The amount on hand will be bigger just after pay-day and will dwindle to zero about the time he receives more pay. It is this necessary interval between receipt of income and its expenditure that constitutes the first reason for holding money.

Money is held for the convenience of not having to make up your mind immediately what to buy with your income, and of not being faced with the need to make some urgent but unexpected purchase while without the means to make it. (What is said of the salaried individual is true, *mutatis mutandis*, of the business enterprise.) The amount of money held for this purpose at any time will depend on the habits which have been formed in the past, habits which will have developed in relation to the usual length of the interval between receipt and disbursement. But, given those habits, the amount of money held will depend on the level of incomes and prices. If employment expands and the national income increases, there will be more people receiving income and many people receiving more income, and consequently people will want to hold rather more money in the aggregate. Similarly if employment and the real income of the community remained unchanged but prices rose, and the money income therefore increased, people would want to hold more money. Roughly, it has been suggested, people would want to hold enough more money to give them the same average command over things in general. Equal convenience requires an increase in the amount of money held roughly proportional to the rise in prices.

Precaution. We must next consider problems which arise from accumulation. The typical family does not plan to spend each week's income in the week, each month's income in the month, or each year's income in the year, in which it is received. Most families plan to save out of income, whether it be to provide for some lumpy expenditure in the near future (a holiday or a bicycle) or whether it be to build up a fund to provide for the future. The former type of accumulation is likely to involve an increased holding of money because it would not be worth the trouble, expense, and risk of trying to make profitable use of the accumulated money in the short time involved. The

latter type of accumulation is likely to involve the purchase of
securities, or property, rather than the holding of money. The opportunity to increase their income by judicious investment will lead
most people to prefer to buy insurance, bonds, corporate shares, mortgages, houses, etc., rather than to hold "barren" money. But people
are likely to choose to hold some part of their property in money form
as a precaution against sudden and unexpected need for cash. Of
course such needs can be met by the sale of securities or property,
or by borrowing, but this involves trouble, delay, and some expense.
There is enough advantage in holding some property in the form of
money to compensate for the loss of income which results. The
amount so held is again a matter of habit, based in part on the ease
or difficulty with which those with other forms of property can,
under the existing financial institutions, raise cash quickly when
required. It is likely that the amount of money held on these precautionary grounds has some relationship to the total value of property
held, as the amount held for convenience had some relationship to the
size of income. Given these habits this amount will depend on the
cost of holding it, i.e. on the loss of income through not investing it,
particularly on the rate of interest on the safest and most liquid form
of investment, government bonds. The higher the yield of such gilt-
edged securities the less the amount of money people will choose to
hold idle.

Speculation. Finally, there is the speculative reason for holding
money. If one expects a fall in prices, one may postpone purchase and
hold money in readiness to buy cheap when the fall occurs. This may
happen with reference to purchases of consumers' goods, but it is
particularly important in relation to the security market. Those who
expect a fall in security prices will sell their securities and hold
money with the intention of buying other securities when prices seem
to have reached bottom. Those who expect security prices to rise will
use all the money they can lay their hands on to buy securities in the
hope of speculative gain. It is this speculative holding of money that
creates the most serious difficulties for monetary theory and policy
alike.

The supply of money and the level of incomes and prices. So far
we have been concerned to explain how much money people would
want to hold. It is clear, however, that they *do* hold in fact whatever
the total amount of money happens to be. All the money must be
held by someone, and must be held *voluntarily* by someone. When
one person reduces his stock of money by spending it, someone
else receives it. The aggregate stock of money is not reduced, only

its ownership has changed. We must ask, then, how people come to want to hold in the aggregate the amount of money which is available for them to hold. A completely satisfactory answer is impossible in a brief note, and with the limited apparatus of economic theory and the limited knowledge of economic institutions at our disposal. Some useful ideas can, however, be developed, especially if we are prepared to begin by discussing a simple, but unreal condition where the only reason for holding money is the first of the three reasons discussed above. We rule out for the time being the precautionary holding of part of one's wealth in the form of money and we rule out any speculative behaviour. We admit only that holding of money which gives convenience in the administration of current income. Let us then consider what would happen, under these simple conditions, if the actual amount of money available was more, or less, than the amount which people wanted to hold.

Let us consider first the case where there is *more* money than people want to hold. People will try to reduce their balances by spending more. This will mean *either* a rise in prices (if full employment has already been reached) *or* an increase in employment, output, and money income (if there are unemployed resources available for re-employment), *or*, what is more likely, some rise in prices and some increase in employment (if there are unemployed resources, but not necessarily as efficient as those already employed and not so fluid as to be re-employed immediately in response to increased demand). This process of rising prices and/or increasing money income would continue until the level of income and prices was so much higher that people would want to hold the extra money. Their habits remaining the same, the amount they want to hold depends, we have shown, on the level of prices and the size of incomes. We can now add, under the special simplified conditions of our problem, that the level of prices and incomes is that which leads people to want to hold just the amount of money actually available.

The case where there is *less* money than people want to hold involves the same process in reverse. Each individual wanting to hold more money spends less, prices and/or incomes fall, till with the lower level of prices and incomes people are content to hold the smaller quantity of money.

It should also be noticed that a change in the monetary habits of the people would have similar effect: if people decide that they want to hold less money and the supply of money remains unchanged, their spending drives up prices and/or incomes to the level at which with their new habits they want to hold the old amount of money;

and similarly if they decide that they want to hold more money, prices and/or incomes will fall to the level at which with their new habits they are content to hold the old amount of money. Habits with respect to the amount of money held for convenience in the administration of current income are, as a matter of fact, very stable. What change there is, is likely to be slow and regular.

We may next suppose that some people hold part of their accumulated wealth in the form of money, as a precaution against unforeseen emergencies. Under these conditions we must also suppose that if they have more money to spend they may buy securities as well as, or instead of, goods (they may lend rather than spend). If they buy securities this will drive up security prices and therefore reduce their yield. But with lower yields the inducement to hold earning assets rather than money is less strong; with higher prices of securities the total value of property held becomes greater and if people hold something like a stable proportion of their property in the form of money, they may want to hold more money; and finally, if spending on goods produces any serious rise in prices people may feel that they need more money to protect them against equal emergencies which would now involve higher emergency expenditures. The yield on old securities having fallen, entrepreneurs could expect to be able to borrow cheaper. This might stimulate "real investment," the building of houses, the extension of manufacturing plant, etc. If such "investment" increased, income would increase,[3] and again more money would be wanted. (Modern economists are inclined, however, to minimize the effect of interest rates on investment; certainly small changes are ineffective.)

The addition of the second reason for holding money introduces new variables, the rate of interest and possibly the amount of real investment, but it reveals again a process whereby an increased supply of money creates the conditions under which people want to hold it. Again it may be noted that the habits with respect to the amount of money held for precautionary purposes are relatively stable, changing slowly and with regularity. One warning should, however, be given. There is reason to believe that the equilibrium condition will not be achieved easily and smoothly. When the expansion of income and the rise in prices have achieved the necessary level and the process is checked, there may be a serious rebound. More serious, however, than such oscillation is the possible disequilibrating effect of speculation, to which we next turn.

[3]For discussion of the role of saving and investment in the economy see above, pp. 57-65.

If we now admit the third reason for holding money, the speculative reason, we leave the realm of stable habit and approach the realm of volatile behaviour and we also introduce a disequilibrating factor. That is, we introduce the possibility that an increase in the amount of money may start a process which makes people want to hold less money; this would have the same effect as a further increase in the amount of money and would push the process further, so that people would want to hold still less money; and so on without obvious end. This possibility arises from the effect already considered on the price of securities. Rising prices will lead to the anticipation of further rises and encourage speculative purchase. The rise in security prices which progressively deters people from further conversion of money held for precautionary reasons into securities as the yield falls, persuades people to convert more of the money held for speculative reasons into securities in the expectation of capital gains.

If the amount of money held for the speculative reason is big enough, and the change of sentiment general enough, a cumulative expansion of money income and prices of considerable magnitude may set in. The rise in prices and the increase in output as unemployed resources were put to work would increase the earnings of business, and thus give good reason for expecting a further rise in the price of securities and therefore intensify the desire to hold assets other than money. The effect on "real investment" might be expected to add further to the expansive force. Exactly similar cumulative contraction without apparent limit might take place if the supply of money declined, prices of goods and securities declined, and people sold securities and wanted to hold more money.

It is important to add that the actual movements of expansion and contraction of business cannot be explained by reference to the change in the desire to hold money. This change in itself requires explanation. Usually some non-monetary influence initiates the process of expansion or contraction; the change in the desire to hold money for speculative reasons is a result of that process, but it becomes a cause of acceleration and intensification of the process. A change in people's attitudes towards holding money rarely lights the fire; but once the fire is lit such a change generally sets in and adds fuel to the fire.

The right amount of money. Discussion of the disturbances which occur if there is more, or less, money than people want to hold under existing conditions draws attention to the importance of controlling the supply of money so as to have the *right* amount. We must turn, therefore, to consider what determines the actual amount of money and how likely it is to be the right amount of money. But one must emphasize one point: the amount of money can become too much either if it increases when people do not want to hold more, or if it does not decrease when they want to hold less. The "right" amount changes and a perfect monetary system would provide for the actual amount to adjust to those changes. The speculative holding of money provides the possibility for sudden and drastic changes in the desire to hold money, and a rigid money supply must, in such circumstances lead to the initiation of a process of expansion or contraction, as the case may be, of prices and incomes. Now if we are concerned with the "right" amount of money we must consider whether such a process is desirable, and the following propositions may be stated. First, any wide change in the general level of prices is to be deplored because it involves a change in the real terms of all contracts which call for the payment of money. A rise in prices benefits debtors and hurts creditors. Second, any deficiency in the amount of money which precipitates a decline in money income, through some decline in prices and much decline in employment, is to be deplored for obvious reasons, of which the distress of the unemployed is the most important. Third, though it is not as easy as might appear from this preliminary survey to initiate expansion from low levels of employment simply by providing more money, it is important that expansion to a high level of employment be not hindered by insufficiency of money. When expansion proceeds from lower to higher levels of employment, in response to an increase in real investment, there should be available more money for people to hold as with increasing incomes they come to want to hold more. Fourth, we have to say something about the international implications of these propositions, and especially about the problem of exchange rate stability. These problems are discussed in the next section.

The exchange rate. On the foreign exchange market money of foreign countries is bought and sold like any commodity. Pounds sterling, for example, are bought in Canada with Canadian dollars: (1) by people who want to buy English goods for their own use or to resell in Canada; (2) by people who have borrowed in England in the past and who must regularly pay interest and ultimately repay the principal; (3) by people who want to lend to Englishmen or to buy English securities; or (4) by people who want to travel in England. The supply of pounds sterling comes (1) from people who have sold goods in England; (2) from those who have received interest and dividends on English securities which they hold; (3) from those who have sold securities to Englishmen or who have borrowed from Englishmen; or (4) from English tourists in Canada. These all want to sell their pounds for Canadian dollars. The market is complicated, of course, by the existence of speculators who buy pounds when the price seems likely to rise, and sell when it seems likely to fall. At any time the price established by free bargaining in the market is that which "rations" the available supply according to their readiness to pay amongst those who want sterling.[4] Two problems have to be briefly discussed: first, the influence of the amount of money on the exchange rate; and, second, the effects of changes in this rate, or how we want the exchange rate to behave.

The amount of money and the exchange rate. If the amount of money is more than people want to hold and prices and incomes rise, one may expect that the price of foreign funds will rise too. More spending will mean more spending on imported as well as on domestically produced goods, and more spending on foreign travel. More buying of securities will mean more buying of foreign securities as well as of Canadian securities. More people will want to buy U.S. dollars, sterling, and other foreign currencies, to pay for such things. At the same time there may well be some decline in the amount of these currencies available for sale in Canada, for if Canadian prices rise Canadian exporters will be at a disadvantage in the foreign markets. On the other hand, there is some possibility that the prospects of profit in Canada may attract foreign investors and so provide an increase in the amount of funds available. Similarly if there is less money than people want to hold and prices and incomes fall, one may expect the price of U.S. dollars, sterling, and other foreign currencies to fall as imports decline, as foreign travel is curtailed, and as the purchase of securities shrinks. Again there is the partial offset that foreign lending and buying of Canadian securities by foreigners is likely to dry up as the prospects of profit in Canada become worse.

In general one may expect monetary expansion to put pressure on the exchanges and so drive up the price of sterling and U.S. dollars, which is equivalent to a depreciation of the Canadian dollar on the markets of London and New York. This assumes, of course, that nothing happens simultaneously in the other countries. If at the same time that income was rising in Canada monetary expansion was in progress in Great Britain and in the United States, the expansion of their money incomes would mean more imports from Canada and higher prices for those imports, and so greater supplies of foreign

---

[4]During the war free bargaining was replaced by authoritative rationing under the Foreign Exchange Control Board so as to ensure the maximum purchase of war material from abroad. See below, pp. 77–79.

currencies available to meet the greater demands arising from Canada's expanding incomes. Monetary expansion in company with the great industrial powers involves no pressure on the exchanges; and depreciation of the Canadian dollar may come equally from monetary expansion in Canada out of line with the great powers, or may come from the absence of monetary contraction in Canada when prices are falling and incomes contracting in those countries. One may get out of line by stepping forward when the line does not move, or by remaining motionless when the line falls back.

There is one other buyer and seller in the foreign exchange market whose operations must be noted, the government or its agent the Bank of Canada. In December, 1955, the "official holdings of gold and U.S. dollars" amounted to 1900 million dollars. By selling some of its holdings at a time when Canadians want to buy more U.S. dollars a rise in the exchange rate may be prevented or mitigated: by buying more U.S. dollars to hold at a time when there are more U.S. dollars for sale a fall in the rate may similarly be prevented or mitigated. But clearly there is a limit to the continuance of such buying and selling; the reserve cannot be allowed to fall dangerously low, or to grow extravagantly big. Either the rate must be allowed to rise and fall with the changing demand and supply; or if the rate is to be fixed, monetary and fiscal policy must make us want to buy at that rate just the amount of U.S. dollars that people want to sell at that rate. Judicious use of the reserve, however, may smooth temporary fluctuations, and tide the economy over a period of slow adjustment to new conditions.

Foreign exchange control in World War II. In a wartime economy the need for imports tends to increase while the ability to supply goods for export decreases. The consequent bidding up of the price of foreign currencies is likely to have three undesirable effects. It will increase the cost of imports and the prices of goods made from imported materials, thus making price control more difficult. It will encourage producers to export their goods and profit from selling the scarce foreign currency they receive in return. This drain of exports will create shortages at home. Finally, the depreciation of the exchange rate will encourage speculators to hoard the scarce currencies and drive their prices even higher. Under such conditions the stability of the economy is endangered. Foreign exchange control is thus an important consideration in maintaining other domestic controls. But more important still is the need to conserve scarce foreign exchange for the purchase of things necessary for the prosecution of the war. In Canada it was recognized that the free operation of the

foreign exchange market could not achieve adequate conservation, or
sound enough rationing, even if wide fluctuations in the exchanges
had not been undesirable. The Foreign Exchange Control Board[5] was
set up in the first week of the war to conserve foreign exchange and
to maintain the stability of the exchange rate. War had quickly
destroyed the complicated network of international trade upon which
Canada had relied to get needed supplies, and some foreign
currencies (the U.S. dollar in particular) became scarce.
Normally, Canada had exported more to the United Kingdom than
she imported from that country, and had imported from the United
States more than she exported to them. With the surplus pounds
which we received from our excessive exports to the United Kingdom
we bought, in Britain, U.S. dollars to pay for the excess of
imports from that country. The advent of war, it was clear, would
destroy the relationship. Britain would be faced with an even greater
need than Canada to mobilize and conserve U.S. dollars.
The United States was the great source of munitions of war, and its
neutrality legislation stood in the way of borrowing capital. Foreign
exchange control in Britain early limited the right to purchase
U.S. dollars, except for the purchase of essential imports. The
Canadian balance of pounds sterling, therefore, could no longer be
converted into dollars. (Nor for that matter could it be converted
into goods; for the first few years it was used in part to buy back
Canadian securities held in Britain and, in part, it was merely accumulated. Later the "Billion for Britain" and "Mutual Aid" put an end to
this accumulation.) At the same time that Canada could no longer
expect to convert her sterling surplus into dollars, her own war
demands might be expected to lead to an increased demand for
U.S. dollars. It was obvious at the outset that American dollars
would become scarce to Canadians. American investors in Canada,
fearing that war would tie up their investments in a belligerent
country, might be expected to want to sell their Canadian assets and
secure American dollars.

Under the system of foreign exchange control, American currency
realized from the sale of exports to the United States had to be sold
to the Foreign Exchange Control Board. In turn, this currency was
rationed by permit to importers on the basis of a priority need. People
who wished American currency for non-essential purposes, such as
travel in the United States, were forbidden to buy the currency.

[5]See the *Report of the Foreign Exchange Control Board* (Ottawa, 1946). See
also article by F. A. Knox, "Canada's Balance of International Payments, 1940–5"
(*Canadian Journal of Economics and Political Science*, Aug., 1947); and A. O.
Gibbons, "Foreign Exchange Control in Canada, 1939–51" (*ibid.*, Feb., 1953).

Control was made relatively simple by the existence of a concentrated market for foreign exchange among the small number of commercial banks. By limiting the purchase and sale of foreign currency to the commercial banks, the Board was able to administer the scheme very effectively.

During the early months of the war the system of foreign exchange control conserved sufficient American dollars to provide for imports. In 1940 the rapid expansion of the Canadian war economy increased demand for equipment and raw materials from the United States and, at the same time, increased incomes led to new demands for civilian imports. Two methods were adopted to prevent the rapid loss of foreign exchange. The first method curtailed civilian demand for U.S. dollars. In June, 1940, the War Exchange Tax of ten per cent was imposed on practically all imports from non-Empire countries. In July, 1940, the expenditure of United States' funds for pleasure travel was forbidden. The second method was an attempt to increase the supply of available American dollars by purchasing foreign currency from Canadian holders, by transferring domestic gold holdings, and by the encouragement of industries such as gold mining and newsprint manufacture, which could supply additional goods for export. Despite these measures, the drain continued and it seemed possible that the Canadian war effort would run down for lack of American dollars.

In 1941 the Hyde Park Agreement solved the problem. It was agreed that each country should concentrate on the type of war production for which it was best suited. Canada was able to supply certain types of munitions and strategic materials to the United States to be shipped to the war areas. Also, the United States made considerable defence expenditures in Canada during the critical period. The co-operation of the United Kingdom made substantial amounts of foreign exchange available. As a result, Canada was able to maintain her foreign exchange position with the United States although her imports from that country averaged over one billion dollars a year during the war—over twice the normal peacetime imports.

Stable or fluctuating exchanges? There remains the question, how do we want the exchange rate to behave? Here there is a very wide difference of opinion. The older view is that depreciation is shameful and exchange stability desirable at almost any cost. There seems little doubt that the great expansion of international trade and international investment in the nineteenth century was enormously facilitated, if not made possible, by the stability of exchange rates which resulted (for reasons which are discussed below) from the general adoption of the gold standard. "The international gold standard," says Professor T. E. Gregory, "was thus, historically one of the most important adjuncts to the opening up of the world to settlement and exploitation, and whatever may be said by those who never look at the wood because of the trees, this *creation of a world economy* constitutes one of the great (and beneficial) turning-points in the history of mankind."[6]

The depression of the 1930's precipitated a revulsion against too rigid exchange stability. It was argued that no country should be so foolish as to precipitate the trials of deflation (or inflation) just because such a process has started in the world outside and because that country's money will depreciate (or appreciate) if it breaks out of line. This attitude was in part a product of, in part a contribution to, the newer economic nationalism, and was associated with a growing confidence in the ability of economists to devise policies to maintain a high level of employment, and a realization of the difficulty of securing international action along the desired lines. It seems clear that in some situations insistence on rigid exchange rates may involve a country in too great a sacrifice of domestic considerations. And there are occasions when deliberate depreciation may enable exports to be increased for a short time and thus stimulate recovery. But such behaviour is likely to provoke retaliation by way of higher tariffs, special regulations against "exchange dumping," or competitive currency depreciation, and thus to be rendered nugatory. Complete independence of monetary policy on the part of each of the great powers might undermine international trade to such an extent that the problem of full employment would be aggravated rather than alleviated.[7]

Economists have suggested several ways of combining national freedom with international stability. In 1944 the Bretton Woods Agreement established the International Monetary Fund through which countries could buy foreign currencies for the payment of debts. Members of the Fund set the value of their own currency at a fixed rate in terms of gold or American dollars and agreed that they would not alter this rate without the permission of the Fund. By this means stability was to be maintained without rigidity; any country which was faced with a genuine economic crisis could appeal to the

[6]T. E. Gregory, *The Gold Standard and Its Future* (London, 1932), pp. 10-11.

[7]See A. F. W. Plumptre, *Central Banking in the British Dominions* (Toronto, 1940), chap. XVII. Also, W. T. G. Hackett, "The 'Bank', the 'Fund', and the Canadian Dollar" in *Canada's Economy in a Changing World*, ed. J. D. Gibson (Toronto, 1948).

Fund for permission to manipulate its currency. It should be noted, however, that the Fund was not expected to counteract any widespread economic crisis, and thus the success of the Fund depended on the maintenance of world economic prosperity through other means such as the encouragement of international trade and the stimulation of underdeveloped countries.

Canadian exchange rate, 1946–55. When Canada adhered to the International Monetary Fund it was expected that the Canadian government would return, after the war, to a fixed exchange rate: to a foreign exchange market in which buyers would be free to buy and sell as they wished, but in which the Bank of Canada would stand ready to buy and sell at the "fixed" rate, while the Bank and the government by monetary and fiscal policy influenced the market so that the "holding of gold and foreign exchange" should not increase or decrease unduly. In fact things turned out very differently. In July, 1946, the official rate was raised to par. At this rate Canadians wanted to buy so many U.S. dollars (in spite of the continuing war restriction on capital movements) that the "official holdings" declined drastically, from about 1,500 million dollars in 1945 to less than 500 million dollars in 1947. In face of this loss of reserves various restrictions were imposed on importation of goods and on foreign travelling, and in 1949 the exchange rate was changed back to the war level, the price of the Canadian dollar in New York being again reduced to 91 cents. These measures contributed to an increase in the reserve of foreign exchange: by the end of 1949 the "official holdings" amounted to 1,100 million dollars. Then in 1950 the reserves rose rapidly, largely because of the inflow of U.S. capital. By October the holdings were over 1,800 million dollars. At that point the government gave up its "official rate" and announced that it would leave the market free to find its own level. Shortly afterwards the remaining elements of "exchange control" were lifted. From October, 1950, to November, 1951, the rate fluctuated between 94 and 96. In 1952 the rate climbed steadily, reaching 104 by October; it fluctuated between 101 and 103 throughout the next three years, coming to par at the end of 1955. Throughout this period the reserves of foreign exchange remained relatively steady between 1,800 and 1,900 million dollars; they were used to smooth fluctuations in the market not to influence the trend. Whether fiscal and monetary measures were directed at all to limiting the change in the exchange rate we do not know; but in general the rise in the rate was welcomed as reducing the degree of inflation. With the exchange rate fixed at par there would have been a tremendous accumulation of foreign exchange reserves and the purchase of this exchange would have increased domestic spending power. The funds to buy the additions to the reserve might, theoretically, come from the proceeds of additional taxes; but already the level of taxation was high and budgeting for surpluses unpopular.[8]

Only if income and prices had been allowed to rise still further than they did could parity have been maintained without continued accumulation of reserves: only if various offsetting monetary and fiscal measures had been adopted could the accumulation of reserves have been prevented from leading to that further rise in income and prices.

The actual supply of money in Canada. We must now examine the actual supply of money and the factors which determine its amount. First, we must emphasize the fact that bank deposits subject to transfer by drawing cheques constitute the biggest element in the monetary supply of this, and of all economically advanced countries. Between money in the pocket and a credit balance at the bank we need make little difference. Convenience requires that we hold some cash in the pocket, and some problems arise when we want to hold more of our money in the form of cash and less in the form of a bank balance, but for the moment it is important to stress the similarity of

TABLE I

THE CANADIAN MONEY SUPPLY*

(million dollars)

	1938	1945	1950	1955
1. Currency outside banks	240	1060	1200	1500
2. Deposits payable in Canada				
(a) Demand	730	2060	2770	3740
(b) Time	1660	2870	4560	6090
(c) Other	90	200	620	960
(d) Deduct "float"	−120	−280	−450	−680
3. Total money supply	2660	5910	8700	12610
4. Canadian national income	5200	11900	18200	26600
5. Wholesale price index (1935–39=100)	102	132	211	219
6. Notes and deposits of the Bank of Canada held by the Chartered Banks	250	590	810	860
7. Ratio of Chartered Banks cash to deposits in Canada	10.6	12.2	10.8	8.5

*Source: *Statistical Summary of the Bank of Canada.* For table covering 1938–51 see *Monthly Review,* Bank of Nova Scotia, Feb., March, 1952, "The Supply of Money, I."

[8]See *Monthly Review* of the Bank of Nova Scotia, Sept., Oct., 1952, "Strength in the Canadian Dollar" and Aug., 1954, "Continued Strength in the Canadian Dollar."

these forms of money. Cash for the pocket is provided by notes issued by the Bank of Canada. There is, of course, also some metallic currency for the purpose of small change, silver, nickel, and bronze coin.

Some idea of the amounts involved can be obtained from Table I. It will be noticed that a large part of the notes (or deposits which constitute a right to demand notes) of the Bank of Canada are held in the cash reserves of the Chartered Banks (see item 6). The Chartered Banks must hold such reserves because they may be asked to pay Bank of Canada notes (which alone are full legal tender) to any of their depositors. Because people are willing to hold most of their money in the form of bank balances and do not ask for payment of these obligations in Bank of Canada notes, the Chartered Banks need hold and do hold only a fractional reserve of cash (see item 7).

Currency outside the banks (item 1) represents the amount of money held "in the pocket." In 1938 it still included about 100 million dollars in Chartered Bank notes: these have since been eliminated. The deposits of the Chartered Banks have been divided into "demand" (i.e. current accounts) and "time" (i.e. savings accounts); the "other" deposits are largely governmental; the item "float" represents cheques on other banks included in the statements of the banks—this amount is deducted to avoid double counting. One might expect that money held for income purposes would be in the form of deposits payable on demand, and that precautionary or speculative balances would be largely in the form of deposits subject to notice, i.e. as time deposits. This is not, however, strictly true: many small savings accounts are used for regular payment by cheque and are clearly of the "income" variety, and some precautionary and speculative balances may be held as demand deposits. An inspection of the table will show that the increase in the money supply has been roughly proportional to the increase in the national income: if the money supply in 1938 is taken as 100, the supply in 1945 was 225, in 1950 it was 335, and in 1955, 480; if the national income of 1938 is taken as 100, the comparable figures for 1945, 1950, and 1955 are 230, 350, and 510.

Control of the supply of money: The Gold Standard. In the past, money consisted of some commodity selected as generally acceptable, because of its usefulness or esteem, which the owner therefore could rely on being able to exchange for the things he wanted.[9] Many commodities have served the purpose at various times and places, dried cod in Newfoundland, beaver skins in Canada, tobacco in Virginia, sugar in the West Indies. The metals, and particularly gold

[9]See Adam Smith, *Wealth of Nations* (1776), chap. IV, "Of the Origin and Use of Money."

and silver, have been preferred for the purpose: and came to be very generally adopted. The adoption of one of the precious metals as the money commodity was followed by coinage. The coin is simply an ingot of metal the weight and fineness of which is guaranteed by the integrity of the design impressed thereon. Coinage eliminated troublesome weighing and assaying. Given a metal coinage as money the supply of money was limited by the supply of the metal, but was not exactly determined by the supply since there were other uses for the metal. Gold and silver plate might satisfy the desire to hold money, since they could be melted and brought in for coinage, or be sold to be melted for this purpose, if emergency arose.

The development of a monetary system of this sort must not be supposed to have been the result of deliberate choice of a policy of monetary control based on the acceptance of a monetary theory. The theory was developed later to explain why the system worked and to justify its continuance. The monetary theory of the gold standard starts from the belief that the greatest danger in any monetary system is the danger of over-issue. If the sovereign was able to make money at will, was he not likely, when in financial difficulty, to make money to pay his debts rather than to struggle to raise more taxes and bigger loans? And since the sovereign was usually a big debtor, was he not likely to welcome the consequent rise in prices since it reduced the real burden of his debt? If money was gold coin, and if the amount of gold in each coin was defined and unalterable, the sovereign could only make more money by buying gold of equal value. But the gold content of the coin was itself a matter of royal decree, and many a sovereign lowered the legal gold content of the coin in order to pay his debts more easily. There developed in England, however, after 1688 a sentiment in favour of the maintenance not merely of *a* gold standard but of *the* gold standard under which the pound sterling was interchangeable with 123¼ grains of gold eleven-twelfths fine. Perfect interchangeability was not immediately achieved, but in the nineteenth century coin was freely convertible into bullion and bullion was freely convertible into coin. There was thus no deliberate control of the money supply; it was automatically determined.

A laissez-faire standard. A fall in prices would lower the cost of mining and tend to increase the supply, and *vice versa*, but such adjustment would be very slow. In the main, the rate of supply depended on the chance of discovery, e.g. the discoveries in California in 1847 and in Australia in 1851, or on the chance of technological development, e.g. the development of the cyanide process which permitted the development of the mines of the South African Rand.

There was no reason to expect that the supply would become excessive; there was therefore a safeguard against the danger of over-issue. There was reason to fear that the supply would be inadequate and this fear was the basis of the interest in bi-metallism (the use of two metals, gold and silver) in the last quarter of the nineteenth century. But there was a tendency to underrate the pains of the deflation which inadequate supplies of gold would entail; and there was a strong preference for a moderately inefficient automatic system to any system depending on the intelligence and honesty of governments which could be expected to prove grossly inefficient. The attachment to the gold standard was largely a matter of attachment to "laissez-faire." This attitude was very explicitly stated in the famous Bullion Report of that Select Committee of the English House of Commons which investigated the state of the currency in 1810. "The most detailed knowledge of the actual trade of the Country, combined with the profound science in all the principles of Money and Circulation, would not enable any man or set of men to adjust, and keep always adjusted, the right proportion of circulating medium in a country to the wants of trade."[10]

An international standard. To this plea for an automatic standard was later added the plea for an international standard. When in the last half of the nineteenth century the gold standard spread (displacing silver in one country after another) the result was the establishment of a system of nearly rigid foreign exchange rates. As long as pounds sterling were interchangeable with 123¼ grains of gold eleven-twelfths fine, and Canadian dollars were interchangeable with 25.8 grains of gold nine-tenths fine, the Canadian price of pounds sterling could not diverge much from $4.866. If the price rose more than a small fraction above this it would pay to change Canadian dollars for gold, to ship the gold to England and change it into pounds sterling, and then to sell the pounds sterling in Canada. If the price of sterling fell more than a small fraction below $4.866 it would pay to buy sterling, to use the sterling to buy gold, and to change the gold in Canada into coin. Similarly, since the Canadian and United States dollars had the same gold content, the price of a United States dollar in Canada could not diverge by more than a very small fraction from one Canadian dollar. In this case a divergence of 5/32 of one per cent either way would induce buying or selling of gold. To maintain such a standard the government (or some agent for it) had to hold a reserve of gold (and foreign exchange) and be prepared to

[10]*The Paper Pound of 1797-1821: A Reprint of the Bullion Report,* with an introduction by Edwin Cannan (London, 1919), p. 52.

buy at the fixed rate any amount of foreign exchange offered to it, or sell any amount that was wanted. To avoid undue depletion or expansion of the reserve it was necessary to follow a monetary and fiscal policy which would make such a sale or purchase unnecessary. The importance of this exchange stability came to be recognized as one of the most vital features of the gold standard; its disadvantages were emphasized in the thirties.

What has been said above about the control of the money supply under the gold standard has concealed a real difficulty. As long as people really held their money as gold coin the simple explanation so far given was valid enough. But the development of banking changed the picture: Canada on the gold standard in 1927 had a total money supply of some $2,200 million (Dominion notes, $30 million, notes of the Chartered Banks, $170 million, and deposits in the Chartered Banks, $2,000 million): the total gold held in Canada was about $200 million of which rather more than half was held by the Dominion government and the remainder by the Chartered Banks. To explain the supply of money under such conditions, and to explain the supply of money under present conditions, it is necessary to make a new start. We must ask what determines the supply of bank money, which is the preponderant quantity.

Limits to the expansion of bank money. A bank deposit is a debt of a bank. The creditor can call for payment of the debt in legal tender money if for some reason he prefers to hold such money rather than bank deposits or if his expenditures are the sort that must be made in cash. But he may gladly hold the deposit as a satisfactory form of money and he may transfer part of the deposit by cheque in payment for goods. Any I.O.U. could similarly function as money if there was general confidence that the debtor would pay. Banks are institutions which have established that confidence, so that their I.O.U.'s do function as money. A breath of suspicion would bring the whole structure down: if people, becoming worried, called for payment of their debts in money the banks would have to close their doors, unless the government came to their aid (as it well might) and created enough money of the sort people did want to hold (legal tender) to take the place of the sort of money (bank deposits) which they did not want to hold. Once the government made it evident that such amounts of money would be created, so that people could convert their deposits into it if they wanted, the desire to convert would probably disappear. Cash is dangerous stuff to have lying around, thieves do break in and steal: bank deposits are a safer form of money holding as long as confidence makes them generally acceptable in full payment of debt.

If bank deposits are money, we must ask next what determines the amount of such money. Ability to create money is a temptation. The temptation for the sovereign to create money was offset in most countries in the nineteenth century by the need to buy gold of equal value wherewith to make the money. The modern bank it appears can create money by a stroke of the pen; by acknowledging a debt to Mr. X; by creating a deposit in his name which he can use as money. Actually there is a very definite limit to this ability to create bank money, a limit which we will explain in the next paragraph. What is more serious, and harder to explain, is the danger that the amount of bank money will *shrink* at a time when people want to hold more money. It is easy to explain why the banks cannot create too much money, more difficult to explain why they sometimes create too little.

To those who feel that a bank is really a sort of "cloak room," where you check your money as you check your hat, a deposit suggests that something is "deposited" by the customer and the part of the banker appears passive. But let us consider the various ways in which deposits may in fact originate. (1) Most deposits by customers of the banks consist of cheques and constitute no change in the total amount of deposits held by the community as a whole, but simply a transfer of ownership. (2) Some deposits by customers consist of cash. Largely, however, this is merely a matter of flow in and out: every hour people draw cash to make cash purchases largely from shops which re-deposit the cash in their bank. What people are putting in had just come out, and what comes out is likely to be put back in very short order. As long as the flow in and out is fairly regular, a very little reservoir in the till enables the banks to meet the withdrawals of cash from the deposits of cash: the cash reserves of the bank are not swelled by such expected return of cash. If, however, a section of the community that has previously held cash is converted to the banking habit and deposits an amount of cash which has not come out of the banking system but out of the cash boxes of the people, then the cash reserves of the banks are increased. The public have really deposited something; they have really created that amount of new bank money but only by reducing by an equal amount the cash circulation. The amount of money in the hands of the people, bank deposits plus cash, is for the time being unchanged; but the cash reserves of the bank being increased there will be a subsequent increase in bank deposits to nine or ten times the amount of the increase in the cash reserve. (3) The bank lends to its customers, but instead of handing over cash to the borrower it simply makes an entry in its books showing that the borrower has the amount of the loan "deposited" to his credit. The borrower is in debt to the bank, pays interest and generally gives security for repayment: the bank in return admits indebtedness to the borrower and the bank's debt (whether a deposit or a bank-note) can function as money. It is this creation of deposits in favour of borrowers that constitutes the way in which bank money usually increases and it is the limit to such lending that must next be examined.

The customers of a bank are buying and selling goods, services, and securities. When they buy they draw cash, or they pay by cheque. If they pay by cheque, they may pay to another customer of the same bank in which case nothing but a book entry is required, or they may pay to a customer in one of the other banks in which case the cheque is presented for payment in cash at the Clearing House. But customers are also selling and receiving cash or cheques. They pay the cash into their bank; some of the cheques are from other customers of the same bank and involve nothing but a cross entry in the books, other cheques are on one of the other banks and are presented for payment in cash at the Clearing House. Ideally a bank will so arrange its affairs that the inflow of cash plus the cheques receivable at the Clearing House balance the outflow of cash plus the cheques payable at the Clearing House. It must avoid a continual adverse balance because it would lose its cash and have to sell its earning assets to secure more cash to pay out. It must avoid a continual favourable balance because it would then find itself with an unprofitable large proportion of its assets in the form of cash rather than in the form of earning assets. One can apply to the bank what was said above (p. 69) of an individual. The individual must keep enough money to meet all possible contingencies; but he should keep as little as is consistent with this convenience because if he does not have to hold his money he can spend it and get an income of pleasure or an income of money from the goods or securities he buys. Similarly the bank: it must hold enough money to be able to meet all ordinary demands and even some unforeseen extraordinary demands, and enough to make people feel confident that it has enough to meet all contingencies. But if the bank is to make a profit it must lend, or buy securities; it must hold earning assets. As it lends it creates deposits and subjects itself to an increased outflow of cash and an increase in the amount of cheques payable at the Clearing House. Each bank then will lend freely if cash is on balance flowing in; but in so lending it will cause an increased outflow of cash, and will stop expanding its loans if the position is reversed and cash is on balance flowing out. Such a condition could be achieved theoretically with a minute reserve; the actual reserve of cash is generally around 10 per cent of its notes and deposits, the amount being in part based on estimate of the minimum necessary for safety but being largely a matter of convention. Bankers must respect convention because it is not enough to have a safe reserve; only that reserve is safe that the people consider safe.[11]

The limit to the creation of deposits by any one bank lies, then, in the increased drain of cash directly or through the Clearing House which will accompany any expansion of its loans and thus of its deposits. But suppose that all banks increase their loans: each becomes subject to increased drain of cash as a result of its own expansion, but each enjoys an increased inflow of cash as a result of the expansion of the others. As long as they go forward together they appear to avoid the limit which would operate on each if it tried to go forward alone. Yet there is a limit to the power of all the banks acting together to expand deposits. The limit lies in the increasing need of the people for money in the pocket as money incomes and prices rise under the impact of the increased spending which is occasioned by increased lending by the bank. If people want to hold more money in their pockets the banks must provide it. Nor can all the banks replenish their supplies of cash by selling assets as *one* bank can if there is some other bank with too much cash. When they all want more cash because they have to pay out more cash to the public who want to hold more money in their pockets, they are not going to find a good market for their assets. Even if bargain prices for their assets tended to induce the public to part with some of the cash held for the precautionary reason, the expectation of a further fall in prices would tend to induce the public to hold more cash for the speculative reason, and the deterioration of the banks' balance sheets might further induce people to prefer money in the pocket to money in the bank.

Note issue. If banks are allowed to issue notes, I.O.U.'s payable to bearer, and especially if they are allowed to issue small notes, the

[11]See the statement by the Governor of the Bank of Canada in evidence before the Committee on Banking and Commerce of the House of Commons: "If someone were to ask me why the chartered banks try to maintain a 10 per cent cash reserve, instead of 5 per cent or 15 per cent, or some other figure, I could only reply that the working experience of many years has indicated that 10 per cent is a reasonable ratio which provides sufficient cash to cover any immediate demands, but is not so high as to constitute an unnecessary burden in the form of non-earning assets. The banking system of each country must decide from its own experience what ratio is appropriate, since conditions vary as between one country and another. I might add, however, that in Great Britain it has been the practice for many years to work to a cash ratio of about 10 per cent, the same as in this country, and up until recent years a ratio approximating 10 per cent also represented banking practice in the United States" (*Memoranda and Tables respecting the Bank of Canada extracted from the Evidence of G. F. Towers and W. C. Clark*, Ottawa, 1939; these memoranda provide most useful and relatively simple explanations of the working of the Canadian monetary system).

banks can still meet the demand for cash for the pocket without sacrificing any legal tender from their reserves. They merely change one form of indebtedness, a deposit, into another form, a note, both payable on demand in legal tender money. Before the establishment of the Bank of Canada in 1935 the Canadian banks had the privilege of issuing notes, but only in denominations of multiples of $5.00; and they were free only up to the amount of their paid-up capital to issue with a fractional reserve (beyond that amount they had to have a 100 per cent reserve of gold or legal tender). At one time of the year, the crop-moving period, the demand for money for the pocket being particularly heavy, the banks were allowed to extend their note issue by an amount equal to 15 per cent of their paid up capital and capital surplus. These regulations severely restricted the banks' ability to provide enough notes of convenient size to meet the needs of the people for more money in the pocket, without parting with some of the legal tender money which in those days consisted of Dominion notes, in denominations of $1.00, $2.00, $4.00, $5.00, etc. Bank credit was therefore limited to that amount which was consistent with a level of incomes and prices which would lead the people to hold just so much legal tender money in their pockets as to leave legal tender money for the reserve of the banks sufficient to provide the conventional reserve for that amount of bank credit.

Since 1935 the supply of legal tender money has been delegated to the Bank of Canada and the privilege of note issue by the Chartered Banks has been withdrawn. The ultimate limit to the expansion of bank credit is now, therefore, the readiness of the Bank of Canada to provide notes (or deposits which are interchangeable with notes) on a scale adequate to meet the needs of the people for pocket money and of the banks for reserve money.

There is one other limit to the expansion of bank credit which must be mentioned: namely, the existence of *good* borrowers. Bank deposits expand as loans are made (or securities bought). The bank makes its revenue from interest on its loans, or on its securities. Further the bank has become a debtor as well as a creditor, a debtor to the people to whom its creditors have paid the funds put at their disposal. The position of the bank as a debtor can only be safe if its position as a creditor is safe, that is if its debtors can be relied on to repay their loans, or if their promises to pay (and the securities held by the bank) are marketable. When times are bad there may be many wishing to borrow, but few able to convince the banks of their ability to repay a loan. As some banks reduce loans, in the absence of good borrowers, other banks have to contract in order to avoid the drain of cash at the

Clearing House which would be experienced by any bank that failed to contract in company with the others. In depression it is the lack of borrowers rather than lack of legal tender that constitutes the most serious limit to the expansion of bank deposits; the fear becomes one of too little credit creation, not too much; and the question of a limit to expansion becomes the more difficult question of whether there is any limit to contraction.

The Bank of Canada.[12] It remains to consider the behaviour of the Bank of Canada which provides the small notes which people want in larger quantities as prices and incomes rise, and the additional cash reserves which the banks want to hold against their increased deposits. The system is now essentially a "managed" rather than an "automatic" one; it is the responsibility of the Governor and the directors to do what the Bullion Committee (see above, p. 85) thought no man nor any set of men, could do. In the original Bank of Canada Act there are the vestiges of an automatic system. The provision that the notes (and deposits) of the Bank should be convertible on demand into gold would have forced the adoption of a monetary policy consistent with the maintenance of parity between the Canadian and United States dollars. This provision could be, and immediately was, suspended by Order in Council and so this automatic check was removed. Then there was a provision in the Act that a 25 per cent reserve of gold should be held against the notes and deposits. This meant some restriction on the power of the Bank to expand credit; but in 1940 the clause was suspended and all the Bank's gold was handed over to the Foreign Exchange Control Board. The Bank of Canada is therefore free, for the time being, to behave as it sees fit.

Objectives. As laid down in the preamble to the Act it is the duty of the Bank of Canada "to regulate credit and currency in the best interests of the economic life of the nation, to control and protect the external value of the national monetary unit, and to mitigate by its influence fluctuations in the general level of production, trade, prices and employment *so far as may be possible within the scope of monetary action.*" The phrase "protect the external value of the national monetary unit" is perhaps intentionally vague. If it meant that the Bank must prevent any depreciation, i.e. must maintain stable exchange rates, then the discretion of the Bank would be severely limited. The Bank would have to regulate its credit policy so as to give an income and price structure consistent with the fixed exchange rate, i.e. would have to deflate when the world deflated irrespective of its duty to mitigate fluctuations in prices and employment; or it would have to sell its own

[12]See E. P. Neufeld, *Bank of Canada Operations, 1935–54* (Toronto, 1955).

foreign assets and borrow abroad to meet the increasing demands for foreign exchange at the fixed rate, a line of action which would be feasible for short periods but which could not continue long. Whether the government intended more emphasis to be put on the word "control" rather than on the word "protect," we do not know, but the Bank, with the approval of the government, has felt free to experiment with a policy of flexible exchange rates.

It is clear that the objectives are not necessarily consistent. Stability of prices and stability of employment may be roughly consistent; though there are conditions under which rising prices may be desirable to stimulate employment. Stability of prices and stability of employment are only consistent with stable exchange rates if prices and employment in the outside world are stable, and if no large inflow or outflow of capital is in progress. For a while after World War II the Bank seemed to have another objective, to maintain the value of Canadian war bonds. This meant buying bonds to support the market and thus increasing the cash reserves of the Chartered Banks. Such purchases were at times inconsistent with the objective of stable prices.

Means of control. The Bank of Canada, like other central banks, exercises its function of monetary control mainly by operations designed to increase, or decrease, the cash reserves of the commercial banks. This it may do either by lending more freely to the banks or by purchases of securities in the open market. *(a)* If the banks want to increase their cash they will try to borrow from the Central Bank: the Central Bank may encourage them to borrow by a low interest rate or may discourage them by a high interest rate and by limiting the amount they will lend at any rate. Control via the rate of interest is not very effective, and has been little used by the Bank of Canada. When banks are contracting credit because of the absence of good borrowers they cannot be tempted to borrow more from the Central Bank by a small fall in the rate of interest charged for such loans. When the banks are expanding credit the Central Bank is in a stronger position; but Canadian banks have access to loans in New York, and Canadian business is liable to arrange to borrow from other institutions, or from abroad, if the banks cannot meet their needs. *(b)* The Bank of Canada, like other central banks, may influence the reserves of the commercial banks by buying or selling securities in the open market. If it buys securities it pays with a cheque on itself: the sellers pay this into their accounts in the Chartered Banks which thus find their balances at the Bank of Canada, i.e. their cash reserve, increased. Sale of securities by the Bank of Canada in the open market will have the reverse effect: the buyers will pay by cheques on the Chartered

¹See F. P. Neufeld, Bank of Canada Operations, 1935-54 (Toronto, 1955).

Banks and the Bank of Canada will ask payment in cash thus reducing the cash reserves of the banks. The effectiveness of such a policy on the total supply of money depends largely on the rigidity with which the Chartered Banks adhere to their conventional ratio of cash to demand liabilities: if as their reserves increase they do not lend more freely the open market policy of the Central Bank is rendered nugatory.[13] (c) A new means of control was introduced in the revised Bank of Canada Act of 1954. Prior to that date the Chartered Banks were required to hold cash reserves equal to 5 per cent of their Canadian dollar deposit liabilities. Under the revised Act the Bank of Canada is given power to vary the minimum cash reserve requirements of the Chartered Banks between 8 and 12 per cent, provided that at least a month's notice is given and that the increase is not more than 1 per cent in any one month. (d) Along with these weapons of control goes the power of persuasion: in England the advice of the Bank of England, the "old lady of Threadneedle Street," is taken very seriously; in Canada the Bank of Canada will acquire, indeed is acquiring, prestige with age.

Conclusion. The importance of a sound monetary policy is undoubted. Unwise policies can cause much grief. But it is necessary to end with a warning. Monetary policy cannot solve the problem of depression and unemployment. The possibility that it might was tested in the thirties; it did not work. Dr. Alvin Hansen concludes: "The decade of the thirties offers abundant evidence that cheap money alone is not adequate. Cheap money will not tempt borrowers if there are not available reasonably satisfactory outlets for profitable investment. Cheap money can encourage investment if conditions are favourable. But it will not of itself produce an adequate volume of investment and consumption. This is the lesson we have learned, or which has at least been heavily reinforced, from the experience of the thirties."[14] A long period of reliance on fiscal rather than monetary policy led to some neglect of the importance of the latter and failure to realize its effectiveness in controlling inflation. In the fifties interest in monetary policy revived. Perhaps we are beginning to learn that fiscal policy and monetary policy are complementary rather than competing, and that the optimum mix varies with circumstances.

[13]See evidence of Mr. Towers on the "Effect of Security Purchases by the Bank of Canada" (*Memoranda and Tables respecting the Bank of Canada*, pp. 30-4).

[14]Alvin H. Hansen, *Fiscal Policy and Business Cycles* (New York, 1941), p. 82. Cf. Monteath Douglas, "Limitations of the Financial Factor in a War Economy" (*Canadian Journal of Economics and Political Science*, Aug., 1942).

CHAPTER V

POPULATION

WE have discussed some problems of growth in our simple model, problems arising from the growth of population and from the growth of wealth. We might have noticed that growth of population calls for growth of wealth if the standard of living is to be maintained, and that with a growing population the outlets for new investment are likely to be more obvious and the problem of maintaining full employment is likely, therefore, to be easier than with a stationary or declining population. We now turn, equipped with the tools fashioned while studying the model, to study population growth in the real world. We shall be concerned particularly with the probable trend of population in the next few decades, and with the economic problems associated with that trend. To understand the present, and to peer into the future, it will be necessary to make an excursion into the past. We shall begin with a somewhat detailed examination of the history of population growth in England and Wales, and of the prospects for its further growth. This detailed study of one country is intended to provide an example of methods which must be used in the study of population in any country, an example of a pattern of population growth which can be shown to be very typical, and a discussion of some of the underlying causes of the changing trends. It is followed by a brief discussion of the trend in Europe generally and in the United States of America. We shall then deal with some of the economic problems resulting from population growth or decline, and with some of the policies devised in the thirties to meet the problems of a stationary or declining population. Finally, we shall examine the history of population growth in Canada and the prospects for its future growth. Canada, being a "new" country with an economy extremely dependent on the economies of the older countries, presents some different problems which require separate treatment. What is said about Canada can be said, *mutatis mutandis*, about other new, or pioneer, countries, and, perhaps one should add, about new, or pioneer, regions of some of the older countries.[1]

[1]Much of the material in this chapter has been previously published either in my review article, "The Population Problem" (*Canadian Journal of Economics*

Population growth in England and Wales. We can make only rough estimates of the size of the population of England before 1801, when the first census was taken. It seems clear, however, that the population had been more or less stationary for several centuries before 1700. There may have been fluctuation but there seems to have been no marked trend of growth or decline. In the eighteenth century the population began to grow, and after 1770 the rate of growth was rapid. In 1700 the population must have been about 5½ millions; by 1750 it had grown to 6½ millions; by 1800 it was 9 millions. During the nineteenth century rapid growth continued; the population was 18 millions in 1850 and 33 millions in 1900. Since 1900 the rate of growth has been less; in 1930 the population was 40 millions and in 1940 nearly 41 millions. The rate of growth as shown by the percentage increase of population per decade was 6 per cent in 1751-61, rose to 18 per cent in 1811-21, continued at from 12 to 14 per cent for the remainder of the nineteenth century, and fell to 6 per cent in 1921-31.

The period of rapid growth. A population grows, migration apart, when the inflow through births is greater than the outflow through deaths. We turn our attention, therefore, to the changes in the death-rate and the birth-rate, i.e. the number of deaths, and the number of births, per 1,000 of the population. If the population was more or less stationary before 1700 the birth- and death-rates must have been roughly the same. Both rates were high, probably over 35 per thousand. The death-rate fell after 1700 to 30 per thousand by 1770, and to 20 per thousand by 1820. The birth-rate, on the other hand, remained relatively stationary at the high level of 35 per thousand, or more, till 1840. The resulting excess of births over deaths was the immediate cause of the growth in population which ensued.

The cause of this decline in the death-rate was a decline in mortality resulting from spectacular progress in medicine and public health, the "medical revolution" of the eighteenth century.[2] The death-

and Political Science, Nov., 1939), or in my essay, "Population Problems and Policies" contributed to *Canada in Peace and War,* edited by Chester Martin (Toronto, 1940). The courtesy of the publishers in permitting reproduction of parts of these articles is gratefully acknowledged. The above-mentioned review article was supplemented by a second review article, "On Population" (*Canadian Journal of Economics and Political Science,* May, 1942) dealing with books published between 1939 and 1941. W. D. Forsyth's *The Myth of Open Spaces* (Melbourne, 1942) is a more recent book of special significance to Canadians. *The Future Population of Europe and the Soviet Union,* by F. W. Notestein and others (League of Nations, 1944), the *Report of the Royal Commission on Population* (London, 1949) and Dennis H. Wrong, *Population* (New York, 1956) should also be noted.

[2]Dr. Karl Helleiner has raised doubts as to the effectiveness of medicine in those days and seeks other causes, declining virulence of some diseases, dis-

rate is subject, however, to two influences; first, to the underlying condition of mortality; and second, to the age composition of the population concerned. A decline in mortality could cause, and alone could cause, a decline of the death-rate if the age composition remained the same; but a change in the age composition could cause a change in the death-rate even if mortality remained constant. Obviously a population with a large proportion of young people may be expected to have a smaller death-rate than one with a large proportion of old people. The change in the conditions of mortality is revealed in the change in "mean expectation of life," that is the average number of years that live-born babies may be expected to live. The mean expectation of life in 1750 was about 30 years, by 1850 it had increased to 40 years. This change was not associated with any increase in longevity, the span of life remained unchanged; but the proportion surviving infancy and living through a considerable part of the normal three score years and ten did increase.

If the decline in mortality was the cause of this growth in population, the coincident revolutions in agriculture and industry were necessary conditions. (It has been frequently asserted that the growth began with an increase in the birth-rate in response to the greater ease of providing food, clothing, etc., for a bigger population. This would make these revolutions the immediate causes. The weight of evidence is against this view.[3]) Without the increased productive power, the flood of babies, which the new medicine enabled to survive infancy, could not have been fed, clothed, and housed. The death-rate might have risen as poverty triumphed over medical science. In time, perhaps, the slow operation of those processes of social adjustment, about which we know too little, might have reduced the birth-rate to a level consistent with the low mortality and the limited productivity. But for the fifty years, 1770 to 1820, the increase in productivity resulting from the application of science to agriculture and industry apparently did take care of the increase in population resulting from the application of science to medicine and sanitation. The fact that the death-rate rose a little after 1820 (when one would have expected it to fall because the population had come to include a larger proportion of persons in the early middle ages)

appearance of the plague-bearing rat, etc. See his forthcoming paper, "The Vital Revolution Reconsidered" in the *Canadian Journal of Economics and Political Science;* see also T. McKeown and R. G. Brown, "Medical Evidence related to English Population Changes in the Eighteenth Century" (*Population Studies,* IX, 1955).

[3]See T. H. Marshall, "The Population Problem during the Industrial Revolution" (*Economic History,* vol. I, no. 4).

suggests that the growth of population then became too rapid, that population pressure did develop, and that the positive check did come into operation. A perusal of the report of the Royal Commission on the Health of Towns (1844) suggests, however, an alternative explanation of this check to the fall in the death-rate; the new demands on the sanitary engineer as industrial cities rapidly grew were heavy, and the absence of adequate institutions of local government hampered him in meeting these demands.

The period of declining rate of growth, 1870–1940. After 1870 mortality continued to decline. By 1900 the mean expectation of life was 50 years, and by 1930 was 60 years. The death-rate fell from 22 per thousand in 1870 to 14 per thousand in 1910 and to 12 per thousand in 1930. But in this period the birth-rate, after remaining more or less stationary at a high level for so long, began to fall. From 35 per thousand in 1870, it fell to 24 per thousand by 1910, and to 16 per thousand in 1931. The excess of births over deaths dwindled from 13 per thousand in 1870 to 4 per thousand in 1930.

Like the death-rate the birth-rate is subject to two influences: first, to the underlying conditions of fertility; and, second, to the age composition of the population concerned. The decline in the birth-rate has been the result of a drastic decline in fertility, one measure of which, the gross reproduction rate, is described below (p. 99). Changes in the age composition have had significant effects on the birth-rate, in particular the slowing down of population growth is now producing an age composition less favourable to births, thus reinforcing the depressing influence on the birth-rate of the decline in fertility.

It is generally supposed that the spread of the practice of contraception is the immediate cause of this decline in fertility; but Raymond Pearl considers it "highly probable that the steady decline of total fertility cannot be regarded as due solely, or possibly even primarily, to the operation of those same forces (viz., contraception and abortion). Other and more obscure factors are involved about which almost nothing of a precise and definite character is now known." The extent of involuntary sterility requires investigation; if it is important we must rely on medicine to find means to remedy it. Medicine brought the death-rate down, perhaps it may help to bring the birth-rate up. But even if contraception is really the immediate cause it remains for the sociologists to explain its adoption. There seems little doubt that the purely economic aspect is not the primary one; if it were it would be easier to devise remedies. "The whole atmosphere of the present day," says Mr. Marshall, "is unsympathetic to the parents of many children. In the heyday of the Victorian age, the father of a large family was proud of the fact, and was treated by others as an object of respect. Today he may or may not be proud of himself; but he is apt to be treated by others as a figure of fun or as an object of pity." Or again: "It is not only habits of thought that are weighted against the large family, but also the habitual organization of social life. The large family is not catered for, it does not fit into the modern scheme of things. Houses and flats get smaller, domestic help gets scarcer, holiday makers take to tents and caravans. . . . A man with children is spoken of as a man with 'encumbrances,' and treated as such." Mr. Marshall concludes: "You cannot bribe or terrorize men and women into regulating their most intimate and private lives in a manner contrary to their wishes and to their sense of duty. If people are to have more children, they must want more children. The State can only remove the obstacles to the satisfaction of that want. Nor is it suggested that the remedy lies in removing, if that were possible, the means of exercising that control which has given rise to the situation. The uncontrolled family has gone, never to return. Voluntary parenthood has taken its place."[4] Similarly, Professor Carr-Saunders:

The large family was a consequence of the beliefs, standards, and habits of the time; it was accepted rather than designed . . . it was accepted with resignation as a part of human fate. . . . "The family is rarely a large one," remarked J. S. Mill, "by the woman's desire, because upon her weighs, besides all the physical suffering and full share in all privations, the unbearable domestic toil which grows from a large number of children." There must always have been among women a latent desire to be delivered from this burden . . . it was not so much the absence of knowledge as the presence of moral sentiments, opposed to the discussion, and even more to the employment of contraceptives, which left women in bondage to the large family.

Carr-Saunders quotes a letter from Queen Victoria to the King of the Belgians in 1841: "I think, dearest Uncle, you cannot *really* wish me to be the Maman d'une nombreuse famille, for I think you will see with me the great inconvenience a *large* family would be to us all, and particularly to the country, independent of the hardship and inconvenience to myself; men never think, at least seldom think, what a hard task it is for us women to go through this *very often*." His comment on this letter is: "The great esteem in which the Queen was held by her people was due to the fact that she shared in so many ways the views of her subjects. And in respect of size of family she was no exception." If the fall in fertility has been the result of a change of ideas, moral standards, and social values, we still want to know why these changed. Urbanization, industrialization, mechanization, all appear to have been

[4]See *The Population Problem, the Experts and the Public*, chap. VIII; and A. M. Carr-Saunders, *World Population* (Oxford, 1936), chaps. VIII and IX.

influential; but little can be said about the fundamental causes of this revolution in ideas.

Gross and net reproduction rates. Because of the disturbing effects of changing age composition on death-rates and birth-rates, and because the age composition of the population of England and Wales is changing as its rate of growth changes, the existence at present of a small excess of births over deaths cannot be taken as proof that the force of fertility is at present adequate to offset the force of mortality and thereby to maintain the present population. Dr. Kuczynski[5] has rendered notable service by introducing a simple measure of the degree to which populations have fertility adequate for ultimate maintenance or increase of their numbers which he calls the *net reproduction rate.* This can be defined by reference to the number of female children likely to be produced in the course of their lives by one thousand female babies, if the existing fertility and mortality rates remained unchanged. If they exactly replace themselves by one thousand other female babies the rate is unity; if they produce 1,500 other babies the rate is 1.5; if only 800 the rate is 0.8. In a stationary population the rate would of course be unity; if the rate is 1.5 the population will *eventually* increase 50 per cent in a generation. (The *present* rate of increase is so heavily influenced by the *past* rate and by the consequent present age distribution that the population may for the time being increase though the net reproduction rate is below unity. This is true, for instance, of England. Hence the insertion of the word eventually.) For England and Wales the net reproduction rate in the seventies was 1.5; by the turn of the century it was 1.3; by 1921 it was 1.1; by 1931, 0.8; by 1933, 0.7. In the later thirties the net reproduction rate increased to 0.8; after 1942 it moved upwards and was well above unity in 1946–48. The fluctuation of the rate from year to year in this period has drawn attention to the danger of relying on this "rate" as an indication of how far current fertility is adequate to ensure maintenance or increase of the population. There is some reason to believe that the high figures in the late forties reflect an abnormal proportion of recently married couples, and a tendency to have children earlier. Unless the average size of their completed families increases (it may, but it will be some years before we can tell) the rise in the net reproduction rate for these years may not mean any real increase in "fertility."

Calculation of this net reproduction rate involves recourse to the specific fertility rates (i.e., the number of babies born to women in any

[5]See his essay, "World Population," in *The Population Problem, the Experts and the Public;* also his book, *Population Movements* (Oxford, 1936).

age group per thousand women in that group, almost exactly half of which will be female), and to the female mortality tables which show the number of women surviving at any age out of a thousand female babies. An example calculated from hypothetical figures may facilitate

TABLE I

HYPOTHETICAL SPECIFIC FERTILITIES AND SURVIVAL RATES

Age Groups	Births in each year per 1,000 women of given age	Survivors in each age group from 1,000 female live births
15-19	20	900
20-24	100	875
25-29	125	850
30-34	90	825
35-39	50	800
40-44	20	750
45-49	2	700

understanding. (The figures approximate those typical of Western Europe, but are chosen for ease of calculation.) Suppose, then, that *specific fertility* rates are as given in column 1 of Table I. Suppose that of 1,000 female babies the number surviving to enter each age group be as given in column 2. Then a thousand female babies will yield:

900 women aged 15-19 who will have $\frac{20}{2} \times \frac{900}{1000}$ female babies in each of the five years, or 45 in all.

875 women aged 20-24 who will have $\frac{100}{2} \times \frac{875}{1000}$ female babies in each of the five years, or 218.75 in all.

850 women aged 25-29 who will have $\frac{125}{2} \times \frac{850}{1000}$ female babies in each of the five years, or 265.6 in all.

825 women aged 30-34 who will have $\frac{90}{2} \times \frac{825}{1000}$ female babies in each of the five years, or 185.6 in all.

800 women aged 35-39 who will have $\frac{50}{2} \times \frac{800}{1000}$ female babies in each of the five years, or 100 in all.

750 women aged 40-44 who will have $\frac{20}{2} \times \frac{750}{1000}$ female babies in each of the five years, or 37.5 in all.

700 women aged 45-49 who will have $\frac{2}{2} \times \frac{700}{1000}$ female babies in each of the five years, or 3.5 in all.

This would mean that 1,000 female babies would live to produce only 856 female babies; they would have failed to replace themselves and the net reproduction rate would be 0.9.

Reference should also be made to the *gross reproduction rate*. This is similar to the net reproduction rate, except that it neglects mortality. It reflects the number of female babies which would be born in the course of their lives to a thousand female babies if they all survived to the end of the child-bearing period. In the hypothetical case given above suppose that all the original thousand babies live at least 50 years; they would have 10 female babies in each of the years 15-19, 50 in all; they would have 50 female babies in each of the years 20-24, or 250 in all; and so on. In this case the original thousand babies would produce 1,018 female babies, the gross reproduction rate would be 1.0. The significance of this measure, based on the fantastic assumption of no female mortality before age 50, is twofold. It provides a measure of the decline in fertility, and it indicates the maximum contribution that further reduction in mortality can make towards reversing the trend to decline. For England and Wales the gross reproduction rate was 2.3 in 1870; the rate fell below unity in 1927 and was 0.9 in 1935. The decline in fertility had, this demonstrates, gone so far that no improvement of mortality would have sufficed to counteract it. "Mortality," concludes Dr. Kuczynski, "was the decisive factor in determining population growth in the past. The future population trend will depend on fertility."

Estimates of the future population of England and Wales. A similar conclusion to that reached by calculating the "net reproduction rate" may be reached by estimating the future population on the assumption that the existing conditions of fertility and mortality remain unchanged. Such an estimate was made for England and Wales by Dr. Enid Charles.[6] The materials necessary for making the estimate are, the present age and sex composition of the population, and the present specific fertility rates and specific death-rates. Starting with the number in each quinquennial age group in 1931, and applying the specific death-rate, it is possible to estimate the number likely to survive from each age group to replace those in the next age group five years later. Similarly, knowing the number of women in each of the age groups and the specific fertility rates it is possible to estimate the number of births each year. From the specific death-rates for the early ages it is then possible to estimate how many of these babies will survive to form the low age groups at succeeding censuses. An examination of the results of this calculation reveals that the conditions of fertility and mortality existing in 1931, when the population of England and Wales was 40 millions, would provide for some growth in the thirties, to 40.8 millions in 1940, for an almost stationary population in

[6] L. Hogben (ed.), *Political Arithmetic* (London, 1938).

the forties, with a population of 40.7 millions in 1950; and for continuous and accelerating decline thereafter, to 37.3 millions in 1970, and 28.5 millions in the year 2000.

We must remember that these are estimates of what the population *would* be, *if* conditions of fertility and mortality had remained, and were to continue, as in 1931. In fact we know that through the thirties the decline in fertility continued, and that there was some, though less, decline in mortality. Dr. Charles therefore made another estimate based on estimates of the probable further decline in fertility and mortality. This alternative estimate makes little difference to the estimate for 1940, but shows a substantial decline in the forties, and shows a population in 1970 of 33.8 millions (compared with 37.3 millions in the first estimate) and a population in the year 2000 of 17.7 millions (compared with 28.5 millions in the first estimate).

Since these are estimates of what population *would* be *if* fertility and mortality trends went the way Dr. Charles has assumed, one must consider the reasonableness of her assumptions. So far as the next thirty years were concerned the estimates seemed, at that time, to be very reasonable: the attainment of a mean expectation of life of roughly 70 years by 1965, which is the assumption in the alternative estimate, would be fulfilled only if there was continuous improvement in medical science and progressive elimination of conditions of serious poverty. Any sudden reversal of the decline in fertility seemed most unlikely. When, however, the estimate went beyond thirty years the element of uncertainty became very much bigger. The more obvious the trend of decline the more likely was the adoption of positive population policies calculated to reverse that trend; the longer the trend continued the more likely was the selection of effective population policies. The very publication of Dr. Charles's estimate became, therefore, a factor which might change the underlying assumptions on which it was based, and make it probably an under-estimate in the event, at least so far as the later years are concerned. Why positive population policies might be expected will be clear after we have considered the economic effects of declining population and the strategic, and cultural, effects of differential rates of decline in different countries.

Renewal of population growth, Great Britain. The population of Great Britain was 44.8 millions in 1931. If the expectations of the thirties had been fulfilled this would have grown to about 45.7 million in 1941 and have remained stationary, or declined slightly by 1951. In fact the population of Great Britain was 46.6 millions in 1941 and 48.2 millions in 1947. An examination of the causes of this upsurge may be found in the *Report of the Royal Commission on Population* (1949).

In the thirties there was a net immigration of 650,000 compared with a net emigration of 500,000 in the twenties; this striking reversal of the balance of migration was quite unexpected. The decline in mortality was steady and about as expected except that the decline was rather accelerated in the first half of the decade of the forties by the spread of the sulphanamides and of penicillin. It was the upsurge of births in the late forties, however, that was the principal factor in reversing the population trend: instead of births of around 700,000 annually, and an excess of births over deaths of about 140,000, as in the thirties, births rose to over 930,000 annually in 1946–48, giving an excess of births over deaths of some 375,000. This "flood of babies" is largely explained by the increase in the number of recently married couples: the number of couples married in the previous ten years was 3.4 millions in 1933, 3.7 millions in 1938, and 4.3 millions in 1947. What appears to have happened is that people married earlier; it is not clear that they were marrying more. Nor is it clear that marital fertility had increased. The number of births in the period 1939–48 is very little greater than one would have expected on the basis of 1933 fertility rates. The experience of World War I leads one to suppose that one should deduct some 300,000 from the "expected" figure, and on this basis the Royal Commission concluded that the fertility of married couples might be between 1 and 5 per cent higher than in 1935–38. It is impossible to determine, however, whether fertility really had increased or whether earlier marriage and earlier family formation involved borrowing, as it were, births from the future. An examination of family formation led the Royal Commission to present the following facts and conclusions:

Couples married in the years 1917–28 had had by the end of 1938 a considerably larger number of children, on average, than the couples married in the years 1927–38 had had by the end of 1948. . . . The couples married in 1937–44 had had almost the same number of children by the end of 1948 as the couples married in 1927–34 had had by the end of 1938. . . . Coming after a 60 year decline in average family size, a cessation of the fall over a ten year period would be a sufficiently striking event. When we allow for the disruption of normal family life by the war, however, it may be that something even more important has occurred. . . . In a large and important section of the population the size of the family seems to have been increasing.[7]

This does not mean a return to the large family! It does seem to mean a sufficient increase to promise that for some time to come fears of declining population can be banished. If family size were to stabilize at 6 per cent above the level of the thirties the population would be likely to increase to 52 millions by 1980 and to 52.2 millions by 2000.

[7]*Report of the Royal Commission on Population*, pp. 52–6.

Population growth in Europe. This pattern of population growth associated directly with the decline of mortality consequent on the development of scientific medicine, and indirectly with the increase in productivity resulting from the progressive application of science to agriculture and industry is not peculiar to England and Wales, but is found to be common to all European countries. The dates at which growth began were generally later than in England, and later in the South and East than in the North and West. But of Europe as a whole we can say that the population in 1700 was probably no larger than in 1600, no larger, indeed, than in 1300; that the population did increase from about 110 millions in 1700 to 140 millions by 1750, to 190 millions by 1800, to 270 millions by 1850, and to 410 millions by 1900. During this same period there was a migration of Europeans to other continents, especially to this continent, which is estimated at some forty millions. In Europe generally, as in England and Wales, this era of population growth seems to be approaching an end. The decline of

TABLE II
TREND OF GROSS REPRODUCTION RATES, 1880-1935

	About 1880	About 1895	About 1910	About 1925	About 1935
Over 3..........	Russia	Poland	Bulgaria		
		Russia	Russia		
2.5-3.0				Bulgaria	
				Russia	
2.0-2.5	Austria	Austria	Austria	Poland	
	Denmark	Denmark	Germany		
	England	Finland			
	Finland	Germany			
	Germany	Norway			
	Norway				
	Sweden				
1.5-2.0	France	England	Denmark	Czecho-	Bulgaria
		Sweden	Finland	slovakia	
			Norway		
			Sweden		
1.0-1.5		France	England	Denmark	Czecho-
			France	England	slovakia
				Finland	Denmark
				France	Finland
				Germany	Germany
				Norway	Poland
				Sweden	
Under 1..........					Austria
					England
					France
					Sweden
					Norway

fertility, evident in England after 1870 has become similarly evident in one country after another. This is shown in a table of gross reproduction rates calculated by Dr. Kuczynski and published in a volume of studies entitled *Political Arithmetic.* An adaptation of this table is here presented in Table II; the drift of concentration downward and to the right is very revealing. In 1870 the gross reproduction rate exceeded 2 in every European country but France. By the turn of the century it was less than 2 in England and Sweden and had fallen to 1.5 in France. By 1910 it was below 2 in every country of Western and Northern Europe. By 1925 in only Russia, Poland, and the Balkans was the rate above 2; in the other countries of Europe the rate was between 1 and 1.5. In 1935, Russia was the only European country in which the rate exceeded 2, and it was below 1 in England, Norway, Sweden, Belgium, France, Switzerland, Austria, and Estonia. Dr. Kuczynski concludes that the gross reproduction rate for Western and Northern Europe was about 2 until 1890, and that it dropped below unity in 1931. In Central and Southern Europe it still exceeded 2 in 1922, but by 1935 had declined to 1.5.

This decline in fertility has in part been counteracted by a further decline in mortality; but with the gross reproduction rate less than

TABLE III

TREND OF NET REPRODUCTION RATES, 1895-1935

	About 1895	About 1910	About 1925	About 1935
Over 1.5	Bulgaria Denmark Germany Norway Poland Russia	Bulgaria Norway Russia	Bulgaria Russia Ukraine	Russia
1.0-1.5	Ukraine Austria England Finland Hungary Sweden	Austria Denmark England Finland Germany Hungary Sweden	Denmark Finland Hungary Poland	Bulgaria Ukraine
0.8-1.0	France	France	Austria England Estonia France Germany Sweden	Denmark Finland France Germany Hungary
Under 0.8				Austria England Norway Sweden

unity no improvement in mortality can prevent a decline of population if the present low fertility rates continue. The prospect of decline is shown in the tables of net reproduction rates calculated by Dr. Kuczynski and published in *Political Arithmetic*. An adaption of his table is here presented as Table III. In Northern and Western Europe as a whole the net reproduction rate in 1870 was over 1.3; it had fallen by 1935 to 0.8. In Central and Southern Europe it was in 1935 still 1.5. The rate was between 0.8 and 1 in such countries as Czechoslovakia, Denmark, Finland, France, Germany, Hungary, Latvia, and Scotland; it was below 0.8 in Austria, Belgium, England, Estonia, Norway, Sweden, and Switzerland.[8]

The population of the United States. This pattern of growth and decline is not peculiar to Europe; in the United States a similar trend is found. The population of the United States grew at a spectacular pace before the Civil War; for six successive decades the average decennial increase was nearly 35 per cent. In 1800 the population was 5 millions, by 1850 it was 23 millions, by 1870, 40 millions. Since 1870 the growth has been slower, though still rapid by comparison with European countries. By 1900 the population was 76 millions, by 1930 it was 123 millions. The increase in population was 21 per cent in the decade 1890–1900, only 15 per cent in the decade 1920–30. The decline in the rate of growth was due to a decline in immigration and to a decline in fertility partially counteracted by a decrease in mortality. With population declining in Europe it did not seem likely that immigration would again contribute much to population growth in the United States. The decline in fertility had already gone so far that the net reproduction rate in the thirties was slightly below unity. In an excellent report, *Problems of a Changing Population*,[9] published by the United States government, the conclusion was stated that "if no change occurred in the proportion of persons surviving from birth to different ages, or in fertility rates of women at different ages, population growth would gradually cease." And the report added significantly: "There is good reason to expect that further decline in fertility rates will be more rapid than the rise in survival rates." Even for the United States the end of the era of population growth seemed to be in

---

[8]Dr. F. W. Notestein in the *Future Population of Europe and the Soviet Union* (League of Nations, 1944) argued that while the population of most European countries was not likely to increase much more, and would probably reach a maximum about 1965, the population of the U.S.S.R. was likely to increase quite rapidly: his projection for the U.S.S.R. was: 1940, 174 millions; 1950, 203 millions; 1960, 228 millions; 1970, 251 millions. In some countries a flood of babies has upset these calculations; the pattern is not uniform and the trend of fertility cannot yet be determined.

[9]A report of the Committee on Population Problems of the National Resources Committee (Washington, 1938).

sight; absolute decline was not likely to be evident before 1970 (perhaps later), but in place of an increase of 16 millions in the twenties, the increase in the thirties seemed likely to be about 9 millions, in the forties to be less than 8 millions, and in the fifties less than 5 millions. Indeed one estimate, which did not appear to be based on very unlikely assumptions about the trend of fertility, showed the turning point, where absolute decline would begin, as early as 1960.

Estimates of the future population of the United States. Three estimates of the future population of the United States made in the thirties are presented in Table IV based on three different assumptions as to the behaviour of the three factors of growth. They were, of course, in the event gross under-estimates: in the United States as in Great Britain there came an unexpected flood of babies. It may tend

TABLE IV

ESTIMATES OF THE FUTURE POPULATION OF THE UNITED STATES OF AMERICA

	Estimate (*a*)	Estimate (*b*)	Estimate (*c*)
1940	132	131	132
1950	141	137	142
1960	147	139	149
1970	151	138	155
1980	153	134	158

to promote modesty in again estimating the future population to examine these estimates, and the bases on which they were made. (1) *Mortality.* The mean expectation of life of the live-born baby in Massachusetts was about 35 years in 1789, 38 years in 1850, 46 years in 1900, and 60 years in 1930. Mortality probably declined in the United States as a whole in about the same way as in the State of Massachusetts. It seemed likely that there would be some further decline; therefore the estimates of future population presented in Table IV were based on the assumption that by 1980 the mean expectation of life of live-born babies would be 69 years for males and 71 years for females. (2) *Fertility.* The gross reproduction rate fell from 2.2 in 1850 to 1.1 in 1930. This decline in fertility seemed likely to continue though at a rapidly diminishing rate. The decline in the twenty-five years prior to 1930 was about 34 per cent; estimate (*a*) in Table IV was based on the assumption of a further 13 per cent decrease in fertility in the fifty years after 1930. This would mean a gross reproduction rate in 1980 a little less than 1. "This is slightly less than an average of two births for all women, and slightly more than 2½ per fertile woman. It is approximately the 1930 rate in Massachusetts, Washington, and Oregon, and also in Sweden. In the opinion of the staff of the Scripps Foundation these medium assumptions were more likely to be followed than either the high or the low. It was admitted, however, that there must be a rather rapid change in attitude regarding the desirability of 3- and 4-child families if this medium trend were not to prove too high." Estimate (b) gives the result of assuming a more drastic decline in fertility, viz., 31 per cent. The Committee on Population Problems recognized the difficulty of making an estimate of the future trend of fertility where "the unknown factor is how many children will be wanted."

Immigration. In view of the peculiar difficulty of predicting immigration the estimates (a) and (b) in Table IV made no allowance for migration. Immigration came in waves of varying magnitude. It rose to peaks of 400,000 a year in 1854 and again in the early seventies. In 1882 it rose to a higher peak of 790,000. In the nineties an average annual immigration of 400,000 prevailed, but the number rose rapidly and exceeded a million in 1905-7, 1910, and 1913-14. A temporary law to restrict immigration was passed in 1921, and more permanent legislation in 1924. Immigration from the "Quota" countries was limited to 150,000 a year. In 1930 consular officers were instructed to take into account the condition of depression in applying the clause excluding persons likely to become a public charge. From 1931-5 more people left the United States than entered. It did not seem likely that there would be immigration on any great scale in the calculable future. Estimate (c) in Table IV shows the effect of revising estimate (a) by assuming immigration of 100,000 persons a year after 1940.

Turning now to the facts, we find that by 1951 the population had increased to 151 millions.[10] Mortality had decreased as much as was expected; but immigration was greater than allowed for in estimate (c) and the birth-rate increased from 17 per thousand in the thirties to nearly 26 per thousand in 1947 and seems likely to stay for some time near 24 per thousand. New projections suggest that the population may be 210 millions in 1975!

Age composition of declining populations. Worries about declining population arise in part out of the increasing proportion of the population in the higher age groups which would be found in these declining, or more slowly growing, populations. In England, for instance, the proportion of persons over 60 was in 1930 11 per cent, by 1960 it would be nearly 20 per cent, and by 2000 the proportion would be 23 per cent according to the conservative estimate of Dr. Charles based on the continuance of the fertility rates of the thirties, and 46 per cent according to her radical estimate based on the assumption of continued decline in fertility. This demonstrates the important point that the

---

[10]See J. S. Davis, "Our Changed Population Outlook" (*American Economic Review*, June, 1952).

more rapid the decline, the more rapid the aging of the population. In the United States the proportion of the population over 65 doubled between 1930 and 1950 though the population increased only 23 per cent.

The effects of this "aging" of the population were the subject of much concern in the thirties. One of the early German books on population decline had the significant title, *A Country without Youth.* The Swedish Population Commission discussed the problem most effectively:

A declining population means a relatively greater number of old people and a higher average age even within the generation of middle-aged persons. Because of certain average psychical differences between generations, which have not been well studied, such a difference in age distribution must have important effects upon the whole life of the people, not only economically but even politically and culturally.

In a judgment of this question it is certainly incorrect to underestimate the importance of the calm presence of mind, the patient care, and the greater experience of life which comes with age. But the age distribution already present with a stationary population should give assurance of a sufficient predominance by the older classes which possess these valuable qualities in high degree. The age distribution which comes about with a declining population would, on the other hand, imply serious danger that the nation will be wanting in the other qualities likewise valuable, which belong above all to youth: willingness to sacrifice, courage, power of initiative and creative imagination.[11]

Differential fertility. The decline in fertility was differential in its incidence as between social classes. The classic evidence is Dr. Stevenson's *Report on the Fertility of Marriage* from the English Census of 1911. In it the population was grouped into five classes which may roughly be described as the rich, the upper middle class, the lower middle class, the skilled workers, and the unskilled. The total fertility of marriage of class I (corrected for varying age distribution) was found to be 20 per cent less than the average for the country as a whole; that of class II to be 8 per cent less than the average; that of class III to be 2 per cent less and that of class IV, 2 per cent more than the average; that of class V was 14 per cent more than the average. This wide differential had developed since 1861. In the decade 1851-61 the fertility of class I may have been 10 per cent less than the average; but the differences between the other four classes were negligible, and the slightly greater fertility of the unskilled was more than counteracted by the greater infant mortality.

This modern differential birth-rate has been a source of worry to

[11]Quoted in G. Myrdal, *Population* (Cambridge, Mass., 1940), pp. 160-1.

some eugenists. Doubts as to the association of desirable biological qualities and pecuniary success, realization of the degree of ignorance as to the hereditary transmission of these qualities, and recognition of the difficulty of agreeing on the qualities for which one would breed if one had the opportunity, combine to suggest that this worry need not be serious. And in any case the differential does not seem likely to be permanent. Dr. J. W. Innes in his study, *Class Fertility Trends in England and Wales, 1876–1934*,[12] has shown that equalization of fertilities in classes I - IV had proceeded very far by 1931. He further suggests that the relative isolation of class V should not be exaggerated; its relative fertility decline has kept pace with the others, and if the relative differential between it and other classes has diminished but little, the absolute differences have greatly diminished. It appears likely, then, that the "history of the association of fertility and status in England . . . is simply a reflection of a class pattern of fertility decline." One wonders whether a reversal of the declining trend of fertility will show the same class pattern, with consequent emergence of reversed differential class fertilities. It was not only the class differentials that caused concern in the past. The differences in birth-rates between countries led one economist to suggest the need for a "league of low birth-rate countries"; and within many countries racial problems are complicated by the existence of wide racial differentials in birth-rates. It seems likely that these differentials will disappear in time, but the process may be slow.

Population and wealth. We turn from the history and prediction of the facts of population growth, to opinions about the effect of such growth. In the two or three centuries before the modern era of population growth began there was general ignorance of the actual trend, and general fear of decline. The reason for this fear was largely military and political; the nation-state needed man-power to make it strong and influential. The economic reason is not clearly stated in the economic writings of the time, but it is implied in the theory of exploitation expressed by John Bellers in *An Essay for Imploying the Able Poor* (1714): "Labouring people do raise and manufacture above double the food and clothing they use themselves"; were this not true, "every gentleman must be a labourer and every idle man must starve." It seems to follow that the more "labouring people" the better for the gentleman, the better for the state. This has been described as "a theory of the most advantageous exploitation."

The rapid growth of population after 1770 was barely recognized before it was the subject of apprehension. From Thomas Robert

[12]Princeton, 1938.

Malthus, whose first *Essay on Population* was published in 1798, to John Stuart Mill, whose *Principles of Political Economy* was published in 1848, economists talked of the danger of over-population, and preached doctrines of marital self-restraint in the hope of averting the danger. Malthus did not see how the food supply could be increased as fast as population was increasing: Mill saw that the food supply could be increased fast enough, but thought that it could be done only at greatly increased human cost. But it was not only on economic grounds that Mill's attitude to the population problem was based; perhaps equally important were his political and ethical views on the emancipation of women: "a more important consideration still," he writes to a friend, "is the perpetuation of the previous degradation of women, no alteration in which can be hoped for while their whole lives are devoted to the function of producing and rearing children. That degradation and slavery is, in itself, so enormous an evil . . . that the limitation of the number of children would be, in my opinion, absolutely necessary to place human life on its proper footing even if there were subsistence for any number which could be produced."

It was clear to Mill that historically the returns to human effort in agriculture had been increasing as a result of the improved technique of the agricultural revolution. The "progress of civilization" had partially counteracted the force of the static, but constantly operating, "law of diminishing returns" in agriculture. We were, Mill would have us believe, better off as a result of this progress, but not as well off as we should have been had population not increased, and we were unwise to rely on continual technical progress. This position was very generally accepted and curiously enough, persisted long after the beginning of the decline in the rate of growth, though the rate of scientific and technological progress was becoming more rapid. How late the fear of over-population persisted can be shown by reference to Mr. Keynes's *Economic Consequences of the Peace Treaty*, published in 1920. "Malthus disclosed a Devil. For half a century all serious economical writings held that Devil in clear prospect. For the next half century he was chained up and out of sight. Now perhaps we have loosed him again." Similarly in 1923, Mr. D. H. Robertson in a characteristically whimsical essay, "A Word for the Devil,"[13] wrote: "I do not in the name of the (Malthusian) devil, prophesy sudden cataclysm or even *necessarily* continued degradation; nevertheless in the pie of the world's poverty I detect his smoky finger." To Mr. Robertson it appeared that the standard of living in England "would have been higher if there had been fewer of us."

[13]In *Economic Fragments* (London, 1931).

The optimum population. Edwin Cannan could never accept the doctrine that increasing population *necessarily* meant poverty.[14] "Mill," he said, "coolly assumed that all the improvements which have been made would have been made just the same if the population had not grown. We cannot assume that." This suggestion, that progress in the arts is not unconnected with the growth of population, leads to another, that effectively to utilize the new arts you may need a bigger population. Thus there emerges the idea of an optimum population. Over-population came to mean that the population was greater than the optimum size. The per capita production of wealth in such circumstances could be increased if the population could be reduced. But if it was reduced below this optimum size, per capita production would again decrease. Under-population was thus put on a par with over-population; either involved, if not poverty, at least less wealth than could be enjoyed with the optimum population. It was recognized that the optimum size changed with changing technology, and it was fairly well agreed that modern machine industry had in fact raised not merely the *possible* size of the population, but also its *optimum* size. This concept of the optimum population is elegant and no doubt sound: unfortunately, however, we have not succeeded in developing adequate criteria for determining in any actual case either what is the optimum size, or even whether the particular population is too big or too small.

Population and employment. In the thirties the recognition of the probable decline of population was followed by a complete reversal of the population fears. We used to fear too rapid growth, we began to fear decline, to be worried by the economic consequence of a stationary population, or of one growing too slowly. This new fear was not based on the belief that we were then near, or below, the optimum size. Those who thought about the optimum at all probably felt that many countries in Europe were then over-populated, and that some decline would be an advantage. Many of them, however, were worried because they could see no end to the decline short of extinction, just as Malthus and Mill could see no end to the increase short of "plague, pestilence and famine, battle, murder and sudden death." This particular worry need not detain us. We may note the comment of one critic of the estimates of the future population of England quoted above: "A person of the intellectual power and originality of Dr. Enid Charles should know that she cannot reasonably and scientifically extrapolate a population trend for a

[14]See *Wealth*, chap. IV; also E. Cannan, *A Review of Economic Theory* (London, 1929), chap. IV.

century or more hence without allowing for new forces tending to restore equilibrium on a new level." We may also suggest that the sociologist can explain this cycle of growth and decline in terms of slow social adjustment to two successive innovations, medicine and contraception; the second of which starting as a means of restoring the equilibrium of birth- and death-rates which was upset by the first, became in the end a force making for a new disequilibrium, calling for new adjustments.

The fear of the economic consequences of a declining population, or even of a less rapidly growing one, is a by-product of the development of the theory of employment associated especially with Lord Keynes. Both Mill, when discussing the inexorable law of diminishing returns, and Cannan, when explaining that we might be better off with a bigger rather than with a smaller population, assumed that there would be full employment in any case, or that the degree of employment was independent of the growth of the population. Some there were who thought that more people would mean greater unemployment. But generally the theory of employment was neglected. Modern economists have come to concern themselves properly with the problem of maintaining full employment, and they became worried about the effect on employment of the process of decline, rather than about any fear of the disadvantage of a smaller population. For the maintenance of a high level of employment it has come to be recognized as necessary that there shall be adequate "investment" or "real capital formation," adequate "income producing expenditures offsetting saving." In the past the increase of population provided one of the more important sources of demand for new capital. Indeed, Professor Alvin Hansen has estimated that the growth of population in the nineteenth century was responsible for about 40 per cent of the total volume of capital formation in Western Europe, and for about 60 per cent in the United States. In his presidential address to the American Economic Association in December, 1938, Professor Hansen presented a forcible statement of the problem: "We are thus rapidly entering a world in which we must fall back upon a more rapid advance of technology than in the past if we are to find private investment opportunities adequate to maintain full employment. . . . The great transition, incident to a rapid decline in population growth and its impact upon capital formation and the workability of a system of free enterprise, calls for high scientific adventure along all the fronts represented by the social science disciplines." Professor Hansen expressed similar views before the Temporary National Economic Committee, at the same time that he voiced the doubts, quoted in the last chapter, as to the effect of industrial maturity on the volume of capital formation.

So far as private investment outlets (for savings) are concerned, this requires continuous technological progress, the rise of new industries, the discovery of new resources, the growth of population, or a combination of several or all of these developments. . . . It is not difficult to see that a country experiencing a rapid increase of population requires a vast capital outlay in order to provide housing, transportation, and all the facilities necessary for modern methods of living, such as municipal utilities and the like. The enormous capital outlays of the nineteenth century were, of course, in the first instance conditioned by new technological developments, but they were determined also by the vast growth of population. It seems not unreasonable to suppose—and some rough estimates lead to this conclusion—that approximately one-half of the capital outlays of the past century were due to the growth of population and its expansion into new territory.

Dr. Hansen added: "It is not enough that an economy is simply growing. If the additional amounts of growth are smaller and smaller you have from that fact alone a depressing effect on your economy . . . [because] your plant is built up to a point to take care of growth."[15]

Population growth and mobility. The growth of population promotes the smooth functioning of the economy, by making for bigger, and more regular, capital formation, and by making, as we saw in our study of the model, for greater mobility, i.e. easier adjustment to change. This same ease, or difficulty, of adjustment reacts on the readiness of private people to expand their productive equipment through the less, or greater, risk involved according as mistakes are easily, or with difficulty, corrected. Nor is it only the increased risk to the investor that is serious; mistaken expansion will leave pockets of unemployed for whom movement is difficult, and whose inability to buy will produce further unemployment. On this topic one may quote Mr. H. D. Henderson:

When numbers are growing rapidly, there is such a big increase in the total demand for goods and services, that there is seldom either an absolute decline in the demand for any particular commodity or even an absolute decline in the demand for labour in any particular industry. That certainly was our experience during the nineteenth century. I have found it of interest in this connection to compare the number of people employed in the different industries in England and Wales in 1871 and in 1895. It is not, indeed, easy to obtain exact figures, since there were many changes in classification. But the broad results are striking. In almost every separate industry for which it is possible to make the comparison, and in every

[15]Hearings before the Temporary National Economic Committee, part 9, *Savings and Investment,* pp. 3503–4.

industry of any importance, there were more people employed in 1895 than in 1871. Some industries, of course, grew much more rapidly during the period than others. The numbers employed in engineering, for example, increased by about two and a half times, whereas the numbers employed in textiles increased by only about fifteen per cent. In other words, the shift in the *direction* of the demand for labour as between engineering and textiles was very large. But the aggregate volume of employment expanded in both groups of industries; and this was true, as I have said, of almost every industry for which it is possible to obtain figures. In these circumstances there was no need to move actual workpeople from one industry to another in accordance with changes in the direction of the demand for labour. All that was necessary was that the new recruits to industry should go mainly into the more rapidly expanding occupations. Thus no serious problem of structural unemployment arose. When, however, the working population becomes virtually stationary, and the demand for labour continues to shift its direction, an absolute decline in the numbers employed in certain industries is inevitable. Then it becomes far more likely that many work people in those industries will lose their jobs and will remain permanently unemployed, unless they are sufficiently adaptable to be able to make good in unfamiliar occupations.[16]

Population growth and capitalism. One is tempted to a "population interpretation" of modern capitalism. Edwin Cannan sensed it: Professor J. R. Hicks now toys with it as he wonders in a foot-note at the end of his *Value and Capital* whether the "whole industrial revolution of the last two centuries has been nothing else but a vast secular boom, largely induced by the unparalleled rise in population." Modern capitalist free enterprise may prove to have been a boom system, and the modern trend to something like seventeenth-century mercantilism may be a trend towards institutions appropriate to an era of stationary population. Dr. Gunnar Myrdal drew attention in his book, *Population*,[17] to the effects of "aging."

The shifting of the age distribution *within* the working ages, which will result from the lowering of the population trend, will come to have a restrictive effect upon *young people's opportunities for advancement.* . . .
    . . . people will get discouraged. They will lose their dynamic interest in working life; society will lose the mental attitude that goes with progress. Interest in security will be substituted for an earlier interest in social advancement.
    The peculiar brand of Socialism which is apt to develop under the continued influences of these factors must unfortunately be expected to take on an administrative, bureaucratic, senile character; it will be the bureaucratic administration of the liquidation of a people. Much less takes care of itself in a declining economy than in one that is growing; the bureaucratic

---

[16]See his essay, "The Economic Consequences," in *The Population Problem, the Experts and the Public.*
    [17]Pp. 161–6.

apparatus must therefore increase. This apparatus becomes less dynamic, less effective, not only because it comes to rest principally in the power of old men, but also because of a heretofore unmentioned reason: the best, the most dynamic intelligences cannot come to feel a very great interest in the administration of a liquidation. Even one who was a Socialist in politics, but who has felt the pulse of progress in his veins, who has loved free initiative and advance, must feel cheerless before these prospects. He hardly expected this to be the outlook for Socialism. He would even be tempted to defend private capitalism if by that means he could revivify dynamic progress.

Perhaps Keynes has shown us how to organize to meet the problem. Some of his followers seemed inclined to exploit the new population fear to sell the latest employment nostrum. Indeed this was one of the pleasant features of the new population literature: with Malthus the fear of over-population blocked all social reform; with Myrdal the fear of depopulation became a "crowbar for social reform"; housing, public health, family allowances, education, all considered desirable in themselves became so much more desirable as contributing, possibly, to maintenance of fertility.

We do not know whether the problem of unemployment was particularly severe in the seventeenth and eighteenth centuries. The population was stationary and technical progress slow, so that opportunities for investment must have been limited. But total income was small, so that saving was limited; and saving led to the accumulation of things, the products of labour, gold and silver plate, and improvements to houses and country estates. With the nineteenth century, as income increased saving also increased; and saving began to lead to the accumulation of promises to pay, bank balances, paper securities, things which were not the direct product of labour. But the growth of population at home, and rapid technological progress combined with the opening of new continents to exploitation, provided enough investment to enable the system of free enterprise to function in the nineteenth century, if not perfectly, at least well enough to guarantee its survival. In the modern world the national income which we could enjoy if we were able to maintain full employment becomes bigger, and the potential saving grows faster, while the accumulation of intangibles becomes the most general form of "pecuniary emulation." In these circumstances Professor Hansen told us we must look to technological advance to provide new investment opportunities to make free enterprise "workable." Fifteen years later we find population growing, technology advancing rapidly, defence expenditures high: our worries are concerned with over-full employment, with inflation.

Speculation on the effects of declining population was new, and experience thereof was non-existent. We could not be very confident in our anticipations either of troubles, or of remedies for the troubles. We anticipated trouble from a continuance of Victorian standards of thrift into a period of declining investment. But the standard of thrift might decline, and, what is more important, the distribution of income might become more favourable to a high level of consumption. The proportion of income saved by the rich is, of course, much higher than that saved by the poor. Any shift of income from the richer to the poorer would mean more spending on consumption, less saving, for any given size of the national income. Dr. Hansen told the Temporary National Economic Committee that this "shift to a high consumption economy and a lower savings economy" was already evident in England. This makes strange reading in 1956!

We have here been concerned with the workability under conditions of declining population of the institutions of "capitalism" as we know it. Under strain these institutions are likely to change or to be superseded by institutions more appropriate to the changed conditions.

Population policies. In many European countries positive population policies were adopted. Behind these policies lay generally the military and political interest in man-power for the totalitarian state: perhaps only in Sweden was the economic reason influential, and the liberal doctrine of Malthus and Mill, that the welfare of the individuals in a population is the proper criterion of policy, taken seriously. The following were usual elements in these policies: (1) Repressive legislation against abortion and contraception (Sweden was a notable exception, since along with a positive population policy went state provision of birth-control clinics). (2) Special taxation of bachelors and provision of marriage loans (but in Germany these latter were intended, at first, to take women off the labour market). (3) Family allowances (introduced in France on grounds of social justice but developed and adapted with special attention to their effects on population). (4) In Sweden housing policy was used to promote population growth both by provision of adequate room for larger families, by provision of crèches to relieve the mothers, and by reduction of rent for large families. (5) In Germany an attempt was made to stimulate by propaganda a spontaneous desire on the part of married couples to have numerous children. The effects of these policies seem to have been negligible. "To increase fertility," as Dr. Kuczynski says, "is a gigantic task. Fertility in the territory comprised by Western civilization is so low because most couples want few children. Even if the desire to raise children should not diminish farther, fertility, as a whole, is bound to decrease as the most efficient birth control devices are not universally known. A stop in the downward trend of fertility in the near future is to be expected only from an increasing desire to raise children, and a general desire for more children is hardly to be expected as long as public opinion in most countries does not favour population growth." Public opinion in this matter is changing, "but it is one thing to believe that others should have bigger families, another thing to want a bigger family oneself." It is true that a flood of babies came in the forties, and that fertility may have increased; it is not clear, indeed it seems unlikely, that this change is the result of the population policies here discussed, or of any deliberate policy.

Population growth in Canada. The population of Canada had grown from 2½ millions in 1851 to 11.5 millions in 1941. This growth had not been even but had been marked by two spurts. In the fifties the decennial increase was 33 per cent. In the next four decades the rate of growth was much smaller, and declining. It had fallen to 11 per cent by the end of the century. In the first decade of this century the decennial increase again rose to 33 per cent, but declined thereafter. In the twenties it was 18 per cent; in the thirties it was only 10 per cent. In the eighteen fifties, and in the first quarter of this century conditions existed favourable to a rapid growth of wealth; this meant that rapid population growth *could* take place, and, since immigration was an important source of population growth, it meant that rapid growth *would* take place. For, though we have suggested that birth-rates and death-rates, and consequently rates of population growth, did not respond during the industrial revolution in England to increasing productivity or to increasing wealth, we know that migration is in large measure a response to increased expectation of high earnings in the new country.

The conditions favourable to rapid growth of wealth in a pioneer country are, as was explained in chapter I, high prices for its staple exports and availability of foreign loans at low rates of interest. We noted in chapter III a further reason why high prices of its staple exports are important. Such high prices mean big incomes for the producers of the staples; these incomes are, in large part, spent at home, stimulating production and employment. The effect on its domestic production of a fall in these prices and a consequent reduction in the incomes of the producers of these staple exports would be similar to the effect of their *spending* a smaller proportion of the income previously enjoyed: with prices in the home market partially inflexible less goods could be sold, less goods would be produced, fewer men employed. The effect of a rise in the prices of staples and a consequent increase in the incomes of staple producers would be similar in its stimulating effect on employment to an increase in "investment." Further, the profitability of producing the staples, or things to sell to the producers of those staples, stimulates "investment," expenditure on new plant and equipment, thus increasing still further employment and production. Low prices have the reverse, depressing effect. One important condition of wealth, we have said, is that the resources of the country should be fully employed. This condition is most likely to be fulfilled when the prices of the staple exports are high. These theoretical statements as to the conditions of rapid growth in a pioneer country are supported by the history of Canadian growth.[18]

In the decade 1851-61, the decade of the first of the two spurts in the rate of population growth, the prices of lumber, wheat, and fish were rising; European funds were available at low rates for railway building and other construction; European population growth promised an increasing demand for food while progressive industrialization reduced the numbers growing food. World conditions remained favourable till 1875, but after 1860 Canadian growth lagged: Ontario farm lands were mostly occupied by 1860, and the Homestead Act of 1862 was a prelude to the opening up of the American West. There followed twenty years of falling prices and general depression (1875-95): the prices of Canadian exports fell and large-scale borrowing was impossible. The upturn in prices, and improvement in prosperity which began about 1896 brought a new period of expansion in Canada. The prices of her staple exports were rising, and particularly important was the rising price of wheat. There was renewed interest in foreign investment, and in Canada as a borrower: funds were available at low rates, and steel, needed in vast quantities for railway building, etc., was cheap as a result of technological advance. Western settlement in the United States was nearly complete; and the essential technical problems of wheat production in the Canadian prairie had been solved with the invention of the chilled steel plough, with the development of dry farming practice, with the selection of early maturing wheat, with the completion of the transcontinental railway, and with the establishment of lines of elevators. The rapid growth of the Canadian West in the decade 1901-11 is not, then, surprising. But

[18]See W. A. Mackintosh, *The Economic Background of Dominion-Provincial Relations*, appendix 3 of the *Report of the Royal Commission on Dominion-Provincial Relations* (Ottawa, 1940). Cf. J. B. Condliffe, *New Zealand in the Making*, chap. I.

it is important to notice the stimulating effect of western expansion on other parts of Canada; prairie farmers bought lumber from British Columbia and manufactures from Ontario and Quebec. The high level of exporters' incomes induced heavy spending, and the obvious opportunities for profit and the general optimism induced capital formation on a considerable scale. There was, therefore, general Canadian expansion: but the impetus came from Europe.

Prospects for future growth by natural increase. Looking forward in the thirties it seemed likely that the Canadian population would grow but slowly, and would probably stop growing by the end of the century. Twenty millions seemed likely to be the limit of growth. Professor Burton Hurd[19] made a projection of the Canadian population similar to that of Dr. Charles for England. His estimate was based on the assumptions of no immigration, fertility rates as in the period 1931-6, and mortality rates as in the 1931 Life Tables. The result is shown in Table V. This projection shows a population for 1971 of 15.4 millions. This is a considerable absolute increase, but the rate of

TABLE V

ESTIMATE OF FUTURE POPULATION OF CANADA, ASSUMING NO IMMIGRATION, AND NO CHANGE IN FERTILITY OR MORTALITY

	Population (millions)	Percentage increase in previous decade
1931	10.4	18
1941	11.6	11
1951	13.0	11
1961	14.3	10
1971	15.4	8

growth over the thirty years 1941-71 would be slow[20] compared with that of the previous three decades, and it would be decreasing. Professor Hurd thought that the fertility rates on which this estimate was based were abnormally low owing to postponement of marriage in the depression; he therefore doubted whether the decline in fertility would be greater than could be counteracted by the further decline in mortality. The continued existence of differences between the fertility of rural and urban regions, and between French Catholic and English Protestant regions, suggested the probability of further decline in

[19]W. Burton Hurd, "Some Implications of Prospective Population Changes in Canada" (*Canadian Journal of Economics and Political Science*, Nov., 1939).

[20]The net reproduction rate for Canada was 1.39 in 1930-2 and had fallen to 1.27 by 1940-2. There are wide differences between the provinces: New Brunswick (1.6) stood in 1940-42 at the top of the list, British Columbia (1.07) at the bottom. The rate for Quebec was 1.45, that for Ontario, 1.12.

average fertility as the evening down process, evident in class differentials, took place.[21]

Prospects for future growth by immigration. The difficulty of forecasting migration is much greater than that of forecasting natural increase. Unpredictable technological changes are likely to induce shifts of population within national boundaries and across these boundaries. More unpredictable political influences operate to promote, or more often to prevent, the readjustment of population to changed economic circumstances. It seemed likely in the thirties that Canadian immigration would not be very great in the next few decades. Two lines of reasoning leading to this guess may be noted.[22]

We considered first whether conditions favourable to growth, such as existed in the eighteen-fifties and in the first quarter of this century, were likely to be repeated. The expectation of declining population in Europe, and declining rate of growth in the United States, was not favourable for such repetition. A decline in population would involve reduced consumption of certain staples, e.g. wheat. It seemed likely to involve, as we have seen, a condition of general depression unfavourable for the prices of staples, which are highly sensitive. New policies might, indeed, be devised to counteract these depressing influences, but among these policies economic nationalism seemed destined to be an early selection, and it was calculated to make more difficult the role of the staple exporter. Low prices of staples would cause depression in Canada through reduced incomes of the exporters and so reduced expenditure on consumables and reduced expenditure on the maintenance and improvement of equipment.

Secondly, we noticed that in the decade 1901–11, with the most favourable conditions, and with a flood of immigrants, the average annual increase was only 180,000. In the next two decades with the stimulus of war production and war-time prices, and with the

[21]A rough measure of the decline in fertility has to be derived from the Census in the absence of adequate statistics of births in Canada. The number of children aged 0-4 in each census year per 1,000 women aged 15-45 has decreased from 614 in 1881 to 467 in 1931. This same rough measure of fertility makes it possible to compare fertilities in 1931 among the English and French in Canada, and between rural and urban population. The number of children aged 0-4 per 1,000 women aged 15-45 was in 1931: rural English 480; rural French 751: English in cities over 30,000, 298; French in cities over 30,000, 429.

[22]See also W. J. Waines, *Prairie Population Possibilities*, one of the mimeographed research studies of the Royal Commission on Dominion-Provincial Relations (Ottawa, 1939); also H. F. Angus (ed.), *Canada and the Doctrine of Peaceful Change* (mimeo., Toronto, 1937), chap. II, "The Ability of Canada to Receive Immigration"; and Mabel F. Timlin, *Does Canada Need More People?* (Oxford, 1951).

emergence of new staples such as pulp and paper and various minerals, the average yearly increase was 160,000. It was hard to envisage an absolute increase much bigger than this in the next few decades and natural increase would provide a yearly increase of some 130,000. In the period of rapid growth through immigration, emigration to the United States was easy, emigration of Canadians and re-emigration of immigrants. In the thirty years 1901–31 natural increase in Canada was 3.3 millions, and immigration was 5.1 millions; the population of Canada might then have grown by 8.4 millions. The actual growth of population was 5 millions, so there must have been emigration of 3.4 millions. What Canada lost was, probably, half a million Canadians, and three of the five million immigrants. This suggests that the limit to population growth was not availability of people, but economic absorptive capacity.

Thirdly, we noticed the possibility that migration might be inhibited by political influence: the "struggle for population" in Europe suggested that many nations would be unwilling to accelerate their decline in numbers by permitting emigration, and in the absence of full employment in Canada political pressure would limit the admission of immigrants. It appeared, in conclusion, that unless the problems of economic adjustment were solved, immigration would be likely to reduce the standard of living of Canadians generally, to depress native fertility rates ("substituting the colonist car for the cradle") to increase mortality through the influence of poverty, and probably not greatly to increase the rate of growth over two or three decades.

Renewal of population growth: Canada. The Canadian estimates of future population growth made in the thirties, like those made in Great Britain, and in the United States, have proved very wrong. After 1940 ten years of high employment, high marriage-rates, high birth-rates and renewed immigration led to a 19 per cent increase in the Canadian population (excluding Newfoundland); and in the one year 1951 population grew 3 per cent. The birth-rate which had fallen in the thirties to 21 per thousand was over 27 in every year from 1946 to 1952 and over 28 in 1953; the rate of natural increase rose from 11 per thousand in the thirties to 18 in the late forties and 19.5 in 1953. It is, of course, impossible to determine yet whether fertility has really increased, whether the size of the completed families will be larger. But in Canada as in the United States the high birth-rate has persisted longer than in Great Britain. During this period immigration has continued at a rate of about 110,000 per year. Looking forward in 1956 it seems likely that the population will grow rapidly in the next twenty years: a forecast of 25 millions (including Newfoundland, which had in 1951 a population of some 360,000) in 1975 seems not unreasonable.[23] This depends of course on the maintenance of peace, and of a high level of economic activity. Here the changed population outlook in the United States, and in the world generally, becomes important. In place of the pessimism of the thirties we find optimism in the fifties. "If the picture of world and particularly U.S. demand for raw materials depicted in the Paley Report is at all valid," said the *Monthly Review* of the Bank of Nova Scotia in July, 1953, "the long term outlook for Canada's basic exports is a strong one."

Meanwhile a large part of the non-Western world is experiencing very rapid population growth as the decline in mortality which took place in England over nearly two centuries is telescoped for these countries into a few decades. For them Malthus is more relevant than the population literature of the thirties.[24]

[23]See *The Future Population of Canada 1955 to 1975*, Canadian Economic Research Associates, Technical Reference Paper No. 1 (Toronto, 1955); also the *Monthly Review* of the Bank of Nova Scotia, June–July, 1953 ("Twenty-five Million Canadians") and July, 1954 ("Canada's Changing Population").

[24]See Kingsley Davis, "The Amazing Decline of Mortality in Underdeveloped Areas" (*American Economic Review*, XLVI, 2, May, 1956), pp. 305–18. "The rapidity with which the death rate has declined in most of the underdeveloped areas . . . has been unprecedented. It has never been matched at any time in the now advanced countries. . . . The best known case is that of Ceylon. There the crude death rate fell by 34 per cent in one year (from 1946–1947). This was no fluke because the death rate continued to fall. In 1945 the rate was 22.0 per 1000 population, which was about normal for the country . . . in 1954 it was down to 10.4 per 1000, a reduction of 53 per cent in nine years." The significance of this decline in the death-rate depends on the response of the birth-rate and on the rate of economic growth. In this context it is important to note a further statement by Professor Davis: "The reduction could be rapid because it did not depend on general economic development or social modernization in the underdeveloped areas. It did not depend on training local medical personnel, or local research, or local prosperity. It was an example of a rapid cultural diffusion of death-control techniques which did not depend on the diffusion of other cultural elements, or basic changes in the institutions and customs of the people affected."

CHAPTER VI

WHEAT IN THE CANADIAN ECONOMY

WHEN the Canadian government purchased the territories of the Hudson's Bay Company in 1870, they contained a white population of less than 7,000 (of which 5,000 were half-breeds) and an Indian population of 50,000. The area was given over to the fur trade; barely 9,000 acres were cultivated to supply some food for the fur traders. By 1931 this same area had a population of nearly 2½ million, and had 110 million acres occupied, of which 25 million acres were under wheat. In the twenties it produced on the average 360 million bushels of wheat annually, worth some $500 million. This wheat was mostly for export. Its export over the first thirty years of the century provided a basis for the rapid growth of Canadian wealth and population. It provided a means of paying for imported goods which could not have been made, or could have been made only with great difficulty, in Canada. It also provided a basis for foreign borrowing by promising a means by which foreign money could later be acquired to pay interest and repay loans. In Canada the spending of the incomes of the wheat farmers stimulated production, and so did the spending of borrowed funds to build up the equipment of the farms, to provide transportation facilities for handling the grain, to furnish roads, schools, hospitals, churches, and all the equipment of social life. In this period wheat played the dynamic role in the development of Canada. This has been indicated briefly in the last chapter; it is discussed rather more fully in the first part of this chapter.

But if prosperity and stimulus came through wheat in the period 1900-30, depression and discouragement came through wheat in the thirties. The greater part of this chapter will deal with the later, less happy, phase. Drought and low prices combined in this decade to reduce the value of wheat exports by $200 or $300 million and to reduce the incomes of wheat producers to a point where relief became essential. The drastic reduction of current purchases by the wheat producers, and the practical cessation of expenditure on expanding equipment, had depressing effects on the incomes of other Canadian producers. We shall examine the causes, the effects, and the policies adopted to mitigate the ill effects, of this collapse of the wheat economy. At the end of the chapter we shall consider briefly the problems of wheat in World War II and in the post-war world.

The progress of settlement. The Canadian prairie is the north-central part of the great American plain. The settlement of this plain was a continuous process, the determining factors being physical and economic. Settlement north of the international boundary would probably have taken place at roughly the same date if it had been merely a state boundary. The political element was not completely absent, nor completely ineffectual, but it is unlikely that it had much effect on the timing of the settlement of the Canadian West.

The rapid settlement of the American plain can be explained: (1) by the suitability of its soil and climate for the production of wheat, and the great productivity of virgin soil; (2) by the development of cheap transportation by sea and land;[1] (3) by the development of mechanized agriculture to which the topography of the plain was particularly adaptable and which the short growing season made imperative; (4) by the provision of free, or cheap, land under the Homestead Act of 1862; and (5) by the flow of immigration from eastern North America and from Europe. The part played by the demand for wheat is more difficult to determine. In the period 1870-1900 cheap American wheat, cheap because of its low cost of production, drove English farmers out of wheat production.[2] In such periods expansion was based mainly on the discovery of a cheaper source of supply, rather than on an increasing demand. While American wheat acreage was expanding, the wheat acreage in Great Britain declined from 3.6 million acres in 1874 to 1.4 million acres in 1904, and this in spite of the growing demand for wheat as population grew. Many of the displaced wheat farmers of England, and of eastern North America, joined the stream of settlement which flowed west, preferring to grow wheat elsewhere rather than to grow new products at home. The others turned to develop the production of what were formerly by-products: "the development of the milk trade, dairying, pasture farming, flower growing, market-gardening, poultry-keeping, is," says Lord Ernle, "characteristic of the new period." After 1900 rising prices of wheat, an indication of relative scarcity,

[1]Professor Clapham gives the following estimates of the cost of carriage of wheat from Chicago to Liverpool: 1868-79, 11s. per quarter; 1880, 9s. 1½d. per quarter; 1886, 6s. 2½d. per quarter; 1892, 4s. 3d. per quarter; 1902, 2s. 10½d.

[2]For the reaction on England see J. H. Clapham, *An Economic History of Modern Britain* (Toronto, 1931-8), vol. III, chap. II; also Lord Ernle (R. E. Prothero), *English Farming Past and Present* (London, 1922), chap. XVIII.

accelerated settlement of the better lands and permitted the extension of settlement to less favourable regions. Such extension of settlement was promoted also by technical progress which further reduced the cost as, one after another, the new handicaps which were encountered were overcome. Higher wheat prices thus accelerated the process of settlement which lower costs, through the progress of knowledge, constantly promoted. In this period wheat acreage in England increased a little, to 1.9 million acres in 1914, which "shows how ready farmers were to plant the old staple crop, given the slightest encouragement by price." The growing demand for the new products, as population grew and as the standard of living of the industrial workers rose, had mitigated the effect on English farmers of American competition in wheat; but they had clearly been forced out of wheat, not attracted into dairying.

Settlement and railways. The part played by railway building and its relation to prices must also be noted. The possibility of cheap transportation through the development of the technique of transcontinental railway building was, as we have noted above, a condition of this settlement. The actual building of particular railways to open up particular wheat regions, while a condition of the settlement of those regions, was only undertaken because of the expectation that wheat could, and would soon, be profitably grown there. The rate of railway construction depended on the expected rate of growth of settlement. High prices of wheat raised the expectations of the railway builders and so accelerated the provision of that necessary condition of rapid settlement. The fact that high prices of wheat have been associated with periods of prosperity and optimism makes the connection of high wheat prices and rapid railway construction more intimate, for in such periods investors were in a mood to believe the promise of profitable operation.

The spread north and west. From 1870 to 1895 the trend of wheat prices was downward, and business in general was depressed. The settlement of the American prairie continued, but at a slower rate. The spread of settlement west and north on the American plain is described by H. A. Faulkner:

The frontier stretched in 1860 not far from the 95th meridian. By 1880 the line ran along the western boundary of Minnesota, jutting out in Nebraska and Kansas to beyond the 100th meridian, back to the western boundary of Arkansas and west again through Texas beyond the 97th meridian. The next two decades marked the rapid occupation of Minnesota, the Dakotas, Montana, and western Nebraska, giving warrant in 1890 for the declaration of the Superintendent of Census that the frontier no longer existed. By that time most of our good arable land had been taken up. . . . Good free land might be gone, but after 1890 there was still a large amount of inferior land which, with modern methods, might be made productive, and there was an abundance of cheap land still available; and for those who still desired high-grade free land, it was possible, as thousands did, to emigrate to Canada.[3]

Thorstein Veblen, writing in 1892, stated the position as follows:

While we have by no means reached—or nearly reached—the limit of the possible extension of the wheat area in America, it is probably true that we are fast approaching the point beyond which there is no considerable additional amount of wheat lands equally fertile and otherwise equally available with the last ten or twenty million acres already brought under cultivation. It can hardly be said that the spread of cultivation in America during the past 10 or 12 years has been to less fertile or less available lands; but for the next 10 or 12 years . . . any considerable further spread of the area of cultivation cannot take place without recourse to less available lands.[4]

After 1895 the price of wheat showed a marked upward trend in spite of increasing supplies; the result was an acceleration of railway building, settlement, and the extension of wheat production. The settlers having come to the end of the good land available for homesteading in the United States crossed the border to Canada, the Canadians who had been going to the American prairie went to the Canadian prairie, and a flood of European immigrants went there through Canadian ports. The relative disadvantages of the northern prairie compared with that further south had been partially overcome. The shortness of the growing season as the farmer went further north was met by selecting early maturing spring wheats, just as spring wheat had replaced the winter wheat of the East as settlement spread north on the western plain. "The general introduction of Red Fife wheat by 1900, of Marquis by 1912, and of Garnet and Reward wheats by 1929 mark," says Dr. Mackintosh, "definite stages in the northward progress of wheat growing." The other disadvantage, relative shortage of moisture, was shared by large parts of the American plain and had been met by the development of dry farming, i.e. methods of farming calculated to conserve moisture. The methods for an attack on the Canadian prairie were, then, ready to hand: and the disadvantages were themselves in part advantages, which became more important about the turn of the century. The climatic conditions

[3]*American Economic History* (New York, 1938), p. 436.
[4]"The Food Supply and the Price of Wheat" (*Journal of Political Economy,* June, 1893); see also his article on "The Price of Wheat Since 1867" (*ibid.,* Dec., 1892).

which made it difficult to grow wheat, made the wheat that was grown of a superlative quality. It was hard wheat, and the introduction of the gradual reduction process of flour milling in the last quarter of the nineteenth century enabled the modern miller to make more desirable flour out of hard wheats than out of soft. Hard wheat thus came to command a premium over soft. Before 1880 soft wheat had commanded a premium at Liverpool of 5 to 10 cents per bushel over hard American spring wheat; by 1890 hard spring wheat commanded a premium of from 1 to 5 cents per bushel over soft wheat. Finally, one may notice certain purely Canadian, or political, influences: the completion of the St. Lawrence Canals reduced the cost of carriage at one stage; the provision of adequate aids to navigation, lighthouses, etc., in the Gulf of St. Lawrence brought down marine insurance rates; government support to railway builders accelerated the provision of transportation facilities, and by such arrangements as the Crows Nest Pass Agreement (1897) and the Manitoba Agreement (1901) the government assured low railway rates on wheat; finally, an aggressive immigration policy guaranteed that settlement would not slow down for lack of settlers. Under the influence of a definite upward trend of wheat prices the settlement of the Canadian prairie proceeded steadily in the fifteen years before the War of 1914-18. The upward trend of prices at Winnipeg is shown by the following five-year averages: 1895-9, 76 cents per bushel; 1900-4, 79 cents; 1905-9, 93 cents; 1910-14, 96 cents. The increase in acreage under wheat was from 2½ million acres in 1900 to 10 million acres in 1913.[5]

Acceleration due to war. The war, 1914-18, greatly accelerated the development of wheat production in Canada and in the United States, and the increase continued in the post-war years. War, blockade, and later, social revolution and monetary chaos, combined to reduce the wheat acreage in the European wheat-exporting countries between 1914 and 1921 from some 95 million acres to some 55 million acres. At the same time European importing countries, especially France and Italy, reduced their acreage by about 5 million acres, or 10 per cent. The high cost of marine insurance and freight in wartime put Australia and Argentina at a relative disadvantage, and consequently the task of meeting the European demand for wheat

[5]For a more detailed account of the spread of settlement on the Canadian prairie see W. A. Mackintosh, *Economic Problems of the Prairie Provinces* (Toronto, 1935), especially chap. I, "Economic Trends"; and W. A. Mackintosh, *Prairie Settlement, the Geographic Setting* (Toronto, 1934), especially chaps. II, III, and IV.

devolved largely upon Canada and the United States. In Canada acreage increased by about 12 million acres, and in the United States by about 15 million acres. European importing countries after the war were importing a slightly higher proportion of their wheat requirement, and were importing 98 per cent from overseas where they had before the war bought only 50 per cent of their smaller requirement. This tremendous shift owing to the cataclysm of war was reinforced by technical changes in wheat production on the American plains. The development of the small cheap tractor after 1916 not only reduced cost but also released for wheat production a great acreage of land previously required to grow oats for horses which were used as a source of power. The combine, rather later, partially overcame the handicap of high labour costs; harvester excursions to the West became a thing of the past. The war prices were high: the average price per bushel of No. 1 Northern at Winnipeg was in 1914-15, $1.32; in 1915-16, $1.13; in 1916-17, $2.06; in 1917-18, $2.21; 1918-19, $2.24; in 1919-20, $2.18. It is true that all other prices were rising, so that wheat did not exchange for much more of the things farmers wanted to buy with the proceeds of the sale of their wheat. But the debts of the past, direct debts of the farmers and their indirect debts as taxpayers in the municipalities that had borrowed to build schools, roads, etc., were lightened as the debt charges could be met by the sale of fewer bushels of wheat. High prices were the main stimulus, but patriotic appeal to grow more food for the Allies was a further stimulus, while advancing technique facilitated expansion.

In this war-time extension of wheat production there were elements of weakness. First, it seems likely that under the stimulus of high prices instead of pressing on to the discovery of new good land (of which there was not much left) poorer quality land (which had been passed by) was now broken. Improved technique was reducing costs over the whole American plain; but in spite of improved methods much of this new acreage was scarcely capable of producing wheat at prices low enough to drive Europeans permanently to abandon wheat production on the scale that war made them abandon it. Trouble might be expected, then, when Europe settled down to peace-time agriculture again. Secondly, farmers incurred debts on the basis of war-time wheat prices which would become most burdensome if prices fell. Wheat prices, and prices of things wheat farmers wanted to buy did both fall after the war. The fall in wheat prices immediately increased the burden of these debts, while the greater fall in the price of wheat than in the prices of other commodities was a further blow. The results of these weaknesses were delayed in action by the continual fall in costs with improving technique, and by the slow recovery of Europe, especially of Russia.

Readjustment after the war. The consequences for Canada of the stabilization of Europe's agriculture on a peace-time basis were made a little more serious by the slower rate of population growth, by dietary changes which reduced the per capita consumption of wheat, and by a change in consumers' habits and bakers' techniques which reduced the preference for hard wheat. But political influences enormously intensified the difficulties. European governments were not prepared to allow the competitive struggle to eliminate, or reduce to dire poverty, their wheat farmers. The part played by the food blockade in the last war made clear the military danger of dependence on foreign food without command of the sea. The part played by the peasants in maintaining the social order was equally clear, and gave further reason for assistance to the farmer. Cheap wheat might prove dear in terms of social life. By 1929 only the United Kingdom, Eire, Belgium, and Holland admitted wheat without the payment of substantial import duties. After 1929 the protection of agriculture, and of wheat in particular, became greatly intensified. The story was told by Dr. Mackintosh in an article in the *Queen's Quarterly* in the autumn of 1939:[6]

This rapid movement toward the protection of European grain growers had very wide political and social ramifications. In the period immediately after the war Europe experienced a most violent economic and social disorganization. Bolshevism surging westward from Russia threatened existing institutions throughout the whole of Western Europe. More conservative elements gradually gained the upper hand, but they did so with the support of the agrarian and peasant populations as a balance against the more radical urban populations of those countries. Agrarian protection was not merely a matter of improving the position of one group at the expense of another, it was in the eyes of governments, a major bulwark of order against chaos. . . . From the time of the repeal of the Corn Laws, the United Kingdom had been the great free market for wheat. In 1932, however, having reversed her historic policy, she adopted the Wheat Marketing Act for the protection of her own producers. She imposed a tax on flour, the proceeds of which were to be used to bonus the production of wheat. By this means she gives to her wheat producers a price of about $1.30 per bushel when wheat is selling in Liverpool at about 50 cents. On the average her production seems to have increased by about a third, but she still remains the world's greatest importer of wheat.

Previously, Italy had been the largest importer of wheat, but in the latter half of the last decade Mussolini initiated his "battle of the grain" with the object of raising Italian wheat production. The measures then adopted were greatly extended with the onset of the crisis, and Italian

[6]"The Crisis in Wheat" (*Queen's Quarterly*, autumn, 1939).

imports of wheat have been reduced by about 78 per cent. By these measures the Italian farmer receives about $2.00 per bushel for the wheat grown. Production in an average year seems to have increased by about 25 per cent, while consumption has been reduced about 10 per cent by substituting other grains for wheat in the making of flour.

After Italy, Germany had been one of the greatest import markets for wheat. A multiplicity of protective measures now give to the German wheat producer a price of rather more than $2.00 a bushel. Wheat production has risen spectacularly by as much as 75 per cent, while the mixing of rye, cornmeal, and potato flour in the making of flour and bread has reduced the consumption of wheat. Increasingly, such wheat as Germany imports is drawn from the Danube countries, with which she has her most successful trade agreements.

France has never been so great nor so dependable a market for imported wheat as have Italy and Germany. She was, however, normally an importer to a small amount, and in years of less than average yields she was an important buyer. Imports of about 50 million bushels have in her case sunk to negligible amounts, and in some recent years she has been a formidable exporter.

The progress of this protectionist movement is well shown in Table I, taken from a League of Nations report on *Agricultural Protectionism*[7] which shows the prices paid for home-grown wheat in Germany, France, and Italy as a percentage of the price of imported wheat at Liverpool. In the "liberal" world of the nineteenth century, in which we may include the first quarter of this century, there was a reasonable

TABLE I

GOLD PRICES OF HOME-GROWN WHEAT AS A PERCENTAGE OF THE GOLD PRICE OF IMPORTED WHEAT IN ENGLAND

	Germany	France	Italy
1928	104	118	132
1929	106	116	135
1930	155	148	169
1931	253	291	226
1932	261	276	270
1933	250	243	269
1934	276	300	268

expectation that wheat production would be gladly left to the countries that could produce it most cheaply. For the "liberal" economists, particularly those living in the great oversea exporting countries, it has been difficult to conceive of the reversal of this position as anything but the triumph of unreason, or as anything but temporary. How little the trend was appreciated is indicated by the continued growth in wheat acreage through the twenties: in 1929 the wheat acreage in Canada reached 25 million acres and the wheat acreage in the United

[7]Geneva, 1936.

States again approached the level of 1921, nearly 65 million acres. The conflict arising from these liberal views and a realization of the military and social reasons for preferring *dear* home-grown to *cheap* imported wheat is illustrated in Dr. Mackintosh's article, "The Crisis in Wheat":

It is quite obvious that Europe can obtain its wheat much more cheaply, and feed its populations better by obtaining more of its wheat from overseas and less from its own growers. Under such circumstances Europe would consume somewhat more wheat, but the important gain to her population would not be in additional wheat consumed, though the bread in Italy, Germany, and elsewhere has deteriorated greatly both in nutritional value and in palatableness in the last decade. The great gain which these populations would achieve would be in the release of land for the production of the highly important protective foods—meats, dairy products, and green vegetables. It is here that the great decline in the standard of European nutrition has taken place. The high prices for wheat artificially maintained have diverted land from the growing of other crops and have raised the prices of all feed grains, with the result that it is less profitable to produce livestock and vegetable products. These agricultural activities have suffered while grain growing has expanded. Thus Germany has been for a number of years notoriously short of butter and animal fats generally. Only in a limited fashion has the choice before Germany been Goering's famous "guns or butter." More fundamentally, the choice has been homegrown bread grains and butter. . . .

Such a rational economic solution is fantastic in the world of today where unreason triumphs over reason and politics is dominant over economics. Those countries which were formerly great wheat importing countries are now almost exclusively war economies. Granted the objective of war and military power, their policies with respect to wheat are not completely irrational. By curtailing imports of wheat they can greatly reduce their dependence on potential enemies and unfriendly neutrals. True, they reduce the standards of living of their populations, but that is unavoidable if war is the objective. Even though by some miracle the threat of war should pass, the adoption of such a rational economic policy would be hampered by many obstacles. Great vested groups have been built up behind the protective policy and only in highly stable and politically mature countries can readjustments be made against the resistance of such vested interests. It is difficult to see, when one realizes the political importance of agrarian groups in European regimes, how so great a shift could be accomplished except over a long period.

The enormous increase in the productive power of modern economic society has also to be taken into account: in the nineteenth century the European nations were still poor enough for cheap wheat to be of great significance, in the twentieth century many of them are wealthy enough for the extravagance of dear home-grown wheat to be insignificant.[8]

[8]"It is in the richest and most industrious countries that they [restraints upon imports] have been most generally imposed. No other countries could support

The wheat economy of Saskatchewan. In order to simplify the story, and to draw attention to the special problems which arise from intense regional specialization, we shall restrict our discussion in the greater part of this chapter to the Province of Saskatchewan. This enables us to utilize more fully the excellent study of *The Wheat Economy*[9] by Professor G. E. Britnell. In this province 66 per cent of the land annually seeded to field crops is devoted to wheat, and in some regions this rises to 80, and even 90, per cent. Ordinarily over the whole province 80 per cent of the cash receipts from farming come from the sale of wheat, and, of course, in some regions this rises to almost 100 per cent. Some understanding of the physical and economic basis of this specialization is essential; it will therefore be necessary to examine some of the physical characteristics of the region. We want some explanation of the lateness of the development of wheat production, of the success of that development in the first thirty years of the century, of the extreme concentration of wheat production to the exclusion of alternative agricultural products, and of the hazardous nature of wheat production in Saskatchewan. Though the emphasis will be on the physical factors, it will be found impossible to isolate them from the economic, social, or political factors.

The climate of Saskatchewan. The settled area of Saskatchewan can be divided into three distinct economic zones determined by climate and characterized by soil. The southern zone is the prairie plains, but this in turn requires sub-dividing into two zones. The "Brown Prairie" zone occupies the south-western portion of the province; its light soils with low organic content and thin cover of short grass reflect the light and highly variable rainfall of that region. This is, or should be, mainly ranching country; it represents the fringe of the northern end of the American desert. It was collision with these more arid lands that turned settlement north-west, rather than continuing west. North and east of the short grass prairie lies a transition belt of dark brown soil, whose somewhat heavier soils and heavier cover of short grass reflect somewhat higher and more reliable rainfall. This is the soil, and the climate, of the spring wheat belt proper. North and east again is the "park belt" with taller grasses, and scattered clumps of trees. The soil is darker, with a higher organic content and with a more luxuriant cover, reflecting still higher and more reliable rainfall. Wheat can still be grown successfully, but not wheat of the

---

so great a disorder. As the strongest bodies only can live and enjoy health, under an unwholesome regimen; so the nations only, that in every sort of industry have the greatest natural and acquired advantages, can subsist and prosper under such taxes" (Adam Smith, *The Wealth of Nations*, 1776).
    [9]Toronto, 1939.

SKETCH MAP OF MAIN SOIL ZONES OF SASKATCHEWAN

(1) Brown soils, short grass prairie; (2) dark brown soils, intermediate prairie; (3) black soils, tall grass or park region; (4) gray soils, wooded region.

This map is reproduced, by permission, from G. E. Britnell, *The Wheat Economy,* which also contains interesting photographs of land in these regions (plates 1 and 2), q.v.

same high quality: on the other hand, coarse grains and forage crops can be grown with great success. Still further north is a more heavily wooded region with gray soils, low in nitrogen and phosphorus, unsuited to grain growing.

"In the wheat belt of Canada," says Dr. Mackintosh, "agriculture is carried on close to the minimum conditions requisite for its success. Over the greater part of the region it is necessary to conserve moisture . . . the margin of safety . . . is comparatively narrow."[10] The necessary minimum annual precipitation for wheat production is about 12 inches:[11] the mean annual precipitation on the plains varies from 11 to 15 inches, and in the park belt from 14 to 19. But the amount of rain falling during the growing season is of even greater significance for wheat production, 7½ inches in this season being a minimum requirement. It is found that the proportion of the annual precipitation falling in the growing season increases as the annual precipitation decreases. Thus at Winnipeg out of a total mean precipitation of 20 inches, 12 inches fall between April 1 and September 1; at Medicine Hat out of a total precipitation of 13 inches, 8 inches fall between those dates. Evaporation must also be considered, and loss of moisture from this cause increases towards the region of hot winds to the southwest. But all this is in terms of yearly averages, averages which conceal very different degrees of variability. Dr. Mackintosh finds that the rainfall becomes more variable, and less reliable as it becomes less; and that the warm season rainfall is more variable than the annual rainfall. The result of this climatic variability is, of course, very great variation in the size of crops; and, since the margin of safety is so small, complete crop failures are liable to occur.

As the settler moves north the moisture problem becomes less, but the frost problem more serious. The chief danger is the summer frost. The growing season, the average number of days between the date when seeding is general and the date of the first killing frost (29° or less), varies from 145 days in the south to 130 days in the north. But even in the south the growing season is so short as to require specially early maturing wheat, and this average conceals further variation. Early frosts are an annual hazard. The danger is greatest in the north, but occasionally is more widespread.

Returning to the questions with which we began this section, we see that geographic, especially climatic, conditions give a clue to the

[10]See Mackintosh, *Prairie Settlement, the Geographic Setting*, especially chaps. I and IX.

[11]It is estimated by one authority quoted by Dr. Mackintosh that "under average dry farming conditions . . . each inch of annual precipitation between six and eighteen inches represents about 2.5 bushels of wheat per acre in a crop year."

answers. The development was late because the better lands to the south were first used up and the techniques requisite to exploitation of the more northerly lands were progressively developed as the southern lands were occupied. The development was successful because this climate was peculiarly suitable to producing, with the new techniques, hard wheat, and yields from the virgin land were heavy. But economic and political conditions conspired with climatic conditions to achieve this success: prices were favourable, tremendously favourable during the war, and Europe seemed prepared to allow America to grow her wheat, as long as it was grown cheaply. The extreme concentration on wheat is to be explained largely by the impossibility of other types of settled agriculture in view of the deficiency of water. The choice was ranching or wheat over a wide area. Other cereals need more moisture than wheat, hay crops still more. But even if it had been technically possible to practise mixed farming the cost of transporting the product to the centres of population, and the handicap of the long winter, would have made it economically impossible to compete. Finally, we have seen something of the physical hazards of wheat production; we shall later have to add to drought and frost, hail, rust, weeds, and grasshoppers.

The wheat economy of Saskatchewan, 1926-37. In this section we shall examine in more detail the trend of production and prices and

TABLE II
SELECT STATISTICS OF THE WHEAT ECONOMY OF SASKATCHEWAN, 1926-37

	(1)	(2)	(3)	(4)	(5)	(6)	(7)
Year	Wheat acreage (*million acres*)	Wheat production (*million bushels*)	Wheat yield (*bushels per acre*)	Average price at farm (*per bushel*)	Value of wheat sold off the farm (*million dollars*)	Total value of all produce sold off the farm (*million dollars*)	Net income of farmers after deducting depreciation (*million dollars*)
1926..	13.6	220	16	$1.08	240	289	204
1927..	13.0	253	20	0.97	216	270	184
1928..	13.8	321	23	0.77	256	319	228
1929..	14.4	161	11	1.03	184	243	158
1930..	14.7	207	14	0.47	87	124	34
1931..	15.0	132	9	0.38	44	70	−8
1932..	15.5	212	14	0.35	55	73	−7
1933..	14.7	128	9	0.47	53	73	4
1934..	13.3	114	9	0.61	61	92	20
1935..	13.2	142	11	0.60	75	108	36
1936..	14.7	110	8	0.92	76	119	60
1937..	13.9	37	3	1.05	37	85	23

The data for columns (1)-(4) from G. E. Britnell, *The Wheat Economy* (Toronto, 1939), for columns (5)-(7) from D. C. MacGregor *et al.*, *National Income*, appendix IV to the *Report of the Royal Commission on Dominion-Provincial Relations* (Ottawa, 1940).

the consequent fortunes of the wheat producers, in the highly specialized region of Saskatchewan, and in the most troubled period, 1926–
37.[12] The relevant statistics are assembled in Table II. Wheat acreage
in Saskatchewan grew from half a million acres in 1900 to 5½ million
acres in 1913. During the war, and immediate post-war years, the
acreage increased to 13½ millions, and remained relatively steady between 12¼ and 13¼ millions till 1928. The rise in acreage from 1929 to
a peak of 15¼ millions in 1932 is to be explained in part as the slow
fulfilment of plans laid in the optimistic twenties, partly to the hope
that in the next year a good yield and a good price would recoup the
farmers' losses. The decline in acreage in 1934 and 1935 is probably
to be explained largely in terms of the lack of funds to pay the cost
of cultivation, but also in terms of the discouragement of low yields
and low prices.

Drought. The physical hazards of wheat production and the consequent unintended and unpredictable variation in output are shown in
columns (2) and (3) of Table II. The main cause of the variation in
yield was the prolonged drought in the southern part of the
province where most of the wheat acreage lay. From the point of
view of the province as a whole the fall in yields, and therefore of
output, is serious enough, but when we consider particular districts
great variation is discovered, and the condition of some districts is
found to have been appalling. In 1931 in the large crop districts in the
south yields were from 2 to 6 bushels; only the heavy yields in the
north (23 bushels around North Battleford) kept the provincial average
as high as 9 bushels per acre. In 1932 there was some improvement,
but yields remained below the average. In 1933 the average yield was
slightly less than in 1931; on the plains where 60 per cent of the wheat
acreage is found the yield averaged 4 bushels per acre, in the park belt
with 40 per cent of the acreage yields averaged 15 bushels per acre.
The grasshoppers were especially destructive in this year, destroying
some 18 per cent of the provincial crop, and completely destroying
such crop as there was in some of the southern districts. Again in 1934
the yield in the southern districts averaged 4 bushels per acre, and in
many districts harvests were too poor to return seed. In the park belt
yields remained satisfactory and half of the Saskatchewan crop came
from the one-fifth of the provincial wheat acreage lying in that belt.
Prospects for relief from drought seemed good in 1935, but rust in the
east, continued drought in the west, and frost in the north did tremendous damage. Rust completely destroyed one-quarter of the wheat

[12]See Mackintosh, *Economic Problems of the Prairie Provinces*, chaps. II and
x; also Britnell, *The Wheat Economy*, pp. 48-79, or G. E. Britnell, "Saskatchewan,
1930-35" (*Canadian Journal of Economics and Political Science*, Feb., 1936).

that was growing, and reduced the yield and quality of much more. Drought again hit in 1936, and in 1937 caused the most complete crop failure since the settlement of the country.

The meaning of this long period of drought in what has been, and probably will be again, a great wheat-producing area is brought home by the following description of a journey through part of the district, published in the *Regina Leader-Post* and quoted by Dr. Britnell:

We entered Saskatchewan at Antler . . . and from there to Stoughton, a distance of more than 50 miles, we passed through a landscape of almost incredible desolation. There had been a little rain this season, but the dry and thirsty soil, depleted of its reserve moisture by long continued drouth, had absorbed it without a trace remaining.

The land was as lifeless as ashes, and for miles there was scarcely a growing thing to be seen. Where a scanty herbage had struggled up through the dust, flights of grasshoppers had apparently completed the destruction and then despairing of further sustenance, had flown off to other fields.

In many places the land lay untilled, and often where there were evidences of attempted cultivation, the fields were as black as when they had been turned over by the plough. Gaunt cattle and horses, with little save their skins to cover their bones, stalked about the denuded areas weakly seeking to crop the French weed, which with a malign persistence seemed to be maintaining some sickly growth. . . . The few people in evidence in the little towns appeared haggard and hopeless. For fully 50 miles of the region traversed by the highway which bears the ill-omened number of "13," there did not appear to be one single field that will produce a bushel of grain or a load of fodder. If there was anything of a more productive nature I failed to see it, and I was watching the landscape with care and attention. If the livestock of the district are to be saved they will either have to be moved away altogether or all the feed necessary to sustain them will have to be shipped in.

And as for the people themselves, God only knows what their extremity must be. Perhaps they have been unfortunate in their selection of a part of the country unsuitable for sustained cereal production, or they may be suffering from a combination of unfavourable conditions which comes only about once in a lifetime; but whatever the cause, the land upon which they have depended for sustenance has utterly failed them.

Other hazards.[13] A word may be added about the hazards other than drought, and about the measures taken to deal with them. The danger from frost in the north, and the breeding of early maturing wheats to reduce the risk, have been mentioned above. This danger is greatest in the north, though occasionally as in 1928 the damage extends over the whole province. The loss is largely through a reduction in quality and consequently in price. The plagues of grasshoppers have been

[13]See "Song to the Four Seasons" and "To my Father" in Paul Gerhardt Hiebert, *Sarah Binks* (Oxford University Press, 1947).

recurrent, and since dry weather is favourable for their breeding, this plague is likely to accompany drought. Entomologists can now predict with considerable accuracy the areas liable to attack, and have devised means of meeting the attack. The effectiveness of the defence depends on complete co-operation of the farmers in the threatened districts. The heavy losses in 1933 led to a well-organized campaign of fall tillage and grasshopper poisoning which is estimated to have saved at least 10 million bushels of wheat in 1934. Other insect pests, saw-fly, cut-worm, etc., take their toll, and noxious weeds compete for the scant moisture. The control of these insect and weed threats depends largely on organizing communal action; the individual's power of control is limited. Of the plant diseases the most serious one is rust, a fungus parasite. This disease is estimated to have caused annually damage to the wheat crop valued at $25 million and in some years (1916, 1925, 1927, and 1935) the damage has exceeded $100 million. The breeding of rust-resistant wheats, e.g. Thatcher and Renown, gave promise of reduction in these losses. There remains the "terror of hail" against which no protection avails so far as the community is concerned, though for the individual financial protection is possible through insurance. Hail is local in its incidence so that the loss to some individuals can be spread over the community, and it is sufficiently regular for the risk to be estimated and covered at reasonable cost by commercial, co-operative, or municipal hail insurance.

Variability of price. Fluctuations in price added an economic hazard to the physical hazards: the onset of drought was accompanied by the onset of world depression and low wheat prices. The average price at the farm given in column (4) of Table II tells the story, but a word of explanation is necessary. Earlier quotations of the price of wheat in this chapter have had reference to No. 1 Northern wheat in store at Fort William as sold on the Winnipeg market. The price received by the Saskatchewan farmer for wheat of this grade is subject to the deduction of something like 20 cents for freight and handling charges, and by no means all of his wheat is of this high quality. The crop of 1928 which sold at an average price of 77 cents was an extremely low-grade crop, while the crop of 1932 which sold at an average price of 35 cents graded higher than any crop in the previous twenty years. On the whole the average grade was higher in the years 1929-37 than in the years 1920-8; the fall in the average price received by the farmer is therefore the more striking. The effect of this collapse in price together with the failure of the crops is shown in the reduced gross income from the sale of wheat shown in column (5). In place of a gross income of over $200 million in each of 1926, 1927, and 1928, one finds between 1930 and 1937 a maximum annual income of $78 million, and a minimum of $37 million. The importance of this decline is the greater because of the intense specialization in wheat; ordinarily during the twenties 80 per cent of the cash receipts came from wheat. During the thirties there was some increase in the production of animal products, but low prices of these products and the technical limitations imposed by the climate made this avenue of escape from wheat one of minor importance. The total receipts from the sale of *all* farm produce is given in column (6).

But gross receipts show only part of the picture. The farmer is obliged to spend money to feed and clothe himself and his family, to buy seed, feed, or gasoline, and binder twine, to pay for repairs and to pay his taxes, etc. In addition his plant is subject to depreciation and in most cases he has to pay interest on the debt incurred in the past when building up his plant. All these payments must be met out of the proceeds of the sale of his produce before the farmer can be considered to have earned any *net* income. On the other hand, the farmer gets a house to live in and produces some food for his own use, the value of which must be added to his cash receipts. An estimate of this net income made for the Royal Commission on Dominion-Provincial Relations (1940) is given in column (7). In 1931 and 1932 the result of farm operation was a negative income, a loss, of $7 or $8 million. Two items in these expenses must be noted separately, since they are postponable, and possibly ultimately avoidable. In 1931 taxes were $14 million and interest on past debts $27 million. These were in large part necessarily unpaid, and were added to the debt of the farmer. Later, as we shall see, some relief was secured from the burden of accumulating arrears of taxes and interest. Finally, one must emphasize the inequality in the incidence of this decline in revenue; some farmers continued to have a substantial net income, many had none, many were dependent on relief for food and clothing, or for seed and feed, as the drought dragged on year after year. Another way of estimating the net income of the wheat farmers, less accurate but capable of application by districts, is suggested by Professor Britnell. He estimates that "ignoring all capital replacements for a year or two, a farmer might manage to live without outside assistance on average gross receipts of about $4.50 per acre; to pay taxes, with $5.50 per acre; and to meet debt interest, with $7.00. These returns would not, of course, maintain farm equipment." Consider then the yields of wheat in the southern districts, remembering the necessity of deducting a bushel and a half for seed and the low price received for the part sold. How inadequate the gross cash receipts were in this region must be immediately clear; 4 bushels per acre in 1933 would leave only 2½ bushels for sale at 53 cents per bushel, giving a cash income of $1.32. The story of two crop districts, one in the unfortunate south and one in the more fortunate north, is shown in Table III. In the former the cash receipts in every year but one were inadequate to meet even living and farming costs; in that one year they were still inadequate to meet the debt charges. In the latter in no year did receipts fall below the amount necessary to pay taxes and interest charges, and most years there were substantial sums available to finance repairs, replacements and depreciation.

TABLE III°

AVERAGE CASH RETURNS PER ACRE OF WHEAT SOWN IN TWO DISTRICTS OF SASKATCHEWAN, 1930-7

(in dollars)

	1930	1931	1932	1933	1934	1935	1936	1937
South-central district	3.25	0.61	2.37	1.18	1.28	5.98	2.82	nil
North-eastern district	10.62	7.79	7.11	7.10	9.27	9.32	11.35	9.55

°Data from Britnell, *The Wheat Economy,* p. 78.

Wheat and the price system. Our discussion of the wheat economy has taken us into a world very different from that of our model price system of chapter III. It is, however, similar in that the unit for production is generally the family, and in that the number of small producers is so great that the condition of competition is achieved. No farmer can hope to influence the price of wheat by reducing his acreage or withholding part of his crop. But the contrasts are obvious, especially in the results. That nice adjustment of production to consumption at a price which gives the producers an income roughly equal to that of other producers, which we found in the model, is noticeably absent in the real wheat economy. We turn then to consider the reasons for this failure to adjust through the operation of prices, and the consequence of this failure.

Demand. Consider, first, the problem of demand. Study of the model suggests that if wheat was produced in too great quantities the price would fall, and the fall in price would stimulate consumption. It was pointed out that the readiness with which increasing purchases (and consumption) can be induced by price reduction varies from commodity to commodity. This quality of responsiveness to price is called by economists the *elasticity of demand.* The elasticity of demand for wheat is probably low, although substitution for potatoes, for other grains, and for other foods, is possible. If there were plenty of wheat and scarcity of potatoes, a moderate fall in the price of wheat and a moderate rise in the price of potatoes might change people's consumption habits appropriately. This notion of elasticity involves, however, considering what would happen if the price of wheat fell while the prices of substitutes remained the same, and the incomes of the consumers were also unchanged. But if there is plenty of wheat and plenty of potatoes, a fall in the price of wheat which persuades consumers to buy more wheat and fewer potatoes will force potato growers to lower their prices to resist the inroad of the wheat farmers into their market. Hence the drastic fall in price actually experienced. If other prices may be expected to change, so may incomes. For the world of the thirties was a depressed world with widespread unemployment and greatly reduced incomes. This reduction in general buying power is important in explaining the ineffectiveness of even drastic price reductions to stimulate consumption. With the end of the optimism of the twenties the speculative buyer withdrew from the market, the low price to be effective had to be low enough to stimulate people to buy to consume; none, save governments for political reasons, dared to buy to hold. Finally, a political element was injected: for non-economic reasons many countries maintained high internal wheat prices thereby discouraging wheat consumption at a time when, political and military reasons for not importing apart, wheat could have been cheap and plentiful.

Supply. Consider, next, the problem of supply. Here the essential notion is "mobility." In the model low prices were supposed to induce families to leave the depressed industry and move into a more profitable one. In the real world mobility is very limited, and adjustment largely comes, as we have suggested in chapter IV, by changing rates of entry. Once a man has committed his fortunes to farming, though his expectations are not fulfilled, he will find it difficult, almost impossible, to retreat. He has made a considerable investment, which must be sacrificed if he abandons his farm, for if he cannot make a profit it is unlikely that anyone else will buy the farm in the belief that he could. And always there remains the element of uncertainty, the possibility that the drought may break, that prices may improve. For some farmers there is the chance of alternative products of the farm, and where such possibilities exist adjustment of supply may be quicker. But for the farmer on the prairie plains the alternatives are limited by the climatic conditions; and even where alternatives are possible their prices will also have fallen and will be driven still lower by the increased production. It is necessary to refer again to the general collapse of incomes and the prevalence of unemployment. If the crisis in wheat were a thing apart, if opportunities for employment in the cities were bright when earnings on the farm were falling, there would be considerable movement. But the crisis in wheat was precipitated by world depression and, as we shall see later, a crisis in Canadian wheat has always and necessarily been accompanied by unemployment in the cities of Canada. Movement from the farm in the face of low earnings is too likely to mean movement into the ranks of the city unemployed. Before much movement has taken place further technical development in wheat production, a fall in the prices of the things the farmer buys, and a downward revision of his ideas of the Canadian standard of living, may make the low prices more nearly tempting. Finally, one must notice that in the exporting countries governments are likely to try to save producers from the full impact of the fall in prices; just as in the importing countries the maintenance of prices reduces consumption, so in those countries and in the exporting countries support of prices increases supply, or postpones its decrease. And always in agriculture the supply is only partially subject to human control; you may reduce acreage and have a crop failure.

The impact of low wheat prices on the Canadian economy. The consequences of the drastic decline in the gross incomes, and therefore in the expenditures, of the prairie farmers could be predicted by anyone who had understood our discussion of the problem of saving in the model price system with rigid prices. One may add that it could have been predicted by any student of history, for the relation of unemployment in Eastern Canada to farm incomes in Western Canada has been strikingly obvious for the whole of this century. Perhaps one should add that common sense without the apparatus of the model might have sufficed. But the model has its use. Let us consider, then, the effect of a decline in income in one important sector of the economy if the prices of other Canadian products remain unchanged. They will not remain unchanged, but the effect of imperfect adjustment of these prices to the new low level of wheat prices can be best demonstrated by theoretical consideration of what would happen in the complete absence of such adjustment. If prices remain unchanged the wheat farmers with reduced incomes must buy less: purchases of equipment will be reduced to a minimum in face of unprofitable operations and the consequent absence of cash or credit to make such purchases, and purchases of personal goods will be similarly reduced. The reduced sales will cause manufacturers to reduce their working force. Unemployed workers will buy as little as, perhaps less than, depressed wheat farmers, thus causing further unemployment. Nor is it only the curtailed spending of the farmers' income that is serious. The country has become geared to western expansion; geared to meet the expenditure of borrowed funds to expand railway equipment, to build towns, to equip farms, etc. Such spending is dependent on the prospect of profit; with the decline in profits and the emergence of loss the incentive to new construction will disappear. Reduced purchases of construction materials and of personal goods by unemployed construction workers will be one more phase of the repercussions of the fall in export prices. So with rigid prices one could foresee something approaching economic paralysis, employment at a low level, money incomes shrinking and real incomes shrinking too. In fact there was considerable adjustment of other prices, but the adjustment was delayed and partial. The decline in the national money income of Canada from some $6 billion in 1929 to little over $3.5 billion in 1933 cannot be explained by reference to wheat alone, for other export groups were badly hit too. But the part played by the collapse of prairie incomes was important.[14]

The importance of the adjustment of other prices to the low level of wheat prices is threefold. First, the extent to which the "real income" or the standard of living of the farmer falls with the fall in his money income depends on the magnitude of the decline in the prices of things he consumes. Second, the extent to which it is possible to continue to produce wheat at low prices depends on the extent to which costs can be reduced, which must in turn be largely a matter of falling prices of the things required for production. Third, the extent to which distress on the farm creates more distress in the city largely depends on the extent to which lower prices permit continued sales and therefore continued production. The difficulties of adjustment cannot be discussed here; but they must not be minimized, nor must it be assumed that a simple solution of Canadian unemployment has been indicated. A problem has been stated rather than a solution offered. The magnitude of the adjustment achieved and required is indicated by the fact that while the price of wheat fell about 66 per cent between 1929 and 1933, the average fall in the prices of a large sample of "things farmers buy" was only 25 per cent and many important items fell less than that.

Relief and rehabilitation, 1930–38. The drastic curtailment of the income of the wheat economy consequent on drought and low prices

[14]See the Report of the Royal Commission on Price Spreads and Mass Buying (Ottawa, 1935), chap. II; also V. W. Bladen, "Tariff Policy and Employment in Depression" (Canadian Journal of Economics and Political Science, Feb., 1940); and Monthly Review of the Bank of Nova Scotia, Dec., 1935.

created problems which could not be solved on an individual basis through the operation of the price system. Government assistance on a large scale and of a varied character became necessary. The government had, of course, played a part in the development of the wheat economy; some reference has already been made to its part in this expansion, and further reference will be made below to its regulation of the grain trade. But the part played in the thirties was not the earlier one of assistance to a lusty, growing industry, but one of support to a crippled, indigent industry. It was a part improvised as the play proceeded; there were often several government actors improvising at the same time, and however effective each actor's performance may have been the total effect was scarcely that of a well-knit play. By the end of the decade the part to be played had become more clearly defined.[15]

Relief.[16] The first and most insistent problem was the provision of direct relief. The farmers of a large area were without income with which to buy food, fuel, and clothing for themselves and their families, or to buy seed and feed, gasoline and binder twine to carry on farming in the hope of an income next year. When in 1929 and 1930 drought affected a large area in south and central Saskatchewan support came to these areas from the rest of the province. The provincial government spent several million dollars in road construction, thus giving the farmers a chance to earn some income; it provided free transportation of feed and other necessaries into the drought area; and it guaranteed bank loans to the municipalities for the provision of direct relief. By 1931 the magnitude of the relief problem had increased: the drought area was extended, and its long continuance in some areas used up the financial reserves of the few farmers who had been able to finance themselves through the first year or two of crop failure. At the same time the ability of the province to carry the relief burden was reduced as the extension of the drought and the fall in the price of wheat reduced the total income of Saskatchewan citizens from $450 million in 1928 to $160 million in 1931. The tax revenue of the province was inadequate even to meet the ordinary expenditures of government in spite of drastic reduction in the grants for education and the social services; and unemployment relief in the cities added to its expenditures. To deal with agricultural relief it was necessary for the Dominion government to come to the aid of the province, i.e. for the rest of Canada to support the wheat farmers

[15]See G. E. Britnell, "Dominion Legislation Affecting Western Agriculture 1939" (*Canadian Journal of Economics and Political Science*, May, 1940).

[16]See Britnell, *The Wheat Economy*, pp. 89–99.

in their distress. Over the period 1931-9 the Dominion government provided practically all the money to finance the farm relief programme in Saskatchewan, amounting to some $140 million. Even with this burden taken from its shoulders the Saskatchewan government was not able to make ends meet, and between 1929 and 1935 it trebled its debt. Some details of the relief expenditures are given in Table IV. The amount of relief required each year will be seen to fit very closely the account given above of the varying fortunes of the wheat farmers from year to year. But the amount of relief required as a result of any one crop failure depends, of course, on what went before: if it succeeds a period of good yields and high prices the individual can finance himself; if it succeeds a period of poor yields and low prices even one crop failure may reduce most farmers to the relief level. The personal relief included food, fuel, clothing, medical aid, etc. Food was the biggest item and accounted for half of the expenditures; fuel came next in importance; clothing became more important as the drought continued and clothes bought in better days wore out. The agricultural relief included seed and the expenses of seeding operations, feed and fodder, and freight thereon. Public relief was supplemented by private relief. This was largely organized by the churches, though many other organizations, such as the Red Cross Society, made substantial contributions, particularly in the later years.

TABLE IV

EXTENT OF RELIEF IN SASKATCHEWAN, 1931-9*

Year	No. of families on relief	Relief given by the government (million dollars)		
		Total	Personal	Agricultural
1931-2	60,000	19	6	13
1932-3	32,000	3	2	1
1933-4	50,000	14	6	8
1934-5	37,000	21	7	14
1935-6	26,000	9	5	4
1936-7	38,000	21	9	12
1937-8	69,000	50	20	30
1938-9	57,000	13	11	2

*Data from Britnell, *The Wheat Economy.*

In 1931-2, 250 carloads of fruit, vegetables, and clothing were sent to the drought area. Assistance varying with the intensity of the need continued through the thirties and reached a peak in 1937-8, when 770 carloads of fruit, vegetables, canned goods, blankets, and clothing were distributed. Throughout the period these private efforts were co-ordinated by the Saskatchewan Voluntary Relief Committee which worked in close co-operation with the Provincial Relief Commission.

It is unnecessary to describe the machinery built up to deal with the relief problem, or the principles of its administration, but one principle must be noted. In general, the relief provided was treated as a loan not a gift: for the personal relief a straight promissory note was taken, for the agricultural relief a lien on the crops of the individual in the year of the advance and in the succeeding year was taken as security. The attitude of the Relief Commission was that "the great majority of those in need of relief were not bankrupt, in so far as their assets and liabilities were concerned, or paupers or indigents in the ordinary sense." It regarded itself in 1934 as "supplying short term credit to relieve distress among those in need for what was expected to be a short period." The distress arose from the absence of current revenue owing to crop failure, the general inability to dispose of their assets at any price, and the undesirability of forcing them to dispose of their assets at bargain prices in case they were able, and the unwillingness or inability of banks, gasoline companies, general stores, or neighbours to extend further credit. The piling up of "relief" debt, and the cancellation of part of it, is discussed below.

Relief measures having been improvised from year to year since 1931, more permanent provision for emergencies was made by the Prairie Farm Assistance Act of 1939. This Act provided for a levy of 1 per cent on all grain marketed from farms in Western Canada to be paid into a Prairie Farm Emergency Fund. If this fund proved insufficient to meet the claims on it, the Dominion Treasury would provide the balance. The claims would arise from widespread crop failures. Distress arising from local or individual crop failures could be dealt with by municipal and provincial agencies; but where crop failure extended over a wide area (e.g., 135 townships in Saskatchewan) there would be a claim against the Emergency Fund. If a crop failure area was proclaimed by the Governor-in-Council each farmer in the townships involved would be entitled to a payment of $2.50 per acre on one-half of his cultivated acreage, with a minimum payment of $200, and a maximum payment of $500. The Act also provided a scale of payments from the Fund in any year proclaimed an "emergency year"; where the average yield is 4 bushels or less each farmer can claim $2.00 per acre on half of his cultivated acreage, with a maximum claim of $400; where the yield is over 4 but not more than 8 bushels, each farmer can claim $1.50 per acre on half of his cultivated acreage, with a maximum claim of $300; where the average yield is over 8 but not more than 12 bushels, and if the price of No. 1 Northern wheat is less than 70 cents per bushel, each farmer can claim $1.00 per acre on half his cultivated acreage with a maximum claim of $200; the claim in this case is progressively reduced if prices rule above 70 cents and is withdrawn if the price rises to 80 cents. In the years 1939–53 the 1 per cent levy yielded $75 million, while payments under the Act amounted to nearly twice that amount. The scale of contribution is hard to justify by reference to the risk; especially since the Manitoba farmer, on the average received less than 29 cents for every dollar he paid while the Saskatchewan farmer received $2.50 for every dollar he paid. It should also be noted that the rise in prices made the scale of payments ridiculous.

Before concluding this discussion of relief it should be noted that relief expenditures in Saskatchewan involved a transfer of income from those to whom the operation of the price system allotted a relatively high income. If the transfer was made by taxing the one group and subsidizing the other, one might suppose that the spending of the taxed group was curtailed by exactly the amount that the spending of the subsidized group was increased. One might expect, then, no change in the volume of employment. The transaction would properly be described as a "transfer." But if the increased taxation reduced the savings rather than the expenditures of the one group, or if the government borrowed the funds to pay relief, the spending of the subsidized group might be, in part, additional spending creating additional employment and increasing both the money incomes and the real incomes from which the transfer had to be made. The act of transferring then partially creates the income which is transferred.

Government control of prices.[17] While drought deprived many farmers of any income and called for provision of relief, low prices created distress for many, and difficulty in meeting debt charges for almost all, farmers. But the price system was not left to do its worst; attempts were made by the Dominion government, some of them relatively ineffective, to raise the incomes of those farmers who had wheat to sell. These attempts included a direct subsidy in 1931 of 5 cents for every bushel of wheat sold off the prairie farms; purchase in the years 1930-5 by an agent of the government of wheat to hold off the market with a view to maintaining, or stabilizing, the price; the offer in subsequent years to buy wheat at a stated minimum price

[17]See H. L. Griffin, "Public Policy in Relation to the Wheat Market" (*Canadian Journal of Economics and Political Science,* Aug., 1935); H. S. Patton, "Observations on Canadian Wheat Policy Since the World War" (*ibid.,* May, 1937); V. C. Fowke, "Dominion Aids to Wheat Marketing, 1929-39" (*ibid.,* Aug., 1940).

and to give participation certificates entitling the seller to share in the profits if the government ultimately sold the wheat at a profit. Under the legislation of 1939 this last method was continued but with the minimum price fixed by statute instead of by administrative order, and with a limit to the amount which each farmer could sell at this price. The Canadian Wheat Board would buy up to 5,000 bushels of wheat from any farmer at a price of 70 cents (basis No. 1 Northern, Fort William), the seller to be given a participation certificate entitling him to a share of the profits, if any. This was a guarantee of a minimum price on a substantial part of the crop; if the farmers could get a higher price through the regular channels of trade they were free to do so. There was a further guarantee of a minimum price of 60 cents per bushel for unlimited amounts of wheat sold through co-operative organizations.

More will be said about this government action with regard to marketing in the section of this chapter on the grain trade. It is here referred to, at the cost of some repetition, in order to emphasize its part in the general attack on the problems of the distressed wheat area. It should be clear that such measures, in so far as they involve paying more to the farmers for their wheat than is realized by its sale involve a cost to the Dominion Treasury and ultimately a "transfer" of income from one group of people to another group similar to the "transfer" involved in relief payments; and there is the same possibility of the real burden of the "transfer" being reduced by the stimulating effect on employment, i.e. by the expansive effect on income of the increased prairie spending which it makes possible. The subsidy of 1931 cost the Treasury nearly $13 million. The stabilization purchases rose at one time to $80 million, but the whole transaction ultimately resulted in a profit to the Dominion Treasury of about $9 million. Some "transfer" of income thus occurred in the early years when wheat was being bought, but those who bore the burden of the "transfer" later reaped the advantage of the profit. The later guarantee to purchase any wheat offered at a stated minimum price cost the Treasury roughly $12 million for the 1935 crop, and probably $50 million for the 1938 crop.

Debt adjustment.[18] The rapid development of wheat production on the prairie was made possible by the ease with which money could

---

[18]See Britnell, *The Wheat Economy*, pp. 79–89; G. E. Britnell, "Saskatchewan Debt Adjustment Programme" (*Canadian Journal of Economics and Political Science*, Aug., 1937); W. T. Easterbrook, "Agricultural Debt Adjustment" (*ibid.*, Aug., 1936); Mackintosh, *Economic Problems of the Prairie Provinces*, chap. xii; A. F. W. Plumptre, *Central Banking in the British Dominions* (Toronto, 1940), chap. xii.

be borrowed to buy land, to equip the farm, and to finance the farmer in the developmental period and in subsequent emergencies. Most farmers were in debt, and wisely so. Their debts had generally been incurred so that earning assets might be acquired; the obligation to pay interest and repay principal was not expected to be onerous since earnings were expected to expand by more than the amount of these obligations. Perhaps it was unduly optimistic to expect that wheat would generally sell above $1.00 a bushel; but it was an optimism shared by borrower and lender alike, and there was no means of knowing for certain what would happen. It may have been unduly optimistic to expect rain, but there was no basis for expecting the prolonged drought of the thirties. The pre-war debtors had seen their optimism much more than fulfilled, they borrowed in the hope of dollar wheat and enjoyed years of much higher wheat prices. The borrowers of the twenties were made the more optimistic by this experience; but what had seemed a reasonable burden of interest charges with good crops and wheat over a dollar, became an impossible burden with crop failures and 50-cent wheat. The annual interest charge of the farmers of Saskatchewan was about $25 million, and they were generally under obligation to repay part of the principal annually. These payments were possible from the 1929 gross farm income of $243 million; they became impossible when farm income fell in 1931 to $70 million, and remained impossible as this income slowly rose again to $119 million in 1936, and fell again in 1937 to $86 million. Even if this income had been equally distributed it would scarcely have met the absolutely necessary expenditures for continued operation. In fact, of course, some farmers still had a surplus above their necessary minimum, and continued to pay their obligations; others had no surplus and could not pay their obligations; still others were on relief. Default was inevitable.

Debt continued to grow in the thirties. Arrears of interest were added to the debt; new borrowing was undertaken in the early thirties to tide over the temporary emergency; tax arrears and public relief were added to the debt as a first charge against the land. Whereas the earlier increase in debt had been associated with an increase in earning assets, that of the depression period was associated with deterioration of the physical assets and with grave doubts as to their prospective earnings. The situation called for the intervention of the government to adjust the relations of debtors and creditors; immediately to protect the debtors from unreasonable and impossible demands, but also to protect the creditors' future claims in case prosperity returned. This protection first took the form of "debt postponement" legislation. From 1931 on, various Acts were passed by the Saskatchewan Legislature limiting the rights of creditors to collect their debts. An Act of 1933 required the creditor to secure permission from the Provincial Debt Adjustment Board before he could use the machinery of the courts for such collection; another Act of that year restricted the rights of creditors to collection in any year of the proceeds of one-third of the crop grown in that year less one year's taxes, regardless of the terms of the original contract. All this involved only postponement; arrears were added to the old debt. More drastic measures of debt reduction became necessary as the distress continued.

Some adjustment of debts was made voluntarily by agreement between the parties concerned; but voluntary adjustment was likely to be slow and inadequate. Both the Saskatchewan and the Dominion governments set up machinery to facilitate voluntary agreements, and to arrange compulsory settlements where agreement was impossible. The Saskatchewan Debt Adjustment Board was mainly concerned to give the farmer temporary security of tenure by protecting him from unreasonable court proceedings, but it did incidentally arrange some voluntary settlements involving reduction of debts by about one million dollars. More important was the machinery set up by the Dominion under the Farmers' Creditors Arrangement Act (1934). This provided a cheap equivalent to the ordinary methods of bankruptcy in other lines of business. The farmer in difficulties might make an assignment of his assets to an "official receiver" appointed under the Act. With the help of the receiver the farmer worked out a proposal for submission to his creditors. If agreement could not be secured the case might be referred to a Board of Review: this Board would try to formulate a proposal acceptable to all parties, but if it could not secure agreement the Board might force acceptance of its own proposal. The machinery proved relatively ineffective: the number of individual cases was so great that an enormous staff would have been required to administer it. Actually the number of receivers was small, the proportion of cases referred to the Board of Review high, and there was only one Board in each province. By 1938 about 5,000 Saskatchewan farmers had made "arrangements" involving reduction of their debts by $15 million, and an annual saving of interest to the extent of nearly one million dollars.

In 1936 the Saskatchewan Board persuaded the Dominion Mortgage and Investment Association, representing the creditors, to agree to a "blanket" reduction of debt in the drought area, by promising cancellation by the provincial and Dominion governments of various

obligations which constituted a first charge against the land. By the
cancelling of these government debts the private creditor was given
a better chance of getting some payment in the future; in return he
agreed to reduce his claim. All farmers in the drought area, irrespective
of their particular ability to pay, were given the following concessions:
(1) cancellation of all indebtedness for personal and agricultural
relief incurred before 1935; (2) cancellation of provincial and municipal tax arrears with the exception of taxes due in 1935 and those
becoming due in 1936; (3) cancellation by mortgagees and vendors of
land under agreement of sale of all unpaid interest which had
accumulated down to January 1, 1935. The principal outstanding under
any such mortgage or agreement, together with any unpaid interest
for the years 1935 and 1936, was to be consolidated under a standard
agreement containing provision for interest at 6 per cent, repayment
over a period of ten years, and continued restriction of the creditor's
right to collect to the proceeds of one-third of the crop in the years
1937, 1938, and 1939. The remainder of the province, outside the
drought area, was granted no reduction of debt but might take
advantage of the standard agreement to pay over ten years with
interest at 6 per cent. Private debts in the drought area were reduced
under this agreement by about $30 million, and relief debt and tax
arrears of $55 million were cancelled. But in the next two years
continued distress led to further accumulation of arrears of interest,
unpaid taxes, and relief. In spite of some further cancellation of relief
debts ($10 million) and some further voluntary reductions of debt
($10 million) the debt of the farmers had risen by 1938 back to the
level of 1936, standing at about $525 million.

The difficulty of making any adequate adjustment of this huge
debt is the product of uncertainty as to the future. Creditors know
that under present conditions they cannot expect payment, but they
hesitate to agree to a reduction of their debt now because of present
conditions when those conditions may change for the better. Always
there was the hope that prices would rise and good crops appear.
And in the earlier years there was always the possibility of an inflationary monetary policy being adopted, which would have increased
the ability of the farmers to pay and decreased the purchasing power
of the mortgagees' income. Adjustment seemed to require some provision for readjustment if conditions greatly improved, or got even
worse. In corporate reorganizations in industry this is achieved by
giving the bondholder whose claim is reduced some kind of equity
security entitling him to a share in the profits if any are later made.
Similarly, the farm creditor might have asked for the insertion of a
provision giving him the choice of a stipulated money payment or of an

agreed proportion of the crop. He might then have been readier to agree to drastic reduction in the amount stated in money, and he might well have agreed to restrict his own right to collect in any year to a similar proportion of the crop. He would have become practically a partner in the business. But creditors are conservative, and such agreements would have been novel. They did become familiar in sales of land, but were rarely the basis on which old contracts were revised.

A further difficulty of adjusting this debt arose out of the fact that in large part the lenders are institutional. In one sense this is an advantage, since the number of the creditors is small and they have an association to represent them. It is a disadvantage since they have obligations as debtors as well as claims as creditors. Difficulties arise for these institutions not only through the immediate loss of current income but also through a change in their balance sheet if the mortgages are written down. And the stronger, which could stand the writing down of their assets, will hesitate to urge this policy if they think some weaker companies would be embarrassed. The policy of the association will be that of the weakest members, or if not of the weakest that of the most conservative. It was largely to meet these difficulties that the Dominion government established in 1939 a Central Mortgage Bank, closely connected with the Bank of Canada. This new government bank was to accept half the loss incurred by any co-operating institution in reducing the principal of debts due to it. It was also to make funds available at a low rate to the co-operating institutions, with a view to making new mortgage money available to the farmers at low rates. Operation of this Central Mortgage Bank was postponed at the outbreak of the war. During the middle forties the remaining farm indebtedness was drastically reduced; mortgage companies reported a reduction of 88 per cent in farm mortgage loans in Saskatchewan between 1937 and 1952.

Rehabilitation.[19] The experience of the thirties made it clear that the land in the dry area is not as productive as seemed probable at the time of its settlement; but also that it is difficult to say how productive it is. To doubts of physical productivity were added doubts as to the market. It was estimated that the wheat-exporting countries were producing annually 250 million bushels of wheat in excess of normal requirements. The price might, therefore, be expected to remain low. The countries of Europe which had taken to producing wheat at great cost for social and military reasons showed no signs of reversing their

[19]G. E. Britnell, "Rehabilitation of the Prairie Economy" (*Canadian Journal of Economics and Political Science,* Nov., 1937); Britnell, *The Wheat Economy,* chap. VIII; A. Stewart, "The Prairie Farm Rehabilitation Programme" (*Canadian Journal of Economics and Political Science,* Aug., 1939).

policies; in all the exporting countries, including Canada, curtailment was difficult and was delayed by the measures taken by governments to mitigate the immediate distress.[20] In Saskatchewan the long run adjustment seems to involve: (1) withdrawal from wheat production of lands that are physically unfit for it; (2) reduction of wheat production on land suitable for alternative lines of production; (3) improvement of technique and the equipment of the remaining wheat farmers to enable them to match the low price by a low cost. In part all these things were likely to happen through individual adjustment; but slowly and painfully. Individuals might not have adequate knowledge to make a wise change, or adequate resources to make it successfully. Governments had the necessary financial resources, and may have had adequate knowledge; but neither civil servants nor politicians are omniscient, so uncertainty and the possibility of error remained.

In the early thirties there was a substantial movement of farmers from the drought area to the newly opened areas in the northern part of the province. The movement was voluntary, but was encouraged and assisted by the provincial government. The results were in many cases unhappy. Neither the individuals, nor the government, knew enough about these lands, or thought enough about the difficulties. There was too little knowledge of the soil of the various districts for settlers to choose wisely, or for the government to direct them wisely. Later when soil surveys were made, several hundred farmers were moved from unsuitable to suitable lands. Even if the land were wisely chosen there were difficulties for the settler; the land was fairly heavily covered with trees and was difficult and costly to clear, frosts came early, and wheat farmers do not easily adapt themselves to mixed farming. To the government this northern settlement was expensive because of the necessity of continuing relief while the settlers established themselves, and of providing roads, schools, telephones, and other community services in these thinly settled regions.

The Dominion government by its Prairie Farm Rehabilitation Act (1935) inaugurated a varied programme to promote long-run adjustment. Only some elements of the programme can be noted. First comes investigation. Provision was made for the conduct of a thorough soil survey in the drought area. Laboratory research was pro-

---

[20]Each country delays adjustment in the hope that it will get relief through other countries reducing acreage. In particular the young debtor countries hope that the United States will curtail its wheat acreage. See E. W. Zimmermann, *World Resources and Industries* (New York, 1933): "In a world suffering from a wheat surplus the United States is the logical country to curtail wheat exports."

moted for the investigation of the problems of dry farming, e.g. the moisture requirement of various crops, and the susceptibility of various soils to drifting. Laboratory research was followed up by experimental work in the fields at the Dominion Experimental Farms. An important innovation was the establishment of fifty district Experimental Sub-Stations, privately owned farms associated with the Experimental Farms. They were used to check the results of the experimental farm under ordinary conditions and in various localities. Second comes extension. It is not enough to discover improved techniques; they must be made known to the farmers, and enough farmers must be converted to the new methods to prove their worth to the rest. The sub-stations played an important part in this, and Agricultural Improvement Associations were promoted to this end. Control of land utilization is a third element in the programme. Land quite clearly unfit for growing wheat was set aside as a community pasture. This had the two-fold advantage of withdrawing from wheat production some of the worst lands and providing some pasture for the neighbouring wheat farmers. A fourth element is conservation of water. The possibilities of economical irrigation are very limited, but the government by financing the building of "dugouts" and "stock watering dams" hoped to extend live-stock production. Some such measure was a necessary supplement to the community pasture. The possibility of much development of live-stock production in such a dry area was, however, very limited. The farmer with live-stock is especially vulnerable in drought; he is liable to lose his capital.

The International Wheat Agreement, 1933.[21] An explanation of the low price of wheat involves the international picture, and this in turn suggests need for international action. During the twenties world acreage increased by about 10 per cent, world production by rather over 10 per cent, while human consumption increased by less than 5 per cent. World stocks, which in the early twenties were between 500 and 700 million bushels (providing a safe cushion between regular consumption and somewhat irregular production), had risen by 1933 to 1,125 million bushels. Reduction of acreage was necessary but each country hoped that others would make the reduction. In 1933 the four great exporters (Argentina, Australia, Canada, and the United States) met with eighteen of the principal importing countries and concluded an agreement. The terms of the agreement covered the two crop years 1933–4 and 1934–5. It was estimated that imports of 560

[21]See D. A. MacGibbon, *The Canadian Grain Trade, 1931–51* (Toronto, 1952), chap. II and W. Malenbaum, *The World Wheat Economy, 1885–1939* (Cambridge, Mass., 1953).

million bushels would be required and quotas were established for the exporting countries: Argentina might supply 110 million bushels; Australia, 105; Canada, 200; the Danubian countries, 50; the United States, 47; and the other countries, including Russia, 48. For the following year the four overseas exporting countries were to plan a 15 per cent reduction in wheat production and were to export "15 per cent less . . . than the average out-turn on the average acreage sown during the period 1931–33 inclusive after deducting normal domestic requirements." This was not expected to meet the import requirement and it was provided that the deficit would be made up from the carry over of Canada and the United States. The importing countries expressed an intention not "to frustrate the efforts which the exporting countries are making, in the common interest, to restore the price of wheat to a remunerative level." They agreed to take no action which would increase domestic wheat production and to adopt measures to increase consumption. Finally a Wheat Advisory Committee was established. The terms of the agreement were not kept, and it was not prolonged, but the Advisory Committee did continue to exist. In 1934 Argentina had a larger crop than was expected and, lacking storage facilities, exported nearly 150 million bushels instead of the 110 allotted to it. The other three overseas exporters failed to take steps to reduce acreage by 15 per cent; there was some reduction but this was due to weather conditions rather than to deliberate policy. What agreement failed to achieve was soon after brought about by the weather: a series of short crops brought the carryover down to 566 million bushels in 1937.

The farmers and the grain trade.[22] So far we have considered the wheat farmer's well-being to depend on physical productivity in Saskatchewan and prices, or prospective prices, in Europe, especially in England. But to make wheat grown in Saskatchewan available in the consuming markets of Europe requires a most complicated trade organization. The farmer is interested in the organization of this trade from three points of view. He is concerned that: (1) the highest price be secured in Liverpool, or other foreign markets; (2) the *cost* of handling and selling be reduced to a minimum; and (3) the *price* charged for handling be reduced as nearly as possible to the cost.

[22]D. A. MacGibbon, *The Grain Trade* (Toronto, 1932), is the standard authority. The story is carried forward in his *The Canadian Grain Trade, 1931–51* (Toronto, 1952). A simple account of the trade is given by A. H. R. Buller in *Essays on Wheat* (New York, 1919), chap. II. The development of the co-operative movement in the trade is described in: H. S. Patton, *Grain Growers Cooperation in Western Canada* (Cambridge, Mass., 1928); W. A. Mackintosh, *Agricultural Co-operation in Western Canada* (Toronto, 1924); C. R. Fay, *Agricultural Cooperation in the Canadian West* (Toronto, 1925); L. A. Wood, *Farmers' Movements in Canada* (Toronto, 1924).

The efficiency of the trade from the first point of view is difficult to determine, but doubts on this score have sometimes assailed the farmers and affected their policies. The guarantee of low cost, and the further guarantee that low costs will redound to the advantage of the farmer and not merely swell the profits of the trade, depend, in a system of free enterprise, on competition. The inefficient who must charge high prices for their services, and the efficient who do charge high prices, may be subject to competition of outsiders, who offer to perform the service cheaper. The efficient might well mean those who can get the maximum price in the foreign market as well as those who can perform the trading services at minimum cost. Farmers had reason to believe, however, that competition was not as active as might be desired, and that they did not get in Saskatchewan as high a price for wheat as was justified by the Liverpool price and by the cost of efficient trading. Quite early, therefore, they organized with a view to improving the method of the trade: they have exercised political influence to secure regulation of the trade; they have organized co-operative trading companies which by their competition have forced private companies to bid higher prices for grain, i.e. charge lower prices for their services; and they sought the substitution of a single selling agency for the multitude of traders of the system of free enterprise, experimenting with a co-operative Pool and ending with a state Marketing Board.

Government regulation. As early as 1874 some provision was made for the regulation of the western grain trade by the Dominion government, and in 1889 the system of inspection and grading was established. Extensive regulation under the Manitoba Grain Act (1900) was a response to a growing agitation of the farmers against the elevator companies. The farmers complained that the elevator companies paid lower prices than were justified by the Winnipeg price and the cost of handling, that they frequently cheated in weighing, graded unfairly, and deducted undue dockage. Competition amongst the elevators which might have forced them to pay higher prices was, the farmers believed, restricted by agreement, and the competition of alternative methods of handling was made impossible by the agreements between the elevator companies and the C.P.R. The railway had realized the economies which would result from the extension of elevators for bulk handling of grain: amongst other things by eliminating delays in loading cars it would enable the crop to be moved with less rolling stock. To encourage the development of elevators the railway offered sites on its right of way at nominal rentals, and gave an undertaking that at points where elevators were erected they would discourage the loading of grain through flat warehouses or direct from farmers' wagons. The provision of elevators undoubtedly made possible the handling of grain at low cost, but the agreement to restrict the competing methods took away one of the guarantees that the low cost would benefit the farmer. Agitation led to investigation by a Royal Commission in 1899, and to enactment of the Manitoba Grain Act in 1900. This Act provided for an extension of government regulation. Administration was entrusted to a "warehouse commissioner" with headquarters at Winnipeg. Complaints about weighing, grading, and docking might be sent to him. Provision was made for more adequate inspection of the scales and the right of the seller to have access to the scales was established. To this direct protection by regulation was added indirect protection by regulations intended to restore the competition of alternative methods. The Act required the railway company to erect a loading platform free of charge upon the request of ten farmers in the neighbourhood, and to distribute cars impartially between applicants. Provision for reviving flat warehouses was made, but proved relatively useless.

Association. A very heavy crop in 1901 took the railways by surprise. They had too few cars, and too few locomotives. The result was a "grain blockade"; when navigation closed only 20 million bushels had reached the head of the lakes; 10 million bushels were in storage, and 30 million bushels remained in the hands of farmers most of whom had no facilities for storing it. A product of the annoyance and distress thus caused was the organization of the Territorial Grain Growers' Association in December, 1901. This was in part an answer to the organization of an association of the grain traders, the North-West Elevator Asociation (later, the Manitoba and North-West Grain Dealers' Association), intended to strengthen the position of the buyers in every possible way. The first object of the Grain Growers' Association was to see that the new legislation was enforced, and particularly that the railway fulfilled its obligation to provide loading platforms and cars. The provision of the former was useless if all the cars went to the elevators, as they mostly did. The Grain Growers protested to the C.P.R. against the flagrant disregard of the provisions of the Act, and when their protest was disregarded they brought action in 1902 against the agent of the C.P.R. at Sintaluta. They won their action, and in 1903 procured an amendment to the Act, requiring that cars be allotted in strict rotation according to the order in which the names appeared in the car order book of the agent. Though complaints continued, it was from that time reasonably possible for farmers to load their own car, and there also appeared "trade buyers" whose competition with the elevators was at times salutary. More important still, the new association gained prestige by its achievement. In 1903 the Manitoba Grain Growers' Association was formed; in 1906, after the creation of the provinces of Saskatchewan and Alberta, the Territorial Association was replaced by the Saskatchewan Grain Growers' Association and the United Farmers of Alberta.

Co-operation. Though the provision of loading platforms and the guarantee of cars in rotation provided some check on the elevators, farmers were acutely aware of the limitations of this check. Direct loading was uneconomical, and was only possible for the big farmer: the competition provided by direct loading was inadequate, and regulation by the government could only protect against certain abuses. In some localities farmer-owned elevators were established to secure the economy of bulk handling: a few were successful, more failed. The causes of failure included: inadequate salaries to managers; interference with the management by the farmer shareholders; dependence on borrowed capital; competition of line of elevator companies which paid high prices for grain in that locality, until the farmer elevator closed, and recouped their losses at other points where there was no such competition. To some the solution lay in co-operative marketing: to many this scheme for a grandiose commercial venture semed to imperil the organization at the time when it had begun to make its influence felt. It was left for Mr. E. A. Partridge, his neighbours at Sintaluta, and such farmers as he could convince, to form the Grain Growers' Grain Company.[23] This Company was incorporated in Manitoba with a capital of $25,000 of which $5,000 was paid up; it bought a seat on the Winnipeg Grain Exchange at a cost of $2,500, and commenced business in September, 1906, as a co-operative commission agent. It was intended to follow the usual co-operative pattern, to charge the regular commission, to pay interest on borrowed capital, and to divide profits if any as a "patronage" dividend.

The Grain Growers' Grain Company. The first year of the Company was stormy. The Exchange seized on the promise of a patronage dividend as a breach of their by-law fixing the commission on all grain sold on the Exchange at one cent a bushel. It also complained that propagandist pamphlets issued by the Company offended against "the honour and dignity of the Exchange" and reflected on the methods adopted by certain of its members. The Company, six weeks after beginning to trade, was suspended from the Exchange. There was a reasonable chance that this would kill it

[23]For a popular account of the early struggles of the Grain Growers see H. Moorhouse, *Deep Furrows* (Toronto, 1918).

by preventing the sale of the wheat it had bought with money borrowed from the bank. In fact, the Company went on buying, in spite of an overdraft which grew to $350,000 in February. It continued to make some sales in the East, and the Scottish Co-operative Wholesale Society assisted by making large purchases. The Company enlisted the support of the Manitoba Government which threatened to withdraw the charter of the Exchange. Finally, in April a compromise was reached: the Company abandoned the patronage dividend, and was reinstated on the Exchange. The view has been expressed by Mr. Crerar, who succeeded Mr. Partridge as President of the Company, "that the company might never have survived had it not been for the publicity given by expulsion from the Exchange. In attempting to destroy a small farmers' concern, certain grain interests created a formidable rival."

The attack on the Company was, in part, a reply to the attacks of the Grain Growers' Association on the Exchange. In 1905, Mr. Partridge had been sent by the Association to study the working of the Exchange; his report characterized it as a "combine" with "a gambling hell thrown in." His study had shown him that the commission market was the strategic point for a farmers' company to enter the trade. It also directed the attention of the Manitoba Grain Growers' Association to the affairs of the Exchange. At their annual meeting in 1906, they branded the North-West Grain Dealers' Association as a "conspiracy in restraint of trade," instructed their officers to ask the Attorney-General of the province to take action, and called on the Dominion government to make full examination of the trade by Royal Commission. A Royal Commission was appointed, and an action under the combines clause of the Criminal Code was instituted. The court dismissed all the charges; the Commission exonerated the Exchange, but recommended that the pooling arrangements of the Elevators be prohibited, and that steps be taken to avoid future shortages of cars. The evidence before the court and the Commission did show, however, that competition was far from perfect (though the court considered that the restraint of trade shown was not "undue"). Three restrictions may be noted. First, the North-West Grain Dealers' Association wired to all country elevators belonging to its members the closing prices of grain, and the elevators were forbidden to quote prices while the Exchange was open. To supply price information was a useful service but one which could be the basis of agreement as to prices. The court found no evidence of agreement. The Commission found "an understanding . . . that prices so wired . . . would not be exceeded"; the prices were not always adhered to, and no penalty was provided for a breach of the understanding, "although where a buyer persists in breaking prices he is brought into line by the combined action of other buyers." Second, the Commission found "an agreement between certain elevator companies for the pooling of the receipts or earnings at the different points where their elevators came into competition with one another." A monthly quota was assigned to each elevator, those members who exceeded their quota paid into the pool an agreed amount (from 2 to 4 cents a bushel) and those who did not reach their quota received a like amount from the pool. The pool had lasted two years, but competition had broken out between its members. The Commission felt that the Grain Act should prohibit such agreements in the future; they "constituted a menace to those who had to sell grain to those elevators and tended unduly to limit competition."[24] Third, the restrictive rules of the Grain Exchange were under fire. In this case, however, the apparent restriction of competition involved in limiting the number of members on the Exchange may well have been a condition of maintaining a really competitive market in Winnipeg. The Exchange could work properly only if its members were known to each other and subject to a common discipline. On the floor of the Exchange the conditions approach the perfect competition of theory, with such perfect communication that only one price can rule at any one time.

Co-operative elevator companies. The Grain Growers by their fight for loading platforms and track buying had enlarged the opportunities of the commission agents and thus provided some competition for the elevators. By entering the commission business the Grain Growers' Grain Company had increased this competition. But the "line elevator" companies had great advantages of efficiency in operation, financial resources, and concerted action. The farmers turned their attention to the provision of government elevators. The Manitoba government embarked on a scheme of acquisition and construction of elevators in 1909. The scheme failed: the prices paid for elevators were too high; some of the elevators purchased were at points where business was declining as new railway building diverted the flow of grain to new channels; the government elevators operated on a purely storage basis while all their competitors were engaged in the profitable business of buying and selling grain. The elevators were finally leased in 1912 to the Grain Growers' Grain Company at a rental of 6 per cent of the book value of the property, taxes and

[24]Compare the *Report of the Federal Trade Commission on the Grain Trade,* vol. I: *Country Grain Marketing* (Washington, 1920), chap. XI, "Competitive Conditions in Country Grain Buying."

repairs being met by the government. It is interesting to note that private firms offered higher rentals, but the government did not dare to return the elevators to the line companies in the face of the farmers' opposition. Meanwhile in Saskatchewan a co-operative elevator company was organized in 1911, with government support. It engaged in all the ordinary business of a private line of elevators, thus avoiding the mistake of the Manitoba farmers. The government financed the construction of these elevators by lending up to 85 per cent of the necessary money on mortgage. In 1913 a similar company was organized in Alberta, financed in part by the Alberta government and in part by the Grain Growers' Grain Company which acted as its selling agent. In 1918 the co-operative lines of elevators in Alberta and Manitoba were merged as the United Grain Growers.

The co-operative elevators proved a great success, the rapid expansion of wheat production during the war being to some extent responsible. Between 1914 and 1920 they handled over 20 million bushels annually (35 million bushels in 1917). In part their success must be judged by their financial results. The Grain Growers' Grain Company and the United Grain Growers paid substantial dividends from the beginning. The Saskatchewan Co-operative Elevator Company had by 1922 paid stock dividends to its original holders totalling $28.50, and an annual cash dividend of 8 per cent. The Alberta Farmers' Elevator Company had paid 8 per cent dividends in the two years before its merger. In part, however, the success of these companies must be judged by their effect on the trade generally. It is believed by many that their competition did improve prices paid to farmers at many points. The Saskatchewan Company claimed this in 1915: "It is almost impossible to find any station where the price paid by the private companies is not determined by the price paid by the co-operative elevators. It is hard to say what this gain to the farmer amounts to, but conservative estimates place it at, at least, three cents a bushel." Co-operative elevators have also claimed that their competition has made for improved service as well as higher prices. These claims are disputed, but many members of the grain trade would admit that they set the pace for several years. And there were other satisfactions in co-operation besides the monetary ones.

The Wheat Pool. The twenties saw the rise of a new type of farmers' grain company, the wheat pool. The pool grew out of the Wheat Board of 1919.[25] This was a government body established to

[25]See Mitchell W. Sharp, "Allied Wheat Buying in Relationship to Canadian Marketing Policy, 1914-18" (*Canadian Journal of Economics and Political Science,* Aug., 1940).

market the 1919 crop, as a result of the experience of government control of the trade during the last two years of the war and of the necessity of easing the adjustment to peace. The Board had a complete monopoly; the farmers could sell to it alone. Farmers received an initial payment based on a price of $2.15 per bushel, No. 1 Northern at Fort William, and a participation certificate entitling them to further payments as the grain was sold. They received an additional payment of 30 cents in July, 1920, and a final payment of 18 cents in November, 1920. The Board was unpopular at the time, but there were elements in the system which appealed to a large section of the growers. The price was good, and the low prices of the next few years were liable to be attributed to the absence of the Board, rather than to the fundamental conditions of the market. The fact that the price received did not vary from day to day relieved the farmer of the necessity of studying the market and enabled him to deliver his grain when most convenient. To many it gave "the intense satisfaction of seeing the middlemen and the speculators with their occupation gone." In 1921 with the low prices of the post-war depression a movement for the restoration of the Board swept the prairie.

The Dominion government claimed that in peace time the creation of a Wheat Board would be *ultra vires* of the Dominion parliament, but passed in 1922 enabling legislation to relieve the provinces of any doubts as to their constitutional power. Alberta and Saskatchewan immediately passed concurrent legislation; Manitoba delayed while an election was in progress and then rejected the proposal. Attempts to get a suitable manager for the Saskatchewan-Alberta Board failed, and the scheme was dropped. The farmers then turned to a voluntary co-operative pool. Growers contracted to deliver their whole crop to the pool for a term of years; they would receive an initial payment and a participation certificate; the pool would arrange for the sale of wheat and pay to its members the average price received, grade for grade, for the crop less expenses of operation and deductions for building a reserve. Whereas the co-operative elevator *bought* the farmer's grain, the pool *sold* it for him. The Alberta pool signed up a membership of 26,000 in 1923 and started business. The Manitoba and Saskatchewan pools started business in 1924 with 8,000 and 47,000 members respectively. The three pools then established a Central Selling Agency. For several years the pools had a great success, handling about half the wheat crop: they strengthened the position of the weakest seller and eliminated for the farmer the speculative element; they probably reduced the cost of marketing, particularly by selling direct to foreign buyers; they did not, and could not, however, appreciably affect the price in the consuming markets. Some of the radicals in the organization talked wildly about their intention to use their supposed monopoly power to raise prices, but the officials recognized their weakness in the world market and rejected such grandiose dreams. But neither the co-operative elevator companies nor the pools should be judged purely on their business success. They were highly democratic institutions, membership in which gave a feeling of social security and prestige. Co-operation was a way of life as well as a method of business.[26]

Trouble developed for the pools in 1929. For several years they had made an initial payment of $1.00 per bushel, No. 1 Northern at Fort William, and in each year had paid substantial dividends. In 1928 they cautiously reduced the initial payment to 85 cents, and were able to pay in the end a further 33½ cents. In 1929 they optimistically made an initial payment of $1.00 (the cash price being then $1.44). The subsequent collapse of prices rendered this an over-payment of 18 cents a bushel, involving a deficit of nearly $25 million. The banks which had financed the payment demanded protection, and in February, 1930, the governments of the three Prairie Provinces guaranteed the banks against loss. In 1930-1 similar difficulties developed. With the cash price at 95 cents the initial payment was fixed at 70 cents; in August this was reduced to 60 cents, in September to 55 cents, and in November to 50 cents. Finally the Dominion government had to intervene. To all intents and purposes the government took over the Central Selling Agency, its staff, its wheat, and its debts, and appointed Mr. McFarland as its manager. The pools separated from the agency; they continued to exist as little more than co-operative elevator companies. The Central Selling Agency became an agent of the government through which the wheat market could be supported by "stabilization" purchases.

Wheat Board, 1935–39. With the collapse of the pools the demand for a Wheat Board revived. The Boards established under the legislation of 1935, and 1939, did not, however, provide the sort of institution the farmer had in 1919, thought of in 1921, and still wanted.[27] The Canadian Wheat Board established in 1935 had no monopoly; the farmer was free to sell wheat any way he liked. But the Board announced a minimum initial payment which it would pay for wheat delivered to it, together with a participation certificate. If the initial

[26]See *The Diary of Alexander James McPhail*, ed. H. A. Innis (Toronto, 1940). McPhail was the leader of the Pool movement in Saskatchewan, and President of the Central Selling Agency.

[27]See section on the Canadian Wheat Board, prepared by T. W. Grindley, in the *Canada Year Book, 1939*, pp. 569-80.

payment proved higher than the market price when farmers were delivering grain the Board would get all the wheat; if less the amount delivered to the Board would depend on the attitudes and expectations of the farmers. The initial payment for 1935-6 was fixed at 87½ cents per bushel, No. 1 Northern at Fort William. For some time the cash price was above this and the Board was unable to estimate how much wheat would be delivered to it. By November the cash price had fallen below the initial payment and the Board got all the wheat. In the next two years the Board announced an initial payment of 87½ cents to become effective only if the Winnipeg price fell below 90 cents. The Board thus became an "emergency" institution. In these two years it received no wheat. In 1938-9 the initial payment of the Board was fixed unconditionally at 80 cents and, as the price ruled lower than this, practically the whole crop was delivered to it. The amendments to the Act in 1939 maintained the Wheat Board's emergency character, but removed the discretionary element in fixing the initial payment. The payment was fixed by statute at 70 cents, the deliveries at this price being limited to 5,000 bushels per farmer. The government also guaranteed an initial payment of 60 cents by any co-operative pool.

We have sketched, in outline, the growers' struggle to improve their competitive position *vis-à-vis* the grain trade and to replace the institutions of the individualist trade by co-operative or state institutions. Enough has been said to explain the attitude of the farmers, but too little has been said about the working of the trade to justify any verdict as to the relative efficiency of the alternative methods. That would take us into very difficult terrain. The effect of speculation on the Grain Exchange, for instance, is extremely difficult to determine and has probably been different at different times as conditions changed. But certainly the operations of the Exchange cannot be dismissed as obviously harmful because to the moral grower it seemed "a gambling hell." But if we have said too little about the trade, we have also given too narrow a picture of the activity of the associated growers. The marketing of grain involves the services of others besides grain traders, and pressure has been exerted to enforce lower prices for, and more efficient performance of, many of these services. The pressure has generally been on the state with a view to securing its intervention: the railways, the lake shippers, the Atlantic Shipping Conference, the banks, the loan companies, etc., have felt the pressure. The growers have also realized that their "real" income depends not only on their money income, but also on the prices of the things they buy: agitation for lower tariffs and for action against industrial combines has been, at times, important. The growers operate in a "price system," but they have realized the political forces which operate and have sought to remould these forces to their own advantage.

Wheat in World War II.[28] The outbreak of war in September, 1939, brought improved export sales of wheat. The open market price began to rise and between January and May, 1940, it averaged 90 cents, or 20 cents more than the Board minimum. This situation encouraged the farmers to expand production and in the spring of 1940 two million extra acres of wheat were seeded. Immediately after this, the German *Blitzkrieg* cut off all European markets except Portugal. The Board negotiated block sales to the United Kingdom, but the hopes of big sales were soon dispelled. The statutory price of 70 cents a bushel continued during the crop year 1940-1 but the crop was a record one and the storage problem began to be severe. Accordingly, in March, 1941, the government announced that although the statutory price was to be maintained, wheat deliveries to the Board would be restricted to 230 million bushels a year and each producer would be assigned a quota, or "authorized acreage," of 65 per cent of his declared 1940 wheat acreage. Further, the government would compensate farmers for land taken out of wheat and diverted to summerfallow or coarse grains.

This government programme reduced wheat acreage from nearly 28 million acres in 1940 to 21 million acres in 1941 and to 16 million acres in 1943. The open market price remained higher than the Board price and in 1941-2 the Board received only 44 per cent of farm deliveries. In 1942-3 the initial price offered by the Board was increased to 90 cents, but as part of general price control wheat for domestic consumption was held at 77⅝ cents by means of a drawback paid to millers.

Then in 1943 the situation changed, largely owing to a crop failure in the United States. The open market price rose and threatened the ability of the government to meet its obligations for bulk sales to

[28]For the effect of the war on the wheat market see G. E. Britnell and V. C. Fowke, "Development of Wheat Marketing Policy in Canada" (*Journal of Farm Economics*, Nov., 1949); G. E. Britnell, "The War and Canadian Wheat" (*Canadian Journal of Economics and Political Science*, Aug., 1941); also Harald S. Patton, "The War and North American Agriculture" (*ibid.*); V. C. Fowke, "Economic Effects of the War on the Prairie Economy" (*Canadian Journal of Economics and Political Science*, Aug. 1945), and Max Freedman, "Canadian Agricultural Policy and Export Trade," in *Canada's Economy in a Changing World*, ed. J. D. Gibson (Toronto, 1948).

Great Britain, and to maintain its policy of price control. So, in September, 1943, the Wheat Board was given a monopoly of Canadian wheat marketing. Trading in wheat on the Winnipeg Grain Exchange was forbidden; an initial price of $1.25 for No. 1 Northern was announced; all stocks of unsold wheat in "commercial positions in Canada" were purchased by the Board; and the crop accounts for the previous three crop years were closed out on the basis of the closing market prices on September 27. Thus the farmers at last secured again a government Board to market their wheat. Paradoxically enough it was the threat of high prices that gave them the form of organization they had sought as a protection against low prices. The Board thus established in war has continued to operate in peace.

In 1944 wheat acreage increased to nearly 22.5 million acres and income from the sale of wheat in the three Prairie Provinces rose to nearly 500 million dollars from 200 million dollars in 1943 and an average of 175 million dollars in the five years 1938–42. When income from the expanded production of coarse grains, cattle, hogs, etc., is included total farm income for the Prairie Provinces was just over a billion dollars (in the late thirties it had averaged 300 million dollars). The prairie farmer at last emerged from depression.

Wheat in the post-war world. In the post-war world the Canadian government sought stability for wheat prices through national marketing and international agreement. For eight years it achieved a remarkable stability of price: the total payment for No. 1 Northern was $1.83 on the five-year pool, 1945–50; $1.85, $1.83 and $1.82 for the three annual crop pools 1950–1, 1951–2, and 1952–3. But this stability was delusive. Much of the wheat was sold at what turned out to be bargain prices under the United Kingdom Agreement; and there is little evidence to suggest that our sacrifice of the chance to enjoy high prices has brought us relief from low prices. Stable prices for wheat, it must then be noted, are scarcely a sensible objective in a world of rising prices; United States farmers talk of parity not stability! Finally, Canadian and U.S. carryovers grew to threatening size: the Canadian carryover to 500 million bushels in 1955, the U.S. to 1000 million bushels. World production had again outstripped world consumption.

The United Kingdom Wheat Agreement, 1946.[29] Under this Agreement the United Kingdom agreed to take 600 million bushels over four crop years; the price for the first two years was to be $1.55, the prices for the third and fourth years were to be negotiated having "regard to any differences between the prices paid under this Agreement in the 1946–47 and 1947–48 crop years and the world prices for wheat," but

[29]See MacGibbon, *The Canadian Grain Trade 1931–51*, chap. VII.

were to be not less than $1.25 for the third and $1.00 for the fourth year. This Agreement was clearly made by Canadians who anticipated deflation: it proved a very good buy for Britain! When the Agreement was being negotiated the world price of wheat was between $1.80 and $1.90: on the day when the Agreement came into operation it was over $2.00, and it rose as high as $3.25 during the currency of the Agreement. It has been estimated that the difference between the Agreement price and the world price in the first two years involved a loss to Canadian producers of over $300 million. For the third year a price of $2.00 was negotiated: at that time the world price was $2.40, and it did not fall close to $2.00 until June, 1949. For the fourth year the Agreement price was again $2.00, and again the British had a good buy.

The International Wheat Agreement, 1949.[30] Still seeking stability Canada signed the International Wheat Agreement to run for four years. Its objective was "to assure supplies of wheat to importing countries and markets for wheat to exporting countries at equitable and stable prices." It was signed originally by 38 countries and later by eight more. It provided that Canada should supply 203 million bushels a year; the United States, 168; Australia, 80. The importing countries agreed to accept such amounts of wheat at prices to be negotiated between a maximum of $1.80 a bushel and a minimum which was to decrease from $1.50 to $1.20. This Agreement was renegotiated in 1953 and 1956, but the United Kingdom withdrew. The effect of the Agreement is difficult to determine. The free price was consistently above the Agreement price during the period 1949–53; since then the free price has been within the range of the Agreement.

The wheat situation in 1955–56. World production, as we have said above, in the fifties again outran consumption and carryovers became serious. What happened in Canada and the United States may be briefly stated. The Canadian economy, as Professor Britnell put it, "has been geared for a generation to the production of an average crop of about 400 million bushels of which we have expected to sell abroad not less than 250 million bushels a year."[31] With no increase of acreage we produced 1,800 million bushels in the three crop years 1951–2, 1952–3, and 1953–4: we produced, that is, four and half normal crops in three years. In spite of unusually high exports (nearly 1,000 million bushels, or four years' exports in three years) the Canadian carryover rose to nearly 600 million bushels, of which 200 million were still

[30]See International Wheat Council, *The World Wheat Situation and the International Wheat Agreement* (London, 1954); also MacGibbon, *The Canadian Grain Trade, 1931–51*, chap. VIII.

[31]"The Implications of United States Policy for the Canadian Wheat Economy" (*Canadian Journal of Economics and Political Science*, Feb., 1956).

on the farm, in 1954. A smaller crop in 1954–5 (a little over 300 million bushels) brought the carryover down to about 500 million bushels in 1955, but another big crop (some 500 million bushels) means that exports will have to be abnormally high if the carryover is not to be up again in August, 1956.

In the United States there is a similar problem of surplus, the carryover in 1955 being over 1,000 million bushels. There are several differences. First, acreage under wheat in the United States increased from 63 million acres in 1939 to 84 million acres in 1949. It has been reduced but the bounty of nature has to some extent compensated for the reduction: wheat acreage in 1953 was 79 million, in 1954, 63 million, in 1955, 57 million; production was 1,170 million bushels in 1953, 980 million bushels in 1954, and 920 million bushels in 1955. The significance of these quantities is made apparent when it is seen that domestic consumption runs at about 625 million bushels a year, and that exports from the United States were 70 million bushels a year in the thirties, and 380 million bushels a year in the nine years after the war. The second difference is in price policy. The United States has maintained its domestic price higher than the export price, and has paid exporters a subsidy equal to the difference between export and domestic prices. In May, 1955, this meant subsidies of from 72 to 87 cents a bushel on wheat and $2.41 to $2.58 per cwt. on wheat flour. These high support prices have not made it easier to reduce acreage! The third difference is in the policy of emergency disposal. Under Public Law 480 (the Agricultural Trade Development and Assistance Act) provision is made: "(1) for the sale of surplus commodities for local currency which may be left in the foreign country for development or other purposes; (2) for outright gifts for famine or other relief purposes from surplus stocks; (3) for barter deals of surplus stocks for strategic materials." The Under Secretary for Agriculture said that the Law sought to find a "use for our surplus supplies abroad —over and above what we are able to sell for dollars." At another point he asserted the intention of the United States "of entering into competition for world markets, rather than settling for the role of the world's residual supplier." Competition which entails giving away wheat bought from the farmer at prices much higher than could be obtained in a free market is not easy to meet! Canadians will watch with concern the development of agricultural policy in the United States in the next few years.

What has all this meant to the prairie farmers? Their total cash income had passed a billion dollars in 1944. The figures for the following years are in millions of dollars as follows: 1945, $860; 1946, $850;

1947, $960; 1948, $1,260; 1949, $1,280; 1950, $990; 1951, $1,370; 1952, $1,460; 1953, $580; 1954, $440; 1955, $420. This collapse in farm income is to be contrasted with the buoyancy of income in the country as a whole; and the extent of the collapse of "real income" is, of course, much greater than that in "money income."

What then of the future? Must we have a "fire sale"? Must we abandon a good deal of our low cost acreage so that the United States need not withdraw their high cost acreage? Again I quote Professor Britnell: "We are not out of the woods yet. . . . But is there any reason for panic? Is there any reason why we should throw in the sponge? Is there any reason for a fire sale? We know from past experience in the Canadian West how fast the situation can change; how quickly the substantial surpluses of the thirties and the much larger surpluses of the forties disappeared; how we were sweeping out the corners of the bins in 1937 and 1938 and again in 1946, 1947, and 1948. Like the Pharaohs of Egypt we know that fat years are followed by lean."[32]

[32]*Ibid.*, p. 12.

CHAPTER VII

NEWSPRINT IN THE CANADIAN ECONOMY

In the first quarter of this century the Canadian economy was geared to wheat. Other staple exports had played their part in the earlier development of the country and had, in turn, played the "dynamic" role assigned for a time to wheat. Still other staples have emerged in recent years to challenge the position of wheat. Amongst the earlier staples lumber once played the leading part; another forest industry, pulp and paper, took up the role in the twenties, supported by mining.

Square timber had emerged as a dynamic staple in the Napoleonic Wars, when naval action increased the demand while the "continental system" shut off the supply from the Baltic. In the first half of the nineteenth century "square timber built the Canadian economy." The returns of the trade provided much of the capital for building the roads, canals, railways, and all the varied equipment which a developing new country needs; these returns also provided the basis for borrowing from abroad for still further extension of the necessary equipment. In addition timber ships coming in ballast to Quebec provided cheap passages for immigrants, thus speeding up the rate of population growth. Spending of much of the proceeds of the trade at home stimulated the development of agriculture and the handicrafts. But, as with most of the staples, perhaps more than with any, the demand for timber was highly fluctuating; the economy was therefore subject, then as now, to the shocks of wide fluctuations in export incomes.

The dynamic role passed from timber after 1860, though it remained an important staple. Sawn timber took the place of square timber, the domestic market became more important, and exhaustion of good, accessible timber proceeded apace. The eastern lumber industry suffered from the competition of British Columbia: the completion of the C.P.R. (1885) opened the prairie market to British Columbia; and the opening of the Panama Canal[1] (1917) enabled it to enter the market of Eastern Canada and the United States. But

[1]See H. A. Innis, "Economic Trends" (in *Canada in Peace and War*, ed. Chester Martin, Toronto, 1941).

with the decline of one forest industry in the East has come the rise of another, pulp and paper, to take over the dynamic role. In this role it has another eastern partner, mining.

The emergence of these new staples brought about great shifts in the economic and political centre of gravity of the Dominion. In the era of wheat the prairie was dependent on Europe, and Ontario and Quebec were dependent on the prairie; thus the East and West were integrated for the time being into a single economy. The new staples were largely products of Ontario and Quebec.[2] The East became less dependent on the West, and thus indirectly less dependent on Europe, and more dependent on the United States. The political consequences of this shift were suggested by Professor Kenneth Taylor: "The economic and political bargaining power of the prairies in Confederation is likely to become steadily weaker. . . . The politically isolationist West is drawn by economics to support the maintenance of the tie with Britain and with Europe; while the economics of imperialistic Ontario indicates a probable trend toward Pan-Americanism."[3]

The processes of the pulp and paper industry. The pulp and paper industry involves three stages: operations in the woods with pulpwood as the product, the manufacture of wood pulp, and the manufacture of paper. These three stages may be carried on by separate enterprises, but they have become very generally integrated. The operations in the woods cannot be completely separated from other lumbering operations; many pulp and paper companies operate saw mills to utilize the large timber on their limits, and many lumber manufacturers operate "cutting up" and "barking" mills and sell part of their spruce and balsam logs to pulp and paper mills. From half to three-quarters of the wood is cut by paper producers on their own limits. The trees are felled, cut, and piled in the late summer and fall. In the winter they are hauled on sleighs to the rivers, and, when the ice goes out, are floated down the rivers. On the larger rivers the logs have to be formed into rafts and be towed. The remainder of the wood is purchased from lumber companies or from farmers. That bought from farmers is either hauled directly to the mill or is delivered

---

[2]See W. A. Carrothers, "The Forest Industries of British Columbia" (in A. R. M. Lower, *The North American Assault on the Canadian Forest,* Toronto, 1938). In 1950 Ontario and Quebec produced 75 per cent of the Canadian newsprint; of the rest, rather less than 10 per cent, was produced in British Columbia. The markets of the eastern and western producers can be treated as separate. Competition may develop occasionally on the fringes, but this is unimportant because no considerable consuming centres are to be found on the fringes. This chapter is concerned with the eastern market.

[3]"The Commercial Policy of Canada" (in *Canadian Marketing Problems,* ed. H. R. Kemp, Toronto, 1939, p. 10).

at railway sidings or at points on the river banks. The wood may be delivered to the pulp mill ready for use, with the bark removed and in short lengths of 2 to 4 feet. More is delivered in larger log lengths, which must first be prepared for the mill by cutting into short lengths and removing the bark.

The wood is then made into pulp by either a mechanical or a chemical process. In the mechanical process the wood is held by hydraulic pressure against the face of revolving grindstones and the fibres thus removed are carried away in a stream of water to be washed and screened. A tremendous amount of power is required for this process. The "mechanical" or "groundwood" pulp thus produced contains all the wood substance, a part of which is not durable, and the fibres are generally shorter and weaker than in those of chemical pulp. There are three chemical processes, of which the sulphite process is the most important; in each process chemical action dissolves the non-fibrous or non-cellulose components of the wood, leaving pure cellulose. This substance, unlike the less durable constituents of the wood, is largely unaffected by ordinary chemicals, atmospheric conditions, bacteria, or fungi. For the chemical processes the logs are chipped and then cooked with the appropriate chemicals for several hours under steam pressure. Heat rather than power is needed. Sulphite pulp is used to mix with groundwood pulp in the proportion of about 1 to 4 for the manufacture of newsprint;[4] either pure, or with some mixture of other kinds of pulp, it is made into the better kinds of white paper and paperboard; and the best quality of sulphite pulp is used for the manufacture of artificial silk. Pulp from the "soda" process is an ingredient in the paper for books and magazines; that from the sulphate process, having long, flexible, and strong fibres, is largely used for wrapping papers and paper bags.

The pulp from all four processes leaves the grinder, or digester, as a fluid consisting of water with fibre in suspension. It is screened and thickened, and may then be piped direct to the paper mill in the form known as "slush"; or it may be further thickened and dried, formed into sheets and folded into bundles, or, for export, may be pressed and baled by hydraulic power. In the paper mill the first step is to prepare the pulp in a "beater" in which the various kinds of pulp are combined in the appropriate portions, and the fibres are frayed

[4]Mechanical pulp is cheaper than chemical pulp. For newsprint only enough sulphite pulp is used to give the requisite strength for printing. Because of the presence of the wood fibres the life of newsprint is limited. Newspapers are hard to preserve even for twenty years. The *New York Times* prints a special library edition on rag paper which should last for hundreds of years. Many libraries now use the micro-film to make newspapers available for historians.

and split by mechanical action so as to promote "felting" in the paper machine. After some further preparation, including "loading" with clay, sizing to make the paper ink resistant, colouring, etc., the prepared pulp is stored in readiness for the paper machine. This machine typically consists of three parts, the "Fourdrinier part," the "press part," and the "dryer part." The pulp in very diluted form (almost 99 per cent water) flows onto the "Fourdrinier part," an endless belt of wire screen. As it travels forward much of the water drains through the screen, or is removed by rolls and suction boxes until a weak wet sheet of pulp is formed. At the same time a slight shaking motion promotes interweaving of the fibres. The sheet then passes to the "press part," where an endless belt of felt carries it through the press rolls, and more water is removed. It passes, still over 60 per cent water, to the "dryer part" where steam-heated cylinders evaporate most of the remaining water. It is then cut to the required width, rewound in rolls of about 1,400 pounds, and wrapped with heavy paper ready for shipping.

Early history of paper making.[5] The art of paper making was discovered in China and spread very slowly west: it reached Baghdad about 800 A.D., Egypt about 900 A.D., Morocco about 1100, Spain about 1150, Germany about 1300. The raw material was rags. The process in Morocco about 1100 was as follows. The rags were gathered together and allowed to ferment. They were then boiled with wood ashes, put into bags, and washed in a stream of water. The pulp thus secured was beaten with sticks and then diluted with water to the proper consistency. The sheets of paper were formed by the vatman, who dipped a rectangular flat sieve into the vat of "slush," picking up the right amount of fibre on the sieve, and shaking it to remove some of the water and to weave the fibres. Great skill was required if a sheet of uniform thickness was to be achieved. The sheets thus formed were put on woollen felts; these were piled and squeezed in a press to remove more of the water. They were then dried in the sun and air.

The application of mechanical power to the pulping process was simple and made quite early: even in the twelfth century water power was used in Spain to operate a series of hammers to beat the rags. In 1690 an improved beater using knives was developed in Holland. The paper machine was invented in 1799 by N. L. Robert and was developed by Fourdrinier. "This machine replaced the vatman with a

[5]See L. T. Stevenson, *The Background and Economics of American Paper-Making* (New York, 1940).

horizontal endless belt of fine mesh." The belt then passed between the felt rolls and the sheet was dried as before.

As the use of paper increased, the supply of rags became inadequate. The development of the soda process in the fifties, the mechanical process in the sixties, and the sulphite process in the eighties, permitted the expansion of paper production on the basis of wood pulp. The sulphate process was invented about 1880 but was not used commercially till 1910. After 1923 this process was adapted to the production of wrapping paper and paperboard from southern pine.

Northern migration of the American newsprint industry. As the settlement of the Canadian prairie was simply a continuation of the settlement of the American plain, so the rapid development of the Canadian newsprint industry after 1910 was a northward extension of the American industry. This extension to Canada was the result of the rapidly expanding consumption of paper, and the progressive exhaustion of the available supplies of pulpwood. The United States produced their own newsprint up to about 1910. At that time their imports were little more than 1 per cent of their consumption; by 1921 they were importing about 40 per cent of the newsprint they consumed; they now import almost 80 per cent of their newsprint, almost all from Canada. In 1910 the Canadian newsprint industry was quite small, being confined to the narrow domestic market: production was under 400,000 tons. By 1929 production was nearly 3 million tons; in 1940 it was 3.8 million tons; in 1954 it was nearly 6 million tons and expansion continues. Two preliminary phases of this American recourse to Canada for its paper must be noted. Canada first supplied pulpwood, she then supplied pulp, before she finally began to supply the fully manufactured paper. In 1890 the Canadian production of pulpwood was only 300,000 cords. By 1910 an annual export of pulpwood of about 1 million cords had developed, and export on this scale has continued, rising in some years to 1.5 million. Pulp exports were 200,000 tons in 1908, rose to 800,000 tons in 1920, and remained at about that level throughout the twenties and thirties. Exports of newsprint were only 200,000 tons in 1912, by 1928 they were 2.4 million tons, by 1954, 5.5 million tons. In 1908 two-thirds of the pulpwood and half of the wood pulp manufactured in Canada was for export; in 1936 only 18 per cent of the wood and 17 per cent of the pulp was exported.

Increasing consumption, and depletion of American forests. The expansion of the American market for newsprint was, in part, a function of the rapid growth of population; but the growth in the consumption of newsprint from 200,000 tons in 1890 to 1.5 million tons in 1913 and to 3.8 million tons in 1929 involved an increasing per capita consumption from 8 pounds in 1890 to 30 pounds in 1913 to 62 pounds in 1929 and, after a decline in the thirties, to 76 pounds in the fifties.[6] The basic factor in this increase was the spread of free compulsory education and the consequent increase in literacy. If literacy was the condition of increasing consumption of newsprint, the causes of its increase may be sought: (1) in the political power of the press after the extension of the franchise, and the competition between two well-organized parties to command this power; (2) in the increased volume of advertising[7] associated with the extension of packaging and branding of goods, and particularly with the development of the department and chain stores; (3) in the demand for war news and, later, sporting news; originally these were spontaneous demands to meet which the press learnt a new efficiency in the speedy issue of extras, till it became necessary for them to stimulate the public interest in something to fever heat to provide adequate demand for the extras that they wanted to sell; (4) in the fall in its price resulting from technological advance in the industry. With the increase in newsprint consumption went an increase in the consumption of other kinds of paper, again involving not only growing population but also increasing per capita consumption. With the development of new retailing methods the use of paper bags, paper boxes, and wrapping paper increased. The per capita consumption of paper of all kinds in the United States increased from about 70 pounds in 1900 to 225 in 1929. The bulk of this was made from wood pulp. The drain on the forests was enormous, and involved rapid depletion, and inevitable recourse to the forests of Canada.

The reasons for the development of the newsprint industry in Canada were mainly technical and economic, but political factors may have affected the time and speed of the process. The political boundary may have had some effect on the spread of the industry over the continent.[8] We examine some of the economic and political factors determining its location in the next two sections.

[6]See J. A. Guthrie, *The Newsprint Paper Industry: An Economic Analysis* (Cambridge, Mass., 1941), chap. I, "The Consumption of Newsprint Paper," and chap II, "Pulpwood Resources of North America."

[7]This means bigger papers and also puts an extra premium on wide circulation. The circulation of dailies in the United States increased from 3 million in 1870, to 15 million in 1900, to over 40 million by 1940, and to 55 million, by 1955. See Wickham Steed, *The Press* (Penguin Special; London, 1938), especially chap. VI, "Circulation and Advertising."

[8]Compare the previous discussion of the spread of wheat production north and west across the Canadian border, pp. 125–28, above.

Economies of location in Canada. The essential conditions for the establishment of the newsprint industry were an adequate supply of cheap pulpwood, plenty of good water, a source of cheap power, and satisfactory cheap facilities for transporting the pulpwood to the mill and the paper to the market. These essential conditions were satisfied abundantly in the spruce and balsam regions of the lower St. Lawrence system which were drained by rivers flowing in from the wilderness of the Precambrian Shield. The northern tributaries of the St. Lawrence gave easy access to vast stores of pulpwood, and provided for their cheap transportation. They also provided water for the process of paper making. The surface of the Shield is such that the rivers have frequent "falls" which can be developed as hydro-electric power sites. Cheap power was therefore available. (The development of mining in the north provided a near neighbour ready to buy, or to supply, surplus power; and a reduction in the cost of long-distance transmission of electricity opened up wider markets for power. Newsprint and power tended to become joint products.) The St. Lawrence itself provided cheap navigation both for bringing in mill supplies and for exporting the paper. Railway facilities were also good, and railway rates on newsprint were kept low by the competition of the water route.

Given this combination of favourable circumstances one would expect the expansion in the industry to take place north of the border; but the process was slow. The existing American plants naturally tried to carry on by importing pulpwood; but old plants wear out and become obsolete, and a growing demand calls for increased capacity, and so new plants are built, at last, near the new source of raw material. The cost of transporting pulpwood by rail was very great, and the pulp mill therefore was quicker to locate near the source of wood. When the paper mill followed the pulp mill there were some further, though smaller, economies: the drying and baling of the pulp for transportation, and the breaking of the bales and mixing with water at the paper mill were eliminated, and the cost of transportation of paper was less than that of pulp. The economies being smaller, expansion at the final stage came somewhat later.

The consumption of newsprint in the United States is highly concentrated in regions near the Canadian border.[9] Some seventy per cent of the American consumption takes place east of the Mississippi and north of the Ohio and Potomac Rivers. New York, Chicago, Phil-

[9] See Guthrie, *The Newsprint Paper Industry,* chart 6 on p. 85. This map shows the location of the centres of production and consumption, and demonstrates very clearly the strategic position of Canadian producers in relation to consumers in the United States.

adelphia, Detroit, and Boston are the biggest users. Proximity to the markets supplemented the advantages of cheap wood, cheap power, etc., and contributed to the location of the industry in Canada.

The expansion of the American demand for newsprint was stimulated by the great reductions in price which followed the change, after 1860, from rags to wood pulp as the raw material, and which continued with continual improvement in the mechanical and chemical processes involved. In the sixties newsprint sold at prices varying from $250 to $450 per ton; in the seventies the range of price was from $120 to $250; in the eighties from $77 to $138; in the nineties, from $40 to $68. The price was $45 in 1913.[10] Costs fell even faster than prices, and production expanded. The rapidity of the expansion mainly determined the date at which the industry fell back on the Canadian woods. The rapidity of technological change which was a condition of that expansion in face of falling prices, was also a factor facilitating adjustment of the location of the industry to the new source of wood, for it meant that the rate of obsolescence of the old mills was rapid; new mills had to be built and were built at places dictated

[10]The following table of North American newsprint prices has been very kindly supplied by the Newsprint Association of Canada. (1) *1862-92*. Prices were quoted f.o.b. mill and sometimes differed between different sellers and different parts of the market. The following figures represent average contract prices of leading United States producers.

(Prices f.o.b. mill)

1862	$340.00	1872	$240.00	1882	$120.00
1863	442.40	1873	224.00	1883	114.60
1864	240.00	1874	172.00	1884	110.00
1865	252.00	1875	170.00	1885	104.00
1866	344.00	1876	164.00	1886	95.40
1867	300.00	1877	164.00	1887	83.00
1868	292.00	1878	129.20	1888	80.00
1869	250.00	1879	120.00	1889	77.50
1870	246.00	1880	138.00	1890	68.00
1871	242.00	1881	129.20	1891	62.50
				1892	58.20

(2) *1893-1916*. At the beginning of the period prices began to be quoted on a delivered basis instead of f.o.b. mill. Prices became more uniform, although a number of special quotations still existed. The following prices are annual averages for New York deliveries by leading producers.

1893	$55.00	1901	$36.00	1909	$45.00
1894	45.00	1902	38.00	1910	45.00
1895	45.00	1903	41.00	1911	45.00
1896	45.00	1904	40.00	1912	45.00
1897	36.00	1905	40.00	1913	45.00
1898	36.00	1906	40.00	1914	43.00
1899	36.00	1907	40.00	1915	42.00
1900	36.00	1908	42.00	1916 (Jan-June)	
					43.00

by the new conditions. The new mills, located in Canada, had, therefore, not only the natural advantages of the locality but also the further
advantage of being equipped with the latest machinery. They were
competing with old mills which were not only losing their original
advantages of location, but were also equipped with obsolescent
machinery.[11] So the *expansion* after 1910 took place in Canada. Production continued in the United States on about the old level but the
increase in the demand of the expanding American market was met by
increasing imports from Canada.

Political factors in location. When in the nineties it became clear
that Canadian pulpwood was necessary to supply the American
market, several provincial governments took steps to promote its
manufacture into newsprint in Canada. Ontario, for instance, imposed
an embargo on the export of pulpwood from crown lands (1900), and
offered timber limits and power sites on very favourable terms to
companies that would guarantee to construct pulp and paper mills.
Quebec imposed a stumpage charge of 65 cents a cord on all pulpwood cut on crown lands with a rebate of 25 cents a cord if the wood
was manufactured into pulp in Canada (1901). In 1910 the licences
for cutting wood from crown lands for export expired, and Quebec
then imposed an embargo on export of wood from crown lands. Similar
embargos were later imposed by other provinces. Such measures had
some effect in speeding the migration of the industry to Canada by
making it more difficult for the mills in the United States to obtain
Canadian pulpwood, restricted as they were by these measures to
wood from private lands.[12] On the other hand the Canadian development may have been delayed by the tariff protection enjoyed by the
American industry. This protection was reduced in 1909 from $6.00
per ton to $3.75, plus $2.00 per ton if the newsprint was made from
pulpwood from "restricted" lands (i.e., crown lands subject to the
embargo). In 1911 newsprint was put on the free list, except for the
special levy of $2.00 a ton on that from "restricted" lands. Finally in

---

[11]*The Report of the Federal Trade Commission on the Newsprint Industry*
(Washington, 1917) shows that in Canada in 1916, 30 out of 40 paper machines
had a speed of 600 feet per minute, or more, while only 16 out of the 113
machines of the 16 principal American producers were capable of such speeds.
It shows that 25 out of the 40 in Canada had a width of trim of 140 inches or
more, while only 36 of the American machines had trims of this width: in Canada
there were 9 machines with trims from 170-200 inches, in the United States only
1 machine over 170 inches and none over 180 inches.

[12]C. Southworth, "Newsprint Paper Industry and the Tariff" (*Journal of
Political Economy*, Oct., 1922). In Canada the timber resources are largely owned
by the provinces: in Ontario 3 per cent of the forest land is privately owned, in
Quebec 8 per cent. Only in Nova Scotia (87 per cent) and New Brunswick
(62 per cent) is there a large proportion of privately owned forest.

1913 it was put unconditionally on the free list. The delay in locating the industry in Canada caused by the American tariff was probably small. The press, the customer of the newsprint industry, wields a political weapon; if cheaper paper can be obtained and only a tariff prevents them getting it, the newspapers will not let that tariff last long.[13] We shall notice later that the Canadian newspapers gave evidence of similar power in 1902 when they secured a reduction in the Canadian tariff on newsprint (see p. 223).

Expansion in Canada, 1910-28. The expansion of the newsprint industry in Canada was rapid after 1910, and the expansion was accelerated by the war. The effect of the war was to increase the rate of growth of consumption of newsprint; extras multiplied with the desire for war news; advertising increased as the expanding war incomes of the mass of the people increased retail buying, and as the heavy taxes on profits encouraged business men to increase their advertising appropriations. Prices rose sharply after 1917: the New York price of newsprint rose from $43 a ton early in 1916 to $114 in 1920. (The rise in the Canadian price was greater than in the American price because of the depreciation of the Canadian dollar in 1920.) The profits made during this period provided not only the incentive to invest, but also the funds for investment, as profits were ploughed back for expansion. The expansion was general in the industry, but the production of sulphite pulp increased most rapidly. The production of mechanical pulp increased roughly from 600,000 tons in 1913 to one million tons in 1920, or 66 per cent; that of chemical pulp increased roughly from 250,000 tons in 1913 to 850,000 tons in 1920, or 240 per cent. This is explained by the elimination of Scandinavian supplies of sulphite, and by the use of sulphite, i.e. cellulose, in the making of explosives. This expansion in sulphite production, out of proportion with that of mechanical pulp, constituted an element of weakness for the future.

In spite of a setback caused by the post-war collapse of prices in 1922, when many companies, especially those producing sulphite, went into receivership and were reorganized, expansion continued. The price of newsprint fell from its high of $113 per ton in 1920, to $75 per ton in 1922.[14] With improvement in general business, and

[13]See L. E. Ellis, *Reciprocity 1911: A Study in Canadian-American Relations* (Toronto, New Haven, 1939). Dr. Ellis describes the important part played by the American Newspaper Publishers Association in the campaign for reciprocity and free entry for Canadian newsprint. He also describes the attempts of the American manufacturers of newsprint to secure not only protection for newsprint, but to force Ontario and Quebec to discontinue the embargos.

[14]These prices are based on yearly averages of contract prices of large Canadian producers for newsprint delivered at New York. See *Newsprint in the World Market*, Survey no. 4, Newsprint Association of Canada.

consequent increase in advertising, the price rose to $82 in 1923. Expansion continued through the twenties; in 1928 the Canadian production of newsprint was 2.6 million tons compared with 900,000 tons in 1920, and the annual capacity of the newsprint mills increased from 1.0 million tons in 1920 to 2.7 million tons in 1927 and to 3.9 million tons in 1930. Production, however, did not increase quite as rapidly as capacity to produce. This expansion in production had a depressing effect on prices; by 1928 the price had fallen to $68 per ton. But the fall in prices failed to halt the expansion because costs were falling too, as the technology of the industry improved. In the woods tractors and chutes supplanted horses, and railways penetrated into regions not well supplied with natural water transportation. The method of storing the vast stocks of pulpwood made necessary by the seasonal character of operations in the woods was improved. In making mechanical pulp artificial stones of uniform quality displaced the natural grindstones which frequently had defects. "Magazine" and "pocket" grinders were introduced to increase the capacity of grindstones. New methods in sulphite production decreased the cooking time and increased the yield of cellulose. Economy of power was practised: the peak load was reduced, electric steam boilers were introduced, and surplus power was sold in increasing quantities, thus providing additional revenue. Improved methods of removing water in the paper machine permitted higher speed production of wider sheets. The maximum speed was increased from about 1,000 feet of newsprint per minute in 1920, to 1,350 in 1940 and to 2,000 in 1955.[15] In 1910 machines with a speed of 500 feet per minute were not common; in 1900 the maximum speed was 150 feet per minute. The widest sheet made was not much over 200 inches in 1920; it was 264 inches by 1928, and 350 inches by 1940. In 1910, 120 inches was not common. The average daily capacity of the machines was only 10 tons in 1880; by 1940 it was nearly 200 tons. The cost of transporting pulpwood to the mill, and paper to the market, was reduced by the development of special ships adapted to these tasks.

The depression of the thirties. Expansion continued throughout the twenties in spite of the downward trend of prices. As each new plant was opened prices fell a little more; yet optimism prevailed that costs would fall, that the demand for paper would increase, and that the sale of power would make up for low prices of paper. Then came the crash. With world depression advertising was reduced, and newspaper and magazine circulation fell off. At the same time radio

[15]See C. Wiegman, *Trees to News* (Toronto, 1953), p. 297, for speed of machines at Baie Comeau: 1,475 feet per minute in 1945; 1,715 in 1950. Elk Falls claims the fastest paper machine in the world: 2,000 feet per minute.

was coming to maturity and offering serious competition to the press as an advertising medium. Prices fell still further, to a low in 1934 and 1935 of $40 a ton. The relevant statistics are assembled in Table I. It will be seen (col. 1) that capacity continued to increase in 1930 in spite of the declining sales. This is to be explained by the

TABLE I

CANADIAN NEWSPRINT: CAPACITY, PRODUCTION, AND PRICES, 1924-39*

Year	Annual capacity (*million tons*) (1)	Annual production (*million tons*) (2)	Percentage of capacity utilized (3)	Price per ton (4)
1924	1.6	1.4	86	$79
1925	1.8	1.6	89	77
1926	2.1	2.0	98	70
1927	2.7	2.3	84	70
1928	3.3	2.6	80	68
1929	3.5	3.0	85	62
1930	3.9	2.8	72	62
1931	4.1	2.5	61	57
1932	4.1	2.2	53	48
1933	4.1	2.3	55	41
1934	4.2	2.9	70	40
1935	4.2	3.1	72	40
1936	4.2	3.5	84	41
1937	4.2	4.0	95	43
1938	4.5	2.9	64	50
1939	4.6	3.2	69	50

*Canadian Pulp and Paper Association, *Reference Tables*, March, 1955.

long time which elapses between deciding to increase plant and actually bringing new plant into operation. Faced with falling prices output was reduced (col. 2): this was in part because at the new low prices the least efficient mills could not even cover operating expenses, in part because the mills tried to restrict output in order to prevent or mitigate the decline in prices. The story of these efforts to restrict output is told in a later section. The extent to which the available capacity to produce paper was utilized is shown in column 3; in the worst year of the depression only 53 per cent of the capacity was utilized.[16]

[16]These figures of capacity must be used with caution. The difficulty of defining and estimating capacity was made evident in the efforts to establish a basis for prorating (see below, p. 197). Annual capacity, based on 310 working days, would be given as 4.2 in tons in 1937, but the Newsprint Association in estimating the "possible" Canadian production for 1937 put it at 3.7 million tons. By way of explanation their report said: "Figures of rated capacity . . . are almost meaningless unless studied with many qualifying factors. . . . A mill which may represent effective *machine* capacity may not represent available productive capacity because it lacks immediate wood supply. Another mill may have wood but may temporarily be affected by shortage of water or power. Another mill

Size of the plant and the firm. The unit of enterprise in this industry is large. The individual plant is big and the business unit is often
a combination of several plants. There is a high degree of integration:
the mills own timber limits, carry on operations in the woods, manufacture pulp and paper (80 per cent of the pulp is manufactured in

TABLE II

Size measured by number of employees	Number of establishments of this size		Number of employees in establishments of this size		Percentage of total number of employees in establishments of this size	
	1924	1936	1924	1936	1924	1936
Under 50	33	15	950	475	3½	2
51-200	37	28	4,100	3,000	15	10
201-500	28	27	8,600	9,000	30	30
Over 500	17	23	14,400	17,500	51½	58

integrated pulp and paper mills), and produce hydro-electric power.[17]
For the pulp and paper industry as a whole (including all other kinds
of paper besides newsprint) the distribution of plants between sizes
as measured by the number of employees in the two years 1924 and
1936 is shown in Table II. The increasing concentration of employment
in large plants is probably explained in part by the increasing proportion of newsprint in the total paper production, but some increase in
the optimum scale of operation may have taken place.[18] The relative
importance of the large plants is best indicated by the percentage of
the total number of employees in those plants; there may be as many
small plants as big ones, yet the importance of the small plants may be

may represent theoretical or potential capacity but not available capacity because
of high operating costs; it may lose less money by standing idle than by producing"
(*Newsprint in the World Market*, p. 16).

[17]In some cases the newspaper publisher acquired plants to supply his
own requirements: the *Chicago Tribune* owns the Ontario Paper Company at
Thorold (see Wiegman, *Trees to News*); the *New York Times* had a 49 per cent
interest in the Spruce Falls Power and Paper Company from which it obtained
most of its paper. On the other hand the International Paper Company in 1929
held stock in fourteen daily newspapers to which it had given financial assistance
and from which long-term contracts had been secured. These connections caused
friction with other publishers and were mostly given up.

[18]For the distribution of production between plants of different sizes in the
fourteen leading industries of Canada in 1924, and for a comparison with the
American figures in eight of these industries see V. W. Bladen, "Size of the
Establishment in Canadian and American Industry" (*Contributions to Canadian
Economics*, vol. I, 1928). In 1924 the degree of concentration in large plants in
the pulp and paper industry was rather greater in Canada than in the United
States; the proportion of workers in plants employing over 500 employees was
51 per cent in Canada and only 37 per cent in the United States.

negligible. In 1924 over 81 per cent of the workers were in plants employing over 200 employees; by 1936 this percentage was 88. While the number of employees in the industry increased, and productive capacity increased much more, the number of plants decreased.

The capacity of the mills varied from 10,000 tons a year (Provincial Paper at Port Arthur) to nearly 250,000 tons (the Three Rivers plant of Canadian International). The distribution of the mills between sizes as measured by capacity was, in 1941, as follows:[19]

Under 25,000 tons a year	5 mills
25-49,000 tons a year	4 mills
50-99,000 tons a year	11 mills
100-149,000 tons a year	6 mills
150-199,000 tons a year	8 mills
200-249,000 tons a year	5 mills

The industrial plant is not the unit for business control. The typical business unit, or "firm" as we shall call it, is a *corporation* owning, or controlling, many plants at each of the stages in the process. In the thirties three corporations controlled 45 per cent of the operating capacity in the newsprint industry, viz. Consolidated Paper, Abitibi Power and Paper, and Canadian International Paper. This concentration of the industry in few firms was largely achieved during the five years, 1925-9. It was, like other merger movements, the product of three sets of influences: (1) technical advantages in integration which promised lower costs and therefore higher profits for the consolidation than had been enjoyed by the individuals; (2) the possibility of controlling competition and so maintaining higher prices; (3) the almost insatiable appetite of the public for securities of pulp and paper consolidations to which investment houses were glad to cater. The prospects of increased efficiency were played up in the prospectuses; the possibility of controlling prices had to be handled with discretion; the profits of promotion were crucial. The story of the development of these consolidations, and the present situation can best be illustrated by a brief history of the three biggest corporations.

The Abitibi Power and Paper Company. This company was founded in 1912. In 1926, when its expansion began, it operated a newsprint mill at Iroquois Falls on the Abitibi River, and owned the town site of Iroquois Falls, including the hotel, stores, a hospital, and 215 houses. Power was developed at Twin Falls and Iroquois Falls on the Abitibi River to supply the mills. In 1926 Abitibi acquired a substantial interest in the Manitoba Paper Company (with a mill and power plant at Pine Falls) and the Ste. Anne Paper Company (with a mill, power plant, and timber reserves at Ste. Anne, Quebec). In

[19]According to information supplied by the Newsprint Association of Canada.

1927 it acquired control of the Mattagami Pulp and Paper Company (with a sulphite mill at Smooth Rock Falls and a subsidiary, the Mattagami Railroad Company) and also a power plant at Island Falls on the Abitibi River. In 1928 the continued expansion of Abitibi involved: (1) acquisition of Spanish River Pulp and Paper Mills which owned mills at Sault Ste. Marie, Espanola, and Sturgeon Falls, together with large pulpwood concessions; (2) acquisition of the Manitoba Paper Company and the Ste. Anne Paper Company in which it had already a substantial interest; (3) acquisition of the Murray Bay Paper Company which owned a newsprint mill at Murray Bay, leased an adjacent pulp mill, and had reserves of wood (this inefficient mill was never operated by Abitibi, and was sold by the Receiver for a nominal consideration in 1933); (4) acquisition of the Fort William Power Company which controlled the Fort William Paper Company, with a newsprint mill and reserves of wood, and the Kaministiquia Power Company, which operated a power plant nearby; (5) joint acquisition by Abitibi and Canada Power and Paper of the capital stock of Thunder Bay Paper Company with a newsprint mill in Port Arthur and reserves of wood; (6) subscription of 22 per cent of the capital of Newsprint Bond and Share Company which was formed by a group of newsprint manufacturers to obtain voting control of Bathurst Power and Paper Company. In 1930 Abitibi acquired all the common stock of Provincial Paper, Limited, manufacturers and distributors of high-grade book and writing papers with plants at Roches, Thorold, Georgetown, and Port Arthur. In 1932 it agreed to purchase the whole of the capital stock of Thunder Bay.

The result of this process of consolidation was that in 1932 Abitibi was in control of the following newsprint paper mills:

		Dates installed	Annual capacity (*tons of newsprint*)
(1) Low-cost mills*	— Iroquois Falls	1915–21	186,000
	Pine Falls	1927	78,000
(2) Efficient mills	— Ste. Anne	1927	78,000
	Thunder Bay	1927–8	78,000
	Sault Ste. Marie	1910–12	78,000
	Fort William	1922	52,000
(3) High-cost mills	— Murray Bay	1928	34,000
	Sturgeon Falls	1900–20	46,000
	Espanola	1905–19	100,000
			730,000

*Efficiency ratings are given by the first *Report* of the Receiver. Cf. C. P. Fell, "The Newspaper Industry" (in *The Canadian Economy and Its Problems*, Toronto, 1934, p. 51). Mr. Fell shows the daily capacity of each Canadian company in 1932 classified as "efficient" (A), "less efficient" (B), and "high cost" (C). His rating of Abitibi was: A, 800 tons; B, 900 tons; C 545 tons.

Each of the paper mills made its own groundwood pulp and each, with the exception of Espanola, was equipped for manufacturing sulphite pulp to the extent necessary for its own production of newsprint. The Sault Ste. Marie mill had an excess unbleached sulphite pulp capacity of about 23,000 tons. Power was developed by the company mainly for its own mills at the following places:

	Average generating capacity (horsepower)	
	Hydro-electric	Hydraulic
Twin Falls (for Iroquois Falls plant)	21,500	
Iroquois Falls (for Iroquois Falls plant)	3,300	28,000
Island Falls (for Iroquois Falls plant)	39,000	
Smooth Rock Falls (for sulphite pulp mill at Smooth Rock)	7,300	
Crystal Falls (for Sturgeon Falls plant)	8,200	
Sturgeon Falls (for Sturgeon Falls plant)	1,800	8,900
Espanola (for Espanola plant)	6,700	11,700
Kaministiquia (for Fort William plant)	23,000	
Merritton (for Thorold plant)	850	450

In September, 1930, Ontario Power Service Corporation was promoted by Abitibi to develop power at the Canyon on the Abitibi River. The cost of this development was estimated at $23 million; about $18 million was raised by the sale of $20 million worth of bonds and the remainder was to have been provided by Abitibi. There was also an agreement on the part of Abitibi to purchase power at a price sufficient to make possible payment of interest and sinking fund on the $20 million of outstanding bonds. Abitibi was unable to meet these obligations: it went into receivership in September, 1932, and Ontario Power Service Corporation was thereby forced into receivership in November, 1932. The Hydro-Electric Power Commission of Ontario acquired the properties of Ontario Power Service Corporation in a court sale; the amount realized being less than the claims of the bondholders, Abitibi got nothing. Later Abitibi agreed to turn over its Crystal Falls power plant in settlement of Hydro's claims against it. Sales of newsprint by Abitibi in the period 1928–32 declined more rapidly than the decline in total Canadian sales and the percentage of capacity utilized declined drastically (see Table III). At the date of the receivership only three of the newsprint mills were in operation: the Iroquois Falls mill was operating at 36 per cent capacity; the Sault Ste. Marie mill at 100 per cent capacity; and the Thunder Bay mill was operating at 40 per cent capacity. The remaining mills were closed down. The Murray Bay mill, it appears, had never been operated. Failure to concentrate production in its most efficient mill at Iroquois Falls is explained by need to avoid serious losses from deterioration of inventories of pulpwood on hand at Sault Ste. Marie and Thunder Bay. Substantial quantities of pulpwood were available at Espanola, and Sturgeon Falls, but the costs of conversion were so high that it was not considered economical to salvage them. At Pine

TABLE III*

Year	Sales of newsprint by Abitibi (*thousand tons*)	Percentage of Abitibi capacity utilized	Percentage of Abitibi sales to total Canadian sales
1928†	415	87	17
1929	528	95	19
1930	372	67	15
1931	265	48	12
1932	207	37	11
1933	195	35	10
1934	239	43	9
1935	290	52	11
1936	354	64	11
1937	487	87	13
1938	291	53	12
1939	325	58	11

*From the first *Report* of the Receiver for Abitibi, 1932; and from the *Compilation of Statements and Information* (Abitibi).
†The figures for this year do not include the Thunder Bay mill.

Falls there was little pulpwood on hand, or even available; the low cost of operation was offset by high cost of pulpwood. In 1933 the Sault Ste. Marie mill continued to operate at capacity; the Iroquois Falls mill was operated at 73 per cent of capacity; the Thunder Bay mill was closed down when its stocks of pulpwood were nearly used up. The expenses of carrying the six idle newsprint mills amounted to nearly $900,000 in 1932.

The funds necessary for the acquisition of these companies had been raised mainly by the sale of bonds and preferred shares.[20] In 1930 there were roughly $50 million of 5 per cent mortgage bonds, requiring $2½ million for the annual interest: there were 7 per cent first preference shares with a par value of $1 million and 6 per cent second preference shares with a par value of $35 million. Preference shareholders were entitled, therefore, to dividends of $2,170,000 before any dividend could be declared on the common shares. The net earnings of the company are shown in column 5 of Table IV. It will be noticed that if adequate depreciation had been charged in the years 1932–6 earnings would have been negative. Interest on the

[20]For an elementary discussion of corporate organization and financing see D. H. Robertson, *The Control of Industry* (London, 1922). The significance of the development of corporate enterprise is discussed in A. A. Berle and G. C. Means, *The Modern Corporation* (New York, 1932), especially books I and III. See also C. A. Ashley and J. E. Smyth, *Corporation Finance in Canada* (Toronto, 1956).

bonds was paid till June, 1932; dividends on the first preference shares till October, 1931; dividends on the second preference shares till April, 1931; dividends on the common stock were paid in 1928, but none thereafter.

Abitibi continued in receivership until 1946. Various plans of reorganization were rejected by the bondholders, and in 1940, the

TABLE IV*

CONSOLIDATED FINANCIAL RESULTS OF THE COMPANIES
MERGED IN ABITIBI, 1926–36
(million dollars)

Year	(1) Sales	(2) Operating expenses	(3) Operating profit	(4) Depreci- ation	(5) Net earnings†	(6) Prices of common stock
1926	....	....	8.94	1.70	7.05	....
1927	....	....	8.28	1.62	6.86	....
1928	29.29	21.60	7.69	1.72	6.00	85–37
1929	33.54	24.45	9.09	1.86	7.30	58–35
1930	24.53	17.26	7.27	1.48	4.77	42–8
1931	16.08	10.70	5.38	1.03	3.03	14–2
1932	10.54	8.35	2.19	0.60	1.39	$3\frac{1}{4}-\frac{1}{4}$
1933	8.12	6.97	1.15	0.04	0.79	$4-\frac{1}{4}$
1934	10.01	7.99	2.02	0.02	1.31	$2\frac{1}{2}-\frac{1}{4}$
1935	11.56	9.60	1.96	0.01	1.56	$2-\frac{1}{2}$
1936	14.98	12.04	2.94	0.02	2.46	$7-1\frac{1}{4}$

*Columns (1)-(5) from A Compilation of Statements and Information (Abitibi); column (6) from the Financial Post's Survey of Corporate Securities.

†After adding some miscellaneous revenue, and deducting expenses of idle plant and other miscellaneous expenses, but before paying interest on bonds.

property was ordered sold by the courts, but the bids received were not acceptable. In October, 1940, the Ontario Government appointed a Royal Commission to investigate the situation of the company, and it recommended letting the company work out its own financial situation. As a result, a Moratorium Act was passed to prevent further attempts to force a judicial sale of the property. In 1943 a committee headed by the Hon. F. J. Hughes, was appointed by the Ontario government to work out a plan of reorganization. This plan was finally accepted by the bondholders, shareholders, and creditors and put into effect in 1946.

In the meantime, the stabilization of the price of newsprint at $50 a ton in 1937, and the advent of war, brought higher earnings to Abitibi. Production rose to about 400,000 tons annually, and earnings increased steadily until, in 1944, Abitibi earned $5.7 million, even after making an allowance of $4 million for depreciation. Five distributions were made to the bondholders from 1941 to 1945, totalling $475 in principal and $92.18 in interest for every $1,000 bond. The principal and interest still outstanding were capitalized in a new bond issue which, under the Hughes' plan, was exchanged for the old issue at the rate of $1,100 of the new bonds for every $1,000 of the old.

The preferred shareholders lost their unpaid dividends under the plan, but were compensated for this by a higher dividend rate. The old 7 per cent preferred shares of $100 par value were divided into five shares of $20 par value carrying a dividend of $2.50. The 6 per cent preferred shares of $100 par value were divided and converted into four shares of $20 carrying a dividend of $1.50, and two shares of common stock. The common stockholders received one-half a share for each share of the old common stock held. In 1951 these shares were split into three: the owner of two of the shares for which quotations are given in Table IV would have one of the 1946 shares which by 1951 sold between a high of $60 and a low of $40, and in 1955 would have three of the 1951 shares which sold between a high of $33 and a low of $26 each.

Consolidated Paper Corporation, formerly Canada Power and Paper Company. This is another product of the consolidation movement of 1925-30. Canada Power and Paper was a holding company incorporated in 1928 to acquire control of the Laurentide Company and the St. Maurice Valley Corporation. The Laurentide Company owned a paper mill producing mainly newsprint, sulphite and ground wood pulp mills, timber limits, most of the property comprising the townsite of Grand'Mere, including a hotel and employees' houses. The St. Maurice Valley Corporation had been formed in 1925 to take over the St. Maurice Valley Paper Company and over 85 per cent of the common stock of Belgo-Canadian Paper Company (which in 1925 had absorbed Kilgour Brothers), and a one-third interest in the Anticosti Corporation owning timber land on the island; in 1929 it sold the Canada Paper Company to Howard Smith Paper Mills, receiving in return 20,000 shares in that company. In 1928, Canada Power and Paper Company jointly with Abitibi acquired control of Thunder Bay Paper Company (this was terminated in 1932 when Abitibi agreed to take over sole control). In 1929, Canada Power and Paper acquired control of Port Alfred Pulp and Paper Corporation, and the Wayagamack Pulp and Paper Company. The Port Alfred Pulp and Paper Company had been incorporated in 1924 to acquire the Bay Sulphite Company; in 1926 it had acquired the remaining one-third interest in the Anticosti Corporation. In 1930, Anglo-Canadian Pulp and Paper Mills was taken into Canada Power and Paper, but the union was short-lived. In 1931, Canada Power and Paper defaulted on its bonds and was reorganized as Consolidated Paper, while Anglo-Canadian became again an independent company. As with Abitibi the expansion of Canada Power and Paper had been financed largely by bonds and preferred shares: bond interest in 1930 required nearly $5 million and the preferred dividend called for $1.8 million. In 1929 interest was paid and the preferred dividend earned and paid while a substantial allowance was made for depreciation: in 1930 interest was paid and preferred dividends paid though not quite earned even when no allowance was made for depreciation. In 1931 earnings did not permit payment of interest, and in 1932 and 1933 there was a small operating loss. Consolidated Paper had a daily capacity of some 2,000 tons, compared with 2,200 for Abitibi. It operated five newsprint mills:

Grand'Mère (Laurentide)	Daily capacity	390	tons of newsprint
Cap de la Madeleine (St. Maurice)	"	263	" "
Shawinigan (Belgo-Canadian)	"	642	" "
Port Alfred	"	480	" "
Three Rivers (Wayagamack)	"	170	" "
		1,945	" "

According to Mr. C. P. Fell none of these mills could be rated low cost, but some three-quarters of the tonnage was produced in mills of reasonable efficiency.[21] The company also sold wrapping paper, and cardboard. Its power developments were minor: one in connection with the Port Alfred mill (2,500 h.p.), another in connection with the Thunder Bay mill (3,000 h.p.). Laurentide and St. Maurice sold their respective power subsidiaries to Shawinigan in 1928 before the formation of Canada Power and Paper.

Canadian International Paper Company. This is a subsidiary of International Paper and Power Company, an American company which began with the consolidation of nineteen companies in New York in 1898. The American company in the face of depletion of pulpwood reserves in its own territory and the growing imports of newsprint from Canada first acquired timber limits in Canada, and then, in 1921, built a newsprint mill at Three Rivers. With a change in the direction of the company in 1924 an aggressive policy of expansion in Canada was adopted. This policy involved: (1) building new newsprint and pulp mills in Canada located with a view to permanent reserves of wood; (2) abandoning the higher cost American mills, and converting the more efficient to other grades of paper; (3) developing water power to reduce power costs to their mills and to diversify the company's income. In 1925 the bankrupt Riordon properties were bought

[21]"The Newsprint Industry" (in *The Canadian Economy and Its Problems*, p. 51). Mr. Fell gave the total daily capacity in 1932 as 1,780 tons, and rated 1,360 tons in class B and 420 tons in class C.

at auction: these included sulphite pulp mills at Kipawa and Hawkesbury, saw mills, extensive timber reserves, and power sites on the Gatineau River. In 1926 the Three Rivers mill was doubled in capacity, making it the largest in the world; the Kipawa mill was enlarged to an annual capacity of 100,000 tons so that it produced almost half the world's supply of rayon cellulose; at Gatineau a newsprint mill was built. Other subsidiaries included a mill in Ottawa making paper bags; mills at Gatineau and Midland making fibre board; pulp and paper mills, power development and coal mines in New Brunswick; and vast power developments mainly on the Gatineau and at Ottawa. In 1933 the operating revenues of Canadian Hydro-Electric Corporation (the Canadian holding company for the power interests of International Paper and Power) were $9,300,000, of which some $4,570,000 was for power sold to the Ontario Hydro Electric Power Commission, and some $2,800,000 for power sold to International's Canadian paper mills. Through selling power to E. B. Eddy, Limited, of Ottawa, International acquired, but later relinquished, an interest in that company: it also sold power to various public utilities, and sold power retail. A subsidiary of the Canadian International operated in Newfoundland, but this plant was sold in 1938 to Bowater. According to Mr. C. P. Fell, Canadian International had, in 1932, a daily capacity of about 1,800 tons of newsprint, of which nearly 1,200 tons was from low-cost mills.[22]

Other newsprint companies. In addition to the three big corporations, Abitibi, Canada Power and Paper, and International, each of which had a capacity of about 2,000 tons daily, there were two other big producers, St. Lawrence Corporation and Price Brothers. St. Lawrence was a combination of three newsprint companies and had a capacity of about 1,100 tons daily; Price Brothers had a capacity of about 1,250 tons daily and controlled Donnacona, with a capacity of 250 tons. There were also about a dozen smaller companies with daily capacities varying from 37 to 500 tons daily, two of these being controlled by United States newspaper publishers.

Competition in the newsprint industry.[23] The newsprint industry of Canada in 1939 had an annual capacity of 4.6 million tons; at $50

[22]*Ibid.*

[23]See J. A. Guthrie, *The Newsprint Paper Industry* (Cambridge, Mass., 1941), chap. vii, "Monopolistic Elements in the Newsprint Industry," and viii, "Price Determination and Price Policy"; L. G. Reynolds, *The Control of Competition in Canada* (Cambridge, Mass., 1940), pp. 23–6, and p. 99; E. A. Forsey, "The Pulp and Paper Industry" (*Canadian Journal of Economics and Political Science*, Aug., 1935); *Newsprint Paper Industry* (Senate Document, 214, 71st Congress), Washington, D.C., 1930; Charles Vining, *Newsprint Prorating* (a report submitted to the government of the Province of Quebec, April, 1940).

192 INTRODUCTION TO POLITICAL ECONOMY

a ton it was able to sell 3.2 million tons. It was generally believed that sales would prove highly unresponsive to lower prices. An increase in sales would require on the one hand the expansion of consumption in the United States, and on the other hand substitution by the United States of Canadian for domestic, or Scandinavian, newsprint. Only a very substantial fall in price would increase consumption; a reduction in the Canadian price would be met by a similar reduction in the price of United States newsprint, thus adding little to Canadian sales; and if there were not a similar fall in the price of Scandinavian newsprint the additional sale of 300,000 tons would probably be shared between the Canadian and American mills. It seems likely therefore that the Canadian industry made more money by operating at about two-thirds capacity than if it produced and sold (at whatever price it would bring) its total possible output.

Under conditions of competition such as exist in the production of wheat, restriction of output, by agreement between the producers, even if it were obviously in the interest of the industry as a whole, would be impossible. The reason is that there are so many farmers; and each farmer produces so small a fraction of the whole that any individual restrictions would have no effect on the price. Under these conditions each farmer makes the biggest profit if he produces and sells all he can at the market price, however low. Compulsion by the state to reduce acreage is, except in wartime, difficult politically and administratively. State holding of the accumulating surplus has been for wheat what operation below capacity has been for newsprint; and these surpluses and this unused capacity have been alike as threats to an established price.

Conditions in the market for newsprint are different. In the thirties three corporations controlled nearly half the output and there were a dozen others. If the newsprint producers had behaved like the wheat producers the price would have fallen, sales would have increased and ultimately production would have decreased as the less efficient mills were forced out of business. How low the price would have gone cannot be estimated, but the efficient producers believed, probably rightly, that they would be worse off operating at capacity at the low price which would then rule than operating below capacity at the existing price. There was therefore a basis for agreement to restrict output to what could be sold at that price. The number of producers being small agreement was facilitated. But agreement remained difficult; each seller was acutely aware of the advantage to him of increasing production so as to make the existing operating profit per ton on more tons; each was acutely aware, too, of the ease with which his sales would increase if he quoted a price below that of his competitors, for the product is so completely standardized that price is almost the only competitive factor; and the smaller mills might well feel that any increase in their output would cause a relatively insignificant increase in the total. True, the intelligent producer would see the consequences of his action: the mills that lost tonnage to the price cutter would retaliate by a similar cut, and the lower price would become general; at the lower price total sales would be but little greater and the original price cutter would enjoy only a share of this increase; with a minor increase in output and a major fall in price the firm that initiated the change would be worse off than before, and so would the rest. Intelligent foresight might have restrained the mill; desire to avoid the odium of having reduced the profits of the others might have had a similar restraining influence; and fear that the others would take punitive, not merely defensive, measures might have played some part. But desperation, or disagreement as to the appropriate degree of restriction, led mills to initiate price reductions against the general will of the industry; and the presence of very large buyers on the market did, on occasion, promote such action. With big buyers like Hearst in the market with contracts for amounts up to 250,000 tons annually,[24] the temptation to offer a lower price to secure such a contract was, at times, irresistible. How, then, was the price determined? We shall see that the industry followed the leadership of International Paper in the early twenties; attempted organization to enforce a policy of greater restriction than International favoured in the late twenties; fell into a chaotic state where leadership was ill-defined and agreement lacking in the early thirties; and developed, with government support, a system of equal sharing of production between the mills (prorating) making the task of leadership, or agreement, easier.

[24]Almost all newsprint was sold under contracts for a year or term of years, but the price was subject to revision each year, or half year. This might have been expected to impart a measure of stability in the market, and to permit the existence of different prices at the same time as between different buyers and sellers. It was usual, however, for the contracts to entitle the buyer to the advantage of any lower price quoted in any other contract by the same or any other seller. The result was that any seller who signed a contract below the ruling level committed the industry to the lower price. Mr. Martin of the Newsprint Association informed me in 1939 that "nearly all the old price clauses tying the price to that quoted by any mill of 100,000 tons capacity have been eliminated. There is still interlocking in the case of most of the smaller mills but usually the 'price fixing' companies named are Canadian International, Abitibi, Price Brothers, and Consolidated Paper. Moreover, some of the larger mills do not relate their price to any specific seller but merely use a phrase such as 'a generally prevailing price for Canadian paper in the customer's zone'."

Price leadership. Throughout the twenties International Paper exercised price leadership east of the Rockies, though after 1927 its leadership was challenged. This leadership was based on confidence that in establishing its price the general condition of the industry had been considered, and on a belief that International was prepared to take punitive measures against any who would not follow the lead and that it could command the support of other big companies for these measures. The increase in the price for 1923 and the reductions in price in 1924, 1925, and 1926 were announced by International, and followed by the industry in Canada and the eastern United States. In 1927 the organization of a cartel, Canadian Newsprint Company, to handle the sales of fourteen mills indicates some dissatisfaction with International's leadership, or doubts as to its ability to enforce such leadership. However the cartel (which is described below) was unable to restrain its own members from price cutting, and in July, 1928, International again led the industry in a price reduction. In November, 1928, another organization was formed, the Newsprint Institute, to dispute the leadership of International, and the governments of the Provinces of Ontario and Quebec joined in the fray. International announced a New York price of $57 a ton for 1929 but was persuaded (almost forced by the threats of Ontario and Quebec) to raise this price to $62.

Canadian Newsprint Company. This was a company formed in 1927 and owned by fourteen producing mills[25] to act as a cartel. The individual mills might sell only to the cartel. Sales of paper were made by the three sales agencies that had served the individual mills; these agencies bought from the cartel which pooled the orders and allocated tonnage to the member mills on a rated daily basis. The company controlled 50 per cent of the Canadian capacity. It entered into negotiations with the Hearst buyer for a contract to sell 250,000 tons a year. To secure this contract the cartel was at first prepared to agree to a reduction in price; but a change in its officers led to a change in policy. The new officers tried to maintain the old price whereupon the Hearst buying company began to negotiate with individual members. Anglo-Canadian and Brompton broke away from the cartel and signed individual contracts with the Hearst organization at the price previously agreed by the cartel. The cartel dissolved, and International leadership was resumed. International announced a price reduction for 1929 with a reduction for the latter half of 1928 conditional on signing contracts for 1929 at this price.

[25]These mills were: Laurentide, Price Bros., Port Alfred, St. Maurice, Canada Paper, Ste. Anne, Spanish River, Fort William, Abitibi, Brompton, Belgo-Canadian, Murray Bay, Manitoba, Anglo-Canadian. It will be noticed that most of these figured in the amalgamations of the next few years.

The Newsprint Institute. This was an association of Canadian newsprint manufacturers organized in 1928 at the instance of the Prime Ministers of Ontario and Quebec. It included all the producers except International, Spruce Falls (*New York Times* affiliate), Ontario Paper (*Chicago Tribune* affiliate), and the Pacific coast companies; and it controlled about 70 per cent of the Canadian capacity. Its purposes were to agree on a reasonable price, to restrict output to that which could be sold at this price, and to allocate tonnage to the constituent mills on the basis of rated daily capacity. The following statement about the Institute by George H. Montgomery, K.C., its general counsel, was made to the Federal Trade Commission of the United States in 1929; the emphasis on maintaining employment in towns entirely dependent on the industry is important:

Last autumn the premiers of the Provinces of Ontario and Quebec became seriously concerned over the turn of affairs in the newsprint industry, which was in a highly demoralized condition. It had been considerably over developed with the result that in the competition for business contracts were being entered into at prices which afforded no possibility of profit and a price war was actively threatened which seemed likely to spell ruin to a number of the existing mills. Whole communities were being thrown out of employment, as the result of closing down of certain of the higher-cost mills, and as in many instances these communities were not supported by any other industry it is unnecessary to dwell upon the distress which seemed impending during the forthcoming winter. The complaints were so serious and conditions such that the governments could not ignore them and they felt obliged to give notice to the several companies operating mills in their respective Provinces that unless immediate steps were taken by the newsprint companies to regulate their affairs the government would take the matter in hand themselves. The greater part of the wood from which newsprint is manufactured is the property of the Crown and the Premiers intimated in no uncertain terms that they did not propose to allow their forests to be made use of in a manner so prejudicial to the public interest.

The manufacturers were accordingly called together and were addressed by the premiers who informed them that they would have to make some provision for the distribution of the available tonnage on an equal basis so as to afford some measure of employment to all the mill communities as well as to those engaged in the cutting operations incidental to them. The available business was at the time very unevenly distributed so that the premiers' mandate involved the necessity of the mills which were long in business giving up a portion of it to those who were short in order to put them on an equal footing, and this met with great resistance and was naturally only acceded to by the longs under governmental pressure.

The distribution of the business necessarily involved provisions for adjustments so that each mill would receive the same mill net for the tonnage manufactured. A short set of rules was prepared for the conduct of the industry during this period of stress, giving effect to the mandates of the premiers, which rules were approved by them and agreed to, the premiers themselves undertaking to act as arbitrators in the event of any dispute arising. A secretary was appointed to look after the necessary adjustments and this constitutes the so-called Newsprint Institute of Canada. It is not incorporated and might be termed at the most an involuntary association.[26]

In October, 1928, International bid for a Hearst contract, quoting prices substantially lower than its previously announced price for 1929, a price of roughly $57 at New York. The actual price quoted was not known and rumours were circulated greatly exaggerating the reduction. The members of the Newsprint Institute, who would have to meet this price, protested. On November 19, Mr. Ferguson (then Prime Minister of Ontario) issued a reminder to International that there were means of bringing governmental pressure to bear upon it:

It is with regret that the Government finds it necessary to draw your attention to the fact that you are under contract with this Province, that your contract contains a number of important covenants, that many of the companies are in arrears and default has occurred with respect to a number of the conditions and obligations provided in the contract. This condition can not be allowed to continue. I am therefore writing you on behalf of the Government to say that unless the people interested in the operation of this industry take some immediate steps to put the industry on a more satisfactory basis and improve the present situation, the Government will be compelled to give serious and immediate consideration to what action it should take under existing contracts to protect the interests of this Province, its industries, its settlers, its wage earners and its people generally. May I request that you inform me promptly what immediate action is contemplated by your company and the others engaged in the industry to rectify the present situation?[27]

On November 22, Mr. Taschereau (then Prime Minister of Quebec) called Mr. Graustein, the President of International, to Montreal to discuss the situation, and the conferences lasted six days. Mr. Graustein, in evidence before the Federal Trade Commission, said: "Mr. Taschereau told us in vigorous language that the price which was specified in that October contract with Hearst must be raised. He spoke of penalties and pressure; and he was insistent in his attitude."[28] Mr. Hearst's representative was also present and was subjected to great pressure. Negotiations continued till the end of February while publishers took their paper without knowing what the price would be. Finally International and Hearst revised the price in their contract, establishing a price of $5 above the original contract. This price, roughly $62 at New York, was followed by all the producers in Canada and the United States.

In November, 1929, Mr. Taschereau and Mr. Ferguson again summoned Mr. Graustein to a conference. Abitibi and Canada Power and

[26]*Newsprint Paper Industry*, p. 87.
[27]*Ibid.*, p. 41.
[28]*Ibid.*, p. 43.

Paper wanted to raise the price for 1930 by $5, and International was called on to fall in line. Price Brothers and St. Lawrence, however, broke away from the Institute and renewed their contracts at the 1929 price. International followed suit. The action of Canada Power and Paper in offering a bonus of common stock to secure the Hearst contract, a veiled form of price cutting, had considerable influence in precipitating the action of Price Brothers and St. Lawrence. There followed a period of demoralization and secret price cutting. The Newsprint Institute dissolved.[29]

Newsprint Association of Canada. A "committee of bankers" was organized in November, 1931, to try to restore order. It contemplated a further measure of consolidation to secure joint action, and was successful in establishing some voluntary tonnage pools for 1932. Its activities ceased within a year of its formation. In 1933 a new association was formed, Newsprint Export Manufacturers Association of Canada, to co-operate with the code authority in the United States under N.I.R.A. This time International joined the association and contributed to a pool which distributed orders for over 50,000 tons to needy mills. The United States was prepared to impose a dumping duty on Canadian newsprint if a price below $40 was quoted. The new Association proved less effective than was expected largely because the industry in the United States was not allowed to develop its code as it had hoped. In October, 1934, St. Lawrence, a mill which had been a beneficiary of the pooling scheme, broke the attempt of International to establish a $2.50 rise in price for 1935. The Association continued, however, until 1936 when its name was changed to the Newsprint Association of Canada and some changes were made in its by-laws. This Association still functions, but its influence on price policy cannot be determined.

Prorating.[30] The behaviour of the St. Lawrence Paper Company in 1934 was the first of a series of incidents leading to the establishment of a system of "prorating" under joint pressure from the governments of Ontario and Quebec. Mr. Taschereau called on St. Lawrence to extricate itself from its contract and to follow the lead of International; he promised to induce other Quebec mills to give it a fair share of tonnage and threatened to impose penalties in the form of

[29]The degree of utilization of capacity in mills operated by members of the Newsprint Institute and in Canadian non-member mills is shown in a table taken from the *Compilation of Statements and Information* (Abitibi):

	Institute Mills	Non-Institute Mills
	(percentage of capacity utilized)	
1929	81	98
1930	59	93
1931	45	91

[30]See Charles Vining, *Newsprint Prorating.*

increased stumpage dues and loss of cutting privileges. The buyers, however, insisted on maintenance of the contract; the whole industry had to accept the price thereby established; and penalties were imposed on St. Lawrence.

The second incident occurred in December, 1934, when the Great Lakes Paper Company, having lost an important contract to a Quebec Company, decided that it must close its mill. This shut-down would have meant a serious crisis at the head of the lakes where the Abitibi mill was already closed. The Ontario government conferred with Mr. Taschereau and arrangements were made for certain companies to provide tonnage to enable Great Lakes to continue to operate.

Early in 1935 Quebec passed its Forest Resources Protection Act to ensure that the government could impose adequate penalties to enforce its will on the industry. Mr. Taschereau said: "I have made up my mind that it is about useless to negotiate further with the newsprint companies. My experience is that it is very hard to find co-operation and loyalty among firms engaged in newsprint. Legislation is necessary, and it is our intention to take such measures as we may think proper to save this basic industry." In the next year Ontario passed similar legislation. In each case provision is made that in cases of conduct detrimental to the public interest the provincial government may impose penalties so severe as actually to prevent the offender from continuing operations. The industry appointed at this time an independent committee to work out an adequate plan of tonnage distribution and to satisfy the governments of Ontario and Quebec of the industry's good intentions. The committee consisted of Messrs. Howard, Ralston, and Vining. In the summer of 1935 the powers conferred by the Forest Resources Protection Act enabled Mr. Taschereau to restrain Price Brothers from signing a contract for 1936 at the old price at a time when the industry hoped to raise the price. It was necessary, of course, to promise Price Brothers a "fair" share of the tonnage. The accepted notion of fairness was that tonnage should be enjoyed in proportion to rated daily capacity, but it became clear that there was no agreement as to the rating. In his correspondence with Price Brothers, Mr. Taschereau used the phrase "a proration of tonnage in the industry."

Shortly after Mr. Taschereau had intervened to prevent Price Brothers signing a contract committing the industry to a policy of no advance of price for 1936, the Ontario government ran into trouble with Great Lakes Paper. In September, 1935, a plan for reorganization of this company was proposed which involved a number of United

States publishers placing ten-year contracts with a new company of the same name in return for a number of free shares, class B, bearing dividends concurrently with any dividends paid on class A stock. This proposal was regarded by the other manufacturers as a disguised price rebate. It was also feared that the tonnage taken away from other producers would create new "short" situations and contribute to further instability. Mr. Hepburn, Prime Minister of Ontario, intervened and before the reorganization was completed the company was required to give an undertaking to the goverment that the new company would participate equitably with other mills in any scheme of tonnage distribution that the government might require. Though the government intention was clear it was apparently not made clear to the sponsors of the new company. The new Great Lakes Paper Company resisted application to it of the scheme of prorating.

During 1935 the Ontario government became alarmed at the distribution of tonnage between the provinces. This again raised the question of a sound rating of productive capacity in order to determine what was Ontario's "fair" share of tonnage. It raised, too, the question of finding some form of tonnage distribution which would not merely obtain tonnage to relieve occasional acute short situations, but would assure to each province its proper share of employment and public revenue from the industry. The last straw for Ontario was the announcement in December, 1935, that the Ontario Paper Company (*Chicago Tribune*) intended to build a new 100,000 ton mill at Baie Comeau in Quebec. Feeling that they were already losing tonnage unfairly to Quebec, Ontario saw the new mill as adding to the disparity and "their indignation was emphasized by the fact that they were in the throes of the Great Lakes reorganization difficulties in which they felt they were fighting a battle for the benefit of both provinces." For a time it appeared that the provinces might adopt a belligerent attitude toward each other; but in February, 1936, a policy of joint action was adopted. The two governments agreed to such joint action as would enable each producer to secure a fair share of the available tonnage; a fair sharing between the provinces followed automatically. A careful survey of efficient productive capacity was first made,[31] then the industry was told to make arrangements for a fair distribution of tonnage: if a company's efficient capacity was 10 per cent of the total efficient capacity of the industry it was con-

[31]The survey was made by Mr. Paul Kellogg. It gave the industry, according to Mr. Vining, "for the first time in its history, capacity ratings which the mills recognized as accurate, and they were accepted by both governments."

sidered entitled to 10 per cent of the tonnage, or, putting it another way, if the industry was operating at 60 per cent of efficient capacity each mill was entitled to operate at 60 per cent of its efficient capacity. The independent committee which had acted for the industry in its negotiations with the governments agreed to supervise the scheme, and Mr. Kellogg was added as a fourth member.[32]

The provincial governments did not undertake to determine the price of newsprint; indeed price leadership was again assumed by International. But the incentive to break out of line is eliminated if the price cutter cannot increase his tonnage at the expense of others. Prorating seemed therefore to make agreement on restriction of output and maintenance of prices easier; but there remained the difficulty of securing compliance. In the first place publisher-owned mills were exempt, involving 400,000 tons of newsprint in 1938. This reduced the tonnage available for the prorating mills and caused discontent. It also encouraged other mills to tie up with publishers to secure this advantage. In addition there were cases of persistent non-compliance; in Ontario, for instance, Great Lakes Paper maintained a claim to exemption as a publisher-controlled mill, in spite of the undertaking given at the time of reorganization. Such persistent non-compliance led to discontent and sporadic non-compliance amongst other producers. Continuance of the system required greater severity in enforcing compliance.

In view of the difficulty of restraining producers from expanding production there does not seem to have been much danger of undue restriction and unduly high prices. Competition from Scandinavia, and potential competition from new mills in New England, or in the southern states to utilize southern pine, put a very definite upper limit to the price. The unpopularity of the scheme with the press of the United States could not be ignored: the power of the press had been used in the past to discipline the newsprint producers; it might be used again. It is possible that the cost of production of newsprint was somewhat higher as a result of prorating rather than concentrating production

[32]"The Committee has . . . acted as liaison between the two Governments, has provided each Government with monthly statistical reports and has also, by request of the Governments, submitted advice regarding situations arising from non-compliance with requirements. Within its limitations, the Committee has endeavoured to make the Government's policy effective, but it must be made clear that authority and means of enforcement have rested only with the governments. . . . The position of the Committee has not been an enviable one. Manufacturers have looked upon the Committee as representing the Governments, and the Governments have regarded it as representing the industry" (*Newsprint Prorating*, p. 27). Mr. Vining was President of the Newsprint Association of Canada, but the Committee was "independent."

more nearly in the hands of the efficient suppliers (taking into account both mill efficiency and cost of power, pulp, etc.).[33] It is urged by the advocates of the scheme that there are not wide differences in cost between the mills; that operating costs per ton are not much reduced by increased scale of operations; and that the necessary elasticity in the supply is promoted by having many mills open and operating below capacity. But even if the scheme did involve higher costs it might be justified on business grounds as a cost of maintaining a profitable restriction of output, and on social grounds as a cost of maintaining employment in communities completely dependent on the industry. One of the dangers of prorating was the possible slackening of initiative and aggressive salesmanship on the part of the individual firms. It is important, therefore, that any restrictive policy should be supplemented by a positive policy of developing new business. Such positive action must be taken by the associated companies. There is some evidence that this need was recognized. "Canadian companies," said Mr. Vining in his submission, "need to be prepared to contend effectively against aggressive and well organized competitors."

In 1932 the total production of newsprint was only 2.2 million tons, or 53 per cent of capacity. As business conditions improved in the United States, the industry began to expand, and by 1936 production had reached 3.5 million tons. In 1937 the newspaper publishers, fearing that the prorating scheme would lead to a price rise, tried to build up stocks at the low price. As a result, production

[33]To this suggestion Mr. Vining replied: "The facts give no support to this statement. In the first place each mill's capacity is determined from time to time on an engineer's formula of standardized operating efficiency. A machine or mill below this standard is rated as zero; the others are rated by their performance record over a specified period. In the case of shutdown machines, the engineers ascertain whether they could be effectively operated within a fixed time; if not, they are classed as not available. The ratings thus made have been recognized as competent by manufacturers highly sensitive to the ratings of their competitors.

In the second place there is a great deal of loose talk and misconception about efficient and inefficient mills. The facts are that machine performances are only part of the cost of producing and delivering newsprint, and they are not the major part. The big items are wood, power and delivery. It is quite possible that a new mill may have lower machine costs than an older mill, but the older mill may have a more fortunate power contract, or it may be better located for delivery, or it may have some particular advantage in its wood supply.

Consequently, the expression 'efficient and inefficient mills' means very little. What is really meant is 'efficient and inefficient suppliers,' i.e., taking into account not only machine performances but the equally or more important factors of wood, power and delivery. Taking these into account, there is a surprisingly even level of costs and mill nets among the newsprint manufacturers in these two Provinces. The advantages which do exist do not always belong to the newest mills" (*Newsprint Prorating*, pp. 62-3).

jumped to 4.0 million tons. In 1938 International was able to maintain price leadership in raising the price of newsprint to $50 a ton. A consequent "strike" on the part of the publishers led to a slump of 1 million tons in sales, but the price held. The fall in production threatened the prorating line, and several minor companies broke out. In general, however, prorating and price leadership were effective in maintaining the position of the industry in 1938 and 1939.

The control of newsprint in World War II. The outbreak of war created very little change in the industry. Scandinavian supplies of newsprint to the United States were cut off, and there was some increase in Canadian exports, but this was balanced by loss of most of the United Kingdom market through shortage of shipping space. As a result, the industry continued to operate at about 80 per cent of capacity. Prorating was continued and price was maintained at $50 a ton until 1943. Heavy demands for other wood pulp products caused a rapid rise in the prices of these products and led to some diversion of the unused newsprint capacity of the industry to their manufacture.

In the early part of the war the increasing need for U.S. dollars placed the Canadian newsprint industry in a prominent position in the war effort. The industry was encouraged to increase production of all types of paper needed in the United States in order to expand exports and maintain essential imports. By 1942, however, the strict rationing of U.S. dollars in Canada, and the signing of the Hyde Park and Ogdensburg agreements had alleviated the dollar shortage, while the accelerated pace of war, the increasingly serious shortage of hydro-electric power fundamental to the manufacture of newsprint, the drain of manpower into war industries, and the demand for paper for war purposes, forced the Canadian government to impose controls on the newsprint industry. Large blocks of power were diverted from the industry and the rest was rationed to it according to the requirements of war. In order to compensate the newsprint industry for the loss of hydro-electric power, and consequent decline in production, the government set up a prorating plan under Wartime Prices and Trade Board Order 222, effective January 1, 1943. This order brought the newsprint industry under the control of an administrator, who allotted production and shipments to the various companies.

Total production of newsprint was fixed by the administrator at the average level of output prevailing from April to October, 1941. Later this level was changed to 90 per cent of the average shipment in the period October, 1941, to March, 1942. Production was thus frozen at about 3.2 million tons. Each mill was allotted a fixed percentage of the total, based on the rated capacity of the mill, orders on the books, past shipments, and other factors. Abitibi was to receive

13 per cent of the total production, Canadian International Paper, 16 per cent, and Consolidated Paper, 13 per cent. The remaining twenty-two companies received smaller percentages in accordance with their capacity.

The percentage allotted to each company was a maximum which might be cut owing to a local shortage of power or sulphite. In this case the administrator could transfer the extra tonnage to another company. The profits from the sale of this extra tonnage were to be put into a fund set up under the Commodity Prices Stabilization Corporation. The company from which the tonnage was transferred could then draw from the fund the profits which it would have received if it had been able to produce the newsprint itself. In this way the burden of war was spread among all the companies.

Demand for newsprint was relatively stable for the first few years of the war, with sales to the United States remaining at about 2.8 million tons a year. However, demand increased sharply when the United States entered the war. Interest in war news and improved business conditions sent newspaper sales upward, while the transfer of much American capacity to the manufacture of other types of paper cut their domestic supply. The burden of increased demand fell upon the Canadian mills. To protect Canadian consumers, the Dominion government limited exports of newsprint to 94 per cent of total production, and rationed newspaper publishers to a percentage of their previous consumption. Pressure by American mills on the Office of Price Administration in Washington led to several price increases during 1943 and 1944, and by 1945, the price of newsprint at New York had climbed to $60.25 a ton. The added 10 per cent exchange on United States funds gave the Canadian mills a net price of $66 a ton, an increase of $26 a ton from the low point of $40 a ton, reached in 1934.

Government restrictions on the production of newsprint were never very severe. The political importance of the press, and the vocal power of newsprint consumers, made it more desirable to stabilize production and attempt to increase the supply of hydro-electric power rather than cut output of newsprint to any great extent. The most important restriction lay in the shortage of pulpwood workers. In 1942 efforts were made to increase the numbers of these workers by special dispensation from military service, a high priority rating, and diversion of farm labour to the woods in winter.

Newsprint, 1946–54. With the end of the war Canadian newsprint entered on a new period of expansion. In Table V some of the relevant figures are brought together. Capacity increased by 1.3 million tons, but the mills operated above capacity year after year and the price rose. Newsprint supplies continued in 1955 to be tight, and still further expansion was planned. The increase in capacity since 1946 had largely been achieved by speeding up existing machines: until 1955 only two new machines had been installed, and those in British Columbia; in 1955 five new machines were under construction. By 1957 the industry should have a capacity of 6.8 million tons. At the same time producers

TABLE V

CANADIAN NEWSPRINT, 1946–54

Year	Capacity (million tons)	Production (million tons)	Operating ratio (per cent)	Price (U.S. dollars)
1946	4.6	4.5	97	72.25
47	4.7	4.8	102	88.50
48	4.9	5.0	102	97.67
49	5.1	5.2	101	100.00
50	5.2	5.3	101	101.00
51	5.4	5.5	102	111.00
52	5.5	5.7	103	121.00
53	5.7	5.7	100	126.00
54	5.9	6.0	101	126.00

in the United States have increased their capacity from 0.8 million tons in 1946 to 1.3 million tons in 1954; and an additional 400,000 tons capacity is likely to be added by 1957. One may well ask whether supply will not outrun consumption at high prices, and how responsive to lower prices consumption would be. Growing population and a resumption in 1955 of the growth in per capita consumption in the United States, and unsatisfied demands in the rest of the world, suggest that no great surplus capacity will develop as long as income and employment are maintained. It would be no great hardship to operate for a few years at 90 per cent of capacity with fairly high prices while consumption caught up: depression, on the other hand, would mean low prices and a much lower operating ratio. Meanwhile the newsprint companies have made substantial profits: Abitibi had net profits of $13 million in 1951 and $10.6 million in 1954; Consolidated Paper, $12.9 million in 1957 and $11.8 million in 1954.

The company town. The pulp and paper plant must be located near the source of wood, and, therefore, generally far from the centres of population. To provide the necessary labour supply it is necessary to provide a town for the workers to live in. Spruce Falls Power and Paper Company, for instance, was located at Kapuskasing in the midst of 5,000 miles of spruce forest. In the first great war a prison camp was located here because it was so far from anywhere that prisoners had little chance of escape. At this inaccessible point the company needed a labour force of about 1,000 men. They therefore built an entire town of 35 blocks, with 2 community centres, 3 churches, public and high schools, and 325 company houses. There were in addition many privately owned houses. Its population in 1940 was 3,500. The company's investment in the town was nearly $5 million. The town was organized as a municipality. This is the company town at its best, based on the liberal policy of the company and the steady employment in the publisher-owned mill which has been able to run continuously near capacity.[35]

The story of Espanola is less happy. In 1928 it was a flourishing community of nearly 4,000. There was no municipal organization, the town being governed autocratically by the Spanish River Pulp and Paper Company. The company had built the town, provided the water and electricity, laid sewers, built streets and sidewalks. It established and maintained good schools; and even built the churches (with the exception of the Roman Catholic church, which was built by private subscription, including a generous contribution from the company). The workers' houses were leased for $17.50-$22.50 per month. They were comfortable, well-built houses with all conveniences including a furnace. Water and electricity were free, and there were no taxes since the company ran the town. The stores, the bank, the skating rink, theatre, community hall, the hotel and boarding houses were all owned by the company and either operated or leased by it. Such complete control of the town, even when associated with the provision of considerable material benefits, is a threat to political democracy and to trade union development. On the outskirts of the company town proper, as of most company towns, were settlements of Poles, Italians, and French Canadians. Here were the families of the mill's unskilled labourers who had bought land from the government, or squatted on such land, and built their own shacks. They did this partly to provide cheaper accommodation and to be able to keep a cow or some chickens; partly because houses in the town were scarce and were given by preference to the skilled workers. In 1930 the mill was closed and has never operated since. Some of the skilled workers were moved to other Abitibi mills; others left in search of employment. In 1940 there were 1,200 left, of whom 1,000 were on relief. The company continued to maintain the water supply and the electricity supply, and kept the school open. Espanola gives a lesson in the danger of a town depending on one mill.[36]

The price of newsprint and the standard of living in Canada. The fall in the revenue from the export of newsprint from over $140 million

---

[35]See "A Typical Company Town" (*Saturday Night*, Feb. 24, 1940).

[36]This account is based on an essay by Mr. R. H. Ripley, a student at the University of Toronto in the late thirties.

in 1929 to little over $70 million in 1933, at a time when the prices of our principal imports were falling but little, involved, quite obviously, a reduction in the national income of goods and services available for current consumption or for accumulation. Canada as a whole must have been worse off, but we want to know which particular Canadians were worse off. First, consider employment. In 1929 there were 33,500 employees on salaries and wages in the pulp and paper industry; in 1933 there were 24,000. The worst sufferers were those who lost their jobs and were unable to find others: for them direct relief became necessary. Second, consider wages. Those who remained employed drew wages at rates from 10 to 20 per cent lower. Some indication of the rates of wages for various occupations are given in Table VI. It is

TABLE VI

WAGES PER HOUR FOR SELECTED OCCUPATIONS IN THE
PULP AND PAPER INDUSTRY

Occupation	1929	1933	1940	1950
Beatermen	$ .44	$ .35	$ .50	$1.08
Machine tenders	1.30	1.05	1.48	2.20
Back tenders	1.11	.82	1.32	2.00
Finishers	.45	.36	.54	1.10
Grindermen	.41	.37	.53	1.10
Digester cooks	.80	.65	.87	1.47
Labourers	.37	.30	.45	1.00

*Data from *Wages and Hours of Labour in Canada,* Dominion Bureau of Statistics. The figures given are the medians of the small sample printed in the report.

necessary to emphasize that these are average rates; there is a good deal of variation between persons, mills, and particularly between provinces.[37] In 1950 the number of employees was 52,000; employment was good and wages had risen; the wages of the less skilled had risen more, proportionately, than those of the more skilled, the wages of Quebec workers more than the wages of Ontario workers; the average income of wage earners in the industry, which in 1933 was $1,100 in Ontario and $900 in Quebec, was about $3,000 in both provinces in 1951.

[37]In 1929 wage rates of skilled labour in the industry were on the average 8 per cent higher in Ontario than in Quebec; of semi-skilled, 18 per cent higher; and of unskilled 29 per cent higher (Guthrie, *The Newsprint Paper Industry*). By 1950 wage rates in the two provinces had just about equalized (G. Schonning, "Union-Management Relations in the Pulp and Paper Industry of Ontario and Quebec," unpublished doctoral thesis in the library of the University of Toronto).

Third, consider operations in the woods. The production of pulp-wood fell from 6½ million cords in 1929 to 4¼ million cords in 1932. In good times and at the peak of the season 75,000 men may have been employed in the woods in the production of pulpwood. The decline in production involved, therefore, a substantial addition to the unem-ployed, or deprived farmers of a source of additional income at a time when farm prices were desperately low. Those who continued to secure employment in the woods received wages on the average 20 per cent lower than in 1929. Fourth, consider the owners of the plant. In 1934, 54 per cent of the total capacity of the industry was in the hands of mortgagees who were receiving no return on their investment. A further 5 per cent of the total capacity belonged to companies that had paid no dividend for two years and which operated at a loss in 1933. Finally, we must remember the effect on employment in Canadian industry, and on prices in Canadian agriculture, of the decline in the money incomes of all the groups directly connected with the pulp and paper industry. A direct reduction in the national income of $100 million originating in the newsprint industry might well account, directly and indirectly, for a total reduction of the national income of $300 million.[38]

Trade Union organization. Much has been said in this chapter about organizations of employers to maintain prices, and employees clearly stood to gain from their success. Both parties are interested in the size of the pie. But there are divergent interests too: each wants the biggest possible share of the biggest possible pie. Workers try through organization in unions to influence this division. In the newsprint industry they are organized in three unions, two international and one national and Catholic. The International Brotherhood of Paper Makers has some 7,000 members; it is a "craft" union recruited from the more skilled workers. The Union of Pulp, Sulphite and Paper Mill Workers has 33,000 members: it is an "industrial" union with a high proportion of unskilled workers. The Fédération Nationale de Travailleurs de la Pulpe et du Papier has about 12,000 members: it is an "industrial" union affiliated with the Confédération de Travailleurs Catholiques du Canada. In 1955 almost all workers in the industry were members of a union and were covered by a collective agreement. This is a com-paratively recent achievement: in 1940 less than 60 per cent, and in

[38]Cf. pp. 118, 143–44 above. It should be noted that the effect of a decline in income from wheat and pulp and paper will not necessarily be the same. If much of the income of the owners and creditors in the pulp and paper industry was saved, a decline in income would have that much less effect on employment. Cf. A. F. W. Plumptre, *Central Banking in the British Dominions* (Toronto, 1940), chap. xv.

1930 probably less than 25 per cent were organized. In his study of union-management relations in this industry Dr. Schonning character-izes four periods.[39] The first, 1914–20, was "marked by the struggle for union recognition and by autocratic management"; it was a period of "hostility and conflict." The second period, 1921–30, saw the develop-ment of "paternalism," departments of industrial relations were set up, company "welfare" schemes inaugurated, works councils or company unions were fostered. Dr. Schonning characterizes this period as one of "competition for workers' 'loyalty.'" The third period, 1930–6, saw the emergence of a co-operative and business-like attitude upon the part of the unions. The change in the character of the speeches of the president of his union, Mr. Burke, was striking: in 1918, "you are fighting for freedom just as much as the soldiers on the battlefields in the revolutionary war"; in 1936, "economic facts cannot be laughed off or ignored. . . . Were an international officer of a labour union to ignore economic facts and rely solely upon an appeal to passions or emotions, he would soon lead his union to disaster." The final period, 1937–50, was one of rapid expansion of union membership and the development of mature collective bargaining. Yearly multi-employer, multi-union wage conferences have become customary, one in Ontario and two in Quebec. In 1948, for instance, eleven Ontario firms met to negotiate a contract with nine international unions, the two paper mill unions, and seven mechanical craft unions. In Quebec, Canadian International Paper Company insisted on bargaining alone but five other Quebec firms negotiated joint contracts with their unions. Negotiations were opened first in Ontario where relations were smoother; the Ontario settlement was then used as a "pattern" in the Quebec negotiations.

[39]Schonning, "Union-Management Relations in the Pulp and Paper Industry."

CHAPTER VIII

COMBINES AND PUBLIC POLICY

IN this chapter we shall be concerned with competition and monopoly in Canadian business, and with the policy of the Canadian government in dealing with the problems which arise therefrom. Fundamental to the discussion are certain ideas which have been introduced in the section on the hypothetical handicraft model in chapter III,[1] and that on the grain trade in chapter VI.[2] Competition was there treated as a guarantee of low prices: first, because it provided a stimulus to efficiency and thus kept cost low; and, second, because supply would increase to the point where the price fell as low as the cost. This second proposition was based on two things. First, since each individual produced an insignificant proportion of the total supply he could not affect the market price by any restriction of his own output, and would, therefore, find it most profitable to produce to capacity. Second, entry of new competitors to the trade was supposed to be easy; if the few existing producers working at capacity were able to sell their product above its cost and so make excess profits, their number would be quickly increased, the total output would grow, prices would fall, and profits return to the general level. This guarantee of low prices is usually considered from the point of view of the consumer; but it is well to remember that the consumer is also interested in prices as they affect his income. Competition limits the power of individuals to "sell dear," and also the risk of their having to "buy dear." It is egalitarian in its effect. Monopoly means privileged groups with higher earnings; those excluded from the privileged group will depress earnings and prices in the trades they perforce follow. The privileged sell dear and buy cheap. One should also remember that the competitive equilibrium of our model was shown to be a relatively "sensible order":[3] monopoly in the model would produce a different and less satisfactory order. The monopolized goods would be produced in smaller quantities, and the competitive goods in larger quantities, than if competition ruled throughout. If men could leave the competitive

[1]See pp. 44-9 above.
[2]See pp. 156–61 above.
[3]See pp. 51-2 above.

trades and enter the monopolized trades they would produce higher priced (i.e., more wanted) goods, in place of lower priced (i.e., less wanted) goods. Finally, be it remembered, competition guarantees flexible prices, and we have indicated the importance of price flexibility in maintaining full employment in face of a decline in spending, whether resulting from an increase in thrift or a decrease in export incomes.[4]

In our model we assumed competition to exist. In our study of the earlier history of wheat we found competition to exist amongst the producers: in the thirties though government action very greatly affected the price, no individual producer could influence it by withholding supply: in the forties the Wheat Board became the sole seller of Canadian wheat in a competitive world market, and held large stocks in order to influence the price in that market. In our study of newsprint we found competition of a different sort, competition between a few large producers, each of whom by his action in increasing or decreasing production did affect the market price,[5] and with this sort of competition there naturally developed devices for limiting, restricting, or controlling such competition. The governments of Ontario and Quebec fostered the development of agreements to restrict the output of newsprint; but we shall find that the Dominion government has tried to prevent the development of such agreements in Canadian manufacturing industry and to dissolve agreements that have been made.

Competition of monopolists.   Competition and monopoly are generally thought of as at opposite poles; and properly so if one is thinking of the contrast between Courtaulds (Canada) Limited, the sole producer of rayon (viscose) yarn in Canada, and the tens of thousands of wheat producers. It is important, however, to notice that monopolists are subject to the competition of producers of substitutes. Thus Courtaulds must meet the competition of Canadian Celanese, the sole producer of cellulose (acetate) yarns in Canada, and both must meet the competition of the producers of cotton, wool, nylon, and real silk. These are all different commodities; substitutes yet not perfect substitutes for one another. For some purposes one material is so superior to the others that it will be used even though the difference in price is big; for other purposes the two materials may be so nearly equal that a slight difference in price will decide which is to be used. The monopolist producer of the one must decide how far he wants to push the sales of his own product on the fringes of markets of the others. If he decides to compete he has various weapons: he may lower his price, openly or in many indirect and secret ways; he may improve

[4]See pp. 59–61 and 143–44 above.   [5]See pp. 191–93 above.

the quality and attractiveness of his commodity, or its container, or of the services which are rendered along with the sale; or he may increase his advertising and sales effort in order to persuade reluctant buyers of the superior qualities of his product. If he were a lone monopolist in an otherwise competitive economy this would be simple; but in the real world his competitors may be monopolists too. When they see him encroaching on their markets they retaliate, using the same armoury of weapons. So war is declared: prices are cut, expensive gadgets are added, advertising appropriations are increased. The expense of this competitive warfare is a strong inducement to patch up terms of peace, though it is usually an armed peace. It is these expenses which are in mind when reference is made to the "wastes of competition."

Competition between monopolists is active, and can be well described by analogies from warfare. Under "perfect" competition, such as we supposed to exist in our model, the individual competitor is passive. He adapts himself passively to the market; he can sell all he can produce at the market price and need not raid other markets with price concessions and advertising campaigns. Under such conditions of perfect competition, there is paradoxically no competition in the active, belligerent sense in which business men think of that word. The "decline of competition" in the last half-century appears to some to be better described as the "rise of competition." The passive "perfect" competition has declined; active, fierce, "monopolistic" competition has risen or increased in scope and intensity.

How widespread is the development of this active, fierce competition, and, consequently, of agreements to restrain its ferocity, cannot be understood if we think only of great monopolists such as Courtaulds and Celanese. In modern industry most producers are monopolists in some degree. Their product is not quite identical with that of their competitors and some buyers have a preference for dealing with them. They pack their product in a distinctive container; they distinguish it from similar products by a brand, or trade name; they cater to a particular locality or class of buyer. Though monopolists, they are but weak monopolists; if they raise their price much buyers will desert them and buy instead the almost identical product of their competitors, packed in a different type of container, sold under a different trade name, or at a somewhat less convenient place. Each of these weak monopolists is subject to the active competition of other weak monopolists producing very close substitutes. For them, too, the expense of competitive warfare is considerable and the inducement to patch up terms of peace is strong. But, since the number of competitors is large and their relative strength is uneven, agreement on terms of peace is difficult and the durability of any agreement is likely to be slight.

Entrance to the trade. Every monopolist must consider the potential competition of new entrants to his trade, or of new producers of close substitutes, if profits are tempting. He must train his guns not only on his actual competitors, but also on the paths of entry to the trade. It has been the avowed policy of the government of the United States to keep these paths of entry open by laws restraining "unfair methods of competition." But the paths are often narrow and steep, and the defences remain strong. In some cases the main deterrent is the enormous capital investment necessary to establish a competing plant; in some cases the enormous outlay necessary to break down the existing preference and build up sales of a competing product; in some cases strategic patent rights bar the way; in some cases the fear that aggression will be met by fierce resistance and retaliation may deter the most venturesome. In other cases entry is easy, and agreements between those already in a trade are continually upset by new entrants. The strong monopolist is he who produces something for which there are at present no close substitutes, who is not threatened by the possibility of someone else beginning to produce the identical product, or a close substitute, and who is protected by a substantial tariff from attacks by potential foreign competitors.

Competition and technological progress.[6] At the beginning of this chapter the importance of competition as a guarantee that freedom of enterprise would be consistent with the public good was explained with reference to the "handicraft model." This explanation drew attention to important elements: but it ignored others and it could prove misleading. It was essentially an analysis of a static world, with given technology and given resources. In such a world "cheapness" is achieved by forcing all producers to adopt the least-cost methods then known and to sell at prices equal to those costs. Plenty is achieved by such an allocation of existing resources that more of the more wanted goods are produced. Competition guarantees these conditions. But in the real world revolutionary reductions in cost and spectacular increases in plenty flow from innovation in technology and from investment. It is by this process of innovation and investment that our real national income has been and is growing so rapidly. It therefore becomes a major objective of social policy to maintain an atmosphere favourable to innovation. This requires competition: indeed the case

---

[6]See V. W. Bladen and S. Stykolt, "Combines Policy and the Public Interest: An Economic Evaluation" in W. G. Friedmann (ed.), *Anti-Trust Law: A Comparative Symposium* (Toronto, 1956).

for competition in the English Classical Political Economy was based on the belief that it would provide conditions under which innovation, enterprise, and technological advance would be promoted. In the words of John Stuart Mill: "To be protected against competition is to be protected in idleness and mental dullness." But if innovation requires the stimulus of competition, it does not require the perfect competition of our model, and it was not that sort of competition that the classical economists had in mind. Professor Lionel Robbins puts it this way: "It is clear that the claims of the Classical Economists for competition . . . do not rest upon any very precise or mathematical conception of static equilibrium. . . . Their conception of the mechanism of the system of Economic Freedom was surely a conception of something more rough and ready, something much more dynamic and real, than these exquisite laboratory models."[7] To our first proposition that competition provides the stimulus for innovation we now add a second proposition, that too much competition (competition too much like that of the "exquisite laboratory" or "hypothetical handicraft" model) may inhibit innovation. Professor Joseph Schumpeter has made the most persuasive plea for the necessity of some restriction on competition in the interest of innovation in his *Capitalism, Socialism and Democracy*.[8] In a picturesque phrase he reminds us of the degree of risk and uncertainty involved in innovation: "Long range investing under rapidly changing conditions, especially under conditions that change under the impact of new commodities and new technologies, is like shooting at a target that is not only indistinct, but moving—and moving jerkily at that." The one certainty seems to be the destruction of the profits of innovation as competitors adopt the innovation and, what is more important, make new innovations. Similarly Professor J. M. Clark[9] indicates the necessity for slowing up the process of adjustment: the problem is one of the "relative speeds . . . of the initiator's gain . . . and of the neutralizing process whereby rivals follow the initiator's lead and destroy his differential advantage as his action becomes standard practice. If a potential innovator expects neutralization to be complete before he has recovered the costs of innovation, his incentive to innovate vanishes." So Schumpeter suggests that "perfectly free entry into a *new* field may make it impossible to enter it at all. The introduction of new methods of production and new commodities is hardly conceivable with perfect—and perfectly prompt—competition from the start." And Professor J. M. Clark describes the perfectly competitive

[7]*The Theory of Economic Policy* (London, 1952).
[8]New York, 1942.
[9]"Competition and the Objectives of Government Policy" in E. H. Chamberlin (ed.), *Monopoly and Competition and their Regulation* (London, 1954).

model as one "from which competitive progress would be ruled out." This then involves a dilemma: long run competitiveness is necessary to promote innovation and to ensure that the public enjoy the fruits of such innovation; some degree of monopoly in the short run is the outcome of innovation and at the same time a necessary condition of further progress."

One final point should be made: if competition creates the atmosphere for innovation, innovation is the most important and effective source of competition. Again it is to Professor Schumpeter that we turn for a vigorous statement of this position, a statement of the difference between the road to cheapness and plenty that one is thinking of when discussing competition in the static "model" and the alternative road that one must explore in the dynamic real world.

> The problem that is usually being visualised is how capitalism administers existing structures, whereas the relevant problem is how it creates and destroys them. . . . In capitalistic reality as distinguished from its textbook picture, it is not that kind of competition which counts but the competition from the new commodity, the new technology, the new source of supply, the new type of organisation . . . competition which commands a decisive cost or quality advantage and which strikes not at the margins of the profits and the outputs of the existing firms, but at their foundations and their very lives. This kind of competition is as much more effective than the other as a bombardment is in comparison with forcing a door, and so much more important that it becomes a matter of comparative indifference whether competition in the ordinary sense functions more or less promptly: the powerful lever that in the long run expands output and brings down prices is in any case made of other stuff.

Failure to recognize this aspect of competition leads many to underestimate the real competitiveness of the modern world and to overestimate the need for government action to ensure enough competition.

Monopoly and oligopoly in Canada. Strict monopoly, in the sense of control by a single firm of the whole supply of some distinct commodity for which there is no perfect, or nearly perfect, substitute, is relatively rare. Professor Lloyd Reynolds[10] identified a number of cases in the middle thirties, two of which, Courtaulds and Celanese, have already been mentioned. Canadian Industries Limited had a monopoly of explosives and ammunition, and also of certain chemicals such as anhydrous ammonia, liquid chlorine, liquid sulphur dioxide, and caustic soda. Brunner Mond was the sole producer of calcium chloride and American Cyanamide was the sole producer of calcium cyanamide and sodium cyanide. Anaconda Brass was for some time the only pro-

[10]See *Control of Competition in Canada* (Cambridge, Mass., 1940); also V. W. Bladen, "Monopoly and Competition in Canada" in E. H. Chamberlin (ed.), *Monopoly and Competition and their Regulation.*

ducer in Canada of brass, copper, and nickel silver in rods, sheets, and tubes. Page Hershey Tubes, Limited, had a monopoly in the production in Canada of seamless steel pipe but had Canadian competitors for its other products. Similarly, Kelsey Wheel Company, Limited, appears to have had a monopoly in the production of hubs for automobiles, but there were other producers in Canada of wheels, rims, and brake drums. These are only a few examples. There must be a considerable number of commodities, of more or less importance, produced by only one firm in Canada. Although several firms may produce a commodity, each may have a complete monopoly in some region; only where the market is national in scope, and where the competition of foreign products is limited by tariffs and transportation costs, is the number of firms in Canada a true criterion of monopoly.

In other industries, as in newsprint, the number of firms is relatively few, and the bulk of the product comes from a very small group. This is called "oligopoly" and it is a very common condition. Three automobile firms produce over 90 per cent of the output of their industry. Five firms produce 85 per cent of the agricultural implements. In fruit and vegetable canning, and in meat packing, two firms have a preponderant influence. Seven firms make all the sugar. Two firms produce 90 per cent of the tobacco products. Where the number of firms is so small informal agreement is common, and this frequently involves accepting the leadership of the strongest company. Where the number of firms is larger more formal trade associations may develop.

In manufacturing industries it is usually found that no one producer has complete control of production, yet, nevertheless, maintenance of prices and consequent restriction of production are to some extent achieved. This maintenance of prices may result from several factors. (a) The intelligent realization by each of a small number of producers in an industry that price cutting by him will result in price cutting by others, and that his revenue from sales may therefore decrease instead of increase. Each would cut prices and increase output to capacity if he thought the others would *not* do the same, or if the others were doing the same. But each will maintain, or raise, prices if he believes that his action will induce others to do the same. (b) Decisions to maintain prices based on careful consideration of the effect on the profits of the individuals are fortified by the development of *sentiments* favourable to restriction, e.g., tacit acceptance of the impropriety of "spoiling the market," a feeling that strong price competition is "unfair," and the general use of phrases such as "chiselling"

and "cut throat competition." (c) In the development of such sentiments the cost accountant plays an important part. Conventional or
standard costing systems suggest to the individual producers the impropriety of reducing prices "below cost," and the adherence of the
other producers to the same system gives some assurance that they too
will be conscious of this impropriety, and will interpret "below cost"
in substantially the same manner. (d) Finally, fear of the consequences
of not following the *leadership* of some big competitor may keep the
smaller firms in line.

The role of trade associations.[11] The part which trade associations
may play under these conditions of imperfect competition, or quasi-
monopoly, may be sketched in broad outline as follows. An association
may enable the few producers to act as a perfect monopoly; but usually
differences of strength, differences of efficiency, and jealousies of one
kind and another will make some departure from the line of pure
monopoly inevitable. However, an association controlling prices and
production may achieve very nearly the monopoly price and monopoly
profit. Where such effective monopolistic control is impossible, an
association may promote more or less effective restriction along the
lines of the tacit agreement referred to above. By educating the individual business man to realize that his action in holding prices up
will probably lead competitors to keep them up too, the trade association may keep prices from falling as much, and as frequently, as they
would through competitive action. Whereas before the trade association had done this "educational" work the decision of one of several
firms to hold up prices would be suicidal, afterwards a situation
develops where the abandonment of price competition is the most
profitable course for each of the firms. But at the higher prices consumers can buy less, and the output is almost as much restricted by
this method as by direct agreement. By all kinds of propaganda, by
developing friendly relations, by drawing up codes of "fair" competition, etc., an association can promote the sentiments favourable to
restriction. By judicious promotion of the use of standard forms of
cost accounting, an association can reinforce the existing effect of cost
accounting as an element in tacit agreements to maintain prices and
restrict output. An instance of this is the insistence on the propriety of

[11]Adapted from a note in the *Canadian Journal of Economics and Political
Science*, May, 1938: V. W. Bladen, "The Role of Trade Associations in the
Determination of Prices." See the *Report of the Royal Commission on the Textile
Industry* (Ottawa, 1938), chap. viii, for a description of the activities of the
trade associations in that industry. Cf. A. R. Burns, *The Decline of Competition*
(New York, 1936), chap. ii, "The Trade Association and Industrial Institute,"
for a discussion of similar activities of trade associations in the United States.

taking raw materials into cost at "replacement" value during a rise in raw material prices. Finally, through an association, the "leader" or "leaders" have an opportunity to educate the smaller firms to follow them. In such ways the existence of trade associations clearly strengthens forces making for restriction of production and the maintenance of prices. Such restriction of production in periods of deflation and depression will be euphemistically referred to by the trade as "serving to limit over-production."

Provision of statistical information to their members is one of the most general functions of trade associations; this is at first sight innocuous and legitimate. The effect of much of this "statistical" work, and its clear intention, is to "rationalize"—i.e., restrict—production. The object of exchange of statistics of production, sales, stocks, etc., is clear even when the moral is not pointed. The Broad Silk section of the Silk Association of Canada had a survey of the capacity of the industry made in 1932 apparently "with the intention of impressing each member with the danger of over-production. Monthly reports of deliveries, production, and stock on hand were commenced, and the moral was sometimes pointed, as for instance in the circular sent out from the Silk Association's office in May, 1932. 'Is there overproduction? If so, is there a cure? How about a shut down for an agreed period? Could anything be done about night shifts? Would you attend a meeting to discuss this matter?' "[12]

Exchange of information about prices involves somewhat different problems. The usual excuse for this exchange of prices is the existence of "phantom" competition. The form letters reporting prices—e.g., for full fashioned hosiery—start, "owing to the fact that misrepresentations are being made as to prices at which full fashioned hosiery is being sold by mills, and the terms under which it is sold, with the result that the entire industry is being demoralized, we are giving you the lowest prices at which we sell certain specified goods to anybody in Canada under any circumstances. We have no objection to your disclosing these prices to other hosiery manufacturers. We give no undertaking not to increase or decrease these prices . . . but do undertake to notify you on the day we make such changes so that your information will always be correct."[13] There is little doubt, however, that such "open price" associations are intended to do more than provide a

[12]*Report of the Royal Commission on the Textile Industry* (Ottawa, 1938), p. 144.

[13]*Ibid.*, p. 139. Cf. a similar letter in the woollen and worsted cloth industry in which the manufacturers undertake to "notify you in writing at least three days before we quote or sell below the lowest prices herein given to you" (*ibid.*, p. 141).

defence against the reprehensible tactics of buyers; they are made in the hope, and expectation, that they will maintain higher prices. By agreeing not to change their prices without due notice, it is impossible for anyone to secure that advantage which comes to the firm that cuts first, in the period before the others fall in line. This must surely reduce the likelihood of price reductions. Further, if the names of those intending to reduce prices are circulated, pressure can be exerted to persuade, cajole, or frighten the price cutter into abandoning his policy. Then, too, the formality of reporting price changes must help to impress the members with a feeling of the seriousness of their action, and of their obligations to other members of the industry.

Trade associations have been very much interested in "fair trade practices" or the elimination of "unfair" competition. Under the general heading of "fair trade practice" they have been concerned with: (*a*) agreements to make no allowances for freight but to charge f.o.b. mill; (*b*) agreements as to terms of payment, discounts, etc.; (*c*) agreements to eliminate all kinds of bonuses and rebates, advertising allowances, unnecessary refinishing of merchandise, gifts of merchandise as premiums, etc.; (*d*) proper marking of merchandise, i.e., as "discontinued lines," "seconds," etc.; (*e*) proper definition of "wholesale" and "retail" customers. In a *competitive* society the adoption of such "fair trade" practices would be socially desirable; for competition among buyers is on a healthier basis if easy comparison of prices is possible; and standardization of the product and of terms of sale facilitates such comparison. The establishment of these practices, however, is, in fact, a phase of the decline of competition. Having agreed to maintain the list price, or having become thoroughly imbued with the "unfairness" of cutting list prices, many firms are likely to evade the agreement by giving special discounts, allowances, etc., to get business. A really effective agreement to maintain prices must, therefore, include full details as to terms of sale. Insistence on "fair trade practices" is not confined to those groups which have made price agreements, but in the other groups "fair trade" and restriction of competition are equally synonymous. Where there is a strong sentiment against spoiling the market, i.e., a strong prejudice, against price cutting, there is less prejudice against disguised price cutting. This is partly irrational, but is partly based on the belief that being secret such disguised price cutting will not be met by the competitors. Price cutting by giving special discounts and allowances involves discriminations between customers which is undesirable, but discrimination in favour of first one, then another customer, till the terms have become general, appears to be the way in which prices are in fact whittled down.

Canadian legislation against combines, 1889–1923.[14] The first serious attack against combines in Canada developed in 1888. Trade associations existed before that date, of course, but for various reasons their importance was then increasing. Modern large-scale industry producing for a national market was emerging and with it the pattern of competition was bound to change. The change was accelerated by the need to restrain competition and avoid a collapse of prices in face of the decline in sales resulting from general depression. This need was particularly great in those industries which had expanded under the National Policy of protection. The influence of the United States must also be noted, both on the development of combinations and the development of an anti-trust, or anti-combine, sentiment. The Canadian Act of 1889 was in a sense a by-product of the agitation which produced in 1890 the Sherman Anti-trust Act in the United States.

The inquiry into alleged combines, 1888. A Select Committee of the Canadian House of Commons[15] was appointed in 1888 to investigate alleged combines in manufactures, trade, and insurance. The Committee found sufficient evidence to justify legislative action for suppressing the evils arising from these and similar combinations and monopolies. The subjects examined were: sugar and groceries, coal, biscuits and confectionery, watch cases, barbed wire, binder twine, agricultural implements, stoves, coffins, oatmeal, eggs, barley, and fire insurance. In every case except two, viz. agricultural implements and barley, associations were, or had been, in existence. A brief description of some of the combines investigated by the Committee follows.

The Dominion Grocers' Guild was formed in 1884 with nearly one hundred members. Its main purpose was to prevent price cutting and to dictate resale prices. Its powers depended on agreements with the sugar refiners to give preferential terms to its members, and upon similar agreements with the manufacturers of tobacco, starch, baking powder, etc. The sugar refiners seem to have sold at one-third of a cent per pound less to members of the Guild and to

---

[14]Much of the material in this, and following, sections has been previously published in two articles, "Combines and Public Policy" (*Proceedings of the Canadian Political Science Association,* Toronto, 1934, vol. IV), and "A Note on the Reports of Public Investigations into Combines, 1888-1932" (*Contributions to Canadian Economics,* Toronto, 1932, vol. V). Cf. the accounts given in J. A. Ball, Jr., *Canadian Anti-Trust Legislation* (Baltimore, 1934) and Reynolds, *The Control of Competition in Canada,* chap. vi. See W. H. Hamilton, *The Pattern of Competition* (New York, 1940), for an excellent discussion of the anti-trust policy of the United States; also W. H. Hamilton and I. Till, *Anti-trust in Action* (Monograph 16, Temporary National Economic Committee, Washington, 1940).

[15]The report is printed in the *Journal of the House of Commons,* 1888, vol. XXII, appendix 3.

have imposed the condition that not more than one-quarter of a cent per pound advance should be charged on granulated sugar when resold to the retailer in lots of fifteen barrels or over, and three-eighths of one cent advance on smaller lots. The Guild was fighting for better terms; it wanted a complete boycott of non-members, or, failing this, a discrimination of one cent a pound against them; it also wanted a higher profit on resale, viz. three-eighths of a cent on lots of fifteen barrels and over and one-half of a cent on smaller lots. In its dealings with the sugar refiners it agreed to a maximum mark-up in order to get support for its own agreement on a minimum mark-up. The agreement with two starch companies provided that these companies would sell to the wholesale trade only, at uniform prices, and would support the wholesale trade in a minimum advance to the retail trade of one-half of a cent per pound on common laundry starch, three-quarters of a cent per pound on most other types, and one cent per pound on rice starch. The wholesalers agreed not to sell the product of any starch manufacturer who refused to adhere to this agreement. The Committee reported that this Guild was "obnoxious to the public interest, in limiting competition, in enhancing prices, and by the familiar use of its growing and facile powers tending to produce and propagate all the evils of monopoly."

Professor W. J. Ashley, then at the University of Toronto, came to the defence of the Grocers' Guild in an article in the *University Quarterly Review*.[16] Whereas the Committee found no agreement between the sugar refineries, Professor Ashley maintained that one refinery, the Canada Sugar Refinery at Montreal, dominated the market and that the other three followed its lead. The tariff shut out foreign competition. There existed, he maintained, an agreement to cut down production of sugar in equal proportions if necessary to maintain the price. Professor Ashley considered that the Committee had under-estimated the prevalence of price cutting and especially of the use of sugar as a "loss leader" in the retail trade. It was the retailers hampered in their use of sugar to secure trade, rather than the consumers concerned over the cost of living, that objected to the Guild. Viewed in relation to these conditions the actions of the wholesalers appeared rather as reasonable self-defence than as unwarranted aggression. The rules of the Guild seemed to Professor Ashley to make it harder for the big to kill the small, and this he thought "not a bad thing." We cannot argue here to a conclusion, but the paradox may be noted that free competition seemed likely to lead to the triumph of the few and the big, or monopolistic; re-

[16]Reprinted in *Surveys Historic and Economic* (London, 1900), pp. 361–77.

striction of competition was defended as promoting the survival of the many and the small, or competitive.

The Committee found that associations of coal dealers existed in many towns. In Toronto the six importers and fifty retailers were members of the coal section of the Toronto Board of Trade. The association fixed the price to be charged to the consumer and allowed a profit of seventy-five cents per ton to the retailers. A strict surveil-lance of the dealers was maintained, detectives being employed for this purpose. Three fines of $1,000 had already been imposed, which were divided as follows, one-sixth to the general funds, five-sixths to the importers. When public tenders were called for, the association agreed on the price to be charged and then the privilege of filling the contract was awarded to the member who offered the highest premium. This premium was divided among the importing members. To avoid suspicion, other tenders were put in at higher prices. On one occasion Messrs. Gooderham and Worts imported 259 tons of anthracite from Buffalo. The Toronto association was able to stop the shipments and collected $1,000 fine from the colliery. Similar associations existed at Montreal, London, and Ottawa. In 1910, Mr. Mackenzie King, when urging the importance of publicity, said that the publicity given by this report to the activities of the Ottawa coal dealers led to a considerable reduction in the price of coal.

The manufacturers of coffins and the dealers in undertakers' sup-plies had agreed with the Undertakers' Association to sell only to members of that organization. To become a member and enter the trade required the assent of the three undertakers nearest to the proposed place of business of the new member, and of two-thirds of the executive committee. "The inevitable result of this exclusive con-trol is exorbitant charges to the bereaved families." The manu-facturers of barbed wire attempted to maintain uniform retail prices by giving a reduction in price to those that conformed. Five manu-facturers of cordage and binder twine, who between them controlled most of the market, had organized a pool in 1884, and reorganized it within a few months of its dissolution in 1887. Their agreement provided for uniform prices and the establishment of a quota for each firm. Firms exceeding their quota paid a fine of one and one-half cents per pound, those producing less than their quota received compensation of like amount. The oatmeal millers' association con-sisted of twenty-four mills with similar arrangements as to quotas, fines, and compensation. The association had arranged for ten other mills to close by paying their owners from $300 to $800 a year (a total of $6,300) for not producing. The twenty-five mills which were outside the association were said to have small capacity and to follow its price policy.

The criminal law, 1889. The publicity given to combines by the investigation of 1888 made legislative action necessary and it was taken in 1889. Rejecting the view of the Liberals that the cause of the trouble was the tariff and that the appropriate remedy was reduction of the tariff, the Conservatives decided to force people to compete by making combination a crime. The "Act for the prevention and suppression of combinations in restraint of trade" read, in part, as follows:

1. Every person who conspires, combines, agrees or arranges with any other person, or with any railway, steamship, steamboat, or transportation company, unlawfully
   (a) to unduly limit the facilities for transporting, producing, manu-facturing, supplying, storing or dealing in any article or commodity which may be the subject of trade or commerce; or
   (b) to restrain or injure trade or commerce in relation to any such article or commodity; or
   (c) to unduly prevent, limit or lessen the manufacture or production of any such article or commodity, or to unreasonably enhance the price thereof; or
   (d) to unduly prevent or lessen competition in the production, manu-facture, barter, sale, transportation or supply of any such article or commodity, or in the price of insurance upon person or property;
is guilty of a misdemeanour and liable on conviction. . . .

The sponsors of the Act were disappointed in its effects.[17] In 1891, Mr. Wallace said in the House of Commons: "We have some reason to find fault with the Attorneys General of the various provinces for not having seen fit to enforce the law." Similarly Mr. Sproule, when moving the first reading of his bill to amend the combines clause (1889), said: "This law has been on the statute book many years and efforts have been made from time to time to get the Attorneys General of the provinces to prosecute . . . they all raise the same objection that it would be impossible to secure a conviction under the law as it stands." The law, which had been incorporated in the Criminal Code as section 520, in 1892, was amended in 1899, the qualifying words "unduly" and "unreasonably" being omitted. In 1900 the clause was again amended, the qualifying words "unduly" and "un-reasonably" being replaced, but the word "unlawfully" being omitted. This made it easier to secure a conviction. In this form it remains;

[17]See Reynolds, *The Control of Competition*, pp. 133–5, for a description of the emasculation of the original bill in its passage through Parliament. "A more half hearted statute," says Dr. Reynolds, "can scarcely be imagined. Members of a combine could not be convicted unless the Crown proved that they were 'unduly' doing something which was already unlawful at common law."

for many years it was section 498 of the Criminal Code (since 1955 it has been section 411). Though there were in the ten years after 1900 a number of prosecutions under this clause, it is doubtful whether its existence had any material effect on the structure of Canadian business.

The Customs Tariff Act, 1897. In 1889 the Liberals had maintained that the tariff was the root of the problem of combines. It is not surprising, therefore, to find a Liberal administration providing for the reduction by Order-in-Council of the duties on any article where the manufacturers or dealers were combining to "unduly enhance the price . . . or in any other way to unduly promote the advantage of the manufacturers or dealers at the expense of the consumers." This was done by the Customs Tariff Act of 1897 which provided that, if there was reason to believe that a combination existed, the Governor-in-Council might order an investigation by a judge of the Supreme Court, of the Exchequer Court of Canada, or of any superior court in any of the provinces. If the judge reported that such a combine did, in fact, exist and if it appeared that such disadvantage to the public was facilitated by the duties imposed on a like article when imported, the Governor-in-Council was to place the article on the free list, or so to reduce the duty on it as to give the public the benefit of reasonable competition in such article. This regulation was slightly revised in the Customs Tariff Act of 1907 which stated that the Governor-in-Council might (not must) reduce the tariff in such cases. The Combines Investigation Acts of 1910 and 1923 each included a clause providing for a reduction of the tariff as penalty, or remedy. This method of controlling combines in protected industries seems sound, but it has only once been invoked. In 1902 the Canadian Press Association complained of a combination of paper manufacturers and dealers unreasonably enhancing prices. An investigation was held and the report gives an interesting picture of the competitive condition of the trade. A combine was found to exist and the prices were found to be unreasonable. An Order-in-Council (February 11, 1902) reduced the duty from 25 per cent to 15 per cent ad valorem.[18]

The Inland Revenue Act, 1904. The smaller Canadian manufacturers of tobacco found it difficult to compete with the American Tobacco Company of Canada because of its policy of giving preferential terms to those who dealt exclusively in its products. The dealer agreed to sell only at the prices fixed by the company; if he did not discriminate against the company's cigarettes in favour of those of other manufacturers, he was to receive a commission of 2 per cent

[18]See the *Report of the Royal Commission in re the Alleged Combination of Paper Manufacturers* (*Sessional Papers of Canada*, 1902, no. 53).

on the amount realized from cigarettes consigned to him; if he handled the company's cigarettes exclusively he was to receive an additional commission of 6 per cent. Any violation of these terms meant forfeiture of the commission earned on previous sales which had not yet been paid. The American Tobacco Company of Canada was incorporated in 1895 and acquired certain brands of cigarettes then manufactured in Canada, which were much in demand. In 1897, J. M. Fortier laid information under the Criminal Code against the company because of this exclusive dealing contract, but the court held that the conditions were not unlawful. A Royal Commission appointed in 1903 found that the exclusive contract system existed, that it was not illegal, that it operated to the disadvantage of the other manufacturers, but that there was no evidence of the company enhancing the price or lowering the quality. Parliament decided to give the competing manufacturers relief; the Act to amend the Inland Revenue Act provided that the minister might declare forfeited any licence authorized by the Act where the manufacturer of any goods subject to excise sold on condition of exclusive dealing or on terms which made it more profitable for the purchaser to deal exclusively with that manufacturer. It is said that the appearance of several new brands in the shops gave evidence of the success of the measure.

The Combines Investigation Act, 1910. In 1910, Mr. Mackenzie King introduced a new measure, the Combines Investigation Act. An agrarian revolt was developing against the policy of protection and against the monopolies which were supposed to flourish under such protection. The cost of living was rising and was attributed to those two factors, protection and monopoly. A deputation led by Mr. E. C. Drury, then a high official in the Grange, waited on the government at Ottawa in 1909 to ask that a special officer be appointed to investigate monopolies and that the tariff be reduced on such articles as were found to be monopolized. Then in 1909 the "merger movement"[19] got under way and created new anxiety; though the investors had probably more reason for anxiety than the consumers. This Act of 1910 provided a new machinery for investigation; any six British citizens might make application to a judge for an investigation of an alleged combine. The judge was to hear their application within thirty days, and, if there appeared good cause, he was to order an investigation

[19]According to the *Report of the Royal Commission on Price Spreads* (pp. 28 and 331) there were 58 consolidations in the four years 1909-12; the number of firms entering into these consolidations was 244, and the issued capital of the new companies was $361 million. In the previous nine years (1900-8) there had been only seven consolidations, involving 81 concerns and having an issued capital of $31 million.

by a board of three members, one appointed by each party and a third selected by the first two. Their report was to be published. Mr. King rightly believed in the value of publicity; he had emphasized it in his Industrial Disputes Investigation Act and now returned to it in dealing with combines. One of his complaints against the combines clause in the Criminal Code was that it stifled investigation and publicity. In introducing his Act, Mr. King said: "The necessity of branding as criminals any body of men joined together for commercial purposes before you find out whether or not they have been guilty of a criminal offence is a step which many men will hesitate to take . . . therefore this measure [the Combines Investigation Act] does not propose to place those parties in the position of defendants in a criminal court, but treats them as persons whose business for the time being is being examined into just as is the business of a railway company or a bank to see whether or not it is being carried on in a fair and proper manner." In addition to publicity the Act provided penalties: (1) the tariff might be reduced by Order-in-Council; (2) application might be made to the Exchequer Court for revocation of patents; (3) "any person reported by a Board to have been guilty . . . and who thereafter continues so to offend is guilty of an indictable offence and shall be liable to a penalty not exceeding one thousand dollars for each day after the expiration of ten days or such further extension of time as in the opinion of the Board may be necessary." This is a most important change of policy. Instead of conducting an investigation to accumulate evidence for a criminal prosecution for acts which the business men concerned probably did not know to be anti-social, or criminal, a new method is adopted of investigation to determine whether certain acts are against the public interest, in the belief that, if they were held to be so, most business men would desist from them. If they did not desist, then the sanctions of the criminal law would be invoked.

The defects of this Act have been well summarized by Dr. Reynolds: "complainants were obliged to make out a *prima facie* case before a judge. To do this required more knowledge, courage and money than the average consumer possesses. The complainants were openly named throughout the proceedings, and were therefore open to future retaliation. The procedure was cumbersome, and could be obstructed for long periods by skilful lawyers. Finally, no machinery was provided to ensure compliance with the orders of the Board."[20]

The United Shoe Machinery Company, 1910. There was only one investigation under the Combines Investigation Act of 1910, that of

[20]*The Control of Competition in Canada*, p. 139.

the United Shoe Machinery Company.[21] This company leased machinery to the manufacturers of shoes, payment being made by a royalty per pair of shoes manufactured or by the sale of certain materials above the market price. The machinery was leased subject to the condition that the lessee used no related machinery not leased from the company. This precluded competition except from another company which supplied a full line of machinery. There were manufacturers in Europe who could supply a full line of machinery, but the freight was high and servicing would be inadequate. Out of 145 shoe manufacturers, 138 leased machinery from the United Shoe Machinery Company. Competition was also possible in some minor machines which were not covered by the agreement. The majority report held that the United Shoe Machinery Company was a combine and that competition in the manufacture and supply of shoe machinery in Canada had been unduly restricted. It was recommended that the company be given six months to revise its methods of business, after which it would become liable to a penalty for every day that it continued to offend. The minority report, by the company's representative, maintained that the company had not used its powers unreasonably. Before the expiry of the six months the company made some changes in the form of their leases. The changes do not appear to have been considered satisfactory, but no further action was taken.

The Board of Commerce and the Combines and Fair Prices Act, 1919. During the War special powers were given to the Minister of Labour by Order-in-Council to deal with the problems of profiteering arising from scarcity and inflation due to the War. This involved some control of prices and profits. In 1919, after the report of a Select Committee of the House of Commons appointed to investigate the cost of living, two new Acts were passed: the Board of Commerce Act and the Combines and Fair Prices Act. A permanent Board was established and empowered to restrain and prohibit the formation of combines. It was given power to investigate and, where it found a combine to exist, it was to issue an order to "cease and desist." Failure to obey such an order would constitute an indictable offence and prosecution would be recommended to the Attorney General of the province concerned. No prosecution under this Act, or under section 498 of the Criminal Code was to be begun without the written order of the Board. Such permission it was obviously intended to withhold prior to investigation, and generally after investigation if

[21]See the *Labour Gazette*, Nov. 1912, for the reports of the Board of Investigation. Cf. J. P. Miller, *Unfair Competition* (Cambridge, Mass., 1941), p. 197. The Supreme Court of the United States held similar tying arrangements by the United Shoe Machinery Corporation to be violations of the anti-trust laws.

the practices complained of were discontinued. Under the "fair prices" part of the Act, power was given to deal with profiteering in the necessaries of life; direct regulation taking the place of stimulation of competition.

The members of the Board were Judge H. A. Robson, Mr. W. F. O'Connor (who had served as Cost of Living Commissioner, 1916-18), and Mr. James Murdoch (a trade union official). The combines section of the Act received little attention, most of the Board's activity being concerned with "fair prices." In the first six months it issued fifty "orders" and made more than seventy-five decisions. Most of these were concerned with retail trade often in particular localities: the retail price of sugar was frozen at 16 cents, the retailers' profit on pork products was limited to 25 per cent, and the milk producers and distributors of Toronto were restrained from advancing the price of milk. The Board undertook a task of detailed supervision of prices which was beyond the capacity of its limited staff, and which was well-nigh impossible in view of the inflationary character of the monetary and financial policy of the government. It is doubtful whether it secured compliance with its orders. The government was not sympathetic to the policy of the Board, and lent a ready ear to the complaints of the harassed business men. The Commissioners resigned in 1920, and in 1921 the Privy Council held the Acts unconstitutional. It was the "fair prices" part of the Acts which was held clearly unconstitutional as interfering with "property and civil rights in the provinces."

The Combines Investigation Act, 1923. In 1923 a new Combines Investigation Act was passed, similar to that of 1910, but differing in some important respects: (1) Application was to be made to a Registrar. He was to make an investigation and report to the minister, who might order a further investigation by the Registrar, or by a commissioner appointed for the purpose. It seems to have been intended by those responsible for the Act to provide a preliminary hearing by the Registrar in place of the hearing by the judge, followed by an investigation by a commissioner. In practice this method seems to have been followed, though there is nothing in the Act to indicate that the hearing by the Registrar was to be in any sense "preliminary." If a sort of grand jury hearing is to be held, it is preferable that this should be by a special official, the Registrar, with a training in economics, rather than by a judge. Unfortunately, however, the further investigations were usually conducted by commissioners, appointed *ad hoc* and generally selected from the legal profession. The curious Board of three members of the Act of 1910 was dropped. It was cumbersome, but indicated the hope of agreement by conciliation.

(2) "Every person is guilty of an indictable offence who is a party to . . . a combine." This is a reversion to the policy of 1889 and an unfortunate change from the Acts of 1910 and 1919, which made it an offence to continue to act in a way which had been held to be detrimental to the public.[22] (3) If no action is taken by the Attorney General of the province, the Solicitor General of Canada may allow information to be laid. This seems to be an improvement, assuming that the Dominion government was sincere in its legislative aims.

Administration of the Combines Investigation Act, 1923-31. Up to 1931 ten reports of investigations under the Act of 1923 were published. Some general indication of the scope and character of the proceedings under the Act may be given. The first report (1925) was concerned with a jobber-broker combine in the distribution of fruit and vegetables in Western Canada. The parties injured were the farmers of British Columbia. The Commissioner found a combine to exist and charged the members with various forms of fraud. There followed a successful prosecution for conspiracy to defraud and for offences against the Secret Commissions Act; the charges under section 498 of the Criminal Code and under the Combines Investigation Act were not pressed. A fine of $25,000 and one day's imprisonment was imposed on each of four individuals, and

[22]See J. Finkelman, "Combines and Public Policy" (*Proceedings of the Canadian Political Science Association*, 1932, vol. IV, p. 173): "One of the gravest faults of the whole legislation is that owing to the uncertainty and obscurities of the law a person may be accused and convicted of having committed a criminal offence when he was doing no more than what he considered desirable to forward his own interests in the manner generally approved in the industrial society in which he operates. The line between what is legal and what is illegal is very fine, and his guilt or innocence may depend to a large extent on the social and economic views of the registrar, or the commissioner, or the judge and jury. It is highly desirable in the interests of justice that the offender be not punished unless he has been warned that his conduct is unsocial and until he is given an adequate opportunity of reorganizing his enterprise." Cf. also the remarks of L. M. Singer (the organizer of the Amalgamated Builders Council and other Guilds) in *ibid.*, p. 174: "Every court and every jury may reach a different decision upon the same facts. Until they speak it is not known whether the accused is a malefactor or a benefactor." Cf. the editorial comment in the *Financial Times* (Aug. 1, 1941) on the conviction of a group of tobacco manufacturers and wholesalers: "The 'crime' for which the companies have been convicted is one that has been considered for many years good business and merchandising policy." I have argued on many occasions that a combination of two procedures had merit: where the parties must have known that they were operating to the detriment of the public, invoke the penalties of the criminal code, fine them for past actions; where the parties may reasonably have felt that they were not operating to the detriment of the public though public investigation leads to the conclusion that they were, invoke the procedure of the Act of 1910, require them to change their policies and fine them only if they continue to offend. See my Submission to the Royal Commission on Canada's Economic Prospects (1955), "Competition and Monopoly and their Regulation in Canada."

a similar fine on each of four companies indicted. British Columbia has since passed an Act to govern sales on consignment intended to prevent some of the evils revealed by the report, particularly the operation of jobber and brokerage houses. The second report (1925) was concerned with coal dealers in Winnipeg; no combine was found to exist. The third report (1925) was concerned with the marketing of New Brunswick potatoes. An agreement between two groups of shippers was found to have unduly depressed the price to the grower of potatoes. The Porter interests appear to have indulged in many unfair practices in order to maintain their control of the supply, but their aggressive salesmanship had opened up new markets. The Attorney General of the province took no action. The fourth report (1926) dealt with bread baking in Montreal, and found no combine to exist. The fifth report (1926) dealt with the distribution of fruit and vegetables in Ontario; no combine was found but some marketing practices prejudicial to the growers were disclosed and remedial legislation was enacted by the province. The sixth report (1927) was concerned with an association of wholesale and retail drug stores and manufacturers of proprietary articles sold by them (Proprietary Articles Trade Association). The association proposed to enforce maintenance of resale prices by retail druggists by a system of boycott. The report held the arrangement to be in contravention of the Act and the association thereupon dissolved. The seventh report (1929) dealt with the Amalgamated Builders Council, an association of plumbing and heating and sheet metal contractors in Ontario. The Council was held to be a combine, and a successful prosecution followed. Several other associations organized on similar lines by the same organizer dissolved as a result of the judgment against the A.B.C. viz. the Canadian Millinery Guild, the Canadian Furriers' Guild, the Canadian Cap Manufacturers' Guild, and the Amalgamated Garment Manufacturers' Council. The eighth report (1930) dealt with the Electrical Estimators' Association, an association of electrical contractors in Toronto; again a combine was found to exist and a successful prosecution was undertaken. The ninth report (1931) was on motion picture distribution in Canada; the Commissioner held that Famous Players Canadian Corporation and others connected with the motion picture industry had contravened the laws against combines but those charged in the ensuing prosecution were acquitted in the Ontario courts. The tenth report (1931) dealt with the bread baking industry and failed to disclose a combination detrimental to the public.

It would be unfair to judge the value of the Combines Investigation Act solely by reference to its published reports and successful prosecutions. There are many complaints which are not followed up after preliminary investigation: in some cases there is no solid basis for the complaint; in other cases voluntary dissolution of the agreement is secured. In 1927, about the time of the publication of the sixth report (that on P.A.T.A.), the Registrar contributed a description of his work to the *Canada Year Book:*

Over one hundred complaints have been received and dealt with since the enactment of the measure. Many of these have related to the basic industries or manufacturing, but most have arisen as a result of rapidly changing methods of distribution, the development of chain stores, co-operative buying agencies, department stores, mail order business, and the growing practice of direct selling. The points involved in these cases have included the principles underlying resale price maintenance, price-fixing by manufacturers and by distributors, exclusive dealing arrangements, withholding of supplies for various reasons, and other methods alleged to be in undue restraint of trade and against the public interest. Adjustments have been secured in certain instances without recourse to publicity or litigation, where such a course was obviously in the public interest. Evidences are many also of the restraining effect of the mere existence of the statute and the provision of adequate machinery for investigation under it. In this respect, as in the cases which have been dealt with by means of negotiation, publicity and prosecution, the Combines Investigation Act provides an effective safeguard against combines likely to operate to the detriment of the Canadian public.[23]

[23]The Commissioner kindly provided the information on which the following table of expenditures on the administration of the Act is based. Expenditures for each year are given to the nearest hundred dollars.

1924-5	$ 40,500	1932-3	$31,200
1925-6	91,900	1933-4	38,800
1926-7	59,600	1934-5	13,200
1927-8	27,800	1935-6	14,300
1928-9	34,100	1936-7	15,400
1929-30	55,600	1937-8	21,800
1930-1	101,500	1938-9	52,500
1931-2	28,800	1939-40	45,300
		1940-1	61,800

The permanent staff of this department for the first year was approximately 1½ persons. It was increased to 3 in 1925 and was 8 in 1941. With the increase in the staff the use of special comissioners declined and the cost of particular investigations was thereby reduced. The cost of prosecutions, where these were borne, as in the majority of cases, by the provinces should be added. The Annual Report of the Director of Investigation for 1955 shows the staff of the investigation branch as 43, including 15 Investigation Officers besides the Director. To this should be added, for comparison, the three members of the Restrictive Trade Practices Commission and their staff of four. See W. H. Hamilton, *The Pattern of Competition* (New York, 1940), for expenditures on the anti-trust division in the Department of Justice in the United States. "A statute lives by appropriations and Anti-trust has never been the favourite of Congress. T. R.'s 'big stick' —by which respect for the law was to be dinned into the heads of the mighty —was a division of five attorneys and four stenographers. In 1903 only

The Bennett régime, depression, and codes, 1931–35. Between 1931 and 1934 the Registrar conducted investigations into alleged combines of manufacturers of radio tubes, manufacturers of fruit baskets, dealers in anthracite, buyers of leaf tobacco, manufacturers of rubber footwear, and distributors of gasoline in Ontario. A change in the attitude of the government towards the administration of the Act with the accession of the Conservatives to power is suggested by the fact that not one of these reports was published when presented: that on tobacco buying was made public a year after its presentation as a result of considerable pressure from the House of Commons; that on anthracite was made in 1933 and was published in 1936 after the return of the Liberal administration; the others were never published. Some results were, however, obtained. The Canadian Basket Pool was prosecuted, pleaded guilty, and was fined; five importers of British anthracite were convicted and fined $30,000 and costs; and though the Province of Ontario refused to prosecute manufacturers of radio tubes, it appears that the manufacturers were led by the investigation to reduce prices greatly throughout Canada.

To the Conservative government of that day monopoly had become less frightening; unfair competition appeared the greater danger and any severe competition was treated as unfair. The reason for this change of attitude lay in the severity of the depression; similar conditions in the United States led to the development of "codes" under the National Industrial Recovery Act and opinion in Canada was strongly affected by the American experiment.[24] The Honourable H. H. Stevens, for several years Minister of Trade and Commerce, was the leading exponent of these views. His denunciation of "unethical" or unfair competitive practices and of abuses of economic power by mass buyers such as department stores, chain stores, and meat packers led to the appointment in 1934 of a Special Committee of the House of Commons

---

$100,000 was available to police all of American industry. It took thirty years for the annual budget to make the grade to $300,000. And it was not until 1939 that the preservation of the free and open market became so dear to the hearts of the people that they were willing to pay $1,000,000 a year for it. An establishment all complete with a couple of hundred attorneys, stenographers enough to go round and a sprinkling of economists is the creation of the last few years" (p. 58). To the appropriations for the anti-trust division of the Department of Justice should be added those for the Federal Trade Commission; these amounted to nearly $1 million annually in the twenties, averaged $1.7 million in the thirties, and amounted to $2.2 million in 1940.

[24]It should be noted that the programme in the United States included many measures intended to raise the money incomes of primary producers and wage earners as well as to maintain industrial prices. The special danger of Canadian imitations of the codes was that they would hinder the adjustment of domestic prices to the new low levels of export incomes.

(later reorganized as a Royal Commission) on "price spreads and mass buying." The proceedings of the Committee give ample evidence of the strength of the sentiment in favour of codes restrictive of competition. *The Report*[25] is curiously inconsistent in its attitude. In chapter II, where the influence of the economic advisers of the Commission is evident, stress is laid on the dependence of the domestic price level and of employment in domestic industries on the level of money incomes of the export groups, and on the need for flexibility of domestic prices in view of the high variability of these incomes. "Unfair" competition is shown to develop in the period of adjustment to reduced export incomes, and a distinction is drawn between competition which may seem unfair to the victims but which is beneficial in its effect on the public, and competition which is both unfair to the victims and "detrimental to the public interest."

With simple competition, the producer has no alternative, but to reduce his price in face of a shrinking market. On the other hand, with imperfect competition, the individual producer in industry may well find it more profitable to maintain his selling price even though this involves restriction of his output. There is, therefore, a strong disinclination to enter into any serious price competition because there is a strong sentiment against spoiling the market. But there is, at the same time, a strong urge to increase sales so as to make some use of idle plant, and reduce the heavy overhead costs typical of modern industry. This urge to increase sales without serious price reductions is often the explanation of the intensified competition which breeds unethical practices. It is the fierceness of the struggle, not any unusual depravity in the men concerned, which leads to the adoption of such practices. No one business man can afford to follow the dictates of his conscience and refuse to conform. If he did, he would be eliminated. The only way out is for all the members of a trade or industry to agree to ban certain unethical practices, or for the state to force them all to agree to such abandonment. Such an agreement, however, often will involve conflicting loyalties, loyalty to the particular group of producers and loyalty to society at large. If the agreement is mainly one not to compete, but rather to share the advantages of monopoly, other groups in society have nothing to gain. If, however, the agreement makes survival depend more on efficiency to serve the public and less on predatory strength, the public interest is served. Certainly, in any regulation of "unfair" competition the public interest must be paramount. The purpose of competition is to select those servants who can carry on social production most efficiently and any practice which hinders this purpose is undesirable and should be recognized as unfair.

In other parts of the *Report* the views of Mr. Stevens were stated with less qualification so that the three Liberal members who signed a memorandum of reservations stated that the *Report* failed "to follow logically the statements and implications contained in chapter II."

[25]*Report of the Royal Commission on Price Spreads* (Ottawa, 1935).

The Royal Commission on Price Spreads recommended the creation of a federal trade commission to consist of five members with a status similar to that of the Board of Railway Commissioners. The commission was to be given the following duties: (1) administration of the Combines Investigation Act which was to be revised to make its terms applicable to "single unit monopolies as well as to combinations in restraint of trade"; (2) regulation of monopoly in those industries where competition could not be enforced; (3) approval and supervision of agreements where unrestricted competition had proved demoralizing; (4) prohibition of "unfair competitive practices," and especially "such practices as discriminatory discounts, rebates, and allowances, territorial price discrimination and predatory price cutting"; (5) protection of the consumer by administration of legislation with reference to consumer standards, misleading advertising, etc.; (6) protection of the investor through the regulation of new issues; (7) general economic investigation. As a result of these recommendations the Conservative government included in its "new deal" legislation of 1935 three items relating to combines. First, it established a Trade and Industry Commission with functions more or less like those recommended above with the exception of the regulation of existing monopolies and the regulation of new security issues. It was further provided that the three members of the Tariff Board should constitute the new Commission. This may have been merely a temporary expedient till the constitutionality of the Commission was established; otherwise it would have to be considered deliberate sabotage. The Tariff Board was too busy to undertake the additional duties; and, as Dr. Reynolds has said, "its confidential relationship with business men unfits it for the role of policeman." Second, the Combines Investigation Act was revised to transfer its administration to the new Commission. The revised Act provided that documents produced before the Commission during an investigation could not be used as evidence in subsequent criminal proceedings. This very greatly weakened the Act. Third, a new clause was added to the Criminal Code (section 498A) prohibiting discrimination between buyers "in respect of a sale of goods of like quality and quantity," local price cutting and the sale of goods at unreasonably low prices "for the purpose of destroying competition or eliminating a competitor."

Revival of the Combines Investigation Act, 1936-40. The Liberal government was returned to office in 1935 and proceeded to restore the old combines policy. The section of the Trade and Industry Commission Act legalizing price agreements supervised by it was held by the Supreme Court of Canada to be unconstitutional along with many other items in the "new deal" legislation. The Commission continues to exist, but its sole remaining function is the administration of the "Canada Standard." The Combines Investigation Act was again amended: its administration was put back under the Minister of Labour, and the Registrar was given enhanced status as a commissioner; the limitation as to the use of documents imposed by the Act of 1935 was eliminated.

The definition of combine was amended in 1935 to make it cover monopoly as well as agreement. It was not clear, however, whether the courts would interpret it to cover such cases. Indeed it is rather hard to treat a monopolist as a criminal if it is not his own fault that he is the sole producer. The intention of those who framed the Sherman Act in the United States and the combines legislation in Canada was to keep open the channels through which new competitors entered trades. In the cases in the United States in 1911 against single unit monopolies such as Standard Oil and American Tobacco the basis of the attack was that "a higher degree of control over the market associated with a clear intent to use this power to exclude competitors transgressed the bounds of legality. Certain practices such as rebates, local price cutting, restrictive agreements not to compete, exclusive dealing arrangements with distributors, espionage, and the sponsoring of fighting brands or bogus independents when undertaken by firms holding a dominant position appear in the guise of coercive, exclusive or predatory practices."[26] This seems to be the limit to the use of criminal law in controlling monopoly, viz. to restrain the monopolist from practices which prevent competition from arising. If the monopolist, as such, is to be controlled it seems necessary to institute direct regulation, and in Canada such regulation is probably *ultra vires* of the Dominion government. If the above interpretation of the intention of the legislation is correct more attention should be paid in the future to the restraint of "unfair competition," i.e., of means by which the entrance of new competitors is blocked.

Under the new régime three reports were issued (in addition to the Anthracite report made in 1933 but issued only in 1936). Each of these investigations was made by the Commissioner himself. There was still provision for the appointment of special commissioners to conduct investigations, but this seemed likely to become exceptional. The first report was concerned with the resale price maintenance policy of Imperial Tobacco. The Commissioner held that its policy contravened the Act; a conviction was secured and fines of $221,500 were imposed, but this decision was reversed by the Alberta Court of Appeal. The second was concerned with "paper board shipping containers." The

[26]Miller, *Unfair Competition*, p. 33.

Commissioner found a combine and the Ontario courts imposed heavy fines. The third was concerned with a jobber-broker combine in the distribution of fruit in Western Canada. The Commissioner held that a combine existed, but the British Columbia court acquitted the companies. These reports, together with two of the earlier reports related to them, are reviewed below, after which the later history of combines administration will be discussed.

Report on an Alleged Combine in the Distribution of Fruits and Vegetables, 1925.[27] Though some fruit and vegetables were sold directly by the producer to the consumer (C.O.D., by parcel post or express), and some consigned by producers directly to jobbers for sale on their behalf, the bulk was sent in carload lots through brokers, acting as agents for the grower, for sale to the jobbers in the Prairie Provinces. The Nash interests were, in 1925, by far the most powerful group of distributors in Western Canada. They consisted of forty-five incorporated companies operating brokerage and jobbing houses in all the principal western towns, and were closely associated with the eighty-four Nash American companies. The most important feature of the Nash organization was the combination of brokerage houses with jobbing houses. "The brokerage house," said the Commissioner, "is not a natural ally of the jobbing house for the brokerage house should be the house of the grower; the jobbing house that of the distributor. The grower must by the very nature of things have a broker to market his goods, who must be his servant, not the ally or business associate of the distributor" (p. 13).

The competitive strength of the Nash organization forced the more important independent jobbing houses in 1922 "to adopt some form of organization in order to obtain a supply which would be safe from discrimination as to quantity or quality, and generally to meet the Nash interests on even terms. . . . Organization was effected by taking over the Growers' Sales Agency, Ltd. . . . This gave a brokerage connection, similar to that of the Nash interests." Between these two organizations there developed in 1923 severe competition in securing supplies in British Columbia and in selling in those markets in which there was no local understanding as to prices. This competition does not appear to have lasted long. The Commissioner found that: (a) "there were definite understandings in different places in 1923 and 1924 as to the prices at which certain commodities such, for example, as berries were to be sold. In some cases the jobbers agreed among

---

[27]*Investigation into an Alleged Combine in the Distribution of Fruits and Vegetables, Interim Report of Commissioner* (Ottawa, 1925). The page references in the text are to this *Report*. The Commissioner was Mr. Lewis Duncan.

themselves to take on berries at 75 cents a crate profit"; (b) "the Nash interests and the Growers' Sales Agency Ltd. agreed to close the Edmonton office of the Growers' Sales Agency Ltd. in order to reduce competition"; (c) "agreements and understandings among those in the trade were the rule rather than the exception" (p. 16). In practically every important centre there was a local fruit jobbers association which met regularly to discuss supply and prices:

Depending upon the amount of cooperation and a good feeling among the members, a more or less full disclosure is made of supplies coming in; arrangements are made to bring in and divide pool cars and prices are discussed. Local changes of price generally occur after these meetings, the retail trade waiting for the decision of the jobbers. The evidence on the record is mainly to the effect that what is discussed is "what would be a fair price"; that there is no hard and fast agreement to maintain the price which is finally accepted by the members as fair; but there is a general understanding to sell at not less than the agreed price unless special circumstances warrant members in cutting prices [p. 14].

The greater part of the *Report* was devoted to the peculiar evils of the jobber-broker combination. Section B of the *Report* (pp. 21-42) is concerned with the "operation of the broker in the jobber-broker combine." The broker is, the Commissioner pointed out,

the agent of the grower by whom he is paid, and to whom he is under the duty of acting with perfect good faith. In addition to this general duty the law has imposed certain specific duties, the main ones being the following: (a) to render full and true returns to the growers . . .; (b) not to merchandise or make any secret profit; (c) to take no more than the agreed remuneration; (d) to remunerate any agents or sub-agents out of its own remuneration unless the contract clearly provides otherwise; (e) to act solely in the interest of the grower in obtaining the highest possible price for his products [p. 21].

The Commissioner found "many cases in which there has been deliberate and flagrant disregard of these duties." (1) "Information was deliberately withheld." (2) "It was a common practice to make returns which did not truly and precisely disclose what had occurred." The broker was supposed to sell at a definite price and deduct certain agreed charges, often he appears to have sold on consignment but reported a sale. (3) "There is no doubt that Mutual (Vancouver) Ltd. merchandised and took profits over and above its commission." The Commissioner quotes a statement of the manager that Mutual (Vancouver), Limited, was "a merchandising broker" and that merchandising by brokers "was a common practice of the trade." "This," said the Commissioner, "is petty thieving; but systematic" (pp. 26-36). (4) "Cases have been found of heavy rebates ostensibly given on account of condition, while the condition as shown by the prices obtained and profits made did not warrant any such adjustment." (5) The brokers appear to have discriminated against particular jobbing houses, both as to price and as to supply.

Section C of the *Report* (pp. 43-64) is concerned with the activities of the Nash combine in its relations with the associated growers and with the other jobbers. "Nash officials took a definite interest in the policies of the various growers' associations, and the personnel of the executives. While they were interested in organization up to a point, it was not to their interest to have the growers too well organized and . . . attempts were made to break up and divide different associations" (p. 44). Relations with other jobbers involved discrimination by the broker in favour of its associated jobbers which enabled them to undersell their competitors, and to use their great competitive strength to enforce their price leadership. Section D of the *Report* (pp. 64-108) deals with a series of incidents illustrating further the type of activities already discussed.

The Commissioner concluded:

that the Nash combination of jobbing and brokerage houses is a combine which is operating and has operated detrimentally to the interests of the Canadian public . . . [and] that while other combines within the meaning of the statute exist, such as the self-defensive combine of the Growers' Sales Agency Ltd., and the local associations of jobbers who meet to discuss prices and supply, still the Growers' Sales combine would dissolve into its constituent elements if the jobber-broker connection were made unlawful; and that the price fixing arrangements of the local associations of jobbers are made more permanent . . . by the threats of the Nash brokers and supervisors to discipline any price cutter by depriving him of his supply [p. 120].

He recommended changes in the law to deal with special evils of the jobber-broker combine, but also stated his opinion "that many of the existing evils could be removed by the establishment of a nation-wide grower-owned selling agency. It would lie with such an agency, while obtaining the best price for the growers, to give a maximum distribution without wasteful overlapping, and to develop a rational and unified export policy" (p. 121).

Report on an Alleged Combine of Wholesalers and Shippers of Fruits and Vegetables in Western Canada, 1939.[28] Two combines were

[28]*Investigation into an Alleged Combine of Wholesalers and Shippers of Fruits and Vegetables in Western Canada: Report of Commissioner* (Ottawa, 1939). See also note on the *Report* by C. A. Ashley in the *Canadian Journal of Economics and Political Science*, May, 1940. The investigation was made by the Commissioner under the Combines Investigation Act, Mr. F. A. McGregor. Page references in the text are to this *Report*.

alleged to exist. First, there was an alleged combine of prairie jobbers and British Columbia shippers, Western Grocers, through a wholly owned subsidiary, having secretly purchased a 50 per cent interest in the Lander Company, a holding company which in turn controlled several shipping agencies in British Columbia. Second, there was an alleged combine of jobbers on the prairie, Western Grocers, Consolidated Fruit, and Macdonald's Consolidated, which together controlled some 80 per cent of the wholesale fruit business on the prairie, having, it was alleged by the complainants, entered into agreements to regulate supplies, to fix prices, and to eliminate the competition of certain independent jobbers (p. 1).

With very few exceptions the growers (of whom there were nearly 2,500) did not pack their own fruit. The bulk of the fruit was packed by packing agencies. Most of the packing houses (76 out of 88) were also shippers. A number of the co-operative shippers (23) sold through a central sales agency, Associated Growers of British Columbia. Thirteen independent shippers sold through Sales Service, Limited, a company formed in 1926 to provide a central selling agency at a time when the co-operative movement in the Okanagan Valley was declining and the number of independent shippers was increasing. Four other independent shippers, usually referred to as the "Foursome," had a loose association for joint selling. Associated Growers controlled nearly 40 per cent of the shipments to domestic markets, Sales Service about 19 per cent, the "Foursome" about 20 per cent.

The shipper is the agent and consignee of the grower. He receives fruits and vegetables for disposal in the most profitable markets. "As the grower's agent the shipper has certain moral and legal responsibilities" (p. 11). It is usual to pool the products consigned to a particular warehouse. It is the shipper's responsibility to decide what price to accept for his client's products, to adjust claims made by jobbers, and to distribute the sales receipts equitably amongst the growers who participated in each pool.

The shipper usually employs a broker to represent him, and to act as sub-agent for the grower, on the prairie. This is necessary because of the distance which separates buyer and seller, and of the difficulties which arise from the perishable nature of the goods and the volatile nature of their prices. The broker solicits orders, reports on the state of the markets, maintains goodwill for his principal's products, investigates complaints and adjusts claims. "His legal position in relation to the shipper corresponds to that of the shipper in relation to the grower" (p. 22). "The fruit brokerage business of the prairie provinces is dominated by C. H. Robinson Ltd. and Canadian

Fruit Distributors Ltd., with United Brokers having a fair share of the business in the four cities in which the branches operate" (p. 23). C. H. Robinson had the business of Sales Service, Limited; Canadian Fruit Distributors was a subsidiary of Associated Growers and handled its business; United Brokers received a substantial part of its business from the "Foursome." The weakness of the broker's position is indicated by the fact that C. H. Robinson and Canadian Fruit Distributors "give 75 per cent of their brokerage earnings to jobbers in proportion to the tonnage purchased by them" (p. 25). The Commissioner raised a serious question as to the legality of such action, and added that it was "evidence of the inordinate strength of the bargaining position of these jobbers" (p. 26). Attention is drawn to the method of the California fruit growers who employ full-time salaried agents to represent them in the important prairie cities.

There were eighty fruit jobbing houses operating in the Prairie Provinces, but of these sixty-five were included in three chains: Western Grocers (30 branches), Consolidated Fruit (17 branches), and Macdonald's Consolidated (18 branches). Western Grocers had "a broad supervisory interest in the management and policies" of the 675 independently owned members of the group of Red and White stores; and through a subsidiary it had a big investment in Shop Easy Stores, Limited, operating a chain of twenty retail stores, largely in Winnipeg. Macdonald's Consolidated was a subsidiary of Safeway Stores which operated 140 retail stores. Consolidated Fruit was controlled by P. Burns which controlled a chain of food stores in Alberta, the Jenkins Groceteria Company.

It is important to notice how late is the final sale of the fruit. The grower's apples are handled by packers and shippers as his agents; they employ sales agencies, and these in turn brokers. Even the apparently final sale to the jobber is subject to revision if the price falls drastically before he sells them, or if they move slowly and so deteriorate in stock. Even the retailer may get such adjustments, which are passed back to the grower. If prices rise after the jobber has bought there is no adjustment in favour of the grower. When the growers' agents allow discounts for quantity or adjustments for spoilage or price decline, it is the growers' money that is being given away without consultation. It may be good business to make generous allowances, but it is in the growers' interest that they should be no more generous than is necessary. If the grower's representative were his salaried employee there would be no doubt whose interest would prevail. Under the existing arrangements, as will be shown below, there is no such certainty.

In 1936 Dominion Fruit, Limited, a subsidiary of Western Grocers, bought a 50 per cent interest in the Lander Company, a fruit shipping company which controlled Sales Service, an important selling agency. "The relationship was secretly established and maintained, and growers using these shipping agents are said to have known nothing of it until it was disclosed at a public meeting two months before application for the present investigation was made" (p. 39). To secure secrecy the shares that were acquired were held by nominees of Western Grocers in trust for them. "It is difficult to see how the relationship between Dominion Fruit and the Lander Company—that is between jobber and shipper—can be reconciled with the fact that the shipper is the servant or agent of the grower charged with the legal and moral duty of representing the grower's interests in dealing with the jobber. . . . If the jobber has a substantial interest in the shipper, the shipper cannot be expected to exercise independent control as an agent of his grower-principal, he is placed in a position of having conflicting responsibilities" (p. 57). These problems are analysed under three heads: (a) *Floor stock protection.* "While the investment may not have substantially affected floor stock protection policies there seems little doubt that the close relations between Sales Service and Western Grocers predisposed Sales Service toward demands for 'protection' by Western Grocers" (p. 54). (b) *Condition claims.* It was claimed that such claims were relatively unimportant and that Sales Service had not changed its policy after the acquisition of shares by Western Grocers. The Commissioner admits the difficulty of determining whether the corporate relations of these companies did influence decisions in these matters, but adds, "these relations encourage Sales Service to give a maximum of attention to such claims and to yield at points where, if the parties were independent of each other, the claims might be refused" (p. 55). (c) *Quantity discounts.* The problem is here complicated by the fact that Associated Growers and other shippers gave Western Grocers similar quantity discounts to those given by Sales Service. The Commissioner shows his disapproval of this discrimination because of its effect on the independent shippers and jobbers. He reiterates the impropriety of an alliance between the agent who decides to allow the discount and the buyer who receives it. But he is unable to prove that the quantity discounts given to Western Grocers were the result of this investment in Sales Service (pp. 55-63). In summing up, he expresses his belief that "the wide use of secret quantity discounts . . . by Sales Service Ltd. forced smaller independent shippers to compete with this unfair practice" (p. 81). It should be emphasized that there came to light no evidence of the malpractices which had been rife in the Nash organization.

The brokerage house of C. H. Robinson, which depended for the greater part of its business on Sales Service, was threatened by the connection between Sales Service and Western Grocers. Western Grocers threatened to eliminate the broker and pay the brokerage to the jobber. C. H. Robinson therefore agreed to pay Western Grocers "all of C. H. Robinson's net profits less only a net of $2.00 per car reserved to the brokerage company after the deduction of expenses, taxes, etc. . . . The effect of this agreement was to have the broker pay an outright gratuity . . . of over $14,000 to Dominion Fruit for the two years 1936 and 1937" (pp. 65-6).

The *Report* also discusses the alleged combinations of jobbers (pp. 67-74). Though agreements "to purchase fruit and vegetable supplies in common by way of pool cars are evident . . . there was no evidence obtained which indicated that as such they prevented or reduced competition" (p. 78). Discussion of selling prices was regular but appears "to have resulted at most in 'marks to shoot at' and not in price agreements, to which participants gave real support" (p. 78). The Commissioner, therefore, found no combine amongst the jobbers; but reported that Dominion Fruits, Western Grocers, Sales Service, and Lander were "parties to the formation and operation of a combine within the meaning of . . . the Combines Investigation Act" (p. 81).

Report on an Alleged Combine in the Paperboard Shipping Container Industry, 1939.[29] This *Report* deals at length with the activities of Container Materials, Limited, "whose members and associated companies represent all but one of the manufacturers of corrugated shipping containers," and more briefly with those of the Shipping Case Material Manufacturers' Association, "which comprises the four principal Canadian manufacturers of the paperboard used in the production of these classes of shipping containers." Between these two organizations there was a close relationship; two members of the former were also members of the latter, and both were administered by Messrs. Hardy and Badden, "a Toronto firm of trade association executives." This relationship is shown to have been a source of strength to both parties.

The *Report* opens with a brief description of the development of the paperboard shipping container industry, and its earlier efforts to control competition. In 1914 there were only four or five firms in the

[29]*Investigation into an Alleged Combine in the Manufacture and Sale of Paper-board Shipping Containers and Related Products: Report of the Commissioner* (Ottawa, 1939). The investigation was made by the Commissioner, Mr. F. A. McGregor. The following account is adapted from a note on the *Report* in the *Canadian Journal of Economics and Political Science*, May, 1940. Page references in the text are to the *Report*.

industry and the future of this type of container was uncertain; by 1919 there were seven firms; by 1925, nine firms. In the next five years there was a rapid increase in the number of manufacturers and in the capacity of the industry; the number of firms in 1930 was nineteen and the output had nearly doubled since 1925. In the four years 1930-3 output remained at about five and a half million containers, in the next four years, 1934-7, output was again doubled. In the early twenties, with few firms and a growing demand for the product, no formal association was necessary, but "the majority of manufacturers agreed upon a common method of figuring prices" (p. 9). The entry of a new firm in 1925 led to active competition but "prices were soon established at a lower level" (p. 9). Steady growth in demand enabled the established firms to maintain prices in the years 1927-9 in spite of the entry of new firms offering containers at lower prices. With the onset of the depression the problem of maintaining prices became more serious; an association of the manufacturers was organized (under the "secretarial guidance" of Messrs. Hardy and Badden) and a price list, involving reductions of 10 to 15 per cent, was adopted. This association collapsed within a year and prices fell by 1931 to about 55 per cent of the pre-depression level. To meet this situation a new and more effective organization was established, Container Materials Ltd.

The new method of organization involved the incorporation of a Dominion company with Mr. Badden as president and secretary-treasurer, with Mr. Hardy as vice-president, and with the manufacturers as shareholders. Each manufacturer "agrees that during the currency of this Agreement it will not manufacture for or sell to any person, firm or corporation other than the Company except as agent for the Company any corrugated and, or, solid fibre board products for use or resale within the Dominion of Canada" (p. 16). The company, on its part, appointed the manufacturers as "its agent for the sale within the Dominion of Canada of corrugated and, or, solid fibre board products manufactured by the said Party of the Second Part and contracted for by the Company" (p. 18). The manufacturers gave the officers of the company right of access to their plants and to their records in order that they might satisfy themselves that the agreements were being fulfilled, and there was provision for deposits "to guarantee observance of the agreement and to provide a source from which penalties may be paid" (p. 16).

Under the direction of Container Materials, Limited, a quota system was established, providing a cash penalty for those manufacturers who exceeded their allotted quota of sales and cash compensation to those who failed to secure the allotted proportion of total sales. Under the agreement in 1931 the penalty or compensation, commonly called the pool tax, was 15 per cent; this was raised to 25 per cent in 1933, and to 30 per cent in 1934. In September, 1938, the rate was reduced to 10 per cent (p. 21). No explanation is given in the *Report* of this action: one would like to know whether it was an indication of competitive forces causing stresses in the organization; what was its relation to the 25 per cent fall in prices between January and October, 1938; and whether either had any relationship to the fact that this investigation was in progress. "The quota system is essentially based on the proposition that once a firm establishes itself in an industry it is entitled to a share of the total business. . . . By protecting the marketing position of each member it has served to bolster a system of rigid control of prices and to provide an incentive to manufacturers to continue to submit to the restrictions imposed by the combination" (p. 27).

The methods by which Container Materials, Limited, exercised its control over prices are described in detail in section v of the *Report*. The provisions for frequent audit and regular affidavits from salesmen; the use of the "price figuring" manual, the regulations as to "delivered prices," "non-test" boxes, and quantity discounts, etc., are all carefully described. Section vi is concerned with the action of Container Materials, Limited, in buying off prospective competitors. This is most interesting and important. In 1934 it bought the machinery of the Quebec Paper Box Company, and in 1935 that of Building Products, Limited (a manufacturer of roofing and insulating products in the province of Quebec which had added solid fibre shipping cases to its line of products in 1928). Building Products, Limited, bound itself not to manufacture or sell shipping cases for five years. The price paid for these two lots of machinery was $80,000, when sold by auction to the members of Container Materials, Limited, it realized less than $6,000! In 1936, O. and S. Corrugated Products Company of Toronto loomed as a potential competitor. With them an arrangement was made providing "that in the event of your sales in the nine months ending December 31, 1936, being less than $150,000, and in the year 1937 being less than $200,000, that you would be compensated in each period at the rate of 20 per cent on the difference between your actual sales and the above figures" (p. 59). Between April 1, 1936, and April 30, 1938, their sales amounted to some $80,000, and their compensation for limiting production amounted to some $70,000! The cost of preventing entry of new competitors has to be fitted into the theory of value under monopolistic competition.

The operations of the Shipping Case Material Manufacturers' Association, described in section VIII, cannot, for reasons of space, be discussed here. Reference must, however, be made to the possibility of this association assisting Container Materials, Limited, in its efforts to restrict freedom of entry of new firms into the corrugated box industry. "No proof has been found of concerted action on the part of the two combinations to restrain any firm from establishing a corrugated box plant" (p. 81); but there have been requests for assistance in "dissuading some firm that was going into the field" (p. 81), and the "Hendershot Company of Hamilton was charged a premium on its purchases of paperboard for a period in 1934, shortly after it entered the field" (p. 81).

The conclusion of the Commissioner is "that both these associations have operated and are likely to operate to the detriment and against the interest of the public and are therefore combines within the meaning of the Combines Investigation Act" (p. 89). It is important to notice, further, that the industry has enjoyed substantial tariff protection, before 1930 of some 25 per cent against imports from the United States, in the years 1930-5 of some 35 to 50 per cent, and in spite of successive reductions as a result of the trade agreements of 1935 and 1938 the protection was still at least 25 per cent (pp. 48-50). A comparison of the trend of prices in Canada and the United States is given which shows that "the level of prices in the United States has been lower in relation to prices prevailing in 1926, than the level of prices in Canada on the same basis" (p. 46). Unfortunately, no direct comparison of the prices of similar products at the same time in the two countries is made, and no reference is made to the possibility of using the tariff to control the monopoly condition in this industry.

Report on the Proprietary Articles Trade Association, 1926[30] This association consisted of 157 manufacturers, 28 wholesale druggists, and 2,732 retail druggists representing between 80 and 90 per cent of the retail drug trade of Canada. Its main object was "the taking of such steps as the Association may be advised are legal and not detrimental to the interests of the public . . . to deal with unreasonable and unfair cutting of prices, and to give advice and render assistance to its

[30]*Investigation into the Proprietary Articles Trade Association: Interim Report of Registrar* (Ottawa, 1926). In the preparation of this *Report* the Registrar was assisted by Dr. W. A. Mackintosh. The Association complained that they had not had the opportunity to present their case fully. The Minister of Labour, though maintaining that the Registrar's inquiry had been fair and adequate, appointed Mr. L. V. O'Connor as Commissioner to make further investigation. The *Final Report* of the Commissioner was published in 1927. Its conclusions were similar to those of the *Interim Report*. Page references in the text are to the *Interim Report*.

members in preventing substitution" (p. 6). It proposed to establish standard margins (33⅓ per cent for retailers and 16⅔ per cent for wholesalers) on all the articles on its list. These might not be established immediately but they were the ultimate aim of the association. Wholesalers and manufacturers agreed to withhold supplies of *all* listed articles from any dealer who sold *any* article below the list price, or who sold to anyone who resold at less than the list price. Quantity discounts were provided, but such saving might not be passed on to the public in lower prices. The dealers agreed that when asked for an article on the list they would not attempt to sell any other article in its place: "by implication they are bound to hinder the sale of non-listed proprietary articles" (p. 8).

The problems with which the trade was faced were two: (1) the trade was highly competitive because of the multiplication of drug stores and the development of new types of merchandising with the rise of chain and department stores; (2) there existed a certain amount of predatory price cutting.

The drug store which wants to increase its business may compete by offering better service, by more attractive arrangement of goods in the window and in the store, by advertising, or by selling at lower prices. Any considerable price appeal on the whole range of products is only possible if operating costs are considerably lower than the average, but great advertising effect may be secured by reducing the prices of some well-known article below the advertised price and even below the actual cost to the retailer. The *Report* gives some examples:

A well known case is that of Pepsodent tooth paste with an advertised price of 50 cents, frequently sold by chain and department stores for 29 cents, although it is stated that it costs the small retailer 33 cents and the department store 30½ cents. Eno's Fruit Salt, advertised at $1.00 and retailed for 69 cents by certain stores, is in a similar position. . . .

Objection to this type of price cutting may come from the manufacturer whose product is treated as a loss-leader:

It increases his sales in the price cutting establishments, but hinders his sales in those establishments which maintain prices. His product may have the goodwill of the public, but it lacks the goodwill of the dealer since it is a "cut price article," an article which can only be sold in small quantities at the advertised price or in larger quantities at a price which allows little or no margin of profit. The dealer in such cases occasionally ceases to stock such an article, or more commonly hinders the distribution by offering substitutes for it to prospective customers. Thus the manufacturer has his channels of distribution clogged [p. 17].

However the Registrar suggested that "manufacturers have aided price cutting through giving 'inside prices' to the chain and department stores to enable them to carry their goods as leaders" (p. 16), though he found it difficult to determine to what extent this had been done. He also suggested that the association was promoted by the wholesale and retail merchants, that the manufacturers were "not by any means unanimous in their approval of price-maintenance," but once a considerable number joined the association the remainder were "virtually compelled to join" (p. 19).

The effect of "loss-leaders" on the independent drug stores was held to be irritating rather than fatal: "it is not as wide-spread in its extent or effects as is alleged" (p. 17). The real trouble lay in the efficiency of the newer types of retail store: "the secret of their success lies in mass merchandising and its economies rather than in the 'trick advertising' of 'price-leaders'" (p. 17). But the field of the chain stores and department stores is limited to the large centres of population. The neighbourhood stores and stores outside large cities serve a clientele which chain stores cannot reach.

The chain stores have made and will continue to make inroads on the unit store; they have found progress easy because of the slackness and inefficiency of many small merchants. Naturally, such inefficiency, in the face of keen competition, has been responsible for business failures. From the viewpoint of the public interest this should be regarded not necessarily as an evil . . . but as a beginning in the solution of the problem of the excessive number of drug stores. . . . The unit store has been stimulated by the new competition to greater efficiency . . . it can hold its own in the field even without any artificial protection designed to guarantee profits and to prevent price competition [p. 17].

To this one should add that the guarantee of a high "mark-up" is not a guarantee of high profits to the operator: it is a standing invitation to others to enter the trade and so to spread the available business over more stores, to reduce turnover for each, and to keep the profits of the operators low in spite of high mark-up and high prices to the consumer.

The supreme objection to P.A.T.A., with its fixed margins, was that it tended "to restrict trade to the traditional channels of distribution, whatever less expensive methods may be in existence or may in the future be devised. Despite the admittedly excessive costs of modern distribution, it penalizes all experiment in merchandising looking to the reduction of costs of operation and prices to the consumer" (p. 29).

New agencies . . . have arisen which make economies in distribution as Henry Ford made them in manufacturing. . . . These agencies cannot serve the whole population any more than every person will be satisfied with a Ford car. They do, however, serve large numbers, and they do so at a reduced cost. The reduced cost in most cases means also reduced service but the consumer is in many cases willing to dispense with additional service. . . . The distributor who pioneers and devises more efficient means of distributing goods increases his business by reducing his prices and so passing on part of his economies to the consuming public. If other distributors are to maintain their position they must effect similar economies or persuade the public that they offer greater service and that the greater service is desirable [p. 27].

By contrast, under the rigid prices of P.A.T.A. the low cost distributor cannot pass on to the consumer any of his economies and must compete by elaboration of service rather than reduction of price.

The Commissioner concluded:

In so far as such price cutting does not result from savings in operating expenses, but represents selling below costs for mere advertising purposes, it would seem to be unfair to the manufacturer as well as to competitors. If all price cutting were of this type, and if this were the only type of price cutting to be restrained by the P.A.T.A. there would be less occasion for public concern. But the remedy applied by the P.A.T.A. has the effect unfortunately, of preventing not only predatory price cutting but any reductions in price, regardless of the substantial variations which have been shown to exist in the operating costs . . . of different stores. . . . The P.A.T.A. has been organized in answer to a real and vexatious problem in drug merchandising, but it goes far beyond the cause for legitimate complaint [p. 29].

Report on the Distribution of Tobacco Products, 1938.[31] Imperial Tobacco Company of Canada and its subsidiary companies produced 75 per cent of the Canadian total. The remainder was divided between W. C. Macdonald (the strongest of the independents, producing something like 15 per cent of the Canadian total), Benson and Hedges (Canada), L. O. Grothe, Rock City Tobacco Company, the Royal Canadian Tobacco Company, H. Simon and Sons, and some other smaller producers. The usual channel of distribution was from manufacturer to jobber, or wholesaler, who in turn supplied retailers. The exact number of wholesalers handling tobacco was not known: there were in 1930, 264 wholesale tobacconists, but in addition an unspecified number of wholesale grocers and other wholesalers handled tobacco; Imperial Tobacco sold to nearly 700 wholesalers in 1938. There appear to have been "approximately 60,000 retail outlets for tobacco products

[31]*Investigation into an Alleged Combine in the Distribution of Tobacco Products: Report of Commissioner* (Ottawa, 1938). This inquiry was made by the Commissioner, Mr. F. A. McGregor. In an annex are printed a study of the economics of resale price maintenance by Professor C. A. Curtis of Queen's University and a brief memorandum on the law relating to this subject by Professor J. A. Corry of Queen's University. Both these studies had been made for Imperial Tobacco Company and were produced in evidence at the request of the Commissioner. Page references in the text are to the *Report*.

in Canada, which means that two out of every three retailers make
some sales of tobacco products" (p. 4.). Herein lies the difficulty of
resale price maintenance in this trade: for the majority of dealers
tobacco is carried as a convenience to customers and almost no extra
expense is involved in handling it. The regular tobacconists, by contrast, must cover their expenses almost entirely from the sale of tobacco
products: they are, however, few in number and generally buy direct
from the manufacturers at wholesale prices. Imperial Tobacco had
sponsored a scheme for maintaining fixed prices in all retail outlets for
the tobacco products of all manufacturers. The mark-up allowed by
Imperial Tobacco varied for different products but it was roughly 10
per cent for the jobber, and 18 to 20 per cent for the retailer. The
arrangements for maintaining retail prices at levels which secured
these margins of profit were the subject of complaint as involving
undue restraint of trade.

Imperial Tobacco required wholesalers, and such retailers as had
the privilege of buying direct from it, to sign an agreement "to promote
fair practices and to eliminate unfair cut price competition among
Jobbers and retail Dealers." They agreed to "sell Imperial Goods or
Goods of other distributors or manufacturers, regardless of quantity,
only to Dealers and only at the respective Jobbers' Selling Prices." They
further agreed that they would not "sell or supply Imperial Goods or
Goods of other distributors or manufacturers to any Dealer who is
selling . . . at prices other than the respective Retail Prices," and they
undertook to notify Imperial Tobacco of the name of any such dealer.
"These provisions," comments the Commissioner, "appear to extend
far beyond any reasonable interest which the Imperial Tobacco
Company might have in the prices at which the products of its own
manufacture were resold to retailers and consumers. They appear to
amount to a highly unwarranted regulation of the distribution of the
products of other manufacturers, with the effect of substantially eliminating price competition in the wholesale and retail trade of practically
all tobacco products throughout Canada" (p. 25). When this written
agreement was first introduced, in 1934, it was more drastic and comprehensive. Wholesalers were required to secure a similar signed agreement from every retailer buying Imperial Tobacco products from them.
Each retailer agreed to furnish a statutory declaration or affidavit as
to the details of any sales about which the wholesaler might be suspicious, as well as a general undertaking to adhere rigidly to the agreement. Other terms of the agreement, with reference to return of
damaged stock, for instance, were extremely onerous, and there was
considerable opposition in the trade. Later the agreement with the

wholesalers was made rather less severe and a new method of policing the retailers through jobbers' associations was inaugurated.

The Northern Alberta Tobacco Jobbers' Association was one of thirteen such associations covering the Dominion and operating on substantially similar lines. The jobbers agreed to sell tobacco only to retailers "who are maintaining prices and carrying on orderly merchandising." They agreed not to sell at prices less than those set out in the manufacturers' price lists, and not to grant any discount in any shape or form. The agreement specified many of the forms of discount or rebate in detail, and a memorandum circulated in 1936 and reproduced in the *Report* (pp. 13-16) sets out in elaborate detail the practices which were forbidden. The agreement also covered the appointment of an "Investigating Committee" to be the disciplinary body of the association. Where a breach of the agreement was found the committee might "recommend to the manufacturers that they sell him [the offender] only at Jobbers' Selling Prices for such period as the Committee may deem advisable, or at the option of the Manufacturers they close his account for the same period" (p. 10). Two cases in which these penalties were imposed are discussed in the *Report* (pp. 19-23). Entry to the wholesale trade in tobacco was blocked by a further agreement, more or less informal, with Imperial Tobacco that no additional accounts would be added to the jobbers' list without the consent of the local association. The failure of Merco Wholesale, Limited, to secure supplies from Imperial Tobacco is described (p. 13). This was an Edmonton wholesale grocery house owned largely by some fifty retail merchants in Alberta and Saskatchewan but supplying many others besides its shareholders. "An order sent direct by Merco Wholesale Limited to the Imperial Tobacco Company in Montreal accompanied by a certified cheque for $1,150, in payment for the goods ordered, was returned with the reply that 'we have no account with you and are unable to accede to your request at this time'" (p. 13).

The Commissioner held "that a combine exists in the distribution of tobacco products" and that the Imperial Tobacco Company and the Northern Alberta Tobacco and Confectionery Jobbers' Association have been parties to this combine. His conclusion that these trading methods have enhanced the degree of monopoly power attaching to Imperial Tobacco seems to be well founded. Though it is not discussed in the *Report*, it seems clear that Imperial Tobacco had exercised its power as a price leader, and that the exercise of this power was dependent on its ability to detect immediately any cut in retail prices or any increase in the margins to jobbers or retailers. If known they could be met, if met they were probably not worth making.

The Commissioner published, as an annex to the *Report,* a study of resale price maintenance made by Professor C. A. Curtis for the Imperial Tobacco Company. Professor Curtis argued that the effect of this practice on the retailers was to increase the number of outlets, diminish the sales per outlet, and increase the margin of profit on each sale. Efficient retailers were prevented from passing on the results of their efficiency and competing for increased sales by lower prices. The consumers were required to pay higher prices, were furnished with more retail outlets and with more service, probably more than they wanted or would willingly pay for. The effect on labour in the manufacturing industry, he believed to be negligible. The effect on the grower was doubtful: if it really benefited the manufacturer it might result in higher prices for leaf, but higher earnings would attract new farmers into tobacco production and raise the rent of tobacco lands. If the maintained price reduced the consumption of tobacco the net effect on the grower was likely to be bad. The manufacturer, in Professor Curtis's opinion, derived no substantial benefit from the system, except such intangible advantages as come from a contented group of wholesale and retail dealers. In this judgment he disagreed with the Commissioner who considered that the monopoly position of Imperial Tobacco was strengthened. Professor G. A. Elliott, in a review of the *Report,*[32] suggests that there is a further advantage in the multiplication of retail outlets. "In the absence of special knowledge it seems possible that convenience of acquisition may be a significant factor affecting not only the consumption of the confirmed smoker but also the rapidity with which the habit is developed. If this is true, then the maintenance of retail margins by increasing the number of retail outlets and consequently the convenience of acquiring tobacco, may stimulate sales more than higher prices diminish them."

The Combines Commission, 1939–53. In World War II as in World War I, it was necessary to resort to direct control rather than to rely on the indirect control of effective competition. Some of the problems involved in this direct control have been discussed above in chapter II. Here two things only are to be noted. First, the Combines Commissioner became the Enforcement Administrator of the Wartime Prices and Trade Board. This meant that the staff of the Commission was held together and indeed strengthened. When the time came to abandon direct control the Commission was ready to revert to its old

[32]See his note on the *Report* in the *Canadian Journal of Economics and Political Science,* May, 1939. It is interesting to note that in the United States "the manufacturer encourages price cutting, and the merchant who sells other things cannot afford to have the buyer walk out of the shop because it does not carry his favourite brand." The dealer is therefore "forced to carry the article upon the thinnest of margins" (Hamilton and Till, *Anti-Trust in Action,* p. 15).

task. Second, during the war it became necessary to encourage concerted action on the part of producers and distributors. Quicker and more effective action could be secured when the administrator could communicate with a single organization representing the whole trade rather than with a host of independent units. The Commissioner was very much concerned lest this experience of concerted action in a controlled economy in war should make the control of monopoly more difficult in the decontrolled economy of peace. In an article in 1945 he said:

These business groups play an important part in the war-time control of their respective industries, but the last word, the ultimate control, lies not with them but with government. Government is the senior partner, holds the majority of voting shares, in a partnership that is highly useful and indeed necessary in war-time. Is there a danger that, when government retires from the business of direct control, the junior partner, trained in these war-time ways and well organized, will seek to take over the control business as a going concern? Surely it is obvious that the problem of monopoly in the years ahead of us is not going to be made easier by reason of the particular kind of recognition and impetus that has been given to trade organizations in the war years.[33]

The Cartel report. At the time of the conclusion of the financial agreement between the United States and Great Britain, and the settlement of the lend lease claims, certain proposals for the expansion of world trade and employment were put forward by the United States and accepted as a basis for international discussion by Great Britain. These proposals related to: (*a*) the reduction of trade barriers, tariffs, quotas, prohibitions, etc.; (*b*) the mitigation of the restrictive policies of certain governmental "commodity agreements" such as those operating in rubber, tea, and tin; (*c*) the control of private agreements to divide the world market, or restrain competition between national groups, agreements which have come to be known as "cartel" agreements. The establishment of an International Trade Organization, as an agency of the United Nations, was an essential part of these proposals, providing a forum for the working out of agreed policies and an agency for investigation and control. The high hopes of 1945 have scarcely been fulfilled, but here our concern is not with the fortunes of the I.T.O., but with the report which was the result of Canadian preparation for these discussions. *Canada and International Cartels* is a report of the Commissioner following an inquiry by a small committee.

[33]F. A. McGregor, "Control of Prices in War and Peace: Some Contrasts" (*Commerce Journal*, May, 1945); also, V. W. Bladen, "The Combines Investigation Act and Post War Reconstruction" (*Canadian Journal of Economics and Political Science*, Aug., 1944).

It is, of course, particularly concerned with those "cartels" which affect Canada.

However much one dislikes private agreements to restrict competition in international trade, it is hard to accept the *negative* policy of "anti-trust" unless it is part of a *positive* programme including: (*a*) a strong international full employment or expansionist policy; (*b*) a readiness to administer temporary schemes of restriction for particularly depressed industries or regions by general agreement and under international auspices, while a long-run solution is sought; (*c*) international assistance, including provision of funds for investment, and technical knowledge and personnel, for adjustment of depressed regions; (*d*) administration by international authority of stabilization schemes (possibly "buffer stocks") to prevent wide fluctuations in the prices of important raw materials.[34]

To those who lived through the "Great Depression" it must surely be clear that restriction is a child of depression. Collusion and cartels are just particular manifestations of restrictionism. The tariff, we have said, was the mother of trusts: but we now add that tariffs and trusts, together with import quotas, foreign exchange regulations, and international commodity agreements, have a common parent, depression. Attack on one manifestation of restriction, the combine, is of doubtful value, and is probably not politically possible. To combat the restrictions of depression one should combat depression. Most restrictions will give way under the pressure of expansion: with high level employment, profits come generally from expansion, not from restriction. This is why a positive programme concerned with full employment is properly a part of a "cartel" policy. What is said here about the international sphere is quite as relevant to the domestic scene, and perhaps as frequently ignored.[35]

Post-war reports. In the early post-war years the Commission was active in investigation, and six full dress reports were issued. The *Report on Dental Supplies* (1947) described the operation of a closed association of dealers based on an agreement with the manufacturers for exclusive supply. The association was a regional group of the American Dental Association. Its members were prosecuted and acquitted. The *Report on Optical Goods* (1948) was similarly concerned with restriction of competition between distributors based on manu-

[34]See V. W. Bladen, *Canada and Cartels,* Behind the Headlines series, vol. VI, no. 1 (C.I.I.A., Toronto, 1945); also "International Cartel Policy" in *Canada and the World Tomorrow* (Toronto, 1944); and "Proposals for the Expansion of World Trade and Employment" (*International Journal,* vol. I, no. 2).

[35]See V. W. Bladen and S. Stykolt, "Combines Policy and the Public Interest: An Economic Evaluation."

facturer support, but in this case that support depended on patent rights. The *Report on the Bread Baking Industry in Western Canada* (1948) showed three "chain" bakery companies as holding a predominant position in the various markets in the West: for instance in Calgary they, and one local company, produced 87 per cent of the total bread sold; in Vancouver the chains with one other baker produced 72 per cent; in Regina and Saskatoon they produced 87 per cent. Further, in each province the chains exercised influence on the Master Bakers' Association which provided for fixing prices, for the maintenance of resale prices, for uniform tenders, and for some division of territory. Six firms were prosecuted and convicted; they have appealed. The *Report on the Flour Milling Industry* (1948) similarly showed concentration of control in a few large corporations and efforts on the part of these corporations to control competition through the Canadian National Millers' Association. The difficulty of "containing" competition is well illustrated by the frequent disputes within the Association. In these last two reports on bread and flour, is found evidence of the correctness of the Commissioner's expectation that the experience of war-time co-operation would create difficulties for peace. The *Report on Flour Milling* was withheld from publication by the Minister owing to a disagreement as to the Commissioner's findings with regard to the behaviour of the Millers in war-time. This issue need not be discussed here. Failure to publish the report, as required by the Act, led to the resignation of the Commissioner, Mr. F. A. McGregor. This precipitated parliamentary debate and publication of the report. The public reaction to the resignation of the Commissioner was evidence of strong support for the anti-monopoly policy.[36] The *Report on Flat Glass* (1949) dealt with an association of jobbers dominated by two large firms, one of which was owned by the leading United Kingdom producer and the other about to come under the control of the leading United States producer. Agreement between those two parent firms was discussed in the Cartel report. The parties to the agreement pleaded guilty and were heavily fined. The *Report on Matches* (1949) told the "story of successful efforts by an international cartel to establish a monopoly of the wooden match industry in Canada and to prevent as far as possible the resurgence of any competition." This report is most interesting for its discussion of the methods used to make entry to the trade difficult, almost impossible. Five firms were prosecuted, convicted and fined; in addition, the import duties on matches were reduced.

[36]See *The McGregor Controversy and the Combines Act* (Winnipeg Free Press Pamphlet, no. 29).

The MacQuarrie Committee Reports and resale price maintenance.
Following the resignation of Mr. F. A. McGregor a committee was
appointed to study the legislation. An interim report on Resale Price
Maintenance in October, 1951, led to legislation prohibiting this
practice. This act of 1951 was incorporated in the revised Combines
Investigation Act of 1952: it became section 34:

(2) No dealer shall directly or indirectly by agreement, threat, promise or
any other means whatsoever, require or induce or attempt to require or
induce any other person to resell an article or commodity
    (*a*) at a price specified by the dealer or established by agreement,
    (*b*) at a price not less than a minimum price specified by the dealer
       or established by agreement. . . .
(3) No dealer shall refuse to sell or supply an article or commodity to any
other person for the reason that such person
    (*a*) has refused to resell or to offer for resale the article or commodity
       (i) at a price specified by the dealer or established by agree-
          ment. . . .
(4) Every person who violates subsection 2 or 3 is guilty of an indictable
offence and is liable on conviction to a fine in the discretion of the court or
to imprisonment for a term not exceeding two years or both.

Thus a practice which had been frequently attacked by the Combines
administration, the propriety of which had been in dispute since W. J.
Ashley defended it in 1888 and the legality of which (when not
collectively enforced) had been in doubt, was singled out for prohibition. This is an important change. Mr. McGregor discussing the legislation in 1951 said:

Neither statute [the Combines Investigation Act and section 498 of the
Criminal Code] comes within the category of "specific" legislation, a type
which is more appropriate to a policy of public regulation, in which specific
rules governing every phase of commercial activity within the field of
control are a necessity. It rather establishes general principles of reasonableness which should govern the behaviour of business groups which are
presumed to be subject to competition and not to specific regulation. In such
legislation there is no place for a long and rigid statement of possible
offences.[37]

Before leaving this topic we may note that reports have been issued
dealing with resale price maintenance in four cases: soap in Montreal
(1953)—there was no prosecution but the parties were warned that
they would be prosecuted if they persisted; household supplies in
Chicoutimi (1953)—the parties were prosecuted and nominal fines
were imposed; china and earthenware (1954)—the parties were

[37]See Mr. McGregor's excellent paper "Preventing Monopoly—Canadian
Techniques" in E. H. Chamberlin (ed.), *Monopoly and Competition and their
Regulation.*

prosecuted and fined; television sets in Toronto (1954). Then in 1955 the Restrictive Trade Practices Commission published a *Report of an Inquiry into Loss Leader Selling*. The inquiry was concerned with the question whether, if competition required the prohibition of resale price maintenance, loss leader selling should not be prohibited as a form of "unfair" or "predatory" competition. The Commission found that "grave loss leading had been quite exceptional and sporadic in nature, clearly insuffiicent to warrant new legislation for suppression or control." A dose of depression might change the picture!

The final report of the MacQuarrie Committee (1952) recommended important changes in the Combines Investigation Act which were largely implemented in the revision of 1952. The new Act and its administration will be discussed below, after a glance at the crop of reports of investigations which were completed in 1952–53 under the old legislation while Mr. T. D. MacDonald was Commissioner.

The reports of 1952–53. The *Report on Rubber Products* found evidence of restriction of competition and detriment to the public in all six of the divisions of the industry: mechanical rubber goods, tires and tubes, accessories and repair materials, rubber footwear, heels and soles, and rubber clothing. Of agreement and "collusion" there was ample evidence. Prosecution and conviction followed, and the first restraining order under the Act of 1952 was imposed. Whether the conviction has substantially changed the competitive situation may be a legitimate subject of doubt: and one may also raise doubts as to whether there was substantial "detriment." The reports of this period are more concerned to provide the basis for prosecution in the Courts where agreement *"per se"* was held criminal, and detriment was assumed rather than proved, than to examine the economics of the industry in order to determine whether there had been "detriment," and whether prosecution would serve the public interest. Some divisions of the industry seem to have been and are still, in fact, highly competitive. The *Report* gives some indication of this. "Distrust, however, was common and deviation from the industry arrangements were frequent and this distrust and these deviations left a considerable degree of price competition alive. But it was not the frank and open competition that achieves the effects expected of competition in Canadian industry" (p. 682). I am more impressed by the competitiveness than by the absence of "frankness." But even if there were detriment, has a remedy been found? This is an industry in which there are few firms and some very big ones: it is likely that some restriction of competition will be achieved by "tacit" agreement and "leadership." Perhaps the degree of restriction is no more than is needed to give the feeling of security necessary for the programme of expansion and innovation which is evident in most sections of the industry. Perhaps it is too great, perhaps there is serious "detriment"; but the *Report* gives little basis for an assessment from this point of view. In any case careful study would make it clear that the degree of competition is different in different divisions of the industry and has been different at different times.

The *Report on Electrical Wire and Cable Products* (1953) was made by a Special Commissioner, Mr. H. C. Goldenberg. He found "that competition in the sale of wire and cable products has been unduly prevented or lessened and that agreements and arrangements having, and designed to have, this effect have operated and are likely to operate to the detriment or against the interest of the public." Prosecution and conviction followed. Having made some study of this industry[38] I have doubts about the need for and the effectiveness of this action similar to those I have with reference to rubber. Such study, with the limited time and limited access to materials available to the private investigator, cannot provide a basis for a confident assessment of detriment; it enables one to judge the *Report* rather than the industry. It makes one aware of the absence from the *Report* of the evidence necessary for such assessment. One feature of the *Report* which may be noted is its worry over uniform prices: but surely since the industry is producing standard products prices must be uniform; competition requires such uniformity. The real problem is whether they are uniformly too high, not whether they are uniform.

The other reports in this period were on *Fine Papers* (1952) and *Coarse Papers* (1953). In these cases, too, there were successful prosecutions. Evidence of collusion was clear; detriment was assumed by the Commissioner and the court; what detriment there was and how satisfactory the remedy will prove cannot be determined without much further study of the industry. Finally there were reports on *Bread and Other Bakery Products* (1952) concerned with the Winnipeg market, and on *Maple Products* (1953) concerned with the Quebec market. The former involved a refusal of union drivers to deliver bread to a cut-rate chain store. "Wiser counsels in the union prevailed"; so no action was needed. The latter found that no combine existed: "the parties have not been shown to account for a sufficiently large part of the market." They will be kept "under observation."

The revision of 1952. The important changes in the Combines Investigation Act of 1952 were three: the establishment of a Restrictive

[38]See V. W. Bladen and S. Stykolt, "Combines Policy and the Public Interest: An Economic Evaluation."

Trade Practices Commission; the introduction of a new remedy, the "prohibition"; and the removal of the limits to the size of fine that the court might impose. Possibly more important than the formal change in the procedure of investigation and report was the explicit requirement that the Commission's report shall "appraise the effect on public interest of arrangements and practices disclosed in the evidence and contain recommendations as to the application of remedies provided in this Act or other remedies" (s. 19 (1)).

The new procedure involves division of labour between the Director of Investigation and his staff and the Commission. The Director, when requested by six citizens, when directed by the Minister, or on his own initiative when he believes that a "combine" exists, is authorized to conduct investigations. It would appear from his Annual Reports that almost nine out of every ten investigations opened by the Director are closed without reference to the Commission. When there appears to be a serious problem of restriction the Director prepares a Statement of Evidence and refers the case to the Restrictive Trade Practices Commission. After consideration of the Statement, examination of witnesses and argument by counsel, all in private, the Commission reports to the Minister of Justice. Such report "shall within thirty days . . . be made public, unless the Commission states in writing to the Minister it believes the public interest would be better served by withholding publication, in which case the Minister may decide whether the report, either in whole or in part, shall be made public" (s. 19(3)). The next step is for the Minister to decide whether prosecution should be undertaken: this clearly involves a legal opinion as to the probability of success in the court; but it would seem also to require a political and economic decision, involving the exercise of discretion, based on the appraisal of the effect on the public interest which the report must contain. It would appear to have been the intention of Parliament that prosecution should not follow when detriment is not found, even though the courts could find sufficient evidence of collusion to lead to conviction since they pay attention only to collusion *per se* and assume that there must have been consequent detriment. It is not yet clear whether the Commission or the Minister will accept this position, and it is not even clear whether Parliament will, on second thoughts, maintain what appears to have been its intention. Exercise of discretion at this point seems to be in the spirit of the original legislation. It would not be "irresponsible": the Minister must, unless advised otherwise by the Commission, publish the report and may be questioned in the House on his decision to prosecute or not. Only if such discretion is exercised is there any reason why the Commission should take seriously its duty to appraise, and its other, perhaps more important, duty to think of appropriate remedies, and, one would hope, to exercise some ingenuity and imagination in seeking such remedies.

Leaving the size of fine to the unlimited discretion of the court was intended to "put teeth" into the Act. The introduction of the prohibition was probably intended by some to make possible, in appropriate cases, the procedure of the 1910 Act which provided for penalties if practices found to be detrimental were continued. As I have said above (p. 228) it seems reasonable to distinguish cases which were clearly and seriously detrimental to the public, and which the parties must have known to be detrimental, from cases where the parties may, in good faith, have considered there to be no detriment, where indeed such detriment was not clear, but where it would seem wise to require some change. For the former, punishment seems appropriate; for the latter, prohibition. But others perhaps intended the prohibition to be, and the administration and the courts have made it, an additional penalty, another way of sharpening the "teeth" of the Act. In a Submission to the Royal Commission on Canada's Economic Prospects[39] I have suggested that the Minister might experiment with a return to the "conciliation" philosophy of Mr. King.

There may well be cases where the evidence of detriment to the public does not justify prosecution, but an element of doubt exists and some action is called for. In such cases the Minister might well consider calling into conference the firms concerned in an attempt to determine what changes in institutions are necessary to make competition more active, more effective, while still leaving it "workable." It is in such conferences that the Board of Trade in Britain seeks remedies for doubtful situations brought to light by the Monopoly Commission. The Canadian Minister with a variety of "clubs" available, fines, restraining orders, tariff and patent revision, should not find it difficult to secure consent for any reasonable arrangement. Indeed only on the assumption that business men will accept "reasonable" arrangements has free enterprise any future, or the Combines Act any hope of success.

Reports of the Restrictive Trade Practices Commission.[40] Four reports on cases of resale price maintenance and the *Report on Loss Leader Selling* have already been noted. The *Report Concerning*

[39]For further discussion of current combines policy and for criticism of some of the views presented here see L. A. Skeoch, "The Combines Investigation Act" (*Canadian Journal of Economics and Political Science*, Feb., 1956) and the Submission on this subject to the Royal Commission on Canada's Economic Prospects made by Professors Britnell, Buckley, Fowke, and Timlin (published as *Workable Competition and Monopoly*, University of Saskatchewan, 1956).

[40]See S. Stykolt, "Combines Policy: An Economist's Evaluation" (*Canadian Journal of Economics and Political Science*, Feb., 1956) and "In Defence of the Canadian Consumer," (*The Business Quarterly*, Summer, 1956).

Alleged Price Discrimination between Retail Hardware Dealers in North Bay involved the discrimination clause of the Criminal Code 498A. The difficulty of establishing discrimination is illustrated by the case: the report was inconclusive and counsel advised against prosecution "in view of the local and technical nature of the case and the fact that it would be the first prosecution under section 498A." Two reports have been concerned with the retail sale of coal, one in Timmins (1954) and one in Winnipeg (1956). In Timmins there appears to have been substantial reduction of competition, the important element in which was the readiness of the supplier to withdraw supplies from dealers who would not maintain prices. The remedy would seem to be, in part, to require the supplier to treat dealers equally. In Winnipeg no similar tie-up with the suppliers was found, and fuel oil seems to have provided plenty of competition. In appraising the effects the Commission said:

The preparation, circulation and use of Price List Guides did not eliminate price competition entirely but did result in substantial curtailment in such competition. In principle such arrangements and activities are likely to prove detrimental to the public interest, by removing in large measure the protection afforded, by freely operating competitive factors, against arbitrary prices. In this case some enhancement of prices did occur. On the other hand conditions in this industry, e.g., ease of entry as a seasonal occupation, but more especially the definite threat of fuel oil competition since 1946 and the increasing seriousness of actual competition from fuel oil since 1950 have limited and greatly curtailed the extent to which prices might be enhanced. . . . Under these circumstances the Commission is unable to say that the arrangements and practices carried on by the Exchange and its members in connection with the preparation, issue and use of Price List Guides have resulted in actual public detriment of a substantial nature.

The final conclusion that the practices "are likely to operate against the public interest" could be considered as an argument that these practices are against the interest of the coal dealers, for there seems to be a curious concern lest fuel oil and natural gas should make further headway.

If coal dealers are to have any hope of retaining a substantial share of the market in this area, every effort must be made to improve handling methods and over-all efficiency. Competition from oil and gas will provide a spur for such efforts, but the Commission believes that competition between the coal dealers, including price competition, will also be necessary.

The problem of the allocation of tenders is more difficult: the Commission was convinced that this practice raised prices on this class of business. It should be remembered that for these big buyers, too, oil was available. One other report dealing with retail sale is that on

Gasoline in the Vancouver Area (1954). Under the regulation of the provincial Control Board margins had been fixed; they were lower than the trade would have liked, but they were uniform. After control of the sale of gasoline was ended in 1951 the dealers agreed on a uniform mark up of 20 per cent. The Commission recommended "a judicial restraining order."

Four reports have dealt with manufacturing industry. In the *Wire Fencing* industry there are two powerful, fully integrated companies and three smaller companies. From 1933 to 1951 the Association of fence manufacturers established common list prices: three common price zones were established in Ontario, Quebec and the Maritime Provinces in which goods were sold on a "delivered price basis"; on shipments to Western Canada the price was based on the same railway freight rate though the goods might be shipped from widely distant points in Ontario and Quebec. In June, 1952, the arrangements for price agreement were discontinued. In November, 1952, "Stelco" issued a new dealer price list; "Dosco" followed except for the zoning of the Maritimes; Stelco later fell in line on this zoning. It appears that Stelco furnished Dosco with a copy of its list for special customers. "It is evident," says the *Report*, "that exchange of price lists between competitors would not be engaged in with the expectation that such disclosure of information would be used by the recipient to offer a more advantageous price to the customer. It is also evident that to the extent that the exchange of price information results in the adoption of common prices by competitors, the effect is much the same as that which would follow the establishment of common prices by prior discussion." But one may wonder whether "exchange" of information was necessary: would not such information have become quickly known through trade channels? The *Report* continues: "There are industries in which the pricing pattern is described as that of price leadership. . . . It is not contended that such a pattern is being established in the woven wire fence industry and, in fact, the few instances of independent action of large and small manufacturers in the brief period which has elapsed since the abandonment of joint arrangements suggest the contrary." Surely these instances simply indicate that the price leader cannot impose any decision on the group, any more than he could when he sought leadership in the association. There may well be too little competition in this industry, but it is hard to believe that an order enjoining "exchange of information" will have any effect in making it more competitive. The use of local price cutting to eliminate a new competitor in Montreal seems to have deserved more attention and condemnation than it received:

but predatory or "unfair" competition as a weapon to establish and maintain monopoly is hard to deal with under our constitution, however important control of it may be.

In the *Transmission and Conveyor Equipment* industry uniform prices were established by an Institute. "One of the allegations . . . is that . . . general pricing instructions designed to produce uniform practices in pricing complete units have been prepared, largely by Link-Belt, sometimes without discussion but at other times following discussion among the members of the Institute, and have been published and distributed to the Institute." The Director of Investigation found that "the evidence indicates that prices as determined by the pricing material were high." (In view of the refusal to consider whether prices are reasonable as a defence, it is interesting to find consideration of them as unreasonable as part of the attack.) After 1950 competition from the United States became more effective but the Commission did not believe that reliance could be "placed upon such competition alone to prevent the detrimental effects which the Commission has found in the common pricing practices of the members of the Institute." They place more reliance on a judicial restraining order. Whether this will help, whether oligopolies need institutes, remains to be seen.

The *Asphalt and Tar Roofings Report* describes a set of arrangements for establishing uniform prices which the manufacturers claimed was simply an "open price" association providing each member with full knowledge of prices charged by others rather than providing for determination of these prices by agreement and for adherence to these prices. The *Report* properly notes that many of the practices are probably discriminatory and violations of 498A: e.g., quantity discounts have been based on total purchases from all manufacturers not on the quantity purchased from an individual manufacturer. Some consideration is given in this and some of the earlier reports to "freight equalization" as involving regional discrimination. Again a judicial restraining order is suggested: the manufacturers should be enjoined from "meeting, discussing, arranging, accepting, or reaching an agreement or understanding on prices, terms and conditions of sale, transportation charges" and from exchanging information. Whether the discriminating practices would disappear if agreement was enjoined, or whether some of the practices need to be enjoined, is difficult to say.

The last report to be considered is that on the *Sale of Beer*. This raises very difficult questions. It describes the evolution of an oligopoly in Ontario and Quebec, as Canadian Breweries, Labatt's and Molson's became dominant. It finds the mergers of the thirties "objectionable" "because of the purposes sought to be achieved and because of the methods employed for achieving them. . . . The consumer was deprived of the benefits which otherwise might have been expected to flow from the normal interplay of competitive factors in the market. . . . The public has been and is still deprived of the opportunity to choose from a wide and diversified range of brands, types and qualities of beer, the number of brands acquired in Ontario having been reduced deliberately by the Company [Canadian Breweries] from 150 to 9 only." This sounds shocking; but we then learn that the Company is not "in substantial or complete control of the brewing industry . . . to the detriment and against the interest of the public. . . . It is faced with strong and increasing competition from two large brewing enterprises, John Labatt's Limited and Molson's Brewery." The process of merger was, as might have been expected, a road from the old fashioned competition of small local breweries to the new fangled competition of large national breweries. It is strange to find that the remedy suggested is to prevent Canadian Breweries from taking part in the same process in the Western provinces in the next few years.

Governmental restriction of competition and regulation of monopoly. While much space has been devoted in this chapter to the policy of the Dominion government in promoting competition, it must not be supposed that this is the sole element in Canadian policy in relation to combines. An examination of the policies of the provinces would reveal an astonishing variety of governmental restriction of competition, and permission to associate voluntarily to restrict competition is granted by the Dominion government to trade unions and cooperative associations of farmers, fishermen, etc. The problem here is too much competition and the policy is one of restriction. By contrast there are the "natural monopolies" where competition is out of the question and where public regulation of price and quality of service gives the consumer the protection which competition is supposed to provide in other industries. In some cases public ownership is found to be a simpler solution than public regulation of private monopoly.

Prorating in newsprint. The action of the Ontario and Quebec governments in promoting prorating in newsprint has already been discussed, but one may now consider these arrangements in relation to the combines policy of the Dominion government. Its policy is directed against combines which have operated or are likely to operate to the detriment of the public. In applying the policy it is assumed that any agreement sanctioned by a province or a municipality will be in the public interest; the central government will not question the wisdom of the local government in the conduct of its local affairs. The newsprint arrangement was not, therefore, subject to attack under the Combines Investigation Act. It might further be argued that the newsprint prorating agreement was intended to enhance, or maintain, the price of newsprint against the foreign consumer and was therefore in the interest of the Canadian public. The United States, which has followed a similar policy of promoting competition and "trust busting," exempts by the Webb-Pomerene Act (1918) associations of exporters from the operation of anti-trust legislation, provided that such associations are not "in restraint of any [American] competitor of such association" and that they enter into no agreement and do no act which "artificially or intentionally enhances or depresses prices within the United States . . . or which substantially lessens competition within the United States." Whether the Canadian legislation gives similar freedom to associate for export trade is not clear; but assuming that the public referred to in the Act is the Canadian public, it seems likely that it does. The provincial governments emphasized the social need for spreading employment, but cannot have been unaware of the effect of the arrangements on the price. They were also impressed with the fact that pulpwood was an exhaustible and non-perishable resource; if you did not give away your wood in a bad year you might be able to sell it when prosperity returned.

Newsprint is a rather unusual case of restriction of competition under provincial auspices. The more usual cases concern weak groups of small producers, where the reasons for restriction of competition are similar to those which lead the Dominion government to exempt trade unions and producers' co-operatives from the penalties of the combines legislation. The schemes are supposed to provide reasonable defence rather than means of aggression. They go further than permitting association; they usually make the agreement binding on all the trade whether they have subscribed to the agreement or not. There is also usually some protection of the public through a requirement that the agreements be approved by some public authority.

Milk Control Board of Ontario. This Board determines for some ninety urban markets in Ontario the price at which the distributors must buy milk from the farmer and the price at which they must resell to the consumer. This price used to be the result of an agreement between the milk producers' association and the distributors approved on behalf of the consumer by the Board, or, in the absence of an agreement between the parties or where the parties agreed on a price considered unfair to the consumers, the result of arbitration by the Board. Since 1954 it has been established by a "formula" relating it to the Wholesale Price Index for Canada, the Weekly Earnings Index for

Ontario, the prices of certain goods used by Ontario farmers, and the prices of butterfat, cheese, and other milk products. It is an offence to sell milk for less than the established price; the farmer may not compete for a bigger outlet by offering milk cheaper, nor may the distributor compete for a bigger share of the market by offering milk cheaper at retail.

Entry to the distributing trade is limited by the necessity of obtaining a licence. "No license shall be granted to a milk distributor unless the Board is satisfied that the applicant is qualified by experience, financial responsibility, and equipment to properly conduct the proposed business, and that the issuance of the license is in the public interest." The last clause enables the Board to prevent that wasteful multiplication of outlets which might result from the fixed margin of profit. In many markets, however, the number of distributors is unduly large and the wastes of a competitive struggle which must take the form of offering more service, or differentiated milk, instead of standard milk at a lower price, are considerable. There seems to be a strong case in such markets for choosing between competition and monopoly in the distribution of milk rather than the present hybrid; and if monopoly were the device, municipal ownership would have to be considered.

Competition among the producers of fluid milk is also limited. The price at which they may sell is determined and this has been, at times, relatively tempting to those dairy farmers who sell cream to dairies or whole milk to the cheese factories. To supply the fluid milk market requires more skill, a bigger investment, and higher operating costs both in money and trouble. Some differential may therefore exist between the fluid milk price and the prices in the other markets without any desire on the part of the cream producers to enter the fluid milk market; indeed some differential must exist if producers are not to withdraw from the fluid market. In a free market there would be a definite limit to this differential. Before the depression of the thirties the price of fluid milk was the result of negotiation between the associations of producers and distributors; the price was generally maintained a little above the competitive level and supplies were constantly being transferred from the manufactured to the whole milk markets. In the depression prices fell first in the manufactured market; the resulting price disparity made it easy for distributors to obtain supplies of milk outside the ranks of the organized producers. Having obtained cheap supplies some of the distributors began to increase their business by price cutting; the other distributors had to meet the cut prices. A price war ensued; prices to the producers fell to a point where the supply of fluid milk to the cities was endangered and in one province after another control schemes were introduced, that of Ontario in 1934.[41] The prices set by the Board were somewhat higher than those ruling in the manufactured market, and the differential was probably high enough to tempt some producers to try to break into the market, but entry was no longer free. It is true that the producer does not require a licence, as does the distributor; but effective restriction on entry is imposed by the distributors. It is to their interest to have enough, but not too many producers under contract. It they have too many, too much of the milk will be surplus and their clients will be discontented and agitating for higher producer prices. There is, therefore, a closed circle of farmers attached to distributors enjoying at times monopoly profits. It is provided in the Act that the distributor may not terminate the purchase of milk from a producer without just cause, and it is generally provided in the agreements that the producers' association shall nominate new producers if more are to be given contracts. Mr. Justice Wells in his report as Royal Commissioner on Milk in 1947 suggested that the Act had achieved the result sought in 1934: the producers and distributors had established a price satisfactory to them. "In view of the conditions which prevailed at that time, little thought seems to have been given to the position of the consumer, who quite naturally was taking advantage of the situation to obtain milk as cheaply as possible, and who was, in fact, obtaining it at prices at which it could not possibly be produced and distributed if costs were to be met." He went on to say that "the special interests of the consumer have not been given the weight later experience might have suggested was desirable."

Natural monopolies. Finally, one must notice certain cases where monopoly is inevitable or highly desirable. Obvious examples are the public utilities of the city: water, gas, and electricity. The telephone is another. Railways may compete between some points; but between most points there cannot be two railways and where there are two they are likely to agree not to compete in rates. Even on the road the transport authorities grant exclusive franchises for particular routes in return for a guarantee of regular service. Wherever such monopoly conditions naturally exist, or are created by government, there is likely to be some regulation of rates, or public ownership: in Toronto water and electricity are provided by public bodies, gas by a private company required by law to reduce rates if its profits exceed a certain amount. The Bell Telephone is subject to the regulation of the Board of Trans-

---

[41]See W. M. Drummond, "Price Raising in the Dairy Industry" (*Canadian Journal of Economics and Political Science,* Nov., 1935), especially pp. 560-2.

port Commissioners, as are the railways.[42] Buses in Ontario are regulated by the Department of Highways.[43]

Regulation of monopolies has been concerned almost as much to protect the public from discrimination as from exorbitant charges. Under perfect competition there cannot be two prices for the same commodity or service: every competitor would want to sell his product in the higher priced market. But a monopolist may sell part of his produce in one market at a high price and the remainder in another market at a lower price, as long as the buyers in the high priced market cannot go to the low priced market to buy. The Criminal Code has tried to prevent monopolists from selling cheaper to the mass buyers, on the grounds that this is unfair competition. The Canadian tariff is particularly heavy on goods that are "dumped," i.e., sold by a foreign monopolist at lower prices in the Canadian than in his home market, on the ground that this is unfair competition for the Canadian manufacturer. The Interstate Commerce Commission in the United States and the Canadian Board of Railway Commissioners (now Transport Commissioners) were both constituted largely to control discrimination in rates as between persons, places, and commodities. Discrimination between places and commodities continues, but it is discrimination based on public policy not on private advantage.

Public ownership has been referred to as a method of dealing with natural monopolies; the postal service is an obvious example. It will be found, however, that public ownership in Canada is more generally thought of as a device for securing capital for very large-scale undertakings which seem desirable for national development but which do not offer sufficient attraction to business enterprise. Ontario Hydro-Electric is an example. The Canadian National Railways is the product of the failure of private enterprise in such a development project.[44]

[42]See W. T. Jackman, *The Economics of Transportation* (Toronto, 1926) and A. W. Currie, *Economics of Canadian Transportation* (Toronto, 1954).

[43]See the *Report of the Royal Commission on Transportation, Province of Ontario* (Toronto, 1938). "The Public Vehicle Act grants the Department of Highways the right to approve or prescribe fares. The Department insists that the rates charged by all operators between the same points shall be equalized, and that where no competitive transportation exists, an operator's rates shall not be unduly out of line with his rates in areas where such does exist. There is no standard rate" (p. 147).

[44]It is beyond the scope of this *Introduction* to discuss the problems of rate determination, or of maintenance of efficiency, in regulated or publicly owned enterprises; but reference may be made to one good brief examination of this subject. See J. C. Bonbright, *Public Utilities and National Power Policies* (New York, 1940).

CHAPTER IX

THE WAGE EARNER IN MODERN INDUSTRY[1]

IN the "model" of chapter III, the problem of wages was eliminated by making each family produce and sell some one commodity. The earnings of the workers were determined when the prices of their products were determined; and, under the conditions of perfect competition, perfect mobility, and economic rationality, there assumed, the prices of the products would be such as to give equal earnings to all. In the wheat economy, which was examined in chapter VI, the problem of wages could again be ignored. The typical wheat farmer produced with the aid of his family and employed no wage earners. Again we could relate the earnings of the workers directly to the price of their product; but it became necessary to take account of the variation in individual output. The price of wheat being low and the output being drastically reduced by drought, the incomes of the wheat farmers were so low that state support became necessary. Mobility was highly limited and expectations as to the future of prices and yields could not be formed rationally on the basis of adequate data and understanding. In chapter VII, on the newsprint industry, we again ignored the problem of wage determination. This would have been illegitimate if it had not been intended to discuss the problem in more general terms later in the book. In that chapter we discussed the fortunes of the industry as a whole, but ignored the problem of the division of the product of the industry between workers, bondholders, and owners, and between different kinds of workers. We noted the fact that there are over 50,000 employees in the pulp and paper industry of Canada, and that almost all of them are employed in plants with over 200 employees. Nearly half of them are employed by one of the three biggest corporations. We noted, too, some of the average

[1]See H. A. Logan, *Trade Unions in Canada* (Toronto, 1948). For some discussion of the wage earner in the war-time economy see H. A. Logan, *Canada's Control of Labour Relations*, Behind the Headlines series, vol. II, no. 2, (C.I.I.A., 1941) and his article, "The State and Collective Bargaining," in the *Canadian Journal of Economics and Political Science*, vol. X, no. 4. See also A. Andras, *Labour Unions in Canada* (C.C.L., Ottawa, 1948).

hourly rates of wages paid, varying in 1940 from 45 cents for common labour to $1.50 for expert paper machine tenders. In 1950 these rates varied from $1.00 to $2.20. But nothing was said to explain why these wages were established. They were related, of course, to the price of paper, for they had to be paid out of the revenue from its sale; but the relation was not simple and direct. It is to the explanation of some of the influences determining wages that we turn in this chapter. With the price of paper and the cost of living higher, wages are of course also higher in 1956.

The theory of wages.[2] In order to examine the operation of the economic forces which influence the level of wages in the real world of labour it is usual to set up another model, like that of chapter III, but with a class of capitalist employers who buy equipment and materials, borrow capital, hire workers, organize production, and sell the product. The model becomes rather complicated and it is not intended here to develop fully the conditions of equilibrium for such a system. It is important, however, to notice the two main conditions which would assure the existence of a determinate equilibrium wage. These two conditions are (a) perfect mobility, (b) perfect facility of substitution. By perfect mobility is meant the condition where labour not only can move easily between occupations, but where labour does so move in search of higher earnings: it is this sensitiveness to differences in earnings that is the essence of the concept.[3] Similarly, by perfect facility of substitution is meant not only that the employer can easily produce the same commodity in many different ways involving different amounts of the various agents of production, but especially that such substitution does take place in response to differences in the relative price of these agents: again it is the sensitiveness to these price relationships that is the essence of the concept. Given these conditions one can state: (a) that any agent of production must receive in any occupation as much as it could earn in the alternative occupations to which it could move, and can receive no more; (b) that the earnings of any agent of production relative to the other agents must be such as will induce no employer to substitute more of it for the other possible agents, nor of the other agents for it, in the production of the commodity in question. It has been demonstrated by economic theorists that the operation of these two forces suffices to *determine* wages, i.e. that under these conditions there is only one wage for any type of labour that can persist without itself inducing such movement or sub-

[2]See V. W. Bladen, "What is an Economic Wage" (in *Industrial Relations*, papers presented at a conference on industrial relations at Queen's University, Kingston, 1937). See also M. Dobb, *Wages* (London, 1927).
[3]Cf. pp. 44–45, above.

stitution as would change the wage. The assumption of perfect mobility may be said to flow from the assumption of economic rationality on the part of the worker, the assumption of perfect facility of substitution from the assumption of economic rationality on the part of the employer. The one will not work at a lower paid job if a higher paid job is available; the other will not employ a higher cost method of production if a lower cost method is available, and which is the lower cost method will depend in part on the relative prices of different kinds of labour, different kinds of equipment, different raw materials.

Mobility and substitution in the real world. These two forces, mobility and substitution, operate in the real world of labour, but only roughly and in the long run. If a considerable difference exists in the wages of similar types of labour in different occupations one may expect an increase in the number of workers in the higher paid occupation and a decrease in the lower paid occupation;[4] this will lead to an increase of wages in the lower paid occupation and a decrease in wages in the better paid occupation, till the differential between the occupations is so narrow that no further change is induced. This change will be brought about partly by actual movement from the one trade to the other, but more by a change in the rates at which young persons seeking their first jobs enter the two trades. There is some mobility, but labour is sluggish. This sluggishness is explained in part by ignorance of relative earnings and ignorance of the possibilities of entering the higher paid occupations, in part by the costs of moving, including the cost of training for the new trade, the money cost of moving to a new locality where the occupation is available, and the psychic cost of uprooting the family and transplanting it to the new environment. There are also artificial restrictions on entry to some trades built up to assure the continuance of higher earnings for the privileged members of those trades, e.g. unnecessarily long apprenticeship. Similarly, if a considerable difference exists in the cost of the two methods of production, the one using more, the other less, of some particular type of labour, one may expect substitution, i.e. a change to the lower cost method. But factories are built and equipped for production by methods which seem the most economical, taking into account the relative price of unskilled and skilled labour, and of various types of

[4]See Edwin Cannan, *Wealth* (London, 1923), chap. xii on "Incomes from Work": "We must notice that pecuniary remuneration is not the only thing which people with free choice between occupations think it worth while to consider. They are guided also by their estimate of the agreeableness or disagreeableness of the work to be done and the various conditions accompanying it" (p. 195). Consideration of this point led Alfred Marshall to say that there was a tendency to equality of "net advantages" rather than to equality of "money wages."

machine at the time the plans are made. If later these relative prices change, the plans for new factories may be affected, but the old factories may find it cheaper to continue without change until the time comes for renewing worn-out equipment. Again, the sluggishness in substitution could be explained under the headings of ignorance and cost of change.

In theory, i.e. in the theorist's simple model, wages are determinate because mobility and substitution act perfectly; in the real world they are only broadly determined, or more accurately they are indeterminate within determinate limits. Indeterminate because these forces do not act perfectly, but within determinate limits because these forces do operate to some extent. There are upper and lower limits beyond which wages cannot go without inducing movement or substitution, and therefore beyond which wages cannot go for long. The longer the period under consideration, the narrower the gap between these limits, the more nearly determinate the result. The equilibrium wage of the theorist may be looked on as the wage that would be established if these influences operated quickly, or as that which would be established if the existing conditions continued unchanged long enough for them to operate fully, i.e. for the limits to close up completely. It may be noted, however, that the longer the time necessary for this result to be achieved the more likely is it that many of the fundamental conditions will change and that a new long-run equilibrium wage will have emerged before the old long-run equilibrium wage has been achieved.

Wages and the price of the product. The demand for labour is derived from the demand for its product; one would expect therefore a close relationship between the price of the product and the wages of labour in any trade. The relationship is in fact complicated by the two facts that the agents of production are jointly demanded and are capable of use in many alternative trades. The first complication limits us to saying that the combined earnings of all the productive agents jointly engaged in a trade will be determined by the price of their joint product; but how this price will be divided between them is another question. The second complication leads us towards an answer to this question, but also leads on to some consideration of the reverse influence of the price of the agents on the price of the product.

An imaginary case may be used to demonstrate these relationships. Suppose that the demand for some commodity, say cotton cloth, was to increase. Suppose, too, that the industry was already operating at capacity. The supply of cotton cloth could not be increased until new equipment was provided; the price of cotton cloth would therefore rise to ration the available supply. Suppose the cotton operatives then asked for higher wages. The industry could afford to pay higher wages, but would it have to pay them? This would depend on the degree to which mobility and substitution would operate. If the wage were raised would it attract workers from other trades and so increase the supply in the market that the wages would again be driven down? Or would there be a reserve of unemployed labour anxious to accept jobs at the old rate? If the wage were raised would it induce the manufacturers to revise their methods of production so as to employ less of certain types of labour and more of other types, or to use more automatic devices, and so decrease the demand in the market that the wage would be driven down? A knowledge of the probabilities of this sort would affect the workers in asking and the employers in granting or refusing a wage increase. Such knowledge would also determine the amount of the increase that would be asked. It might well be that the supply of skilled workers could not be increased quickly even in response to a big increase, and that substitution would only take place quickly in response to a large increase. In the short run, therefore, there would be room for bargaining within wide limits. The limits would be widest for the most specialized of the skilled workers. In the long run the production of cotton cloth and employment in the industry would increase, and the price of cloth would fall to a level which would permit the payment of wages in the industry consistent with the level of wages in the occupations drawing labour from the same sources. This would happen whether or not wages had risen in the short run: if they had not risen at first the high profits in the industry would induce expansion, manufacturers would have to attract more workers and would probably have to raise wages for this purpose, but prices would fall and wages settle back to the equilibrium level; if they had risen the inducement to expand would be a little less, at first, but the influx of new workers would drive down wages and so induce further expansion till the same result was obtained. In so far as the supply of labour in a trade is relatively fixed its wages are more closely related to the price of its specific product, but are less accurately determined by economic forces. If we refer back to the information on wages in the Canadian pulp and paper industry (p. 206), we see that wages fell as the demand for newsprint fell, and as the price and output both declined. But a full explanation of the level around which it varied in these years would require consideration of the underlying forces which we have been discussing, and even the variations in these years could only be understood by reference to the decline in wages and in the probability of securing employment in other trades.

Other determining influences. The rates of wages in various occupations are, then, theoretically indeterminate within certain limits; within these limits the actual rate of wages is determined by the influence of custom, chance, bargaining power, and political action. It is necessary to emphasize this in order to counteract the pernicious influence of those who have misused the theory of a determinate equilibrium wage under the simple conditions of the model to suggest that wages are in fact determinate in the real world and that no control of wages is necessary or possible. On the other hand, it is necessary to insist that a knowledge of the limits within which wages are indeterminate is as essential to trade unions and governments as is a sense of justice.

Wages and efficiency. Even these limits are not as rigid in the world of flesh and blood as a study of the theoretical model would suggest. For the workers are flesh and blood, not the standard automata of the model. Their efficiency therefore varies with their pay, but in most erratic fashion. In some cases a higher wage induces greater efficiency in the worker and increases his output; in other cases the higher wage may lead to some relaxation of effort on the part of workers who have had to struggle at the lower wage to maintain their customary standard of living; in some cases it may be that efficiency will depend on the relation between actual wages and the idea of a fair wage in the worker's mind. Let Adam Smith, one of the earliest advocates of the "economy of high wages," speak on the first of these possibilities, the most important from the point of view of the elasticity of the upper limit to wages: "The liberal reward of labour . . . increases the industry of the common people. . . . A plentiful subsistence increases the bodily strength of the labourer, and the comfortable hope of bettering his condition, and of ending his days perhaps in ease and plenty, animates him to exert that strength to the utmost." Or again, "That men in general should work better when they are ill fed than when they are well fed, when they are disheartened than when they are in good spirits, when they are frequently sick than when they are in good health, seems not very probable."

Employers, too, are flesh and blood, sometimes content with a good profit and not seeking to maximize profits as do the rational pawns of the mathematical economist's model. So there emerges the suggestion that if you make him pay higher wages to his employees you may make the employer more efficient. "By hustling the employer and making him pay wages which he cannot afford to pay at the moment if he is to make a normal profit you will have the effect of increasing his efficiency. The average business man is no longer envisaged as the feverishly active and alert figure of the classical economists, who never missed a chance of making a penny if it was humanly possible . . . the new view seems to be that he is a fellow who is easy going and content with a given income and does not bestir himself unduly to increase it to what would be for him the maximum attainable. Therefore in raising wages you bring into activity latent energies in the entrepreneur out of which the additional wages can be paid."[5] Mr. J. W. F. Rowe in his *Wages in Practice and Theory* (London, 1928) has produced some interesting facts and statistics intended to support this point of view.

Neither of these two factors promises complete relaxation of the upper limits to wage movements; but between them they impart some elasticity to the upper limit. One may be a little less timid about the disastrous effects of exaggerating the height to which wages may be pushed. But we have no quantitative data relating to their importance. My guess is that both operate particularly in the sweated industries and that much of the success of minimum wage legislation in sweated industries is to be explained by reference to them.

Why some workers have low paid and others high paid services for sale. The theory of wages has contributed to an understanding of the pricing of various services, and the analysis of the system of prices has been pushed forward to explain the pricing of various types of land, of various types of capital equipment, and of various types of security (or the determination of the rate of interest on loans). This is usually referred to as a "theory of distribution." Professor Edwin Cannan[6] has pointed out that it is only part of the explanation of the determination of the distribution of income between persons, for it leaves out any explanation of why particular people have particular services, particular pieces of land and equipment, or particular amounts of money to offer. A full explanation of differences in wages between different types of labour would require an examination of the innate differences in ability, and of differences in opportunity to

----

[5]J. M. Keynes, "The Question of High Wages" (*Political Quarterly,* Jan., 1930). Mr. Keynes felt that there were "very narrow limits to the practical application of these notions" and expressed grave doubts as to the wisdom of pressing for higher wages in England as long as England was so dependent on international trade. Mr. Rowe's picture of the proper position of the modern entrepreneur may well frighten even the vigorous: "Capital's task should be that of a Sisyphus, and as fast as one stone is rolled up the hill to the feet of labour, another one should be sent rolling down the hill, so that Sisyphus may not rest or even slacken his exertions, for fear lest he be crushed by the accumulation. The stimulus of competition can be, and should be, reinforced by a constant pressure to raise wages" (p. 210).

[6]*Wealth,* chaps. x–xiii.

secure the training required for the more skilled occupations. Such an examination would suggest that the existing unequal distribution of the ownership of property and the consequent unequal distribution of current income is largely responsible for the differences in the kinds of labour which different groups have for sale. The poverty of the poor is their destruction; because their parents were poor many children were undernourished, and had to enter industry at an early age in an occupation which gave maximum immediate earnings but which might prove a "blind alley." On the other hand, one must notice the advantage of the "old school tie," most obvious in an older country like England but not quite absent even in a pioneer country like Canada. Professor R. H. Tawney puts the point cogently:

> We are all disposed to attribute our failures to our circumstances and our successes to ourselves; that the race is to the swift and the battle to the strong and that we richly deserved our victory. But the successful, who had a good start in life, would do well to ask himself what his position would have been if his father had been an unemployed miner or a casual dock labourer. The race is not from scratch, the handicaps are considerable. . . . There is the unequal pressure of mere material surroundings, of housing, sanitation, and liability to disease, which decides that social groups shall differ in their ability to make the best use of their natural endowments. There is inequality of educational opportunity . . . while a favoured minority can cultivate their powers till manhood, the great majority of children, being compelled to compete for employment in their early adolescence, must enter occupations in which, because they are overcrowded, the re-muneration is low. . . . There is the nepotism which allows jobs in the family business to sons and relatives, and the favouritism which fills them with youths belonging to the same social class as its owners. There is in-equality of access to financial information, which yields fortunes of sur-prising dimensions, if occasionally, also, of dubious repute, to the few who possess it.[7]

Whatever the underlying reasons, it is clear that there are different grades of labour between which there may be some movement in the course of generations, but no "mobility" in the sense that movement between them is induced by a widening of the wage differentials. Indeed one may suggest that a rise in the wages of the unskilled would promote, in the next generation, an upward movement by permitting better nourishment, better housing, better training. Within these "non-competing" groups mobility between occupations operates; as between these groups substitution operates, for they constitute different agents of production. The idea of labour as a homogeneous agent is one which is only suitable for the first and simplest model of the theorist.

Wages and employment. So far we have considered wages as a part of the employers' cost and have suggested that the higher the

[7]R. H. Tawney, *Equality* (London, 1931), pp. 157–61.

wage the less is likely to be the number employed. This is roughly true for any one type of labour, or for labour in any one industry. We must notice next a complication which arises from the fact that wages must also be looked on as incomes and therefore as the source of demand for goods and thus, ultimately, for labour. Further, wages are incomes which are peculiarly likely to be fully spent. If, therefore, wages as a whole rise at the expense of property incomes, the total amount spent on consumption goods may rise and the amount of income which people plan to save may decline. The increased demand for consumption goods may encourage manufacturers to extend their plants and so lead to an increase in investment. The increase in the total demand for goods would mean an increased demand for labour even at the new higher wages. But these possibilities are limited in an economy as highly dependent on export trade as is the Canadian economy. For Canada the prices of her staple exports are determined by forces outside her borders and the demand for these goods is not significantly increased by increased spending at home. Wages in the export industries must be consistent, therefore, with the prices of their products in the export markets; and wages in other industries must be roughly consistent with wages in the export industries.

Control of wages. Before going on to discuss the attempts of trade unions and governments to control wages it may be useful to sum up the results of the theoretical discussion. (1) By skilful bargaining, or by government decree, wages may be raised nearer to the upper limit without any unfavourable reactions. (2) By restricting entry to a trade, that particular kind of labour may be rendered more scarce and the upper limit to its price raised; this, however, is at the expense of other trades which must thereby be rendered more crowded. (3) By rules about the introduction of machinery, dilution, etc., the possibilities of substitution may be limited and again the upper limit to wages may be raised. (4) Finally, if there is a sufficient sentiment against accepting employment below the standard wage, so that workers prefer unemployment to employment at a lower wage, and particularly if the union or the state makes some provision for those unemployed, wages may be maintained above the equilibrium level; but this sentiment must exist among possible entrants to the trade or must be combined with restrictions on entry if it is to persist.

Trade unions.[8] The basis of trade union organization may be the craft, the particular industry, or industry in general. The craft union was formerly the dominant form in Canada and the United States but the industrial union challenged its position in the late thirties. Labour

[8]See R. R. R. Brooks, *When Labor Organizes* (New York, 1937); R. A. Lester, *Economics of Labor* (New York, 1941), chaps. xx-xxii.

unions, such as the old Knights of Labor, the Industrial Workers of the World, and the One Big Union have not been serious competitors.

The craft union. The craft union is appropriate to a group of skilled workers who may be employed in a great variety of industries. Such craftsmen, e.g. carpenters, are concerned to limit competition within the craft: their wages are determined, more or less, by the demand for their services in all industries, not by the price of the product of the industry in which they are for the time being employed. If union organization was on industrial lines they would constitute a small minority in each union, and their influence would be the smaller because the personnel of that minority would change as the craftsmen moved from industry to industry and therefore from union to union. Organized as a craft they have a cohesion which the industrial union cannot match; and they have some monopoly powers based on the scarcity of their skill and the discipline of their members. If industrial action is required they can organize an alliance of the craft unions concerned. For dealing with the general interests of labour some central federal body may be set up, such as the American Federation of Labor (A.F. of L.) in the United States, or the Trades and Labor Congress of Canada.

The industrial union. There have always been some industrial unions, or predominantly craft unions with some industrial features, in the A.F. of L. After 1935, however, there was in the United States a great development of industrial unionism under the Congress of Industrial Organization (C.I.O.), which emerged as a rival national organization to the A.F. of L. In 1955 the rival congresses merged. The general argument for industrial organization is that the development of modern technique has undermined the old craft distinctions. Speaking of the automobile industry Henry Ford once said:[9]

43 per cent of our workers require less than 1 day's training
30 per cent of our workers require less than 1 week of training
20 per cent of our workers require less than 1 year of training
 1 per cent of our workers require more than 1 year of training

Modern machine industry employs relatively few craftsmen with skills common to many industries, but many semi-skilled workers on specialized jobs peculiar to that industry. If the mass of unskilled and semi-skilled workers are to be organized, it must be on an industrial basis. The skilled workers who are organized in craft unions may also be at a disadvantage as one union is played off against another, unless successful arrangements have been made for industrial action by an alliance of craft unions. The success of the C.I.O. in organizing the steel workers and automotive workers along industrial lines gave a great impetus to this type of union.

[9]Henry Ford, *My Life and Work* (New York, 1926).

Trade unions in Canada.[10] The American Federation of Labor, and most of its affiliated unions which operated in Canada, recognized the Trades and Labor Congress of Canada as head of the international, craft-union, labour movement in the Dominion. After 1935 the T.L.C. expanded its membership beyond strict craft lines to include many workers associated with a craft but holding semi-skilled or unskilled jobs. In 1938 the membership of the T.L.C. was about 180,000; in 1954 it was almost 600,000. The aim of the T.L.C. as expressed in its constitution is to achieve "legislation in the interests of organized labour in the Dominion of Canada and to assist in safeguarding the social and economic standards of the workers."

In 1940 the All-Canadian Congress of Labour was reorganized as the Canadian Congress of Labour. It took in the Canadian members of the international unions affiliated in the United States with the C.I.O. which had been expelled from the Trades and Labor Congress of Canada as from the A.F. of L. The general aims of the C.C.L. were similar to those of the T.L.C. but at the 1949 convention it was stated that "instead of being directed almost entirely toward the improvement of wages and working conditions it now embraces programs of social security and similar measures, with a view to lessening or eliminating the risks of unemployment, illness, poverty and other preventable evils. Emphasis is being laid upon educational programs so that workers may understand more clearly the economic and political principles upon which the institutions of government and industry are based."[11] In 1938, 50,000 Canadians were members of unions affiliated with the C.I.O.; by 1954, 360,000 workers were members of the C.C.L.

La Confédération des Travailleurs Catholiques du Canada is an independent national organization which is "opposed to control by American Unions."[12] It is made up of 16 federations including barbers, longshoremen, municipal employees, workers in building, clothing, furniture, gloves, leather and shoes, printing, asbestos, pulp and paper, textiles, and commercial establishments. Membership, which is almost completely confined to the province of Quebec, rose from 50,000 in 1938 to 100,000 in 1954. In 1956 the Trades and Labor Congress and the Canadian Congress of Labour, following the example of the A.F. of L. and the C.I.O., merged. There seems a very good chance that the federation of Catholic unions will join this new Canadian Labour Congress.

[10]See H. A. Logan; also the annual reports on *Labour Organization in Canada* published by the Department of Labour at Ottawa, and the statistics of trade union membership in the *Canada Year Book.*
[11]*Report of Proceedings of 1949 Convention of C.C.L.*
[12]*Le Travail,* June 1944.

At the close of 1953 there were over one and a quarter million members of trade unions in Canada, a third of the wage and salary workers in non-agricultural industries. More than one-half of these members were in Ontario and Quebec, about one-tenth were in the Maritimes and the remainder were divided evenly among the four western provinces. The most highly organized province was British Columbia, where almost 40 per cent of non-agricultural workers were unionized, 20 per cent of the total membership was concentrated in Toronto and Montreal, while a further 20 per cent was distributed among nine other industrial centres.

Over 90 per cent of Canadian trade unions are affiliated with one of the central labour congresses: 85 per cent with either the Trades and Labor Congress or the Canadian Congress of Labour, and 10 per cent with La Confédération des Travailleurs Catholiques du Canada. Membership of the congresses was as follows in January, 1954:

Trades and Labour Congress	600,000
Canadian Congress of Labour	360,000
La Confédération des Travailleurs Catholiques du Canada	100,000
Unaffiliated national and international unions	62,000
International railway brotherhoods (independent)	41,000
Unaffiliated international unions	60,000
Unaffiliated national, regional or local unions	100,000

Some indication of the way in which union organization has developed in Canada may be given by listing the largest unions with their congressional affiliates. International Union United Automobile, Aircraft and Agricultural Implement Workers of America (C.C.L.-C.I.O.) had 65,000 members in 1954. The United Steelworkers of America (C.C.L.-C.I.O.) had 70,000; the United Brotherhood of Carpenters and Joiners of America (T.L.C.-A.F.L.) 55,000; the Canadian Brotherhood of Railway Employees and Other Transport Workers (C.C.L.) 33,000; the International Brotherhood of Pulp, Sulphite, and Paper Mill Workers (T.L.C.-A.F.L.) 31,000; the United Mine Workers of America (C.C.L.) 25,000; the United Electrical Radio and Machine Workers of America (independent), 25,000. Canadian trade unions are represented in the International Confederation of Free Trade Unions which speaks for 48 million organized workers in 53 countries.

Trade union policy. The object of trade unions is the improvement of the condition of the wage earners. This they seek to obtain mainly by "collective bargaining" with employers. Such bargaining is concerned not only with improving specific conditions (hours, wages, etc.) but also with putting on a contractual basis many of the personnel policies of the employers so that privileges enjoyed at the will of the employer, sometimes on the basis of long standing custom, may become rights under a collective agreement. The content of a typical agreement will be described below. Many unions still provide "benefits": e.g., insurance against unemployment, sickness, funeral expenses. These, however, have become less important as social insurance has developed and as supplementary insurance has been secured by collective bargaining from employers: in the absence of state health insurance employers have paid, in whole or in part, the cost of group health insurance; employer pension plans supplement the state system of old-age pensions; and supplemental unemployment insurance has been secured and seems likely to spread as a result of the drive for a Guaranteed Annual Wage. The International Typographical Union is an example of full development of "benefit" policies by the union itself: it "cares for its sick, aged and indigent." Unions have also used political action. They have sought to improve their own legal status in order to be able to bargain more effectively, and they have tried to achieve by legislation some improvements in the condition of the wage earners which they have failed to achieve by direct action. In addition to the purely material advantages of union membership there is the advantage which comes from fraternal association with like-minded people, fraternal association in a "movement." The comfort of such association, the joy of belonging to a group, the support to self-respect and self-confidence which comes from an assured status in the group: these men seek in all sorts of societies, in churches, masonic lodges, Elks, and Kiwanis; but for many they are found in the union local. "A union leader, travelling through North Carolina three years after a disastrous strike, was recognized by a group of former union members. They begged her to take them for a picnic, relight their old campfire, lead them in workers' songs, and revive the stories of former struggles."[13]

Collective Bargaining. Essentially, the business policy of the union is to establish collective bargaining in place of individual bargaining, and to arrange for the conduct of collective bargaining by skilled negotiators with a full knowledge of the market. Such a collective agreement or the establishment of a "standard rate," prevents employers from taking advantage of the ignorance or pressing needs of individual workers to employ them at less than the rate ruling in the trade generally; it also raises the rate ruling in the trade. Ability to raise wages may depend in part on skill in bargaining and bluff, but ultimately it depends on the power of the particular group of workers

[13]Brooks, *When Labor Organizes*, p. 231.

by striking to inflict injury on the employer who refuses to meet their demands.[14] The successful use of a strike or threat of a strike, depends on the discipline of the workers and the degree of outside support. Not only must the members of the striking union be prepared to endure the hardships of the fight, but there must be no adequate body of workers outside the trade able and willing to take their places. Picketing has developed as a way of preventing replacement of the strikers. Peaceful picketing to inform strike breakers about the issues and to persuade them not to "scab" is legitimate and legal, but more violent methods of prevention are frequently adopted and involve conflict with the law. Outside support may take the form of contributions to the strike fund from sympathetic unions, or even of sympathetic strikes. The sympathy and support of the general public are also of great importance, particularly where the public suffers immediately and directly from the strike. Skill in presenting the case of the strikers to the public is one of the requirements of the good union leader. Fundamentally the strength of labour's bargaining power depends on the development of a sentiment against accepting wages lower than the standard rate similar to the sentiment against price cutting which animates most employers.

The business policies of the union can be more effectively pursued if recognition by the employers can be secured. The strength of the resistance of many employers who will not recognize a union nor bargain with any but a committee of their own employees is an indication of importance of such recognition. Many strikes in the early stages of organization were concerned to secure recognition of the union rather than to secure immediate wage advances. Provision is now made under federal and provincial laws for a process of "certification." Once the appropriate government board has determined, by a supervised vote or by some other check of union membership, that a union represents a majority of employees in the category concerned, the employer must bargain with it in good faith. Having secured recognition, the union struggles to secure further degrees of union security, the check-off of union dues, the requirement that all shall join the union (the "union shop") or that all shall pay dues whether they join or not (the "Rand formula"). In some trades where the unions are well established employers may undertake to employ only union members ("the closed shop"). In other industries virtually closed shops may exist

14Pressure may also be brought on the employer by refusal on the part of a sufficiently large group of buyers to buy his products. Such a boycott is difficult and probably illegal; but the "union label," registered under the Trade Mark and Design Act, is a lawful device for diverting sympathetic customers to the product of union shops.

through the loyalty of foremen who will not tolerate a non-union man even in an open shop, will find an excuse for not hiring him, or for firing him, or will persuade him to join the union.

The collective agreement. There are some six thousand agreements in effect in Canada affecting over a million and a half workers. Amidst infinite variety a typical pattern can be discerned. The agreement embodies a set of rules to which management and employees are bound to adhere for the term of the agreement, generally one year. It establishes uniform treatment of employees and prescribes the boundaries of management discretion, establishing "management rights" and employee rights. It generally opens with a preamble expressing recognition of mutual interest, for instance: "The successful operation of the mills is hereby declared to be a matter of mutual interest"; or, "Recognizing that the welfare of the Company and that of its employees depends upon the welfare of the business as a whole, and recognizing that a relationship of goodwill and mutual respect between employers and employees can contribute greatly to the maintenance and increase of that welfare, the parties to this contract join together in the following Agreement." Pious phrases, some may say: but they are probably of important ritual significance in the development of co-operation. Clauses are likely to follow which "recognize" the union as the bargaining agent and provide some degree of "union security." No union likes to see non-members enjoying a "free ride" at the expense of dues-paying members, and the strength of the union requires not only the dues but the personal support of the workers. Unions therefore seek some clause which will bring all eligible employees into the union. A closed shop clause may run simply: "None but members of the Union in good standing shall be employed by the Company." It may be qualified by another clause such as this: "In the event that the Union is unable to supply competent men from their present membership, the Company will have the right to employ non-union men, and the Union agrees that, after a reasonable term of employment, men so employed will not be refused admission to the Union." Whatever degree of union security is achieved there may be a clause providing for "check-off," or the collection of union dues by the employer who deducts them from wages and forwards them to the treasurer of the union. Paralleling the union security clause may be one asserting certain "management prerogatives": "The Union recognizes the right of the Company to hire, promote and demote, transfer, suspend or otherwise discipline and discharge any employee, subject to such regulations and restrictions governing the exercise of these rights as are expressly provided in this agreement. . . . The Union further recognizes the right of the company to operate and manage its business . . . [and that] the location of plants, the products to be manufactured, the schedules of production, the methods, processes and means of manufacturing and office operations, are solely the responsibility of the company."

Along with the establishment of wages for all classes of employees the agreement will determine the hours which must be worked at various wages. (A survey of contracts in force in 1951 indicated that a 40-hour week had been secured in nearly a third of the contracts and by over 40 per cent of the employees.) There is then provision for payment of overtime generally at time and a half rates, and for some limit to the amount of overtime that may be required. These provisions may become very complicated in a plant subject to considerable variation in operations, for instance in a meat-packing plant with fluctuation in livestock receipts and in the demand for its products. Regular hours will be scheduled, but workers may be required to work before, or after the schedule: the company may then agree to pay time and a half for hours in excess of the number scheduled, and to pay time and a half for work done one hour after the scheduled quitting time even though the worker may not have worked the full number of hours scheduled for the day. Provision is generally made also for "call-in-time": payment of those called in to work for whom no work is available. A number of holidays with pay will be specified (the number has been increasing) and often double time is provided for those who must work on a holiday. Vacations with pay of various lengths for employees with various lengths of service will be provided. Along with these provisions may be noticed others for sickness benefits, retirement pensions, and (most recent of all) supplemental unemployment pay. In negotiating agreement on all these items the company will be watching the relative cost of additional fringe benefits and direct wage increases (the net cost taking into account, for example, the effect on productivity of any increase in health coming from improved sickness benefits); the union will be watching the relative value set on these gains by its members. Negotiation will involve the content of a "package" in which various items are substitutes for one another.

A vital part of the contract will deal with seniority. This is looked on by the unions as essential to protect their members from arbitrary treatment in layoff, promotion, etc. Some seniority rules would be an integral part of any company's personnel policy; morale in any organization requires some consideration for seniority, and the necessity of justifying any deviation from seniority in promotion may be an important management device for checking favouritism on the part of subordinate officers of the company. But attention to seniority without reference to ability or "merit" would wreck an organization: for some posts it must seek to promote the brilliant young men over the heads of the good longer-service men. The union seeks to protect its members against unfair treatment by writing into the contract the policy of the company, by trying to press the company into giving more attention to seniority, and by establishing some supervision of the seniority lists. One contract reads: "The company recognizes the importance of seniority as a factor to be considered along with merit and ability in all moves, transfers, promotions, lay-offs, reinstatements and recalls but when merit and ability are relatively equal as between employees, then seniority is recognized as the prevailing factor in the making of a selection." This general statement is followed by pages of detailed regulations defining "seniority" and establishing seniority rights in particular circumstances. Special seniority status is provided for union officials. Discussion of a seniority clause with a group of representative foremen indicated serious feelings of frustration in managing their departments as a result of the seniority clause: but the same group showed very strong belief in the principle of seniority in the promotion of foremen!

Vital to the contract is the establishment of a "grievance procedure" through which the rights established by the contract may be defined and enforced in daily practice. The contract establishes general principles: its interpretation in particular cases is often difficult and worker and foreman, union and company, may disagree thereon. The procedure outlined in the contract is usually one involving at least three successive stages. The worker who feels that the contract has not been properly followed or interpreted takes his problem to the "shop steward." If the steward thinks there are grounds for a grievance he will take it up with the foreman. If foreman and steward fail to agree the case is referred to a higher level: the chairman of the bargaining committee may take it up with the senior industrial relations officer of the company. In some cases provision will be made for a case still undecided at this stage to be considered by an officer of the union and an officer of the company. Failing agreement, provision is made for arbitration: the arbitrator's decision must be accepted by both parties since work stoppages are prohibited by law in the case of grievance disputes. The character of the grievance procedures depends on the fundamental union-management relationship in any company: the proceedings can be highly constructive and not purely combative. "This is where many basic problems are decided and ideas for change and further improvement in labour-management relations first make themselves known."[15]

Other parts of the contract will deal with the sickness benefit plan, the pension plan, etc. In each case the rights and duties of both parties under the plan must be clearly defined, the form of management must be agreed, and provision must be made for adjudication of disputes. The provision for the Supplemental Unemployment Benefit in the Ford contract in the United States required fifty mimeographed pages.

Political activities. In North America the union movement has generally stayed out of politics in the sense that it has neither organized a labour party nor allied itself with any other party.[16] It has, nevertheless, sought the attainment of its ends by state intervention, securing that intervention by its influence in both parties, by publicity and by lobbying, and by throwing its weight for or against particular candidates, irrespective of party, according to their attitudes to labour problems. The unions have first sought an assured status for themselves in order that they might pursue their primary business policy of collective bargaining. They are, in a sense, conspiracies in restraint of trade, and were for a long time treated as such. The Criminal Code of Canada, however, specifically exempted them from the operation of section 498. In the United States the National Labor Relations Act (1935) provided that "employees shall have the right to self-organization, to form, join or assist labor organizations, to bargain collectively through representatives of their own choosing, and to engage in concerted activities, for the purpose of collective bargaining or other mutual aid or protection." It declared the following actions by employers to be "unfair labor practices": (1) to interfere with, restrain, or coerce, employees in the exercise of the guaranteed right to organize; (2) to dominate or support, financially or otherwise, a labour organization; (3) to encourage or discourage membership in any labour organization by discrimination in regard to hire or tenure of employment; (4) to refuse to bargain collectively with the representatives of their employees. A Board was set up, with a status similar to that of the Federal Trade Commission, to hear complaints of "unfair labor practices" and to conduct elections to determine, in case of dis-

[15]J. T. Montague, *Labour Unions in Canada* (Current Affairs for the Canadian Forces, vol. 8, no. 9).

[16]An exception is the Canadian Congress of Labour which, since 1946, has passed resolutions identifying it with the policies and objectives of the Co-operative Commonwealth Federation party in Canada.

pute, what organization the employees did freely choose to represent them. The rapid growth in unionism in the United States since 1935 owes much to this legislation. Its influence has been felt in Canada. An amendment to the Criminal Code of Canada made it a crime for an employer to discriminate against a man because of union membership. The Canadian legislation, however, "did not define unfair labour practices as clearly as the American legislation, nor did it set up special machinery for investigating complaints."[17] Under the stress of war by order-in-council (P.C. 1003, 1944) and after the war by legislation (The Industrial Relations and Disputes Investigation Act, 1948) the right of workers to organize and the duty of employers to recognize and bargain with duly certified unions were established. The change in legislation was partly the product of the great change in attitude towards unions in the preceding fifteen years; but it was also a substantial cause of the acceleration of that change.

The conditions of the bargain between employers and employees are not left entirely to free negotiation; the state lays down certain minimum conditions which employer and employee alike must respect. The Factory Acts of the provinces are typical of this type of interference; minimum conditions of sanitation and safety are laid down. Legislation to set up maximum hours and minimum wages has generally been used for the protection of weak, unorganized groups and particularly for women and children. More recently legislation (e.g., in Quebec) has provided that collective agreements may, under certain conditions, be made binding not only on the parties to them but on the whole trade. Elaborate provision for Workmen's Compensation has been made pretty generally and various forms of social insurance have been secured. Ontario provides mothers' allowances for destitute widows, or deserted wives, with dependent children; and, in co-operation with the Dominion government, provides old age pensions. In 1941 a Dominion scheme of unemployment insurance was inaugurated. A comprehensive scheme of health insurance, such as has been common in Europe for many years, has not yet been achieved. The part played by organized labour in securing government action calculated to improve the standard of living of the worker is hard to determine. Generally it has pressed for such legislation; but on occasion it has preferred to achieve its end by bargaining and agreement rather than by legislative enactment because of the effect on the strength and solidarity of the union. Organized labour in Canada has also thrown

[17]*The Right to Organize* (Bulletin 2, Industrial Relations Section, Queen's University, Kingston, 1938).

its weight in favour of free education, adequate provision for vocational training, subsidized housing, etc.[18]

Conciliation. While strikes and lockouts are natural incidents in the competitive determination of wages it became evident quite early that adequate conciliation machinery could reduce their number and intensity. The Dominion government began to provide such machinery in 1900. The Conciliation Act of that year established a Labour Department "to disseminate accurate statistical and other information relating to the conditions of labour." The Department was to promote the establishment of permanent conciliation machinery where possible, and was to intervene in disputes where no such machinery existed to investigate the dispute, and to *offer* its services as mediator or arbitrator. The Deputy Minister of the new Department was W. L. Mackenzie King. Very soon a dispute on the Canadian Pacific Railway drew attention to the peculiar importance of continuous operation of the railways. A new principle was embodied in a special statute to deal with this situation. Under the Railway Labour Disputes Act (1903) the Minister of Labour might intervene of right in case of a railway strike or lockout. He was to appoint a Committee of Conciliation, and if this failed a Board of Arbitration with power to compel attendance of witnesses and production of documents. The arbitrators were to declare "what would be reasonable and proper to be done by both parties with a view to putting an end to the difference." This declaration was to be published in the *Labour Gazette* and was to be sent to the press. It was in no sense binding and in no way interfered with the right to strike. It was Mr. King's belief, however, that a declaration of this sort would have considerable influence in promoting agreement.

A few years later a coal strike in Lethbridge threatened to cause great hardship on the prairies. Mr. King went west as mediator. On his

[18]See J. M. Keynes, "The Question of High Wages." Mr. Keynes having discussed the limits to high-wage doctrines in a country so intimately connected with the international system, urged greater concentration on taxation and extension of the social services as a method of improving the lot of the workers. He urged trade unionists "not to starve the goose that lays the golden eggs before we have discovered how to replace her. We must tax her eggs instead." "It is, to my way of thinking," he said, "a great misfortune that the concerted self conscious efforts of the working class should be so much concentrated on the effort to raise wages, even to the point of being suspicious, as I fancy the Trade Unions are, of alternative methods of bettering conditions. For the main *raison d'être* of a Trade Union as a corporate body is gone if the perpetual struggle for higher wages is to be abandoned." This advice is worthy of consideration: but the programme of social services should be in addition to reasonably high wages and only as an alternative to extremely high wages; and it must be financed from taxes which do not fall largely on the workers themselves, if it is to be, as Mr. Keynes intended, an instrument of redistribution of wealth.

return he drafted the Industrial Disputes Investigation Act (1907). This Act was to apply to all industries where continuous operation was of national importance: to transport, communication, public utilities, and mines. In these industries the right to strike, or lockout, was limited. Thirty days' notice was required of any contemplated change in the conditions of employment. If the changes were protested they were not to be made, nor was a strike or lockout to be declared, until the dispute had been dealt with by a Board appointed under this Act. The Board was to consist of three members, one appointed by each party to the dispute, the third to be chosen by these two or, in the event of disagreement, to be named by the Minister of Labour. The Board was to have power to summon witnesses and call for the production of documents. It was to publish in the *Labour Gazette* a report as to reasonable terms of agreement. To strike, or lockout before the award was made became a criminal offence; but the award was not binding and once made a strike or lockout might proceed. Reliance was placed on investigation and publicity; the weight of public opinion in favour of the award of the Board was expected to have such an influence on the probable outcome of the strike, or lockout, as to induce both parties to accept it. "Light is the sovereign antiseptic, and the best of all policemen." This Act was held to be *ultra vires* of the Dominion government by the Privy Council in 1924; but by enabling legislation in the provinces the Act was re-established throughout Canada except Prince Edward Island. Since World War II compulsory conciliation has spread in most provinces to cover all industry. This development will be discussed below.

Legislation for the promotion of industrial peace must be judged not only by its success in promoting peace but also by its effect on the terms of peace. It is difficult to determine what the effect has been, for to do so involves an estimate of what would have happened if the machinery of the Act had not existed. Two points, however, must be emphasized. First one must notice the difficulty of prohibiting strikes. You cannot make men work against their will; you cannot proceed against thousands of strikers as against a single pick-pocket. To make it a crime to strike may deter strikes because it is the strongest indication of the public disapproval of a strike; but the criminal penalties cannot secure industrial peace. The success of the Act never did depend on the penalties for illegal strikes; nor can it, unless we are to borrow from totalitarian states the concentration camp, the secret police and all its methods, the propaganda bureau, etc. Second, as long as we leave wages to be determined by bargaining between employers and employees, it is doubtful whether we can equitably take the edge off the workers' weapon, the strike, to which he must ultimately be free to resort if the bargaining is unsatisfactory. An examination of the awards of boards established under the Act would probably show that their influence has been generally conservative, mitigating the fall of wages in time of depression and curbing their rise in time of prosperity.[19]

Regulation of labour in World War II.   During World War II the maintenance of industrial peace became extremely important. The conciliation board method of the Industrial Disputes Investigation Act was extended to all war industries. As labour grew scarce, however, there was constant pressure for higher wages. Fearing the inflationary effect, the government, issued instructions to the conciliation boards not to grant increases in wages unless they were below the best level that prevailed between 1926 and 1940. In December, 1939, Order-in-Council 7440 established a basic permanent wage beyond which workers were to be protected by a flat "cost of living bonus" against increases in the cost of the essentials of life. Differing interpretations of the order by the conciliation boards led to considerable confusion and unrest and to demands for a more integrated policy. Finally, in October, 1941, an order was passed stabilizing wages and salaries in all industries as part of the general policy of price control. The new order was to be administered by a permanent National War Labour Board and five regional boards (later nine), which were to grant adjustments in wage rates only where gross inequality or injustice could be shown. As in the previous order, provision was made for payment of a "cost of living bonus."

Aside from wage demands, the issues of union recognition and collective bargaining became more prominent as employment expanded and union membership increased. The problem was recognized in June, 1940, when P.C. 2685 set forth a declaration of principles which "would make for the avoidance of industrial strife." These provided that (1) "fair and reasonable standards of wages and working conditions should be maintained"; (2) there should be no strikes or lockouts but all disputes should be settled by negotiation or by reference to conciliation boards; (3) employees should be free to join trade unions "free from any control by employers or their agents," and to negotiate collective agreements; (4) there should be no coercion or

---

[19]See B. M. Selekman, *Law and Labour Relations: A Study of the Industrial Disputes Investigation Act of Canada* (Cambridge, Mass., 1936). Chaps. III and IV contain an analysis of the principles which appear to have guided Boards in making their decisions. For a discussion of the use of this Act in war time see Bryce M. Stewart, "War-Time Labour Problems and Policies" (*Canadian Journal of Economics and Political Science*, Aug., 1941).

intimidation in influencing a worker to join a union. This order, however, contained no enforcement provision.

As new controls were gradually imposed on the economy and on labour, the government moved towards a wartime labour code. In September, 1941, P.C. 7307 had provided for a strike vote under specified conditions before a strike could legally be called, but a series of strikes took place in the shipyards, and the aircraft and steel industries and in 1943 man-working days lost exceeded one million for the first time since 1925. The National War Labour Board held a public inquiry into the situation and in March, 1944, P.C. 1003 was issued to supersede previous orders-in-council. The order was administered by a Wartime Labour Relations Board, but by agreement with the provinces its powers could be delegated to provincial boards. In the early stages of a dispute, conciliation was to be attempted. Strikes were forbidden until 14 days after the conciliation board had reported to the Minister of Labour. Following American experience, the National Board defined the appropriate unit for bargaining purposes, held elections if necessary to determine bargaining representatives, and was responsible for preventing or punishing unfair practices as defined in the Order. Unfair employer practices included discrimination against union activities or domination of employees' organizations; some unfair union practices were intimidating or coercing employees to join, organizing during working hours, "slowdowns" or other means to limit production without previous use of the laid-down procedure. Where no grievance procedure existed, the Board might establish suitable machinery. The Board had power to impose penalties, including fines, for violations. The Order forced both sides to negotiate in good faith, and alleviated the issue of union recognition. The procedure was criticized as unwieldy, but the Order marked the peak of industrial legislation in Canada, and its effect on Canadian labour can be compared with that of Roosevelt's New Deal labour legislation in the United States.

Compulsory direction of labour to essential industries was not necessary during the early years of the war because a large reserve of unemployed labour was available to fill the new jobs. This reserve was increased by calling on women to enter industry, by asking older men to forego retirement, and by recruiting youths from school. As labour became more scarce, however, the problem of allocating workers grew beyond the scope of the price system and the appeal to patriotism. In March, 1942, the government set up National Selective Service to channel all changes in employment. At first the control was negative: men were prohibited from seeking employment in non-essential industries and employers were prevented from luring skilled workers from necessary jobs. The movement of workers between industries was controlled by permits. A worker wishing to leave his job had to give seven days notice of separation in order to avoid disrupting production. A labour priority schedule was drawn up and workers were prevented from moving from a high priority to a low priority position. In 1943, controls were extended to "freeze" employment of essential workers. Finally, compulsory transfer of labourers from one occupation to another was used, particularly to divert labour into coal mining and agriculture. The emigration of labour was controlled by a system of labour exit permits.

Compulsory allocation of labour was accompanied by measures to increase the supply of skilled labour. Under a War Emergency Training Programme workers were trained in schools and on the job to fill essential positions. The supply of trained technical workers was mobilized through a Bureau of Technical Personnel.

Compulsory conciliation since World War II. In September, 1948, the Industrial Relations and Disputes Investigation Act took the place of both the Industrial Disputes Investigation Act and the war-time Orders. Under this act the Canada Labour Relations Board continues the certification and conciliation work of the Wartime Labour Relations Board in industries within Dominion jurisdiction: the provinces have adopted similar legislation and supervise collective bargaining through their own boards. What follows is based on the experience of Ontario.[20] The procedure involves two stages: first, intervention by a Conciliation Officer; second, the establishment of a Conciliation Board. The Ontario Act requires an employer to bargain with a duly certified union within 15 days of the union's notice that it wishes to negotiate an agreement, or a renewal, or a modification of an agreement. The law requires the parties to "bargain in good faith and make every reasonable effort to make a collective agreement." When it appears that an agreement cannot be reached in a reasonable time, and if 35 days have elapsed since the original notice, either party may apply for conciliation. This assumes that the parties will have been bargaining in good faith for that period, but in fact real bargaining seems to be postponed in many cases till after the conciliation procedures are completed!

Unless the Labour Relations Board has reason to believe that there is further room for effective bargaining without conciliation, the Minister will name a Conciliation Officer (a member of the permanent

[20]I am indebted to Mr. Allan Porter whose unpublished M.A. thesis on "Conciliation in the Province of Ontario" (deposited in the University of Toronto Library) has facilitated the writing of this section.

staff of the Conciliation Service of the Department of Labour). It is his duty to try to promote agreement between the parties; and he must report within 14 days, or such longer periods as the parties or the Minister approve. (In fact he usually takes longer than 14 days.) If he reports that he has been unsuccessful a Board of Conciliation is set up. The Minister requires each of the parties to recommend, within five days, one person to be a member of the Board; upon receipt of this recommendation, or after five days, he appoints two members to represent the points of view of the parties. Within three days these two members may jointly recommend a third person to be chairman; upon receipt of this recommendation, or after three days, he appoints a chairman. (In fact these times are generally exceeded owing to the difficulty of finding acceptable persons free to act.) The Board is required to report within 14 days from the appointment of the chairman, except by agreement of the parties or the Minister. (Rarely is a report made within 14 days.) On receipt of the Board's report copies must be sent to the parties. Until seven days after the receipt of the report by the chairman a strike or lockout is illegal. Conceived as a measure to promote "collective bargaining" and to promote peaceful settlements, there seems some danger that the legislation has become a hindrance to real bargaining, and that it may lose its efficacy as a source of peaceful settlement in emergency situations. Continued study and legislative experiment is necessary. The fact that 300 Boards sat in Ontario in the year 1952 indicates part of the problem: what was surely intended as "medicine" in difficult cases has become "daily food" for all. While some strikes may have been prevented (and possibly many of these would have been of peculiar seriousness in their impact on the public), it has been suggested that "other strikes have been precipitated by conciliation; by the frequently long delays; by the occasional clumsiness of a Board chairman; by the fortunately rare effort by a nominee to urge his party not to agree and to hold out for a better settlement; and by the mere heating up of feelings induced by the irresolution and frustration usually caused by the cooling off period . . . [and by] the apparently debilitating effect [of compulsory conciliation] on collective bargaining."[21]

Labour in the Canadian textile industry, 1938.[22] The following study of labour problems in the Canadian textile industry in 1938 is intended

[21]Allan Porter, "Conciliation in the Province of Ontario"; see for a strong attack on compulsory conciliation, Eugene Forsey, "Conciliation Boards an Unnecessary Evil," in *Information*, Jan.–Feb., 1955; for more favourable evaluation see H. A. Logan, *State Intervention and Assistance in Collective Bargaining: The Canadian Experience, 1943–1954* (University of Toronto Press, 1956).

[22]This section is based on chapter ix of the *Report of the Royal Commission on the Textile Industry* (Ottawa, 1938). The Commissioner was the Honourable Mr. Justice W. F. A. Turgeon. Page references in the text are to this *Report*.

to give concreteness to the generalities on Canadian labour which have preceded it, and to indicate the specific character of the problems of any particular industry. It will be followed by some comment on the labour problems in this industry in 1954. Similar studies of other industries would reveal many different specific problems as well as the essential unity of the problem.[23]

Working conditions. Two characteristics of the labour force in the textile industry must first be noted: first, the high proportion of women; second, the high proportion of young persons. It is particularly important, therefore, to protect the physical well-being of the workers, and particularly necessary to invoke the support of the state since they are unlikely to be able to protect themselves. "The medical examination of workers before employment and periodical examinations thereafter are," in the opinion of Mr. Justice Turgeon, "necessary steps in this direction." He also urged "continued improvement in the facilities for the comfort and cleanliness of the operatives." The work is largely machine tending: but the machines are delicate and complex, work at high speed, and require constant watching, e.g. broken threads have to be tied. There is little muscular effort required of the workers, but both spinning and weaving involve a constant effort of attention, considerable nervous strain, and great manual dexterity.

The physical working conditions in several sections of the textile industry appear to be very unpleasant to anyone visiting a plant for the first time. Some departments require the maintenance of a high degree of humidity for satisfactory operations. The presence of lint and dust in the air is noticeable in the early processes . . . while in practically all departments the machine operations create a tremendous amount of noise. . . . The most serious causes of discomfort evident in the visits made by the Commission to various textile factories were the large amounts of dust present in the opening, carding and spinning rooms of the cotton mills, and the high degree of heat and humidity in the weaving rooms. In addition to these conditions workers testified to the excessive heat which was sometimes encountered when working around some of the textile finishing machines and the presence of deleterious fumes or gases in some of the operations in the manufacture of viscose yarns. The amelioration of excessive heat and humidity and the safeguarding against injurious fumes or dust depend upon adequate systems of mechanical ventilation. Improvements are constantly being made in ventilating systems and what is particularly needed in the textile industry is the progressive adoption of better methods of ventilation. Many of the factory buildings, particularly in the cotton and woollen branches of the industry, were constructed towards the close of the last century or early in the present century, and while improvements are made from time to

[23]Cf. R. A. Lester, *Economics of Labor,* part IV, "Collective Bargaining in Certain Industries." Professor Lester deals with rail and water transportation, bituminous coal, clothing, iron and steel and newspapers, in the United States.

time . . . the conditions in many mills are still below modern standards. In the provision of adequate changing rooms, wash rooms and eating places, many mills leave much to be desired. In many cases workers change from street to work clothes at their machines and must hang their garments on nails on the wall where they collect dust and moisture. It would seem essential that sanitary lockers and separate rooms for changing clothes should be provided in those mills which do not now possess such facilities. Industry needs workers who are healthy and efficient. The lack of comfort, the absence of hygienic facilities and the necessity of entering into the factory room directly from the outside temperature all tend to impair that efficiency and predispose the workers to colds, rheumatism and bronchitis [p. 151].

Hours of work. Though there were some exceptions, the 10-hour day and 55-hour week seems to have been the rule in the Canadian textile industry. This means that the female and child workers were worked roughly to the limit of what was allowed by the Factory Acts of the provinces; the hours of work of adult male workers were not limited by law. In most countries of the world the "regulation normal hours of work" were 48 or lower. Canada took her place along with China, India, and Japan in the group of countries where the normal hours exceeded 48.

Actual daily or weekly hours of work of textile operatives depend upon the level of mill activity and hours are longer or shorter than the regular work-period as the mills become busy or slack. The general practice in the textile industry has been to make no distinction in rates of wages between regular and over-time work and as permits may be secured to work females and children beyond the legal limits the tendency is to work the employees long hours during a rush of orders or when the production in one department fails to keep pace with that in others. If the well-established principle that over-time work should be paid at higher rates were adopted in the industry there would be a strong incentive toward the maintenance of the regular work week which, it is indicated elsewhere, should be shorter than it is now in the textile industry. Recent orders of the Quebec Fair Wages Board provide, in some cases, for the payment of over-time [pp. 153-4].

Wage rates and earnings. Operatives employed on machine work are paid piece rates, others are paid hourly rates. In establishing piece rates for any job the management have in mind a basic wage to be earned in a standard week of operation. "This figure," explained one of the managers, "is based mainly on the type of operative required and the value of such labour in the general labour field." The piece rate is then set so that a good operative working with a full complement of machines and producing as much as can be reasonably expected will earn the basic wage. Only the exceptional operative working under the best conditions would earn more. As piece rates vary with the type of product and the number of machines which the operative is tending it is extremely difficult for the worker himself to keep an accurate record of his own earnings. This leaves the worker "defenceless when mistakes in the calculation of his earnings are made." Mr. Justice Turgeon found "a good deal of justification for the complaint of workers that they cannot determine how their earnings are calculated or at what rates they are being paid," and some evidence of errors being made (p. 155). He recommended the provinces to adopt in their Factory Acts the "particulars section" of the British Act: "In every textile factory the occupier shall, for the purpose of enabling each worker who is paid by the piece to compute the total wages payable to him in respect of his work, cause to be published particulars of the rates of wages applicable to the work to be done, and also particulars of the work to which that rate is to be applied."

The average hourly earnings of textile workers in 1936 were 26 cents in the cotton division of the industry, 24 cents in the silk division, 33 cents in the artificial silk division, 28 cents in the woollen division, and 31 cents in the hosiery division. This average was affected, of course, by the different proportions of women and young persons employed in the different sections, and by the different degrees of skill required. Weekly earnings depend on the number of hours worked as well as the hourly rates: average weekly earnings of males and females in these sections of the industry are shown in Table I.

TABLE I

AVERAGE WEEKLY EARNINGS IN THE CANADIAN TEXTILE INDUSTRY, 1936*

Division		Quebec	Ontario
		$	$
Cotton	males	11.57	14.69
	females	9.57	12.13
Silk	males	12.60	16.65
	females	9.34	11.20
Artificial silk	males	19.56	24.97
	females	13.65	11.23
Woollen	males	16.45	18.04
	females	10.36	12.17
Hosiery	males	19.13	20.29
	females	11.47	12.05

*Data taken from the *Report of the Royal Commission on the Textile Industry,* p. 156.

Minimum wages. Minimum wages for female employees in the textile industry had been established for some time in all the manufacturing provinces except New Brunswick. In 1937, Ontario and Quebec passed legislation providing for the extension of minimum wage orders to cover male employees. The Ontario Minimum Wage Act (1937) gave the Industry and Labour Board authority "to establish minimum rates of wages for all employees and generally to enact such provisions with respect to conditions of employment as may be deemed necessary for the betterment of the physical, moral and intellectual well-being of the employees." The Quebec Act Respecting Fair Wages authorized the Fair Wages Board to determine fair wages and working hours.

The Ontario Industry and Labour Board issued an order covering the textile industry in January, 1938. The minimum wages for the regular weekly hours were: for adult males, $16.00; for boys of twenty, $15.00; of nineteen, $14.00; of eighteen, $13.00; of seventeen, $12.00; of under seventeen, $11.00; for adult females, $12.50; for girls of seventeen, $11.00; of under seventeen, $9.00. Provision was made for payment of overtime at time and a quarter for the first two hours of overtime and at time and a half for all other overtime, and for maintenance of piece rates which would enable a reasonably careful worker to earn the hourly rates which would give the minimum weekly wage when a full week's work was available. Where the Board considered a "learning period" was required the employment of learners might be permitted at rates approved by the Board, "provided that the employer enters into a written contract with each of the learners in a form to be approved by the Board."

Minimum wage regulations for female workers generally provide differential minima according to the age and experience of the worker. Quebec established a new practice in 1935 which facilitated the checking of evasion. This provided that not more than a given percentage of the female workers should be paid less than certain stated rates of pay: in Montreal and district not more than 10 per cent were to receive less than 14.5 cents an hour, not more than 25 per cent less than 19 cents, and not more than 35 per cent less than 25 cents; in the remainder of the province these minima were 12.5 cents, 17 cents, and 21 cents. Mr. Justice Turgeon found that "the cotton companies have conformed to the minimum wage regulations" but the silk industry had "a far less favourable record" (p. 168). In the silk industry in Quebec 20 per cent of the female workers earned less than 17 cents (twice the proportion allowed by law) and only 55 per cent earned 21 cents (instead of the 65 per cent required by the law). In 1938 the Fair Wages Board established minimum wages for all workers in all industries: in Montreal and district 60 per cent were to receive not less than 26 cents an hour, not more than 25 per cent were to receive less than 22 cents, and not more than 15 per cent to receive less than

17 cents; in other cities over 5,000 the minima were 25, 20, and 15 cents, and in the rest of the province were 22, 18, and 13 cents. It also issued a special order dealing with the silk industry; this established a minimum wage of 18 cents an hour, provided that all piece rates should be increased 10 per cent, and decreed increases of hourly rates of from 8 to 20 per cent.

Trade union organization. Though there had been some development of trade union organization in the Canadian textile industry during and immediately after the Great War, it had become of little importance during the late twenties. In 1936, Mr. Justice Turgeon found that organization was "of a very rudimentary character." There were two old locals of the United Textile Workers of America, one in Milltown, N.B., the other in Vancouver. New locals were organized in 1936 at Three Rivers and Cornwall. Efforts were being made to organize locals of the United Textile Workers at various places in Ontario and the Fédération Nationale Catholique du Textile (founded in 1926 but quiescent since 1930) began active organization in Quebec. "The result of this active organization work in both Ontario and Quebec became evident in the following year when organized demands were made upon employers by unions in the two provinces. The refusal of the employers to treat with organized labour led to widespread disputes" (p. 183). The attitude of the employers was made clear in their evidence before the Royal Commission. The President of Wabasso Cotton Company, Limited, said: "The men can belong to any union if they like. We do not ask a man if he belongs to a union or what his religion is, but the Board of Directors refuse to recognize the Union, any Union" (p. 184). The answers of other company officials were evasive or similarly positive in their refusal to deal with a union. "Mr. Binz, President of the M. E. Binz Company Limited, at Montmagny, was the only company executive to express a frankly favourable attitude towards unions" (p. 184). The Commissioner contrasted with this the situation in the English textile trade:

British employers recognize the unions as the spokesmen for labour and have for generations accepted the principle of collective bargaining. . . . In the United Kingdom the conduct of affairs between employers and employees involves the processes of representatives of the two parties meeting in conferences and working out an agreement covering labour conditions, or, failing to reach an agreement, proceeding normally to use some form of conciliation. The development of trade agreements is influenced and guided by technical experts who have been brought up within the unions and subjected by them to impartial examinations before being permitted to act as experts in interpreting the piece rate lists or in determining the nature and extent of allowances. These experts, acting with respective spokesmen for the two parties, make possible the achievement of intelligent results in the bargaining processes and the attainment of a satisfactory agreement provided the basic positions of the employers and employees are reconcilable [p. 181].

Three Rivers Strikes, 1935-6. A strike took place in the mill of the Wabasso Cotton Company at Three Rivers on August 26, 1935, to protest the action of the company in replacing a number of men by girl workers. There was no union; it was a spontaneous outbreak by a group of workers who enlisted the sympathy of a large number of their fellow-workers. The strike was settled through the efforts of the Mayor of Three Rivers and work was resumed on August 28. The company agreed to give preference in employment, as far as possible, to married men and those supporting families. The company also agreed to establish a committee of employees with representatives from each department in the mill and representatives of the management to investigate grievances. The workers were not satisfied that the employer had lived up to his agreement and, having formed a local of the United Textile Workers, presented a series of new demands early in 1936. The company refused all the demands and a strike was called for February 18. The Mayor of Three Rivers tried to bring the parties together and "drafted a plan of settlement which was acceptable to the strikers but was rejected by the company." This plan "greatly modified the original demands of the strikers and did not call for the recognition of the union but merely for a committee of workers." The Mayor having failed, the conciliation officers of the Dominion Department of Labour tried to negotiate a settlement. "Again, however, no plan of settlement could be evolved which was acceptable to the company, which maintained throughout the dispute an uncompromising attitude toward any suggestions which would involve any recognition of organization among the workers, apart from the shop committee already mentioned" (p. 185). The strike was called off on March 2 on the assurance that the Royal Commission on the Textile Industry would conduct an inquiry into the workers' grievances.

The Cornwall Strike, 1936. A strike in the Cornwall plant of Courtaulds (Canada), Limited, started on August 11, 1936. The main demands were for higher wages and for improved working conditions, especially satisfactory measures to deal with the sulphuric acid fumes which occur in certain departments. The workers were practically unorganized, but proceeded to organize a Rayon Workers Industrial Union which affiliated with the United Textile Workers. A conciliation officer from the Dominion Department of Labour intervened. The company refused to negotiate until the international labour organizer was dropped from the committee; it then refused to deal with the committee of the union; finally on September 4 the company negotiated with a committee of the workers and agreed to some wage increases and some improvements in working conditions. The President of the company explained that he refused to deal with the union in Cornwall because the leaders were too "amateurish"; he was also managing director of the parent company in England where he recognized the unions, but he opposed the union in Cornwall because of its "childish tactics." Mr. Justice Turgeon replied:

The essence of Mr. Johnson's criticism is that the union in Cornwall lacked experience. It is difficult to see how this shortcoming could be obviated unless the employers were willing to grant a larger measure of responsibility to the labour organization, for, as the history of labour unions in Great Britain clearly shows, it is only through the acceptance of undertakings by organized labour and the training of leaders skilled in negotiation and administration that unions cease to be "amateurish" and become capable of assuming those responsibilities which rest upon the parties in any joint undertaking [pp. 186-7].

A year later, September, 1937, Courtaulds entered into an agreement with the Rayon Workers Union. The agreement provided "recognition of the union as the collective bargaining agency for its employees who are or may become employees of the union, and that any labour differences involving departmental questions shall be negotiated by the company and the union." The company reserved the right to employ non-union labour. The agreement provided also an increase of wages of 3 cents an hour, time and a half for all overtime in excess of the normal 8-hour day. Work on Sundays and national holidays was banned and an annual holiday of one week with pay was promised.

The Peterborough Strike, 1937. A strike in the Peterborough mill of Dominion Woollens started in June, 1937. It started through the action of an unorganized group of workers, who were afterwards organized as a local of the United Textile Workers. The company refused to negotiate with the committee of strikers on the grounds that the international organizer was not one of their employees, and that the remaining members (most of whom belonged to the union) were not fully representative of their employees. Officials of the Ontario Department of Labour failed to bring the parties together; finally the Prime Minister of Ontario persuaded both parties to leave the determination of wages and hours to the Industry and Labour Board. The employers agreed that any revision of rates by the Board would be retroactive to the date of resumption of work, that there should be payment for waiting time for piece workers and rest periods for female employees.

It was further agreed that negotiations as to other grievances should be conducted by the company and a committee of employees elected from the several departments under the supervision of the Ontario Department of Labour.

Cotton strikes and lockouts, 1937. In July, 1937, a strike occurred at the Canadian Cottons Company mill at Cornwall. A number of the workers had joined the United Textile Workers and the strike occurred when the company refused to negotiate with the union. As at Peterborough, the company refused to meet a committee which included the union official who was not one of its employees. After several attempts at settlement had failed, Mr. Hepburn persuaded the parties to accept a settlement similar to that accepted in the Peterborough strike, namely that wages and hours were to be established by the Industry and Labour Board, and that a committee of employees would be established to deal with other grievances.

Throughout 1936 and the first half of 1937 the Catholic unions in Quebec had been pressing the Dominion Textile Company to enter into a collective agreement. Finally, on August 2, 1937, the Fédération Catholique Nationale du Textile presented demands for higher wages, reductions of hours from 55 to 48. On August 4 the company closed its mills. Negotiations were unsuccessful, but on August 19 the company decided to open its mills. Operations were commenced but the strikers maintained that few of their number had returned to work. On August 25 His Eminence the Cardinal-Archbishop of Quebec appealed to the company and the Fédération to submit to mediation of the Prime Minister of Quebec. Both parties acceded to the Cardinal's wishes and a settlement was reached at Quebec on August 27. The settlement provided for immediate termination of the strike, re-engagement of all employees on the payroll on July 31, establishment of a joint committee of four representatives of the employers, two of the Fédération Catholique Nationale du Textile, and two of other employees of the company, to negotiate collective labour agreements for the various plants of the company. The rates of wages were to be determined by the Fair Wages Board and were to be retroactive to the date of the settlement. So successful were the subsequent negotiations for a collective agreement that the Fair Wages Board was not asked to make an award.[24] Mr. Justice Turgeon said of this agreement: "In view of the earlier opposition of the companies to the negotiation of a collective agreement with their organized workers the successful conclusion of an agreement is a matter of great significance" (p. 190).

[24]The agreement is printed as an appendix to the *Report of the Royal Commission on the Textile Industry,* pp. 273-7.

Labour in the textile industry, Ontario, 1954.[25] It is the purpose of this section to illustrate the great change in union-management relations which has taken place in industry generally: the contrast with the picture in 1938 is remarkable in most industries, but it appears the more remarkable in this particular industry when one recognizes the strain put on these relations by recession. After a period of prosperity in the forties the Canadian textile industry suffered a severe set-back after 1951. Employment shrank between 1949 and 1954 by 20 per cent in most branches of the industry, by 30 per cent in woollens.

In Ontario the majority of the textile workers were members of the Textile Workers Union of America (C.I.O.–C.C.L.): in 1954, it had 72 locals in Ontario. The United Textile Workers of America (A. F. of L.–T.L.C.) had eight locals in Ontario. An independent union, the Canadian Textile Council, formed by officials of the U.T.W.A. who were dismissed for alleged Communist affiliation, had two locals. The difficulties of the unions in recession are greater when competition between rival unions for members is active. On the other hand the attitude of management had changed to one of full recognition of the union's function, and indeed to a recognition of the service the union could perform in helping to adjust to recession. Two sources of possible friction resulting from such adjustment may be noted: (1) the adjustment of piece rates as changes are made in products and in methods in the search for increased sales and reduced costs; (2) the reduction in the number of employees in face of declining sales or increased mechanization. To deal with the first sort of problem, contracts outline a procedure for changing piece rates involving consultation between union and management, a trial period during which the worker usually receives his previous average hourly earnings, and finally, if agreement is not reached, arbitration. In good times small changes in methods may be made without seeking a change in the piece rate: the effect of any one change may be too small to warrant adjustment. The cumulative effect, however, may be to put some jobs out of line. In recession one method of reducing costs is to readjust work loads and piece rates on such jobs. While resisting wage cuts, the union may agree to such adjustments, but it may have difficulty in persuading its members that such action is necessary. To deal with the second sort of problem, the contract contains a seniority clause. The textile unions, like other unions, have sought to increase the importance of length of service and reduce the emphasis on qualifications and

[25]I am indebted to Dr. Sheila Eastman on whose unpublished study, "The Policies of Employers and Unions during a Recession: The Experience of the Primary Textile Industry in Ontario since 1951," I have relied for this section.

ability in determining the order in which workers are laid off. If management questions the ability of a worker, the unions have sought the right to a trial period during which he must prove his ability to meet the regular standard. In recession, when lay offs are more common and management is more concerned with reducing cost, there might well be more friction. It is clear that these and other changes associated with recession give workers causes for complaint. The union as the official channel through which complaints are communicated to management is likely therefore to process more grievances.

The union's policy [says Dr. Eastman] may change. On the one hand, during a recession the union may discourage workers from presenting grievances in order to give management a free hand in increasing efficiency and reducing costs. But to do this it must be extremely strong. . . . It is much more likely that the union's policy will change in the direction of processing grievances more assiduously than usual and carrying a larger proportion to arbitration. In a period of recession it will be difficult for the union to win large economic gains for the workers and, in compensation, it may give increased attention to workers' grievances in an effort to hold the allegiance of its members. Thus there is good reason to expect that the relationship between union and employers will worsen during a recession. It is to the credit of both parties that this does not seem to have occurred in the primary textile industry in Ontario.

There remain problems; there can still be strife, but the chance of peaceful, sensible, and fair solutions has immeasurably increased.

CHAPTER X

CONCLUSION

In the first three chapters of this book much emphasis was placed on the automatic functioning of the price system. The necessity for some political organization to permit the proper functioning of the automatic economic system was noted, but the necessary economic activities of the state were, under the ideal conditions of the hypothetical handicraft model, extremely few. When we turned in later chapters to the study of the real world we found the state playing a very important part in moulding the Canadian economy and influencing the fortunes of various classes in the community. We were studying political economy, not just economics.

Laissez-faire. There was a time when economists and politicians were so impressed with the possibility of the automatic functioning of the economic system that they preached the doctrine of laissez-faire. The agenda of government were reduced to a minimum. Intelligent people from the time of Adam Smith's *Wealth of Nations* (1776) to that of John Stuart Mill's *Principles of Political Economy* (1848) were impressed by the power of competition to destroy monopoly privilege, were amazed at the achievements of business men when free to innovate, were acutely aware of the ineptitude and corruption of the government which had for centuries presumed to regulate and restrict the forces of business enterprise, were supremely confident in the rationality of man and in the goodness of human nature, and were ever conscious of the "natural right" of the individual citizen. In Jeremy Bentham may be found the most extreme examples of this attitude, as for instance in his *Defence of Usury* (1816): "No man of ripe years and sound mind, acting freely and with his eyes open, ought to be hindered, with a view to his advantage, from making such bargain in the way of obtaining money, as he thinks fit: nor anybody hindered from supplying him upon any terms he thinks proper to accede to." But the usury laws of his day, relics of the age of regulation, prohibited lending or borrowing at rates above 5 per cent. Now, says Bentham, suppose a man to be in a position where a loan could save him from great loss, but with no security to offer. He could afford to pay a high rate and no one could afford to lend to him except at a high rate. It would be worth his while to borrow at the high rate. "So he judges who has nothing to hinder him from judging right, who has every motive and every means for forming a right judgment. . . . The legislator who knows nothing, nor can know anything of all these circumstances . . . comes and says to him: 'It signifies nothing, you shall not have the money: for it would be doing you a mischief to let you borrow upon such terms.' And this out of prudence and loving kindness! There may be cruelty, but can there be greater folly?" In 1923 a similar doctrine was expounded by the Supreme Court of the United States of America in declaring invalid a Minimum Wage Act of the District of Columbia: "It forbids two parties having lawful capacity, under penalties to the employer, in contract freely with one another in respect of the price for which one shall render service to the other in a purely private employment where both are willing, perhaps anxious, to agree even though the consequence may be to oblige one to surrender a desirable engagement and the other to dispense with the service of a desirable employee." Bentham was heralding the birth of a period of individualism, Mr. Justice Sutherland was singing its swan song.

The collectivist trend in England.[1] In England a collectivist trend in legislation had become evident by 1870, strong by 1880. By 1900 "the jealousy of interference by the state which had long prevailed in England had, to state the matter very moderately, lost much of its influence, and the belief in the unlimited benefit to be obtained from freedom of contract had lost a good deal of its power." The story of this trend to collectivism is told mournfully in Professor Dicey's *Law and Opinion in England* (1905). When in 1914 he wrote the preface to the second edition his sorrow was intensified. Between 1906 and 1914 legislation of the Liberal government had made the state responsible for the regulation of wages in certain industries; for the payment of old age pensions; for the operation of a compulsory and state aided health insurance and, in some industries, unemployment insurance; for the feeding, medical inspection, and treatment of school children; and for the supply of work class houses. The funds for this social service programme were raised by the extension of progressive taxation. After World War I successive English governments extended and elaborated the schemes of social reform laid down in the period 1906-14. The magnitude of the programme of social services, and the extent of the departure from laissez-faire is shown by the increase in expenditures on the social services from £22 million in

[1]See J. M. Keynes, *The End of Laissez-Faire* (London, 1926); also the discussion of the "decline of laissez-faire" in the *American Economic Review*, supplement, March, 1931; and A. C. Pigou, *Economics in Practice* (London, 1935), lecture v, "State Action and Laissez-Faire."

1891 to £307 million in 1927. At the same time taxes paid by people with incomes under £500 a year increased little if any, while taxes paid by people with incomes over £50,000 a year increased from 8 to nearly 60 per cent of their incomes.

But the breakdown of laissez-faire was apparent in other fields besides that of the social services. The government not only laid fresh burdens on industry but also tried to develop its capacity to bear them. The forcible grouping of the English railways in 1921, the co-ordination of the supply of electrical power under the Act of 1926, the reorganization of the coal mines under the Act of 1931, are examples of intervention in industrial affairs based on a distrust of the efficiency of the entrepreneur even as a profit maker. The growing recognition of the responsibility of the state for the maintenance of a high level of employment in face of a high propensity to save and general reluctance on the part of business to spend on an appropriate scale constituted the most significant element in the decline of laissez-faire in the inter-war period. During World War II the magnitude of the shift of industry from peace to war demands, and the urgent necessity for speed, required an enormous extension of state control and intervention, intensifying and accelerating the collectivist trend. Since 1945, the social services have been still further extended under Conservative and Labour governments.

The collectivist trend in Canada. In Canada a similar trend towards increasing state intervention in economic affairs has been evident since Confederation. This story has been told by Professor J. A. Corry in a memorandum prepared for the Rowell-Sirois Commission, *The Growth of Government Activities since Confederation.*[2] He pointed out certain important differences between the trend in the new and the old countries; in the new countries the state played a more important part in early economic development and yet the sentiment of laissez-faire was in some ways more tenacious and the development of government intervention slower than in England. Professor Corry gives a useful explanation of this difference:

This increase in the functions of government is common to all western countries but it has not always followed the same pattern of development. In those countries which got off to a slow start in the race for industrial expansion and the new countries recently opened for exploitation, the early emphasis was on state assistance to industry rather than on extensive regulation. . . . The opening up of a new country requires more than individual initiative; it requires highly organized co-operative effort to overcome natural obstacles. Private enterprise accumulates capital and organization too slowly for many tasks. The state is the only organization which can

[2]One of the mimeographed appendices to the *Report of the Royal Commission on Dominion-Provincial Relations* (Ottawa, 1939).

command the required capital and integrate co-operative effort on a large scale. Hence it is called upon to assume leadership in important and urgent development. The building of the Intercolonial and the long story of railway subsidies are sufficient illustrations. In a new country, the state is saddled with positive duties of helping people to help themselves. Even though its ultimate function is only that of a referee, it must turn in and help to build the playing field before the game can begin. Thus it has been easy to get agreement on a considerable range of state action in the name of national development. It has covered government ownership of railways and telephones, protective tariffs, bounties and subsidies, the provision of technical and scientific services and the pushing of developmental work of various kinds. *Laissez faire* philosophy, as interpreted in this country, has never objected to the principle of state promotion of national development, however much opposition might be aroused against particular expedients which were subsumed under it.

It should also be noted that the securing of state aid for industry is much easier in those political units where some single industry is dominant. When the great majority of people are engaged in growing wheat, it is easy to get agreement for a broad programme of state action. It must lend money to farmers, subsidize their schemes of co-operation, guarantee loans to the wheat pools and establish moratoria on farmers' debts. The inner logic of the demand for severe limitations on state action is that the diverse interests in society cannot agree on any broad programme and each interest fears a strong state which may be captured by other interests jockeying for advantage. When large areas are predominantly concerned with some single industry, that logic does not apply and it is relatively easy to get agreement that the state should help people to help themselves.

This kind of grandfatherly paternalism which distributes sweetmeats and is sparing of restraint has been a striking feature of Canadian government since Confederation. Subject to this qualification, *laissez faire* was long regarded as the appropriate political maxim. It received powerful confirmation in the everyday scene. The industrious and the thrifty thought they created the opportunity which carried them forward. The self-made men who have moulded Canada saw convincing proof of the maxim in their own success. This belief in a self-reliant individualism was strong enough to postpone any serious attempt at state regulation until the twentieth century and to prevent any significant development of social services other than education, until after the Great War.

It is true, of course, that the relatively late development of industrialism and faith in the constant renewal of opportunities in a new country retarded the demand for state intervention of this kind and the diffusion of responsibility incidental to federalism postponed its adoption even after a demand developed. In the result, we lagged behind England in regulation of economic life and social services. While we have always made much bolder use of state assistance to industry, England went much further than we in providing services, particularly through municipal enterprise [pp. 3-6].

The collectivist trend in political economy. "For more than a hundred years," said Mr. Keynes in 1926, "our philosophers ruled us because by a miracle they nearly all agreed, or seemed to agree on this one thing (laissez faire). We do not dance even yet to a new tune, but a change is in the air." This underrates the change, for the dance has been modified with increasing rapidity during the hundred years in question and the tune has become steadily weaker and confused by counter themes. It also overrates the importance of the tune in determining the character of the dance; the change in the economic dance was an important influence in changing the philosopher's tune. There were, however, other influences which may be briefly sketched.

First among these influences was the diffusion of accurate knowledge of the conditions which called for remedy, knowledge which was provided in England by a succession of Royal Commissions, Parliamentary Committees, routine reports of the growing body of administrative officials, and private inquiries. State intervention was the product of circumstances rather than theory; laissez-faire could not prevail against the facts, once they were known. The Report of Sadler's Committee on the Labour of Children (1832) converted the public to the necessity for a stricter Factory Act, administered by paid inspectors. Appointed to enforce the Act the inspectors did invaluable constructive work and paved the way for a comprehensive code. The appalling revelations of the Health of Towns Report of 1845 led to the Public Health Act of 1848, and further improvements in the law were largely due to the knowledge and experience gained by the medical officers appointed in the large towns. Dr. Simon, appointed first Medical Officer for London in 1848, published a series of reports on the sanitary condition of London which compelled action. While medical officers learnt and taught what could be done, recurrent epidemics stimulated Parliament to pass the necessary legislation; panic was ever the parent of sanitation. These measures did not involve a serious breach in the doctrine of laissez-faire. Children could not be expected to judge their own interest (though it was hard to admit that parents could not be trusted to judge for them) and *laissez-mourir* was no part even of Bentham's doctrine. Further, the Poor Law Commission had recognized the extent to which poverty was due to disease: sanitary expenditure might not increase the rates, if it reduced the burden of poor relief. A more serious departure from laissez-faire was involved, however, in the Merchant Shipping legislation of 1850 and 1854. This was the result of an inquiry made by an official of the Foreign Office into the state of British shipping in foreign ports, which showed that a large proportion of the ships were commanded and navigated in a manner reflecting discredit on the nation; incompetence and drunkenness were rife. So the foundations were laid of an elaborate code of state regulation of shipping, forced on a reluctant government by the pressure of practical necessity. The experience gained by the Board of Trade in administering the early Acts provided the knowledge for further improvement of the law. A last example of how academic scruples fade before unpleasant facts is the influence of Mr. Charles Booth's *Survey of Life and Labour of the People in London* (1903), which did more than any exposition of theory to reconcile the public to drastic measures in the war against poverty.

A second influence was the change in the character of the government. Adam Smith could not foresee the vast improvement in the efficiency and honesty of public officials that was to take place in England during the nineteenth century. The abolition of patronage in the Civil Service and the attraction to that service of a fair share, perhaps more than a fair share, of the brains of the country completely changed the conditions of the problem. It is an obvious, though often neglected, fact that the "agenda" of government cannot be laid down without reference to the character of the government concerned. Professor Pigou puts the point forcibly:

A very important factor in decisions about State action is the quality of the body that would be called upon to act, the intellectual competence of the persons who constitute it, the efficacy of the organization through which their decisions are executed, their personal integrity in the face of bribery and blackmail, their freedom from domination by a privileged class, their ability to resist the pressure of powerful interests or uninstructed opinion. . . . Adam Smith's belief in laissez-faire—so far as he was a believer in it—rested much less upon a theoretical view that, if you leave things alone, they are almost bound to work out right, than upon practical experience that, if you interfere in the sort of way in which governing authorities, as he knew them in his day, did interfere, they are almost bound to work out wrong. . . . [Today] the governing authorities are enormously better equipped for successful action than they were in the days of Adam Smith or in the later days of Bentham. As Marshall has well said, during the last century in England "there has been a vast increase in the probity, the strength, the unselfishness and the resources of Government. . . . and the people are now able to rule their rulers, and to check class abuse of power and privilege in a way which was impossible before the days of general education and a great surplus of energy over that required for earning a living."[3]

To all of this Professor Pigou adds one qualification. The Civil Service may be an institution of "high capacity and unquestioned public spirit" subject to great pressure from persons who can control votes. "Log rolling and lobbying are powerful forces in any democratic country, and when government policy touches private business, they are certain to be called into play. As a result, State action, which, it may be, is

[3]*Economics in Practice* (London, 1935), pp. 125–6.

really needed in the interest of the weak, is most likely to be invoked by the strong." The extension of the franchise has given votes to the weak. The tune is now called, to some extent, by those who suffer most from the maladjustments of a free enterprise economy. It is not surprising, therefore, that they have called, when they have had the opportunity, a new tune.

The final influence to be considered is the change in the intellectual atmosphere. Professor Dicey, himself an example of the survival of laissez-faire as well as the historian of its collapse, saw mainly "a diminished faith in reason and the enthroning of instinct." A diminished faith in *a priori* reasoning there undoubtedly was. Contrast, for instance, Bentham (1748-1832) on "usury" with Senior (1790-1863) on the destruction of unsanitary houses. "The right of the state to prevent a man from doing himself an injury," said Senior, "supposes that the legislator knows better how to manage the affairs of an individual than the man himself does. In the present case this supposition is true." Compare with this W. S. Jevons in his *State in Relation to Labour* (1882) where Bentham's "utilitarian" approach is used to overcome the "natural rights" objection to interference:

I conceive that the state is justified in passing any law which without ulterior consequences adds to the sum total of happiness. Good done is sufficient justification for any act. . . . It is no doubt a gross interference with that metaphysical entity the liberty of the subject to prevent a man working with phosphorus as he pleases. But if it can be shown by unquestionable statistics and unimpeachable evidence of scientific men that such working with phosphorus leads to a dreadful disease easily prevented by a small change in procedure, then I hold that the legislature is justified in obliging the man to make this small change.

The principle is capable of endless extension. The only test is expediency, and since a sound judgment can only be made after experience, experimental legislation is approved.

This empirical acceptance of increasing state activity was reinforced by changes in political and economic theory. New theories of the state, largely influenced by German philosophy, made even the title of Spencer's pamphlet, *Man versus the State*, sound ridiculous. T. H. Green in 1880 was preaching at Oxford the importance of the state in the full development of the individuality of the citizen. French sociology and psychology combined with German philosophy to destroy the atomic theory of society. The development of anthropology and historical jurisprudence contributed to its destruction. The enthusiasm for biology stimulated by the discoveries of Darwin further strengthened the organic view. This enthusiasm for biology also profoundly influenced the method of economic science which had been too much influenced previously by physical and mechanical analogies. The result was less certainty but greater truth.

Influenced by the changing intellectual atmosphere, by the growing experience of social control and increasing knowledge of the facts, economic theory was modified and the economists' suspicion of state interference was mitigated. Economists became more careful in applying theory, valid under certain postulated conditions of great simplicity, to the problems of the real world, and more sensitive to those changes in the characteristics of the real world which undermined views of public policy which had been well founded in the conditions of an earlier time.[4] They came to realize with Alfred Marshall that the "poverty of the poor is the chief cause of that weakness and inefficiency which is the cause of their poverty"; with Professor Pigou that there might be serious differences between cost to the entrepreneur and cost to society; and with John Hobson that a communal investment in the improvement of human equipment might be as profitable to the nation as investment in material equipment. So it appeared that national efficiency called for the measures which the national conscience dictated.

[4]See V. W. Bladen, "Mill to Marshall," in *The Tasks of Economic History,* Supplement I (*Journal of Economic History,* 1941).

INDEX